# Scheduling and Budgeting Your Film

# Scheduling and Budgeting Your Film

## A Panic-Free Guide

Paula Landry

AMSTERDAM • BOSTON • HEIDELBERG • LONDON • NEW YORK • OXFORD
PARIS • SAN DIEGO • SAN FRANCISCO • SINGAPORE • SYDNEY • TOKYO

Focal Press is an imprint of Elsevier

Focal Press is an imprint of Elsevier
The Boulevard, Langford Lane, Kidlington, Oxford, OX5 1GB
225 Wyman Street, Waltham, MA 02451, USA

First published 2012



**Notices**

Knowledge and best practice in this field are constantly changing. As new research and experience broaden our understanding, changes in research methods, professional practices, or medical treatment may become necessary.

Practitioners and researchers must always rely on their own experience and knowledge in evaluating and using any information, methods, compounds, or experiments described herein. In using such information or methods they should be mindful of their own safety and the safety of others, including parties for whom they have a professional responsibility.

To the fullest extent of the law, neither the Publisher nor the authors, contributors, or editors, assume any liability for any injury and/or damage to persons or property as a matter of products liability, negligence or otherwise, or from any use or operation of any methods, products, instructions, or ideas contained in the material herein.

**British Library Cataloguing-in-Publication Data**
A catalogue record for this book is available from the British Library

**Library of Congress Number:** 2011930324

ISBN: 978-0-240-81664-7

For information on all Focal Press publications
visit our website at www.focalpress.com

Printed and bound in the United States

12 13 14 15    10 9 8 7 6 5 4 3 2 1

# Contents

# Acknowledgements

Many thanks to the people who have helped me in the journey of working on and writing this book, I am so grateful — to my parents — first and best examples in all things, to my mother — tireless cheerleader and flag waver, guardian of my spirit and soul — and to my father — endless source of motivation, encouragement, quick to egg on and inspire me at all times. Warmest thanks to Jamie Bauer, constantly supportive against all odds with love and tenacity to spare. Big thanks to my entire family for their love and joyfulness — to Cherie, Doug, Claudia, Lisa, Donna, Tom, Sindi-Rose, Pam, Wayne, Barb, Gary, Breena, Melissa, Joe, Abby, Marina, Libby, Margaret & her boys, Aunt Joyce, Uncle Pete & all their peeps, Uncle Pete, Auntie Gay, Uncle Jack, Auntie Jeannette — & their whole clan. Thanks to every Lindsay — Barb — my muse, Frank, Sharon, Monica, Damon, Nathan, Nana & Poppa, Bruce & the branches from their trees.

Heartfelt gratitude to the many resources around me and their unfailing generosity at every turn by help & example: Stephen R. Greenwald, Marilyn Horowitz, Nicole Bukowski, Bryan Steele, James Weber, Matt Nowosielski, Caitlin Mia Cassaro, Ed Kurpis, Chris Lanzaro, Vern Oakley, Jon Reiss, Rania Ajami, Erick Mullen, Linda Eckert, Claire McLear, Valerie Paehler, Tilokie DePoo, Vinton Thompson, Faye Ran, Humphrey Crookendale, Chris Figueroa, DeAngela Napier, Paul Meyer and all students and colleagues at MCNY, Ithaca (Diane Gayeski & Greg Woodward) NYWIFT (Terry Lawler) & SVA (Sal Petrosino), and all the many filmmakers, vendors and colleagues who helped over and again.

Words cannot express my appreciation to the bedrock of support from everyone at Focal Press — fearless & brilliant leader Elinor Actipis, visionary Michele Cronin, Lisa Jones, Soo Hamilton, Melissa Sanford & the entire team.

# Introduction

What makes a film shoot go well? Organization — with clear goals, a well-planned schedule, and money properly allocated to appropriate expenses. Great production management and preparation may not prevent the chaos or the unexpected twists and turns that ensue during or after principal photography — film production can be as unpredictable as life on earth. Like Brownies, Scouts, mountain climbers, coaches, parents and paramedics, our only defense is to be prepared. Here's where we do that.

This book will give you superpowers. You will learn to worry in advance, see around corners into the future, and develop a sense of urgency — the need for more time, extra money, or more resources.

Whether you're a producer, director, or new filmmaker, looking to expand your skills, you can learn *to schedule and budget your film* with this simple guide — from creating budgets and schedules to allocating resources in an efficient way.

It's not rocket science. It's a series of *steps*, performed *one at a time*. As you do each step a few times, they will become familiar, then you can shape them to *your* liking and tastes, creating a *process that is your own*. Your schedules and budgets may differ from someone else's — influenced by the kind of film you're working on, or the software you do (or don't) use. That's one of the great things about working in film and video — each one is handcrafted, and will have your thumbprints all over it in a fundamental way; the end result that people watch on screen rests upon the schedule and budget.

The following icons will catch your eye. Here's what they mean:

**CYA:** How do you know? Ask! A question now will save time and money later. 

**Tools You Will Need:** Materials to complete the work in the section just ahead. 

**Rule of Thumb:** Generally accepted principles (but not laws). 

**AKA:** Also Known As — many titles, tasks and equipment have a couple of different names. 

Related resources to this topic are free to you on our website. These might include contracts, budget and scheduling forms, video tutorials, software comparisons, and worksheets to complete the exercise as you follow along.  

As with so many others, my journey into filmmaking was circuitous. I carry the skills learned in other arenas (music, business, and teaching) into my work in production, whether working on features, commercials, corporate videos, music videos, or webisodes. Please do that as well! Your life experience, common sense, intuition, and network all contribute to this process. Always be inspired to ask questions — the earlier the better.

This book is modular: you can jump around, work through it in order, or digest one chapter at a time and practice the steps as you go along. My only recommendation is to get in there and participate — the process is totally do-able, and will give you insight and control over your project, setting your current and future films and videos (and you too) up for success.

Please feel free to contact me on the *Schedule and Budget Your Film: A Panic-Free Guide* website — I'd love to hear about your projects and what you're up to.

# About the Website

*Scheduling and Budgeting Your Film* has a companion Web site that accompanies the book. On the site, you will find:

- Further resources to help schedule and budget your films
- Sample and downloadable templates
- Videos from the author that further illustrate key points from the book
- And much more

Please visit: http://booksite.focalpress.com/filmscheduling.com

Please see the Web site home page for registration instructions.

# Chapter One

## *Schedule and Budget Basics*

---

**QUESTION: What is Production Management?**

**ANSWER:** The planning, organizing and managing of the resources and actions required to successfully create a film from a concept or script.

---

Every film is constructed: the result of a careful combination of resources (**AKA:** places, people and equipment), with the common goal of shooting footage that can be edited together to tell a story. Even documentaries and reality television are created, and creation requires planning.

Production management is that preparation, representing the *business* component of *show business* and answering practical questions such as: *When* will that scene be shot? *Who* will shoot it and *where*? *What role* does that actor play and *why* does that equipment need to be purchased, rather than rented? *How much* does each prop cost, and *how many* of those do we need? *Where* is the next location?

Production management is resource management: effectively identifying, organizing and scheduling, locating and pricing, and budgeting and securing everything needed to create a film, so that everything is available, when required, for the best price possible.

When administrative factors are well managed, they contribute to the artistic process of filmmaking. Actors act, the Director directs, and the crew concentrates on the task at hand.

Scheduling and budgeting start once there is a project to manage. It assumes that a Producer has assembled the basic elements of a film such as a script, an end-use plan for the project, and possibly a Director and Key Actor – every project is different.

A Production Manager (PM, or UPM, or Line Producer – we will use these interchangeably) is in a unique position regarding the filmmaking process; they must simultaneously be aware of small details, while maintaining a big picture view. The PM understands the past, present and future of the production, i.e., what's currently happening now, and what's next.

*Scheduling and Budgeting Your Film: A Panic-Free Guide* presents a process to identify every resource needed for a film, and to arrange and price them in the most efficient manner. The schedule and budget that you create may be different from someone else's, but there are basic steps, and a systematic way to approach them, commonly accepted in the industry. This book offers guidelines to understand and streamline that process.

**The Schedule and Budget Relationship**

A film's schedule and budget are interdependent, hinging on the script. If one changes, so do the others.

For example, if you need a piece of equipment that is typically rented by the day, and you add an additional day, your budget will increase.

For a shoot in Manhattan, our Director and DP have requested a Porta-Jib. We call Abel Cine and find out that it will cost $75 per day to rent it. The following schedule in Table 1.1 illustrates how renting this equipment for additional days will incur additional costs.

**FIG. 1.1**

Porta-Jib

**Table 1.1**

| Equipment | Vendor | Days | Cost |
|---|---|---|---|
| Porta-Jib | Abel Cine | 1 | $75.00 |
| | | 2 | $150.00 |
| | | 3 | $225.00 |

This situation brings up questions: in how many scenes will the jib be used? Can we group those scenes together to rent it for the shortest amount of time? Is extra crew required to use the equipment? Will there be any insurance or safety issues? How do we transport the jib? Will it fit in the space at our location – in the elevator, or otherwise? Are there special power requirements? Working in production management raises questions with recurring themes: how will this new factor affect our power resources, human resources, time and monetary resources, and constrictions of physical space, and safety issues?

TIP: One of the fastest ways to reduce your budget is to cut entire script pages, or shooting days, from your schedule. These decisions aren't made in a vacuum; you need the input of your team. Practical considerations require that the Director agree that required scenes can be shot in the time allotted to do so.

For example, if you have scheduled one full day to shoot scene 23 and for some reason the shooting must be extended into the next day, this may impact your budget, i.e., paying for an additional day at that location, extending permits if necessary, equipment rental agreements, employing extras or crew.

It's cause and effect. Additional time, locations, equipment, or people, generally increase time needed to shoot – impacting the schedule and, correspondingly, the budget. The reverse is true; shave time off of your schedule and the budget should go down.

Without a script or detailed concept, creating a film shooting schedule is difficult. And a budget doesn't exist in a vacuum; it is a result of that schedule, i.e., *when* you need certain equipment, or people, and for *how long*.

Film production works on a project basis; crew and cast are freelancers. They must always plan the next job, and may have employment scheduled immediately after your shoot. Extending their planned work time on your project may be out of the question, or tricky to arrange. Together, the schedule and budget set the framework of possibilities for a film and the resources required to create that film.

**Who Manages the Schedule and Budget**

There are many Producer titles, and ultimately one job. Get the best film made, on time and on budget! The Producer's unit organizes time and money to make the film's creation possible.

At the macro level, a Producer *plans* a film project. Regardless of title – Line Producer, Production Manager (PM), or Unit Production Manager (UPM) – the person managing the schedule and budget oversees the *execution* of that plan. The bigger the budget, the larger the Producer's unit. The line between a credit and a job description varies from film to film, but the task of managing the schedule and budget rests upon one person.

A Producer's unit may have one or more of the players shown in Figure 1.2.

Big Hollywood films with multimillion-dollar budgets may employ many people in the Producer's unit. On films with modest budgets – a million dollars and under (way

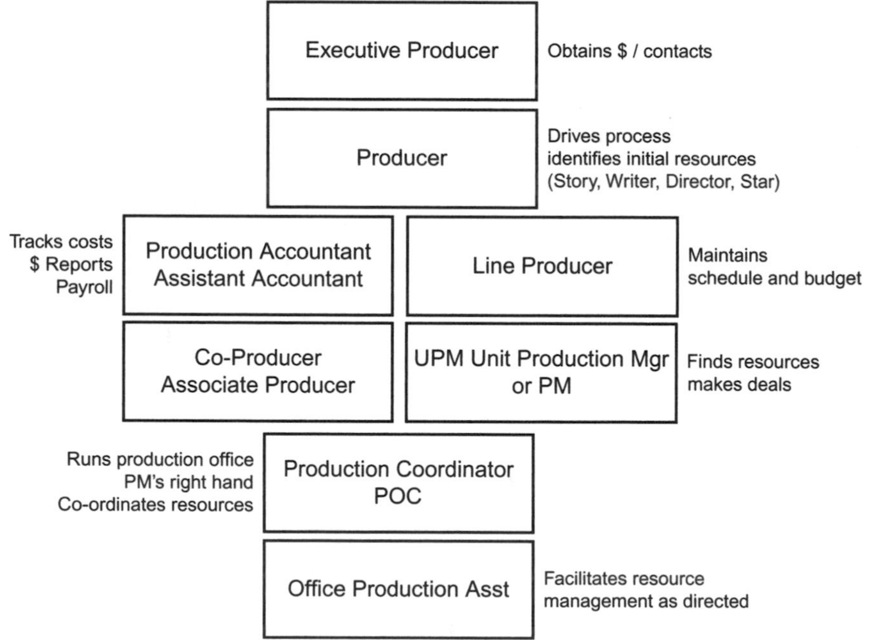


**FIG. 1.2**

Producer's unit

under for many of us) — the Producer and the Production Manager may be one and the same person, assisted by the Production Coordinator and PA.

The distinction between the UPM and LP credit rests with the DGA. A UPM (Unit Production Manager) is an official credit for DGA members (**AKA:** PM), while a Line Producer is not affiliated with a union or guild. On films employing both an LP and PM, generally, the Line Producer maintains the schedule and budget, and the Production Manager locates resources and makes deals. The bottom line is to know *exactly* what is expected of you, what credit you will be given, and put it in an employment contract.

The job of the person managing the schedule and budget involve some mix of:

- Breaking down the script;
- Creating, then adjusting, the schedule;
- Collaborating with the Director, AD, and Production Designer;
- Budgeting the film, and possibly securing locations;
- Facilitating the hiring of crew and cast;
- Execution of contracts, permits, releases, banking, and accounting;
- Arranging travel and housing;
- Coordinating communication with film commissions, studio and/or distribution, and/or banking, financiers, insurance people, any other stakeholders, and;
- Initiating and tracking all the paperwork, i.e., production and status reports.

## A Little History

Many norms in filmmaking go back to the studio system. Prior to the 1950s, studios employed a full-time staff of actors, crew, technicians: definite "units" responsible for specific duties, reporting to a Department Head. This made life simple. This basic structure is still used today. Give people clear things to do, and empower them to carry out those duties. Who does what depends on the film's intended end use, crew experience, and the availability of resources. On small films, many people wear several hats.

Historically, the Line Producer produced "below the line" which, if you look at the budget outlined in Table 1.2, has two parts: Above the Line (initial creative costs), and Below the Line (the cost of making the script). Thus the title, Line Producer.

Modern-day filmmaking dictates that you get your film made any way possible, with whatever resources you can muster. Lean and mean can generate creativity and speed.

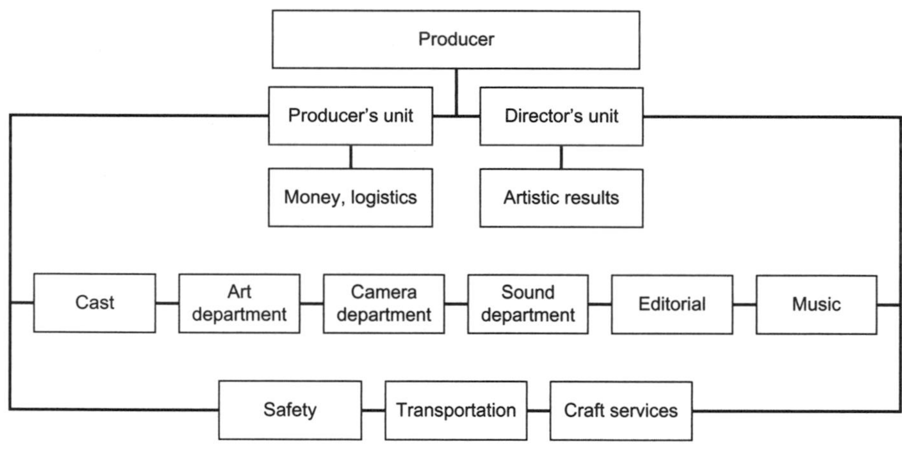


**FIG. 1.3**

Working together, filmmaking units are responsible for explicit tasks

**Table 1.2**

| Account Numbers | Category | Total | |
|---|---|---|---|
| Above the Line | | | The Producer launches and drives the process, starting with Above the Line costs |
| 1100 | Story & Screenplay | $10 | |
| 1300 | Producer | 25 | |
| 1400 | Direction | 25 | |
| 1500 | Cast | 45 | |
| | **Total Above the Line** | **105** | |
| Below the Line | | | The Line Producer (short for "Below the Line" Producer) facilitates the making of the film, through budget and schedule management |
| 2000 | Production Staff | $15 | |
| 2100 | Extra Talent | 55 | |
| 2200 | Sets | 10 | |
| 2300 | Props | 15 | |
| 2400 | Wardrobe, Makeup/Hair | 25 | |
| 2500 | Electrical | 12 | |
| 2600 | Camera | 25 | |
| 2700 | Sound | 25 | |
| 2800 | Locations/Food | 150 | |
| | **Total Below the Line: Production** | **332** | |
| 4000 | Editing | 25 | |
| 4100 | Music | 15 | |
| | **Total Below the Line: Post** | **40** | |
| | **Total Above the Line** | **105** | 105 |
| | Production | 332 | |
| | Post | 40 | |
| | **Total Below the Line** | **372** | + 372 |
| | GRAND TOTAL | **$477** | = 477 |

## Helpful Tools and Software

Scheduling and budgeting can be accomplished with, or without, computers and software. The steps are similar, and the relationship between a script, schedule and budget remain the same, no matter what tools you use. There are advantages and trade-offs either way.

**A Manual and Computer Approach**

Computers were heralded to launch a paper-free work environment, but that hasn't yet happened! Production management breeds a lot of paper, so it helps to get organized.

The process is similar, whether you use a computer or not. The beauty of breaking down a script manually is that you become familiar with the story because there's so much physical interaction – literally. When using a computer, the process isn't necessarily easier, but the automation, duplication, and rearranging saves time, that's why it has become the standard.

If the entire process is to be managed on the computer, it is helpful to print and read the script at least once, to become acquainted with the story and characters.

Tools for the non-computer approach:

- Pencils, colored pencils, ruler, and breakdown sheets
- Calculator
- Production board.

Production boards – a cardboard or wooden chart displaying the schedule, scene by scene, on colored strips of paper – were traditionally used to easily visualize and rearrange the schedule. With the widespread use of computer-based scheduling tools, a production board, while still useful, is only necessary if *you* find it useful.

With a computer, you have several choices, and many programs provide online collaborative features. **Tools You Will Need**:

- Entertainment Partners software, Movie Magic Scheduling and Movie Magic Budgeting are powerful tools, and the industry standard. www.entertainmentpartners.com

- Showbiz makes a robust Scheduling and Budgeting Software. www.showbizsoftware.com
- Scenios is a cloud-based production management suite incorporating tools for post production logging and tracking deliverables. http://scenios.com/
- Final Draft software is an industry standard for screenplay writing, with features for importing into other film production software. www.finaldraft.com
- Jungle Software makes Gorilla software integrating the breakdown, scheduling and budgeting process; available at different price points. www.junglesoftware.com
- Celtx software assists with script writing, pre-production scheduling, and resource management process, and storyboards. http://celtx.com
- WattWenn offers pre-production and production scheduling tools. www.wattwenn.com
- Clever Machine offers multi-user, cloud based, breakdown, scheduling and production tools. www.scenechronize.com
- Microsoft Word and Excel, or word processing and spreadsheet software like Open Office, facilitate the production management process, if set up correctly, but lack the automated features contained in industry software.

All of these programs are available for sale online, and from the software manufacturers themselves. Check out www.masterfreelancer.com, www.writersstore.com, www.amazon.com, and www.filmmakerstore.com. If you're going to use the computer approach, you'll definitely need a printer (preferably color) with lots of ink.

## Basic Steps and Stages

Establishing a system for film scheduling and budgeting helps in several ways; you get to know the project, find opportunities to condense the schedule – creating time efficiencies and save money on the production by experimenting with different budget scenarios.

Basic steps establish a starting point – assigning numbers to scenes and characters that will remain constant, transforming the script into shorthand documents (like production board strips, call sheets and production reports) – so that it is not necessary to read the script through every time to find essential information.

### Scheduling

Without breaking down a script into a schedule, it is easy to miss essential scenes, props, characters and equipment. Without a schedule, there is really no plan, and the resulting budget bears little connection to reality. The initial scheduling process maintains the integrity of data from the script, like GPS leading you toward the completed film. Each day gets you closer. A schedule is the foundation of a production.

Depending on the script, a film shoot can last weeks, or months. Mentally compare the production of the video-game-inspired action film, *Tomb Raider*, starring Angelina Jolie, to an iconic indie film like *The Blair Witch Project*. Actors, costumes, sets, stunts, and locations aside, the *Tomb Raider* shoot lasted 100 days while the duration of *The Blair Witch Project* shoot was approximately eight days. That is not the only reason that *Tomb Raider* was a more expensive film to make, but it is a major indicator. Complicated films take longer to shoot; each additional shooting day costs more. Once every single person, place, or thing, in the script is identified in the breakdown process, assembling them in an efficient order creates a schedule that helps to save money. Think of it as a really great puzzle.

This scheduling process allows you to combine scenes based on similar characteristics (set, time of day, INT/EXT, combinations of cast or equipment), for efficiency.

1. **Read the script completely through** to become familiar with the story and characters. Note questions if you must, but try to give the screenplay your full attention. This first, unbiased impression is similar to how an audience will see the finished film.

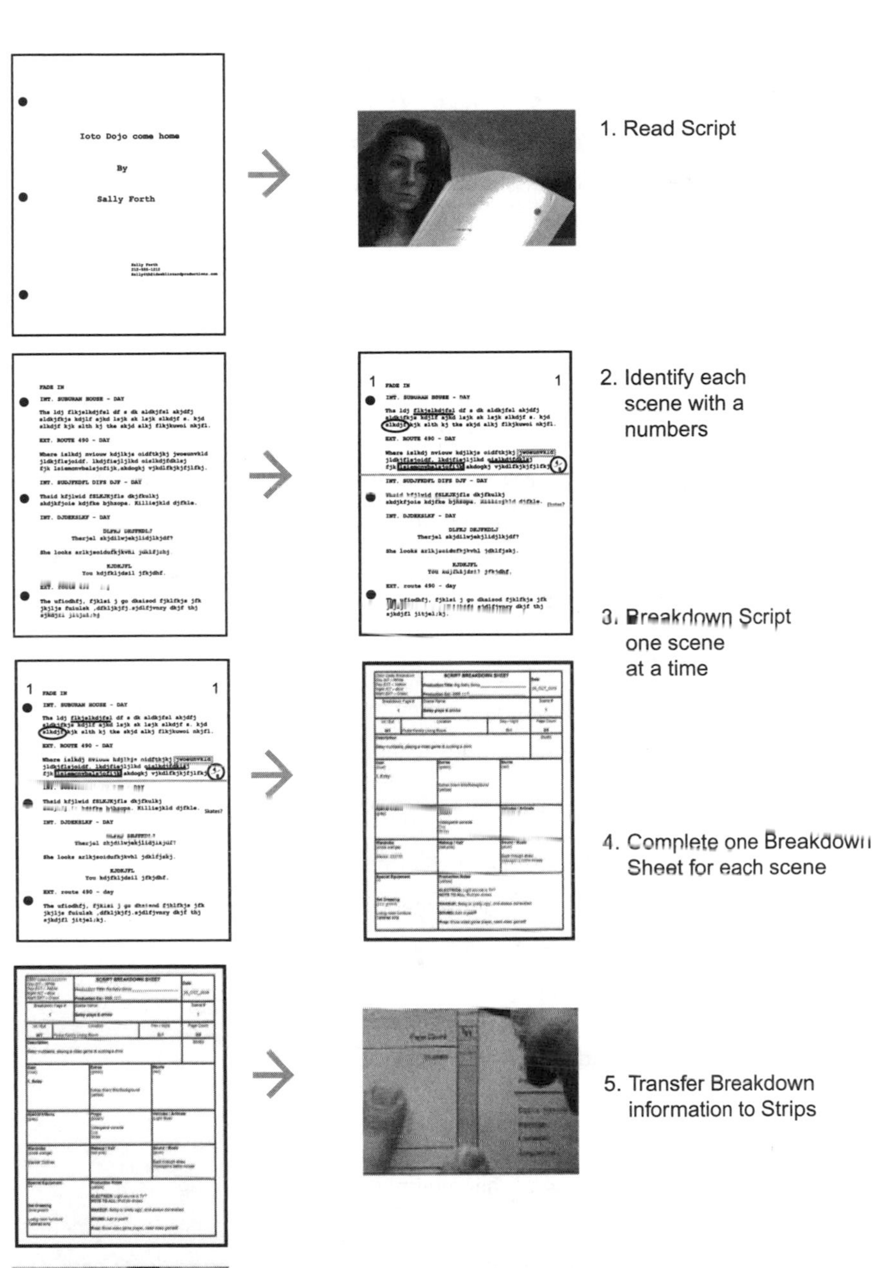
1. Read Script
2. Identify each scene with a numbers
3. Breakdown Script one scene at a time
4. Complete one Breakdown Sheet for each scene
5. Transfer Breakdown information to Strips
6. Rearrange Strips, grouping like things, for the most efficient order

**FIG. 1.4**

Basic scheduling steps

2. **Identify each scene** with a number, one scene at a time, digitally on the computer, or by lining the script on paper, at each Scene Heading showing changes in location. Each numbered scene is a complete unit unto itself. As you insert scene numbers, mark the page into eighths — to show how much of a page the scene takes up.
3. **Breakdown** the script, one scene at a time, marking every resource (i.e., set, cast member, sound, prop, vehicle, as well as any stunt or effect), potentially expensive shot, and all questions, on the script.
4. **Complete one Breakdown Sheet** for each scene, either on the computer or on paper.
5. **Transfer Breakdown Sheets to colored strips** for the production board. (In a film scheduling computer program, this will happen automatically.)
6. **Rearrange strips** around to combine scenes based on identical characteristics, sets, INT/EXT, time of day, cast.

**Budgeting**

Like scripts, good budgets are created and rewritten. As a practical matter, the budgeting process begins with the script, your schedule, and questions for the Producer.

- What format will the film be captured on? Completed on?
- Is it union or non-union? Estimated length?
- Does the film rely heavily on stunts, special effects, animals, kids, huge crowds, specific weather, exotic locations?
- Have any specific resources for the film already been identified?

Answers to many of these questions will point you in a specific direction.

Budgeting is a three-stage process:

1. **Identify and obtain prices** (from multiple sources) in writing: from film commissions (for locations), post production labs (post services), equipment rental houses (shoot), Department Heads and union rate books (cast and crew).
2. **Negotiate** potential deals and present data to your team.
3. **Lock in** your deals with signed contracts (employment contracts, location contracts, permits).

Budgets are structured in layers; the top sheet is an overview, with each successive layer providing more in-depth details. Every item in a budget is assigned an account number, to allow items to be tracked and organized.

Without a completed script, the budget is more of an estimate. The process tends to be fluid; it is important to approach a budget realistically, don't cut it too close! Estimate upwards, giving yourself the flexibility to borrow between accounts later.

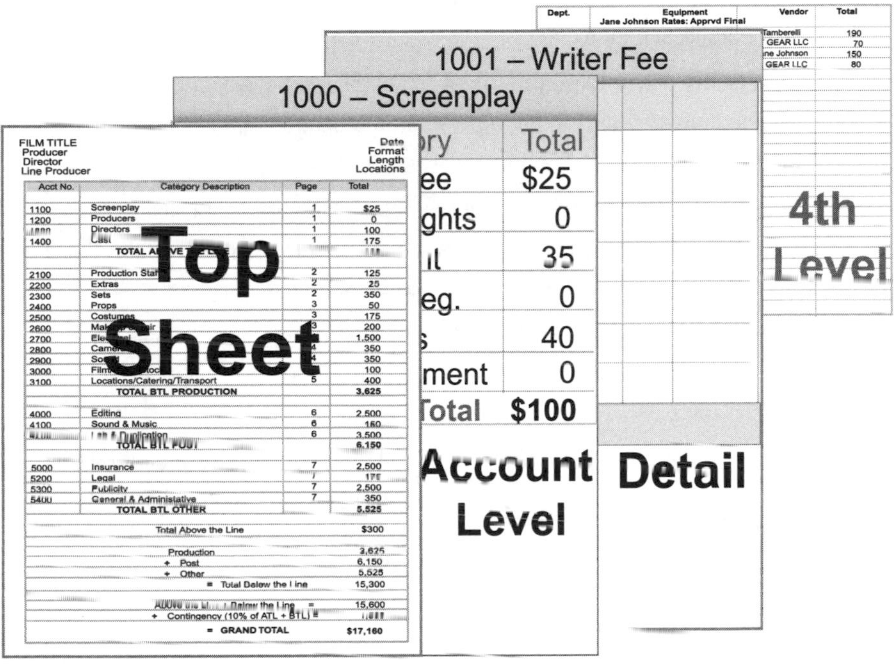


**FIG. 1.5**

Budgets evolve with new information, until they are locked

## End of Chapter One Review

1. Production management is composed of business tasks that efficiently plan the organization, and use of resources, in making a film.
2. Systematic scheduling and budgeting ensures that all of the elements in a script will make it into the film.
3. Regardless of the credit or title given to the person performing the vital task of creating the schedule and budget, the production management process is a set of established steps.
4. Many factors play a role in the final schedule and budget of a film; script changes, crew and cast input, as well as the shooting process itself, all rest upon the foundation of the primary schedule and budget.
5. The basic scheduling workflow consists of reading the script, lining it, breaking it down and completing breakdown sheets, then converting those to scene strips and rearranging those strips for the best schedule.
6. The basic budgeting workflow consists of identifying and obtaining prices for each resource, negotiating deals, and locking in the deals by executing signed legal contracts.
7. The systems of scheduling and budgeting have evolved over a century of filmmaking, but the basics, covered here, remain largely unchanged. The tasks can be done with or without a computer; however, software designed specifically for this purpose can save time and effort.

# Chapter Two

## *Identifying Resources: The Breakdown*

---

**QUESTION: Is There One Way to Break Down a Script?**

**ANSWER:** No. By repeating these steps, and adjusting them to your preferences, you will streamline the process.

Tools You Will Need:

Software: Screenplay file and Final Draft (or Celtx, or other screenplay software) and Movie Magic Scheduling (or other film breakdown/scheduling software)

Manual version: Screenplay and breakdown sheets

---

Just like it sounds, creating a breakdown of a screenplay is the process of *breaking down a script into its basic elements* – identifying every resource needed, scene by scene.

What's a resource?

- Sets and locations
- Cast, extras
- Music / sound effects
- Stunts
- Vehicles, animals
- Set dressing, props
- Make-up / hair, wardrobe.

Basically you do a breakdown so that nobody breaks down on the set! That's a bad joke, but partially true. Improvisation on set should be a conscious decision, or the result of artistic inclination; not an accident because equipment wasn't procured, or set dressing is incomplete.

Why the script breakdown process?

- Scripts are not shot in the exact order they unfold on paper. By accounting for every resource, it is not necessary to memorize the screenplay.

- To maximize the use of resources by:
  a. Identifying, tracking and pricing each resource;
  b. Grouping like things together to save time and money;
  c. Sharing this information as needed.
- To transform technical script information into a flexible form for scheduling.
- **CYA (Cover Your A**)**: So we don't forget, or miss, anything!

Filmmaking is collaborative: any screenplay goes through a fluid process. Once the Producer, Director, principal cast, and Department Heads weigh in on dramatic points and technical issues, the script will change. Your careful breakdown of the script will establish a baseline to start from.

Find out if breakdowns were created previously. The *final draft* of a script (not to be confused with the software) is a misnomer; scripts tend to be continually revised, even with minor revisions, throughout the shooting process, which may affect the schedule and budget.

From script to budget is a four-step, sequential process. This chapter covers the first two stages:

1. **Introduction** to the material: read script through.
2. **Identify resources:** assign scene # and length of scene (eighth of page), each element (within each category—individual cast members, vehicles, props, sets, stunts, sounds, wardrobe/hair/makeup animals, set dressing) in that scene, then transfer information to breakdown form.
3. **Organize resources:** import breakdown information into schedule format and arrange for maximum efficiency (Chapter 3).
4. **Price resources** to create and adjust your budget (Chapter 4).

Each step builds upon the previous one.

*Step 1*

*From Script*

**Introduction** to the material:

**Read** Script through

*Step 2*

*To Breakdown*

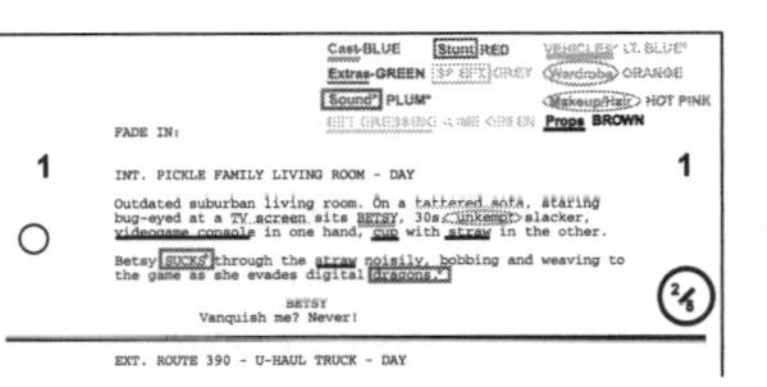


**Identify resources:** assign each scene #, elements in each scene & transfer information to a **breakdown** form – One scene at a time

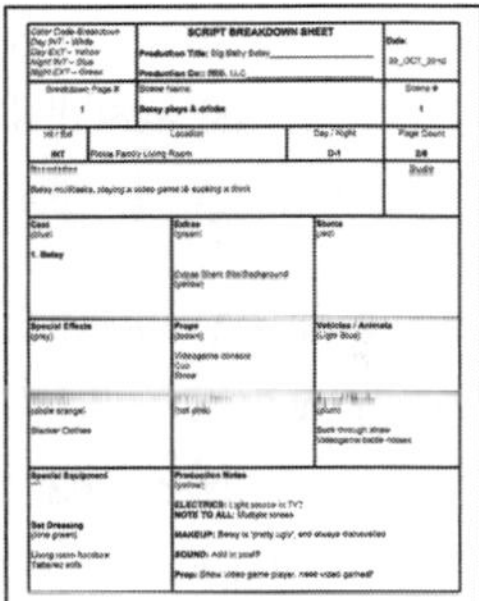

*Step 3*

*To Schedule*

**Organize resources:** import Breakdown info to **Schedule,** consolidate & adjust for efficiency

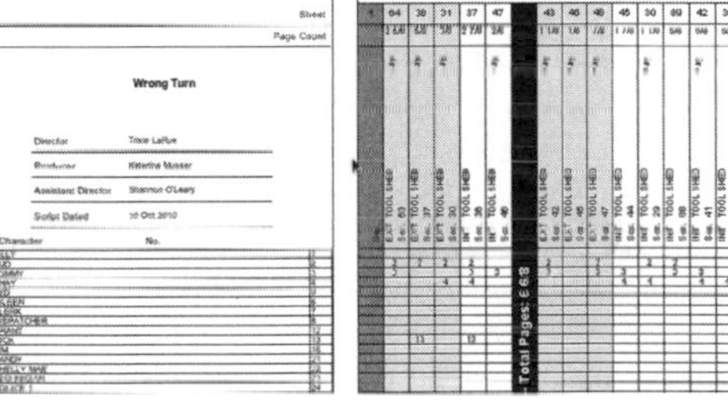

*Step 4*

*To Budget*

**Price resources** to create & adjust **budget**

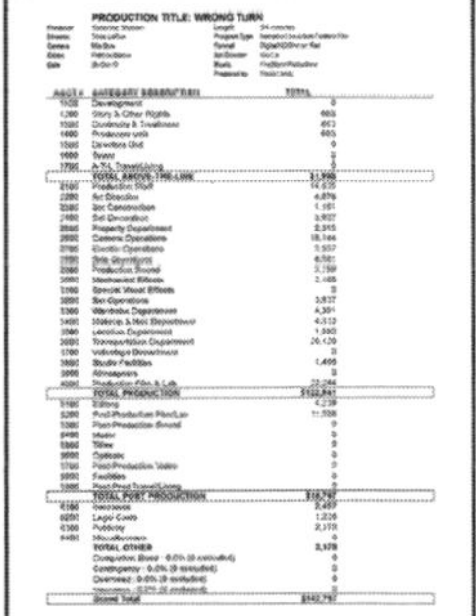

**FIG. 2.1**

From script to budget

## When Is A Breakdown Created?

A script breakdown is completed at one of two junctures:

1. **During development**, a Producer needs to estimate the time and cost investment necessary to make a film, estimate potential profitability, and seek to finance or sell a project. The development process, attaching talent (Director and actors), will significantly affect the script, and therefore the breakdown, schedule and budget.
2. **The project is a go**, and has received the green light. All, or some, financing is committed. In this case, certain parameters (start date, budget range, key crew/cast availability, delivery deadline) may be in place, and the schedule and budget revolve around these factors.

Ideally a breakdown is done when a script is completely finished, polished, everyone is happy with it and any changes going forward will be minor. While a nice idea, that doesn't always happen, so go with the flow. You can only use the information in front of you at any point in time – with the input of your team.

The breakdown process is built upon script components; let's take a quick look at the relationship between them.

## Relationship of Script and Breakdown

The breakdown process is a stepping stone, serving to translate a storytelling form into a technical form – yielding actionable information. The architecture of a script consists of various components.

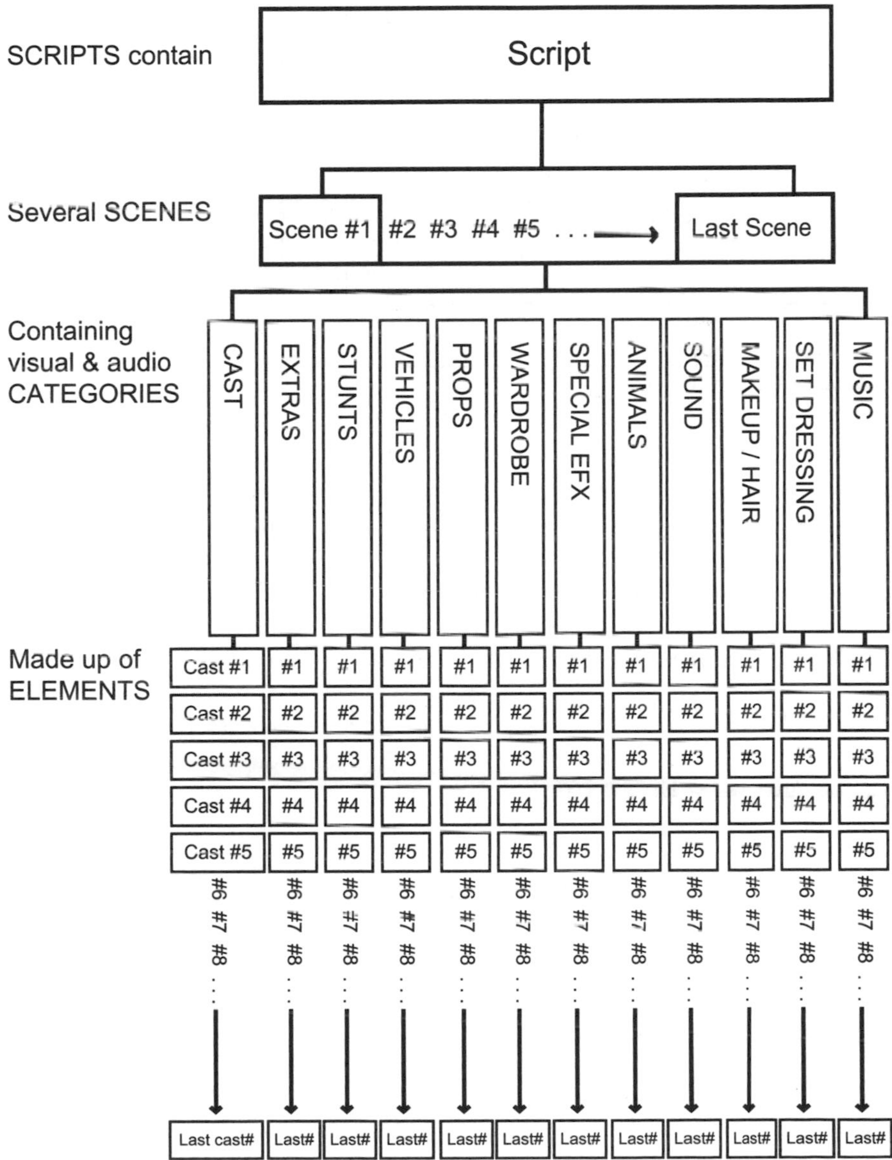


**FIG. 2.2**

Components of a screenplay

The relationship between the script and breakdown is based on the scene as a unit. Most scripts are made up of several scenes. To begin, one scene will be input as one breakdown page.

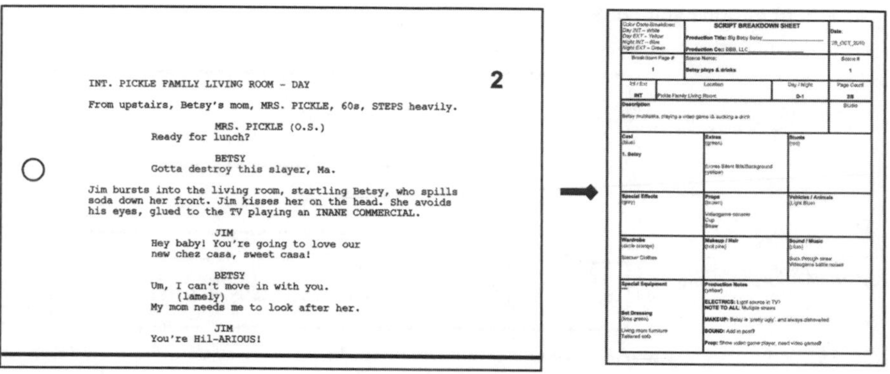

```
                                                                2
INT. PICKLE FAMILY LIVING ROOM - DAY

From upstairs, Betsy's mom, MRS. PICKLE, 60s, STEPS heavily.

                    MRS. PICKLE (O.S.)
          Ready for lunch?

                    BETSY
          Gotta destroy this slayer, Ma.

Jim bursts into the living room, startling Betsy, who spills
soda down her front. Jim kisses her on the head. She avoids
his eyes, glued to the TV playing an INANE COMMERCIAL.

                    JIM
          Hey baby! You're going to love our
          new chez casa, sweet casa!

                    BETSY
          Um, I can't move in with you.
               (lamely)
          My mom needs me to look after her.

                    JIM
          You're Hil-ARIOUS!
```



**FIG. 2.3**

One scene = one breakdown page

**Rule of Thumb**: A *scene* is a dramatic unit of action that *occurs in one physical location* at *one time*. The beginning and ending of a scene is a *Slug Line* (**AKA**: Scene Heading), showing where and when a scene takes place.

Scene #1 might begin with this scene heading:

INT. Southpaw Rock Club, Brooklyn – DAY

Followed by action, characters, dialogue, and end with another scene heading:

EXT. Subway Entrance, 2 Train, Flatbush Ave, Brooklyn – NIGHT

Marking the end of Scene #1 and the beginning of Scene #2.

**CYA**: There is no required *number of scenes* in a screenplay. However, the accepted length of a feature film *script* in *pages* runs from 85–130. *Much longer* or *shorter* than that raises a flag – **so ASK**!

**Rule of Thumb**: *A hidden scene or scene part* doesn't start with a slug line, but is clearly a separate unit – photographs, flashback, flash forward, computer or TV screen insert, historical footage, cutaway shots.

The point of the breakdown process is to identify each element within a scene, categorize it, and position it in a schedule, priced and ultimately used on call sheets, in the shooting schedule and on production reports. You will need to break down every scene — one at a time — whether on paper or using the computer.

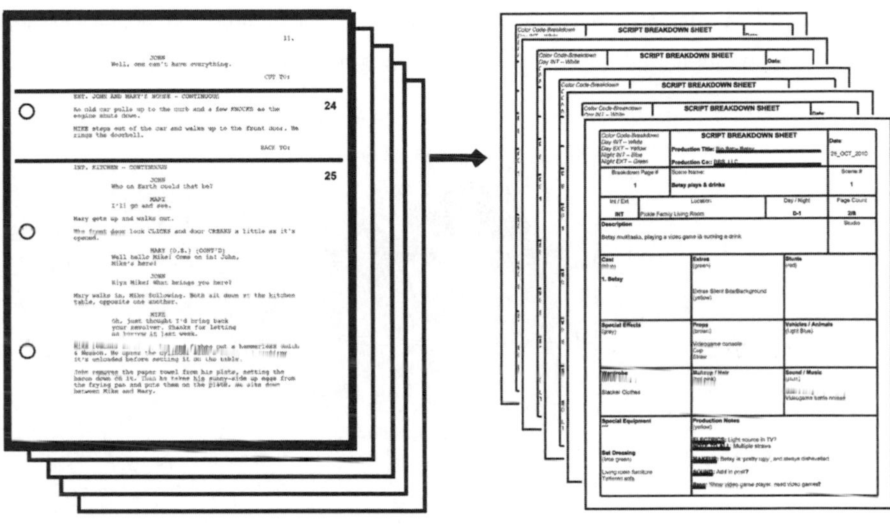


**FIG. 2.4**

# of scenes = # of breakdown pages

It's easier to consider *one scene* as a *unit*, to be moved around inside a schedule, regardless of dramatic order, to find the most efficient timeline. Also, if you are interrupted during this process, it is easy to continue where you left off.

## Script Format

Movies are based on sight and sound; script formatting highlights what is *seen* or *heard*, relaying technical information (like camera directions and scene locations), using spacing, capital letters and margins. This layout makes it easy to "see" a film on paper, but is not conducive to manipulation for scheduling and budgeting purposes. Properly formatted, a script page yields one minute of screen time.

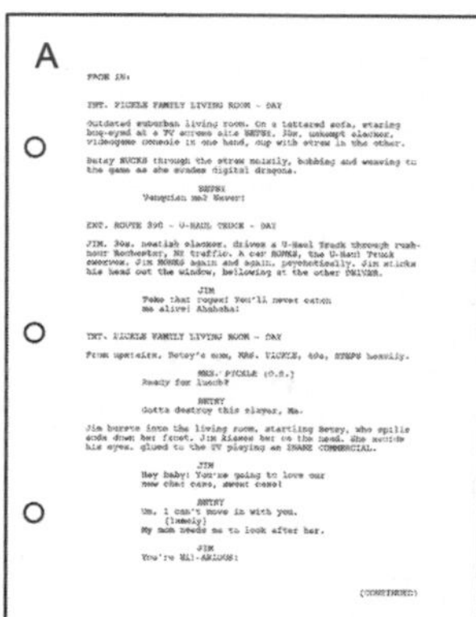
A

FADE IN:

INT. PICKLE FAMILY LIVING ROOM - DAY

Outdated suburban living room. On a tattered sofa, staring bug-eyed at a TV screen sits BETSY, 30s, unkempt slacker, videogame console in one hand, cup with straw in the other.

Betsy SUCKS through the straw noisily, bobbing and weaving to the game as she evades digital dragons.

BETSY
Vanquish me? Never!

EXT. ROUTE 390 - U-HAUL TRUCK - DAY

JIM, 30s, neatish slacker, drives a U-Haul Truck through rush-hour Rochester, NY traffic. A car HONKS, the U-Haul Truck swerves. JIM HONKS again and again, psychotically. Jim sticks his head out the window, bellowing at the other DRIVER.

JIM
Take that [illegible]! You'll never catch me alive! Ahahaha!

INT. PICKLE FAMILY LIVING ROOM - DAY

From upstairs, Betsy's mom, MRS. PICKLE, 60s, STEPS heavily.

MRS. PICKLE (O.S.)
Ready for lunch?

BETSY
Gotta destroy this player, Ma.

Jim bursts into the living room, startling Betsy, who spills soda down her front. Jim kisses her on the head. She avoids his eyes, glued to the TV playing an INANE COMMERCIAL.

JIM
Hey baby! You're going to love our new [illegible], sweet [illegible]!

BETSY
Um, I can't move in with you.
(lamely)
My mom needs me to look after her.

JIM
You're [illegible]!

(CONTINUED)

**FIG. 2.5**

One script page = one minute of screen time

**Rule of Thumb**: industry standard screenplay format:

- Font type: Courier (monospace);
- Font size: 12 point, 10 pitch;
- Printed on one side of letter-sized paper (8.5 inch × 11 inch);
- Specific margins:
  - Top 1 inch
  - Bottom 1 inch
  - Right 1 inch
  - Left (room for brads, holes) 1.5 inches
- Length (85–130 pages) for a feature
- The first time a character appears in a script, the name is CAPITALIZED;
- Writers may capitalize SOUNDS, PROPS, VEHICLES, but not everyone does. It is our responsibility to spot them, whether capitalized or not.

### Metric

For filmmakers working in the metric system, 216 mm W × 279 mm H are the measurements for U.S. Letter Page (8.5 inch × 11 inch). Many writers around the world use A4 paper (216 × 356 mm), the U.S. equivalent of Legal sized paper (8.5 inch W x 14 inches H). The *size* of the page may affect script timing, so measure the page; if it is anything besides standard Letter size, ask your Producer.

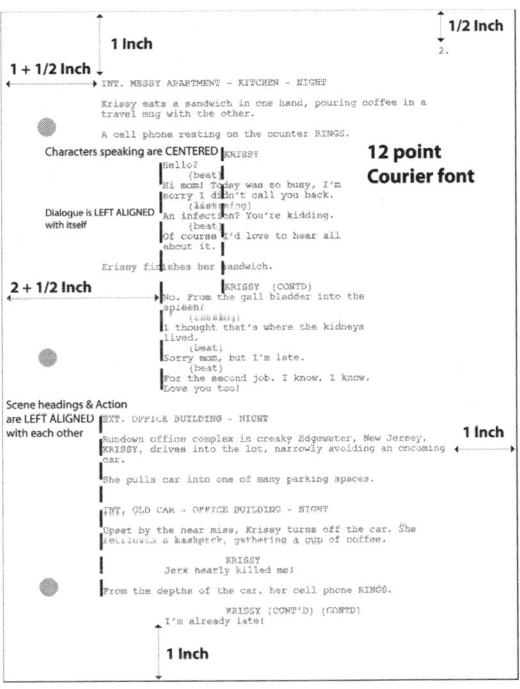


**FIG. 2.6**

Script page margins and alignment

### Rigid Guidelines

These margins and spacing enable a reader to digest information quickly, to tell at a glance where and when a scene takes place, who is involved, and what is happening.

CYA: Use a ruler, check page margins, and/or compare the script you are breaking down with one that you know is correct.

Computerized screenwriting software automatically sets margins, fonts, alignment and format. These programs are widely used, and many incorporate production tools that can assist with the breakdown process, interacting with other software.

Final Draft and Movie Magic Screenwriter are the screenwriting software industry leaders, compatible with most scheduling and budgeting programs. Software continues to improve, and new programs continue to emerge. Using tools *compatible* with your team expedites the work.

**Table 2.1**

| | |
|---|---|
| **Final Draft software** (www.finaldraft.com) Files: .FDR .FDX | **Movie Magic Screenwriter** (www.write-bros.com) Files: .SCW |
| **Celtx** (www.celtx.com) Files: .CELTX | **Story Wizard** (www.scriptwizardsoftware.com) |
| **Truby's (Write A) Blockbuster** (www.truby.com) | **Montage Screenwriting Software** (www.marinersoftware.com) Files: .MONTAGE |
| **StoryO** (www.junglesoftware.com) | |

### Word Processing Software

It is possible to find a template (or create one) for Microsoft Word (www.office.microsoft.com), or Open Office (www.openffice.org), or others.

Not everyone has screenwriting software, but most people can read a .PDF file. It is common for writers to email screenplays in .PDF format for that reason. Adobe Acrobat, Preview, Open Office, and PDF Pen also read this format.

**CYA**: FYI importing files in and out of different screenwriting software can reconfigure page numbers. It is possible for a screenwriting program to change page numbers when it creates a .PDF file. If you are asked to break down a script in the .PDF file format, *ask the Department Head or Producer* for the native file. If you can obtain the screenplay in the original format, it may be quicker and easier to break down those files.

**Rule of Thumb**: If a script format is incorrect, and is the only version available, it is a good investment of time to correct it *before* the breakdown process — even if it means reformatting it yourself. This will preserve the integrity of information once you've assigned scene numbers. Once scene and page numbers have been assigned, *keep them* — these are the legs of your work. Before investing the time and energy to reformat anything, check with the Producer and Department Head.

Note the difference between the feature screenplay page (see Figure 2.7), and the script pages from a musical (see Figure 2.8) and a stage play (see Figure 2.9). In musicals and plays, the visual focus of the page shifts heavily from right to left. In a feature film script, elements are left aligned to the page, or centered.

```
                                                    2.

INT. MESSY APARTMENT - KITCHEN - NIGHT

Krissy eats a sandwich in one hand, pouring coffee in a
travel mug with the other.

A cell phone resting on the counter RINGS.

                        KRISSY
          Hello?
               (beat)
          Hi mom! Today was so busy, I'm
          sorry I didn't call you back.
               (listening)
          An infection? You're kidding.
               (beat)
          Of course I'd love to hear all
          about it.

Krissy finishes her sandwich.

                        KRISSY  (CONTD)
          No. From the gall bladder into the
          spleen?
               (chewing)
          I thought that's where the kidneys
          lived.
               (beat)
          Sorry mom, but I'm late.
               (beat)
          For the second job. I know, I know.
          Love you too!

EXT. OFFICE BUILDING - NIGHT

Rundown office complex in creaky Edgewater, New Jersey,
KRISSY, drives into the lot, narrowly avoiding an oncoming
car.

She pulls car into one of many parking spaces.

INT. OLD CAR - OFFICE BUILDING - NIGHT

Upset by the near miss, Krissy turns off the car, She
retrieves a backpack, gathering a cup of coffee.

                        KRISSY
          Jerk nearly killed me!

From the depths of the car, her cell phone RINGS.

                        KRISSY (CONT'D) (CONTD)
          I'm already late!
```

**FIG. 2.7**

Standard feature film screenplay page

```
   "MY MUSICAL"                                     2.

                               SCENE 1

EXT. MAPLE STREET

                               The hometown firefighter marching
                               band plays a rusty Sousa march,
                               drunken brass players weaving in
                               uneven rows.

                   STELLA
     Which key are we in?

                   TRIXIE
     The key of Sam Adams.

                   STELLA
     That was gone by lunch.

                   TRIXIE
     Ok, the key of Rolling Rock then.

                               A crackling ancient sign over a
                               bar reads THIRSTY'S. The BARTENDER
                               (Handsome Latin, 60s) stands on
                               the sidewalk, giving the drunken
                               crowd the fisheye.

                   STELLA
     Stop stepping on me, you're going to make me
     trip!

                   TRIXIE
     You bumped me.

                   STELLA
     Did not!
                  (then sings)
BLOW IT OUT YOUR SOUSAPHONE
MARCHERS EVERYWHERE
OUR SONG WILL MAKE YOU NEED A DRINK
LISTENER'S BEWARE!

                               Marching band disbands, horns
                               down, scratchy felt hats
                               discarded.

INT. ST. LUCILLE'S CHAPEL

                               Joe waits at the front of the
                               altar, looking around nervously.
                               Organ music plays softly.

                               REVEREND STANTORVSKINI(fat,
                               sweating Ukranian priest) looks
                               anxiously about for the bride.
```

**FIG. 2.8**

Musical page

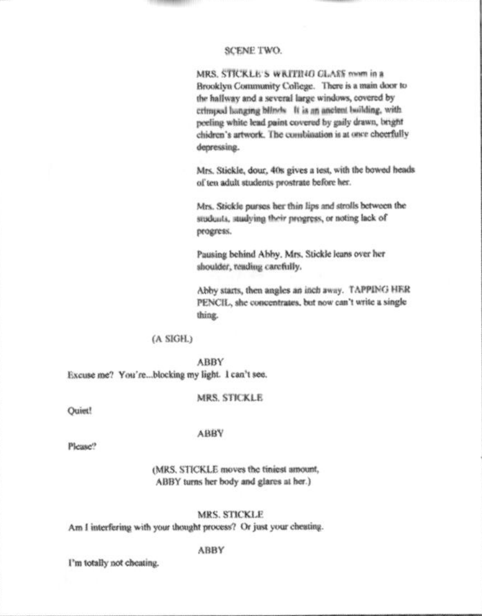

SCENE TWO.

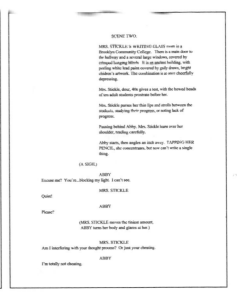

MRS. STICKLE'S WRITING CLASS room in a Brooklyn Community College. There is a main door to the hallway and a several large windows, covered by crimped hanging blinds. It is an ancient building, with peeling white lead paint covered by gaily drawn, bright chidren's artwork. The combination is at once cheerfully depressing.

Mrs. Stickle, dour, 40s gives a test, with the bowed heads of ten adult students prostrate before her.

Mrs. Stickle purses her thin lips and strolls between the studeuts, studying their progress, or noting lack of progress.

Pausing behind Abby. Mrs. Stickle leans over her shoulder, reading carefully.

Abby starts, then angles an inch away. TAPPING HER PENCIL, she concentrates, but now can't write a single thing.

(A SIGH.)

ABBY

Excuse me? You're...blocking my light. I can't see.

MRS. STICKLE

Quiet!

ABBY

Please?

(MRS. STICKLE moves the tiniest amount, ABBY turns her body and glares at her.)

MRS. STICKLE

Am I interfering with your thought process? Or just your cheating.

ABBY

I'm totally not cheating.

**FIG. 2.9**

Stage play page

## Set Up Your System: Software, Colors, Numbers

Creating and using a system is useful in that it can:

- Save time and money
- Avert confusion
- Establish habits for safety checks.

Having said that, any system used in filmmaking is only good if it is:

- Clear
- Used consistently
- Everybody understands it
- Works for accounting purposes.

Establishing a system for this process will foster organization, and build on what you've already done (as opposed to redoing things because they weren't set up right in the first place). Systems combine any variety of colors, software choices, numbering and naming conventions.

Talk with your team. There's no point in buying software, and setting up a project in it, only to have a Producer request something different (although file types are compatible between programs). The breakdown process is an investment of time and effort – get it done right the first time. Once you establish a system, make the information readily available to the parties who need it, and verify that everyone understands it.

Will you do everything manually, by paper, or via production board? Using specific software? Or a combination of software and paper? Using online collaborative platforms? Tools should improve the quality of everyone's work and make the process efficient.

**CYA**: Ask team members if anyone is colorblind or dyslexic, so you can set up a system that will make everyone's life easier. Knowing who has Mac versus PC issues, different versions of software, access to a color printer or not can avert potential roadblocks.

The need for a system goes back to the *length* of a script (too long to memorize, typically shot out of screenplay order). Color and numbering systems establish a shorthand. Imagine a discussion with your Director about greenery. It is cost-efficient to use certain plants in multiple scenes, if possible. It's faster to refer to: "Scenes 24 and 17," rather than "Exterior Garden Party Scene, before the Wedding, and Aunt Mabel's Victorian Mansion, Drawing Room — day."

**Software System**

Computers are great — they can streamline your work and save you time. Computers can also crash, get viruses, software gets buggy, Internet outages plague us, but computers are here to stay, and are an increasingly integral part of production management.

The programs in use for the longest time include Final Draft (for screenwriting) and Movie Magic Screenwriter — they export .SEX (not a misprint) files, used for production scheduling programs. Entertainment Partners production management software is the most widely used, and will be used in our examples. Even if you have a different type of software, the process is similar. Celtx is a popular new arrival with a low starter price point (free).

New production management systems are being developed all the time. Price range, features (whether operating in the cloud or living on your computer), and graphical interface vary.

**Table 2.2**

| | |
|---|---|
| **Movie Magic Scheduling and Budgeting** (www.entertainmentpartners.com) Production management, breakdown & scheduling, budgeting | **Celtx** (www.celtx.com) Screenwriting, breakdown & scheduling |
| **Gorilla Film Production Software** (www.junglesoftware.com/) Production management, breakdown & scheduling, budgeting | **Showbiz Scheduling & Budgeting** (*www.showbizsoftware.com)* Production management, breakdown & scheduling, budgeting |
| **Scenios** (www.scenios.com/) Cloud based breakdown, scheduling, budgeting and production management, with editing logging and workflow component | **Scenechronize Production Tools** (www.scenechronize.com) Cloud based breakdown, scheduling, budgeting and production management |
| **Final Draft software** (www.finaldraft.com) Includes a Tagger program, a breakdown tool to identify elements in the script | **Movie Magic Screenwriter** (www.write-bros.com) A popular screen writing software, with a Tagging feature, a breakdown tool to identify elements in the script |

It is more common to *export* a screenplay for breakdown inside film scheduling and budgeting programs. We will go into further detail on this subject in upcoming chapters. What's important about the computer system you choose is that it works for you and your team, to share information as needed, and keep information private as required.

**Color Systems**

1. Screenplay paper colors indicate revised pages in the script.
2. Breakdown sheet and strip colors indicate time of day.
3. Category color-coding in a script during the breakdown process makes things easy to spot (vehicles, animals, cast, sound, wardrobe, props, make-up / hair).

These systems are unrelated.

1. **Screenplay page colors indicate a revision.** Revised pages are printed on different colored paper so it will be obvious which are new and old pages. These are standard colors (subject to your budgetary constraints). FYI, this is industry practice, but all white paper works too.

**Table 2.3**

| Revision Number | Color |
|---|---|
| Final Draft (what you start out with) | White |
| 1st | Blue |
| 2nd | Pink |
| 3rd | Yellow |
| 4th | Green |
| 5th | Goldenrod |
| 6th | Buff |
| 7th | Salmon |
| 8th | Cherry |
| 9th | Tan |
| 10th | Gray |
| 11th | Ivory |
| 12th | *Back to White again (double white, or neon colors)* |
| 13th | *Blue* |
| 14th | *Pink* |
| 15th | *Yellow, etc.* |

Many screenwriting software programs *ASTERISK* changes in the margin so those changes stick out. Many software programs will do this automatically if set in the screenwriting software. If your Department Head is using word processing software, ask her to *ASTERISK* or indicate changes. Only revised pages are printed, not the entire script. Replace *old* pages with *new* revised ones, and at the end you will most likely have a multicolored-rainbow script.

2. **Breakdown sheets and production board strips indicate time of day and interior/exterior at a location with color.** If you are working *manually* using breakdown sheets, colored paper corresponds to the scene heading, inside (INT.) or outside (EXT.), and either DAY or NIGHT.
   - White: day interior
   - Yellow: day exterior
   - Blue: night interior
   - Green: night exterior.

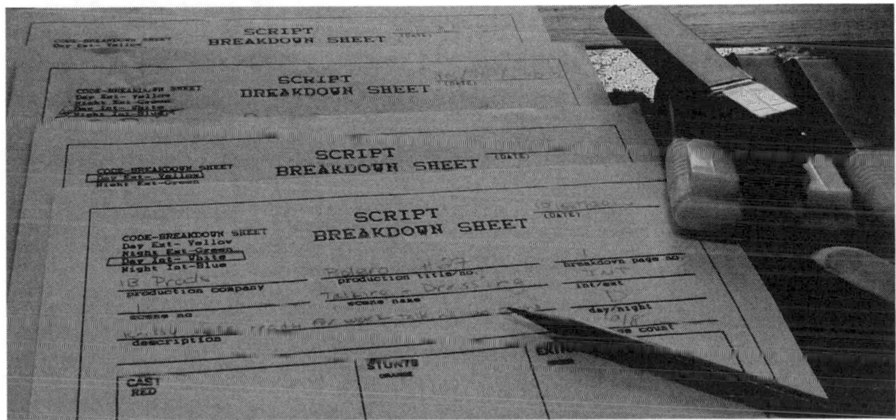


**FIG. 2.10**

Circle corresponding breakdown sheet code

If you are working manually and using all white breakdown sheets, *circle, star, bold* which sheet it is on the top left-hand corner.

3. **Breakdown category color-coding.** The important thing with this system is to:
   - Pick one
   - Be consistent
   - Put a "key" on the first page of the screenplay, for quick reference
   - Make it work for you and your team.

There are two options: a manual approach or a computer approach.

**Manual: All in pencil** (except red pen for stunts), printed script; transfer info to printed breakdown sheets. Pros: cheap, erasable, easy to photocopy.

**Table 2.4a**

| Code | Category |
|---:|---|
| Underline THICK | Cast |
| Circle | Extras |
| **RED underline** | **Stunt/Special Equipment** |
| Underline SKINNY | Vehicles |
| Circle | Props |
| ** | Special Effects |
| Circle** | Costume/Wardrobe |
| Circle** | Make-up/Hair |
| Box | Livestock/Animals |
| Box | Music/Sound |
| Circle | Set Dressing |

**Manual or Computer: In color.** On paper, use markers or highlighters to mark the script. On the computer, use a PDF program (Acrobat, PDF Pen, Preview) to mark the script. Pros: fun, colors make it easy to distinguish information quickly.

**Table 2.4b**

| Color | Category |
|---:|---|
| Orange | Cast |
| Blue | Extras |
| Pink | Props/vehicles |
| Pink UNDERLINE | Set dressing |
| Green | Make-up/Hair |
| Green UNDERLINE | Wardrobe |
| Yellow | Notes |

Another standard option:

**Table 2.4c**

| Color | Category |
|---:|---|
| Red | Cast |
| Green | Extras |
| Orange | Stunt |
| Yellow | Extras/Silent Bits |
| Blue | Special Effects |
| Violet | Props |
| Pink | Vehicles/Animals |
| Circle | Wardrobe |
| *Asterisk* * | Make-up/Hair |
| Brown | Sound Effects/Music |
| Boxed | Special Equipment |
| Underline | Questions, Production Notes |

**Rule of Thumb**: *Cast* and *extras* should contrast to distinguish quickly between them. Crayons or sharpies are not recommended (messy, bleeds through paper).

## Number Systems

Characters and scene numbers condense information in the schedule on each strip. Numbers quickly convey which scene (top row, as in Figure 2.11), and which character appears in that scene.

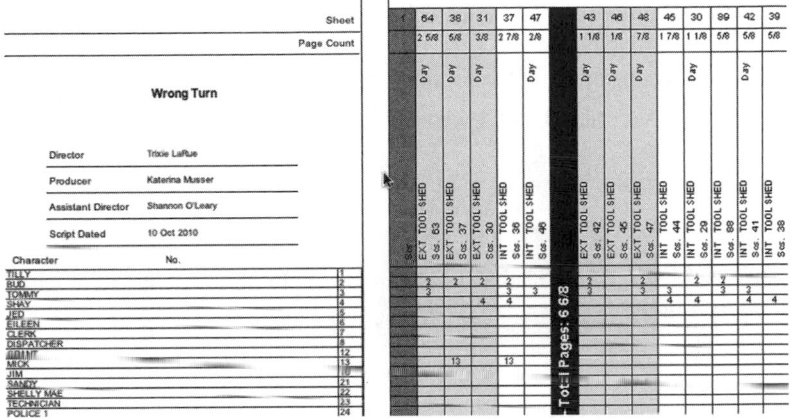


**FIG. 2.11**

Numbers convey information quickly

Scene #
Portion of Script Page
Employing numbers to indicate characters saves us from having to write out the entire name of the character:
"24" takes up much less space than the character's name, "Sindi-Rose Newman Landryski"


**FIG. 2.12**

Scene strip

Set Up Your System: Software, Colors, Numbers

*Set Character Numbers and Keep Them*

It's another one of those things that once you decide, that's it. You can assign a meaningful ID number (easier to remember) to each character, as is common practice, or number characters in the order they appear in the script (the default in scheduling programs). These numbers are political as well, reflecting the leverage of one actor over another (and the universal desire to be #1).

An example of meaningful identification numbers for your cast (1 = most important dramatic character (or actor), descending to least):

Bad guy (or comic relief) = 13

Joker/Wild card = 7

Couple and Pairs = Consecutive Characters – Cops 1, 2 – could be 21 and 22, or 31 and 32, linking them together in your mind.

**Table 2.5**

| Numbers in Order of Appearance | Meaningful ID Number |
|---|---|
| Cop 2 1 | Heroine Suz'n Banthony 1 |
| Main Character Parrot 2 | Main Character Parrot 2 |
| Supporting Character Uncle 3 | Main Character Dog 3 |
| Heroine Suz'n Banthony 4 | Supporting Character Dad 4 |
| Evil, Villainous Clown 5 | Supporting Character Mom 5 |
| Supporting Character Mom 6 | Supporting Character Aunt 6 |
| Cop 1 7 | Supporting Character Uncle 7 |
| Snarky Mime 8 | Superhero Grandma 8 |
| Main Character Dog 9 | Cop 1 9 |
| Supporting Character Dad 10 | Cop 2 10 |
| Spiteful Jester 11 | Snarky Mime 11 |
| Supporting Character Aunt 12 | Spiteful Jester 12 |
| Superhero Grandma 13 | Evil, Villainous Clown 13 |

*Set Page Numbers and Keep Them*

In production, it is not unusual for scripts to continue to change. *Maintain the integrity of your page numbers by locking them.* When material is added and it extends to the next page, the original page numbers remain intact. It's easy to do in a screenwriting program, but you have to make a concerted effort in a word processing software.

For example, once you've locked pages in Final Draft, a new page after 3 would become page 3A, then 3B, 3C, and so forth. Page 3 will remain the same.

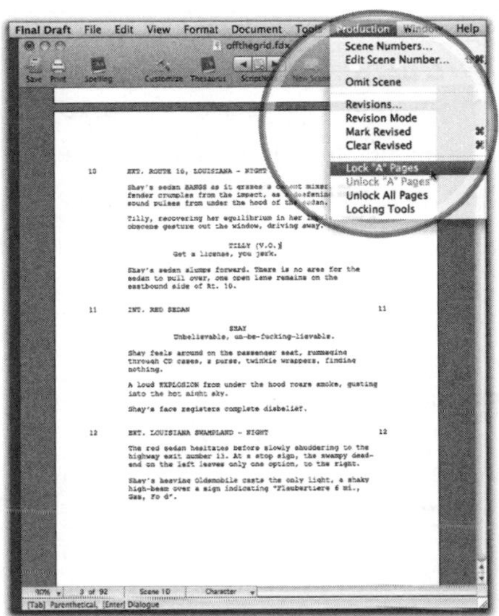


**FIG. 2.13**

Page locked

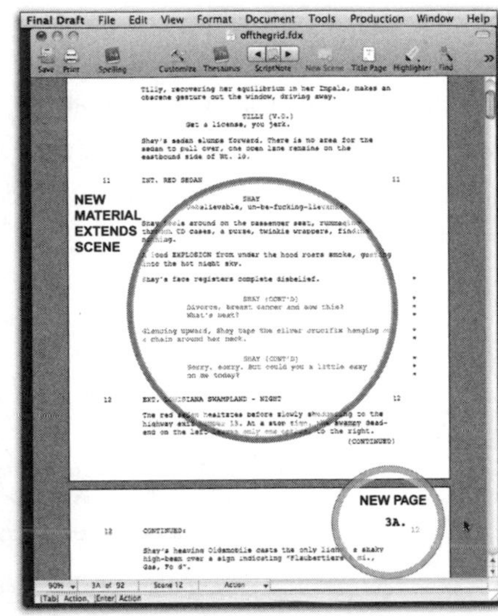


**FIG. 2.14**

Protects page #

The Department Heads you are working with may be familiar with these production tools in their software, but it is a critical part of *your* job to maintain the integrity of scene numbers and page numbers. *Problem prevention* is one reason why PMs and Line Producers are valued, though unsung, heroines and heroes.

### *Set Scene Numbers and Keep Them*

Consistency in scene numbers is important. The principal applied to page numbers applies to scene numbers. Once a scene gets a number, that's it. Scenes are defined by scene headings, defined by where and when the scene takes place. When adding a new scene between scene 23 and 24, the new scene(s) would be numbered 23A. We will go into further detail on this subject shortly.

## Breakdown Forms

Breakdown sheets contain details about each scene in a screenplay, and give us a way to organize, quantify, and inventory resources needed for each scene, one at a time. Depending on where you get breakdown sheets (scheduling software generates them) they look a little different, but serve the same purpose. Use those on our website.

**Table 2.6**

<table>
<tr><td>Color Code<br>***Day INT - White<br>Day EXT - Yellow<br>Night INT - Blue<br>Night EXT - Green</td><td colspan="2">SCRIPT BREAKDOWN SHEET<br>Production Title: <u>Big Baby Betsy____</u><br>Production Co:: <u>BBB, LLC______</u></td><td>Date:<br>18_Apr_2007<br>Script Version: White</td></tr>
<tr><td>Breakdown Page #<br>1</td><td colspan="2">Set<br>Pickle Family Living Room</td><td>Scene #<br>1</td></tr>
<tr><td>Int / Ext<br>INT</td><td>Day / Night<br>D</td><td>Location</td><td>Page Count<br>2/8</td></tr>
<tr><td colspan="3">Scene Synopsis<br>Betsy multitasks, playing a video game and sucking a drink</td><td>Prepared by:<br>Sally Forth</td></tr>
<tr><td>Cast (blue)<br>1. Betsy Pickle</td><td colspan="2">Extras (orange)<br>Extras Silent Bits/Background (yellow)</td><td>Stunts (red)</td></tr>
<tr><td>Special Effects (gray)<br>Light from TV?</td><td colspan="2">Props (brown)<br><br>Videogame console, Cup<br>Straw</td><td>Vehicles / Animals (light blue)</td></tr>
<tr><td>Wardrobe (circle pink)<br>Slacker clothes</td><td colspan="2">Make-up / Hair<br>(underline pink)</td><td>Sound / Music (plum)<br><br>Straw Suck Videogame noises</td></tr>
<tr><td>Special Equipment<br>***<br>Set Dressing<br>(lime green)<br>Living room furniture<br>Tattered sofa</td><td colspan="3">Production Notes (yellow)<br><u>ELECTRICS</u>: Light source from TV? Sp efx?<br><u>NOTE TO ALL</u>:<br><u>MAKE-UP/Hair</u>: Betsy is 'ugly-pretty', and always dishevelled<br><u>SOUND</u>: Add in post? 'cue for actors'<br><u>Prop</u>:<br>1. Multiple straws<br>2. Show video game player, need video games?</td></tr>
<tr><td colspan="4">Director Notes<br>Should empty boxes of Sc #3 be visible in this scene?</td></tr>
</table>

**Rule of Thumb**: The very top of a breakdown sheet (Table 2.7) contains macro information about the current version of the breakdown and schedule:

- Breakdown Color Code, indicating Day or Night/Interior or Exterior
- Production Title/Name, Production Company

- Date breakdown sheet is created
- Script Version color

**Table 2.7**

| *Color Code* | **SCRIPT BREAKDOWN SHEET** | |
|---|---|---|
| ******Day INT – White*** | | **Date:** |
| *Day EXT – Yellow*<br>*Night INT – Blue*<br>*Night EXT – Green* | **Production Title:** Big Baby Betsy<br>**Production Co::** BBB, LLC | 18_Apr_2007<br>**Script Version: White** |

Under this heading information we find the following (Table 2.8) (Mechanics and Logistics of one scene):

- Breakdown Page #
- Set Name in Script
- Scene #
- INTerior or EXTerior
- Time of Day (Day, Night, and sometimes Dawn or Dusk)
- Location (may not know yet, leave blank)
- Page Count (in eighths of a page)
- Scene Synopses – short vivid description of scene
- Name of person preparing breakdown sheet.

**Table 2.8**

| Breakdown Page #<br>1 | Set<br>**Pickle Family Living Room** | | Scene #<br>1 |
|---|---|---|---|
| Int / Ext<br>**INT** | Day / Night<br>**D** | Location | Page Count<br>2/8 |
| **Scene Synopsis**<br>Betsy multitasks, playing a video game and sucking a drink | | | **Prepared by:** Sally Forth |

The lower two-thirds of the breakdown sheet is *inventory*: listing every *element* in its respective *category* in that particular *scene*, and any questions (Table 2.9):

- Cast members (speaking parts)
- Extras (acting parts without dialogue)
- Extras (silent bits – **AKA:** Background/Atmosphere) (Silent background players filling out the scene like real life)
- Stunts (if unsure, put it in Director's Notes at bottom)

- Visual Effects, Special Effects (if unsure, put it in Director's Notes at bottom)
- Props (objects actors handle)
- Vehicles / Animals
- Wardrobe / Make-up / Hair
- Sound / Music
- Special Equipment: (if unsure, put it in Director's Notes at bottom)
- Set Dressing: (objects actors ignore)
- Production Notes (notes about scene for various departments)
- Director Notes (questions about the scene for the Director).

**Table 2.9**

| **Cast** (blue)<br>**1. Betsy** | **Extras**<br>(orange)<br>**Extras Silent Bits/Background**<br>(yellow) | **Stunts**<br>(red) |
|---|---|---|
| **Special Effects**<br>(gray) | **Props**<br>(brown)<br>Videogame console Cup<br>Straw | **Vehicles/Animals**<br>(light blue) |
| **Wardrobe**<br>(circle pink)<br>Slacker Clothes | **Make-up/Hair**<br>(underline pink) | **Sound/Music**<br>(plum)<br>Straw Suck<br>Videogame battle noises |
| **Special Equipment**<br>*** <br>**Set Dressing**<br>(lime green)<br>Living room furniture<br>Tattered sofa | **Production Notes**<br>(yellow)<br>**Security/Teachers/Add'l Personnel:**<br>**ELECTRICS:** Light source from TV?<br>**NOTE TO ALL:** Don't play the video game<br>**MAKE-UP/Hair:** Betsy is 'ugly- pretty', and always dishevelled<br>**SOUND:** Add in post? **'cue for actors'**<br>**Prop:**<br>1. Multiple straws<br>2. Show brand of video game, need video game boxes**?** | |
| **Director Notes**<br>Should empty boxes of Sc #3 be visible in this scene? | | |

Other color codes on the breakdown sheet include:

1. The *paper* color of the breakdown sheet itself.
2. The color of the *category* as identified in your marked script.

**Table 2.10**

| 1 | 2 |
|---|---|
| *Color Code*<br>******Day INT - White***<br>*Day EXT - Yellow*<br>*Night INT - Blue*<br>*Night EXT - Green* | **Stunts**<br>(red) |
| If you use colored breakdown sheets, the code at the top of the Breakdown Sheet communicates what those colors mean.<br><br>Day Interior Scenes are printed on white paper, for example. | Each category section is usually marked by the color that the corresponding item was marked in the script. |

## The Process of Breaking Down a Script

Breaking down a script is a systematic and fun procedure.

1. Read script through, with an open mind, as a spectator.
2. Talk to your team and establish the system you will employ – manual or software-driven? Which software? Decide.
3. Identify scene number. (Start at the beginning.)
4. Mark the portion (in eighths) of a page that the scene covers.
5. Identify resources in that scene – either on paper or with software.
6. Transfer that information to a breakdown form.
7. Go to the next scene (do it sequentially in order, don't jump around), repeat steps 2–6 until you get to the end of the script.

This process can be done manually, by hand, or using computer software, which has become popular and easy to use.

Many screenwriting software programs incorporating production tools can *add* scene numbers (you still have to *check* them) and calculate the eighths of a page (the portion of the page that a scene covers) so you can skip that step.

**Tools You Will Need**: Script, screenwriting program (optional), pencil, your breakdown code.

Manual Version

A. Identify the first scene, draw a line where it ends, and assign it a number (1).
B. Mark 1/8th of a page indicating how much of the page it takes up.
C. Identify each element in the scene.
D. Go to next scene and repeat.

The process using computer software is similar.

Computer Version in Screenwriting Software

A. In your screenwriting software, activate scene #s. Confirm that the number of each scene is appropriate (mark hidden scenes or parts).
B. Identify each element in the scene.

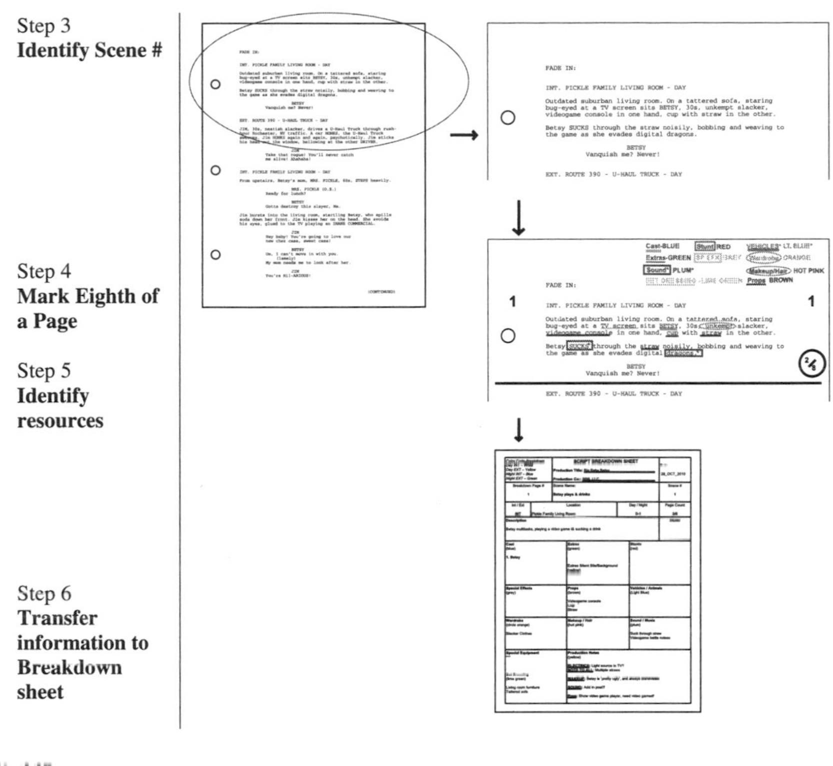


**FIG. 2.15**

Work one scene at a time

C. Transfer element information into a breakdown form.

D. Go to next scene and repeat.

**Rule of Thumb:** Hidden scenes (or parts) don't start with a slug line, but are clearly separate units: photographs, computer screen or TV show inserts, stock historical footage, flashback, flash forward, cutaway shots.

Computer Version in PDF

A. Open script in PDF software (which allows you to mark or annotate it). Identify the first scene, draw a line where it ends, and assign it a number (1).

B. Mark 1/8th of a page indicating how much of the page it takes up.

C. Identify each element in the scene.

D. Transfer information to breakdown form.

E. Go to next scene and repeat.

- When you get to the last scene, you're done with the breakdown process, and ready to move on to scheduling.

**Read Script Completely Through**

Reading a script through once gives you an initial introduction to the material. Put down your pencil, get a snack, get comfy, and read.

This is a good idea for three reasons:

A. You get a first impression; enjoying the story as a spectator.

B. The questions that arise will be confirmed as you commence the breakdown process; and

C. It's hard to go back. After you break down a script, you won't see it the same way. This is the last time you'll see the "forest" for the "trees," before working on it — retaining a lasting impression of the work as a complete story instead of a series of scenes containing elements, questions and puzzle pieces to be moved around.

This may sound obvious, but it's an easy step to skip if you are in a rush. Reading all the way through is helpful because when you start working, you will be ready to ask good questions, which is a critical part of the process. (For example: Is Mrs. Kringle the same character as Sue-Ellen Claus? Is the van in the beginning the same one at the end — didn't it get blown up? Does Ali the dog carry a blanket around in **every** scene?)

If you can read the screenplay in one sitting, even better. If not, that's fine too. In an increasingly digital world, maybe you prefer reading on a computer or iPad tablet — that's great, as long as you can actually read without distraction.

**Number Scenes**

Scene numbers need to remain the *same* once they are set. They are the foundations upon which a schedule and budget are built.

Why not line the whole thing at once? Isn't that what the computer will do? It is tempting, but it takes your attention away from considering each scene carefully. There may be scenes hidden inside other scenes, and you need to ferret them out.

**Before**

2.

CONTINUED:

Tilly hunts down on the floor for the cigarette with one hand, giving up with a shrug. Half a bleary eye on the road, Tilly reaches into the back seat to quiet the suddenly-woken child in the car-seat, swerving.

INT. WHITE IMPALA, BACK SEAT

A dirty BABY, 2, in green wrinkled pajamas with one tiny tuft of hair, CRIES beating chubby fists. The back seat is covered in debris, cigarette cartons, empty beer cans, with the baby's car-seat wedged in between.

TILLY<br>(slurring)<br>Shit. Sh, go back to sleep, almost there.

EXT. ROUTE 10, LOUISIANA - NIGHT

As the child's WAILS increase, the Impala lurches to a stop, blocking the only remaining open lane on the east-bound side of Alligator Alley.

This sudden maneuver forces the aging red sedan quickly approaching from behind, to jerk into the blocked lane. The red sedan scatters traffic cones with the Uhaul trailer it's towing, fishtailing and almost tipping over.

TILLY<br>(V.O.)<br>I said quiet down!

INT. RED SEDAN

SHAY, 20s, in a red baseball cap, has all her windows open in the humid sultry June night, as she slams on the brakes.

Rubber burns on the pavement as Shay is catapulted forward into the windshield, saved at the last minute by her worn seatbelt.

Brakes SCREAM.

SHAY<br>Ahhhhhh!

**FIG. 2.16**

Script page: **before** scene numbers are added

**After**

1 INT. WHITE IMPALA, BACK SEAT 1

Tilly hunts down on the floor for the cigarette with one hand, giving up with a shrug. Half a bleary eye on the road, Tilly reaches into the back seat to quiet the suddenly-woken child in the car-seat, swerving.

A dirty BABY, 2, in green wrinkled pajamas with one tiny tuft of hair, CRIES beating chubby fists. The back seat is covered in debris, cigarette cartons, empty beer cans, with the baby's car-seat wedged in between.

TILLY<br>(slurring)<br>Shit. Sh, go back to sleep, almost there.

EXT. ROUTE 10, LOUISIANA - NIGHT

As the child's WAILS increase, the Impala lurches to a stop, blocking the only remaining open lane on the east-bound side of Alligator Alley.

This sudden maneuver forces the aging red sedan quickly approaching from behind, to jerk into the blocked lane. The red sedan scatters traffic cones with the Uhaul trailer it's towing, fishtailing and almost tipping over.

TILLY<br>(V.O.)<br>I said quiet down!

INT. RED SEDAN

SHAY, 20s, in a red baseball cap, has all her windows open in the humid sultry June night, as she slams on the brakes.

Rubber burns on the pavement as Shay is catapulted forward into the windshield, saved at the last minute by her worn seatbelt.

Brakes SCREAM.

SHAY<br>Ahhhhhh!

**FIG. 2.17**

**After** scenes are numbered (manually)

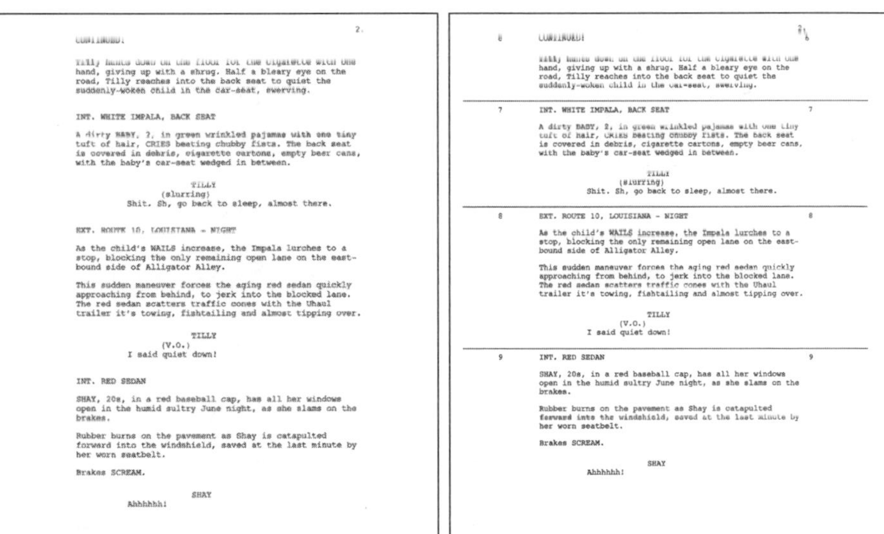

2.

CONTINUED:

Tilly hunts down on the floor for the cigarette with one hand, giving up with a shrug. Half a bleary eye on the road, Tilly reaches into the back seat to quiet the suddenly-woken child in the car-seat, swerving.

INT. WHITE IMPALA, BACK SEAT

A dirty BABY, 2, in green wrinkled pajamas with one tiny tuft of hair, CRIES beating chubby fists. The back seat is covered in debris, cigarette cartons, empty beer cans, with the baby's car-seat wedged in between.

TILLY<br>(slurring)<br>Shit. Sh, go back to sleep, almost there.

EXT. ROUTE 10, LOUISIANA - NIGHT

As the child's WAILS increase, the Impala lurches to a stop, blocking the only remaining open lane on the east-bound side of Alligator Alley.

This sudden maneuver forces the aging red sedan quickly approaching from behind, to jerk into the blocked lane. The red sedan scatters traffic cones with the Uhaul trailer it's towing, fishtailing and almost tipping over.

TILLY<br>(V.O.)<br>I said quiet down!

INT. RED SEDAN

SHAY, 20s, in a red baseball cap, has all her windows open in the humid sultry June night, as she slams on the brakes.

Rubber burns on the pavement as Shay is catapulted forward into the windshield, saved at the last minute by her worn seatbelt.

Brakes SCREAM.

SHAY<br>Ahhhhhh!

**FIG. 2.18**

Script page: **before** scene numbers are added

6 CONTINUED: 2.

Tilly hunts down on the floor for the cigarette with one hand, giving up with a shrug. Half a bleary eye on the road, Tilly reaches into the back seat to quiet the suddenly-woken child in the car-seat, swerving.

7 INT. WHITE IMPALA, BACK SEAT 7

A dirty BABY, 2, in green wrinkled pajamas with one tiny tuft of hair, CRIES beating chubby fists. The back seat is covered in debris, cigarette cartons, empty beer cans, with the baby's car-seat wedged in between.

TILLY<br>(slurring)<br>Shit. Sh, go back to sleep, almost there.

8 EXT. ROUTE 10, LOUISIANA - NIGHT 8

As the child's WAILS increase, the Impala lurches to a stop, blocking the only remaining open lane on the east-bound side of Alligator Alley.

This sudden maneuver forces the aging red sedan quickly approaching from behind, to jerk into the blocked lane. The red sedan scatters traffic cones with the Uhaul trailer it's towing, fishtailing and almost tipping over.

TILLY<br>(V.O.)<br>I said quiet down!

9 INT. RED SEDAN 9

SHAY, 20s, in a red baseball cap, has all her windows open in the humid sultry June night, as she slams on the brakes.

Rubber burns on the pavement as Shay is catapulted forward into the windshield, saved at the last minute by her worn seatbelt.

Brakes SCREAM.

SHAY<br>Ahhhhhh!

**FIG. 2.19**

**After** scenes are numbered (using software)

To turn on scene numbers in Final Draft, open the Production menu.

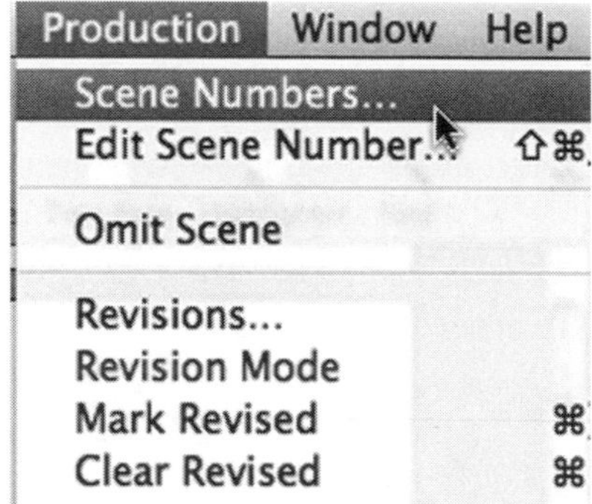


**FIG. 2.20**

Production tools

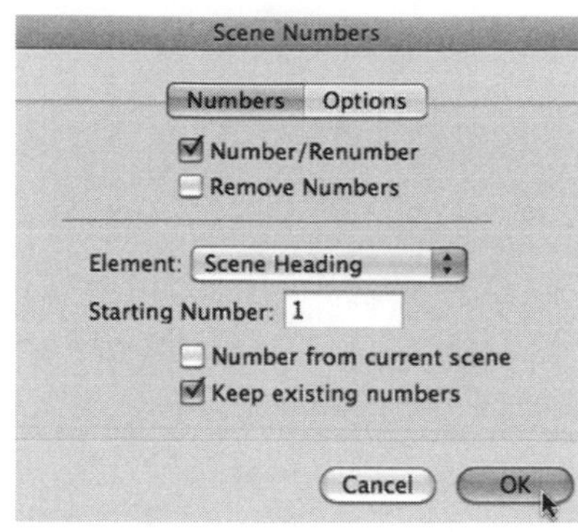


**FIG. 2.21**

Check number

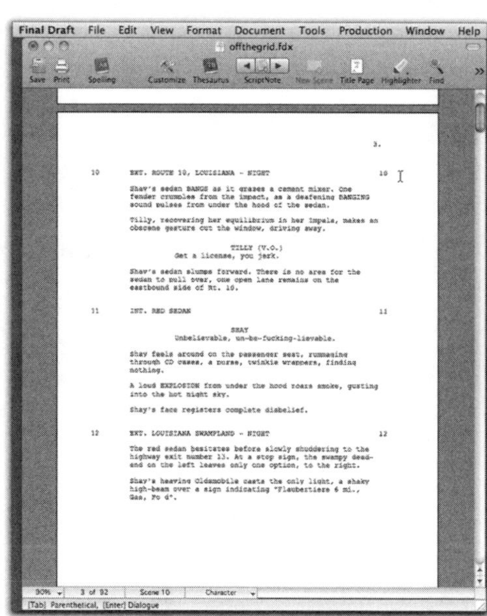


3.

10 EXT. ROUTE 10, LOUISIANA - NIGHT 10

Shay's sedan BANGS as it grazes a cement mixer. One fender crumples from the impact, as a deafening BANGING sound pulses from under the hood of the sedan.

Tilly, recovering her equilibrium in her Impala, makes an obscene gesture out the window, driving away.

TILLY (V.O.)
Get a license, you jerk.

Shay's sedan slumps forward. There is no area for the sedan to pull over, one open lane remains on the eastbound side of Rt. 10.

11 INT. RED SEDAN 11

SHAY
Unbelievable, un-be-fucking-lievable.

Shay feels around on the passenger seat, rummaging through CD cases, a purse, twinkie wrappers, finding nothing.

A loud EXPLOSION from under the hood roars smoke, gusting into the hot night sky.

Shay's face registers complete disbelief.

12 EXT. LOUISIANA SWAMPLAND - NIGHT 12

The red sedan hesitates before slowly shuddering to the highway exit number 13. At a stop sign, the swampy dead-end on the left leaves only one option, to the right.

Shay's heaving Oldsmobile casts the only light, a shaky high-beam over a sign indicating "Flaubertiere 6 mi., Gas, Fo d".

**FIG. 2.22**

Scene #s on

*Set Scene Numbers and Keep Them*

Set scene numbers and *keep* them, even if scenes are deleted (omitted). **AKA:** Delete = Omit

*Delete a Scene*

If the Director wants to eliminate a scene, mark "OMIT scene 89" on the:

- Screenplay (by hand or by computer)
  - Scene before scene 89
  - Scene after scene 89
- Breakdown sheet for scene 89.

This process is similar in screenwriting programs.

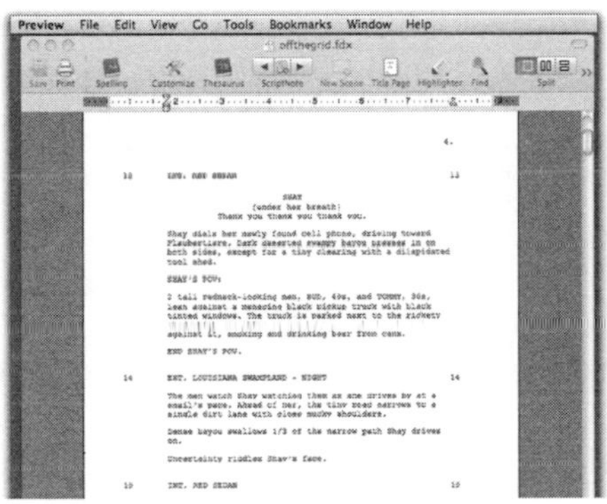


**FIG. 2.23**

Opon

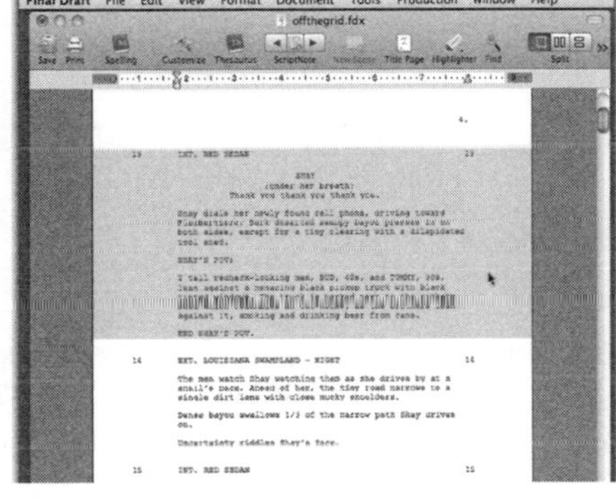


**FIG. 2.24**

Select

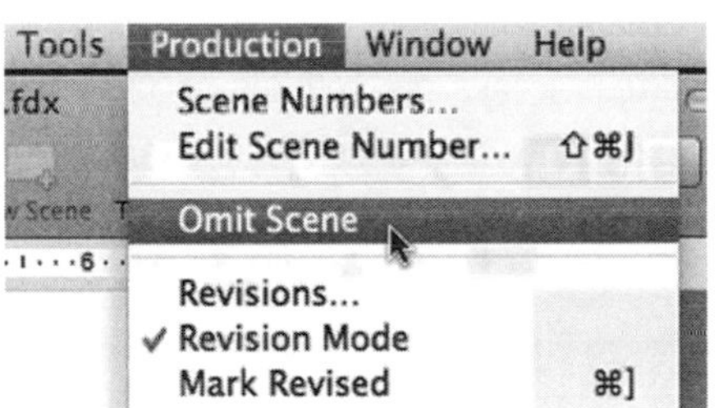


**FIG. 2.25**

Omit

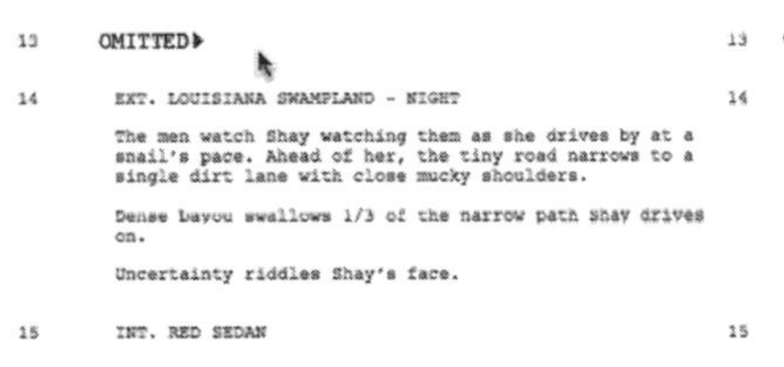


**FIG. 2.26**

Result

*Add a Scene*

If the Director wants to insert scenes, it's not a problem. Add A, B, C up front. For example, the Department Head wrote a new scene, between #16 and #17.

| Existing Scene | |
|---|---|
| 16 | |
| 17 | |

The new scene is #A17.

| **Existing Scene** | **New Scene #** |
|---|---|
| **16** | |
| | A17 |
| **17** | |

Scenes inserted after A17 would be lettered consecutively.

| **Existing Scene** | **New Scene #** |
|---|---|
| 16 | |
| | A17 |
| | B17 |
| | C17 |
| 17 | |

**Eighths of a Page**

Counting segments of a script page as eighths is a way to measure shooting progress, and show how much of a page a scene covers.

Fold a script page, top to bottom, three times to divide it into eighths; each section is about an inch long. Starting at the top of a script page, scenes that are about one fold (1 inch) = 1/8th of a page.

Production management software calculates this automatically. When you are doing this manually, it's an inexact science. The shortest scenes are counted as the minimum, i.e., one-eighth of a page — a guesstimate. When a scene is exactly the length of a page, it's one page (8/8ths). Likewise, for scenes that extend longer than one page, the sum would be:

| Full Page | Partial Page | Total Page Count |
|---|---|---|
| 1 + | 2/8ths = | 1 2/8ths |
| 2 + | 5/8ths = | 2 5/8ths |

A scene that has:

2/8 on the bottom of page 1 &

\+ 2/8 on the top of page 2

= 4/8

No fancy math (for example 1 and 2/8ths pages *would not* equal 10/8ths); don't reduce fractions (2/8ths is not ¼). If a scene isn't quite 1/8th and it isn't quite 2/

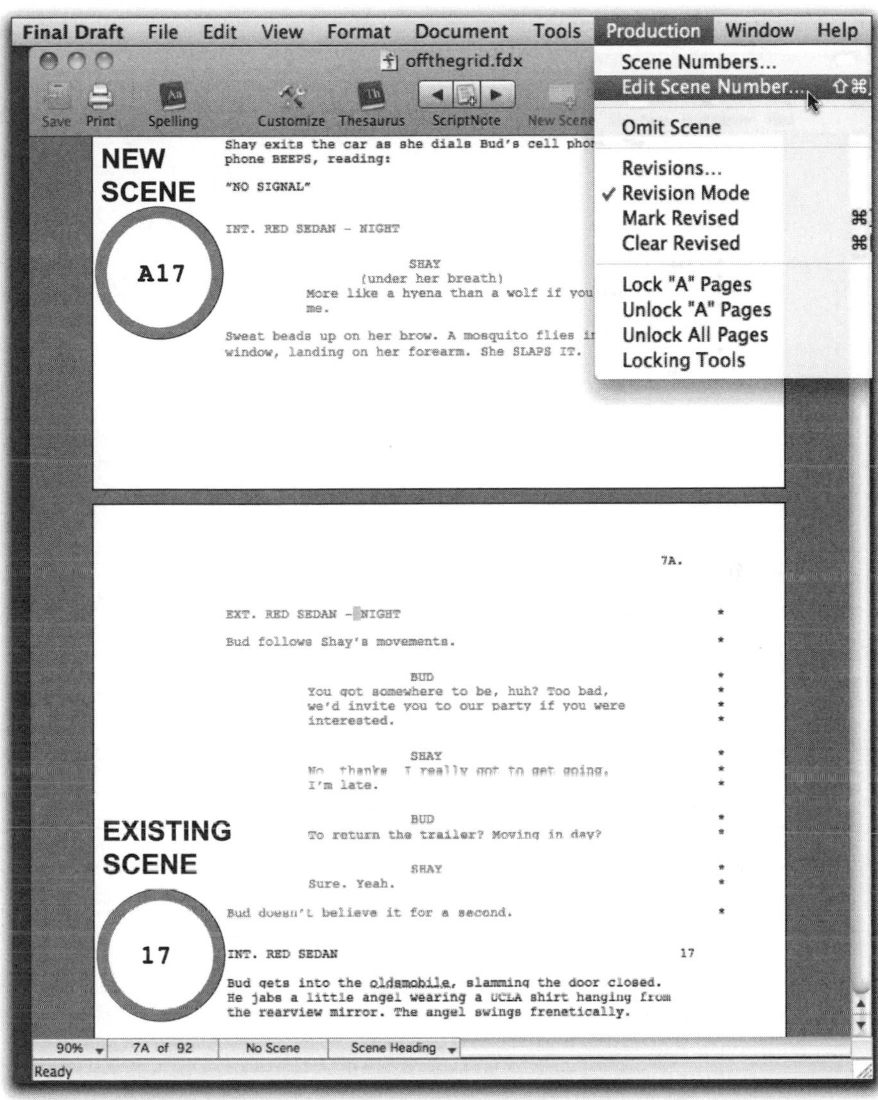


**FIG. 2.27**

Insert scene in Final Draft

8ths, what do you do? Let the material guide you; give stunts and complex scenes more eighths, simpler scenes less. Although this is a matter of occasional debate, keep life simple. Once in a blue moon a page will have more than 8/8ths, which is no big deal. Rarely will all the scenes of a screenplay perfectly line up so that each eighth falls exactly at a scene heading; use your best judgment.

**FIG. 2.28**

Approximate length of eighths of page

### Identify Resources

Identifying resources is the process of marking each element you will need and assigning it to its proper category. Each scene contains one or more visual or audio categories, such as cast, vehicles, props, wardrobe and more.

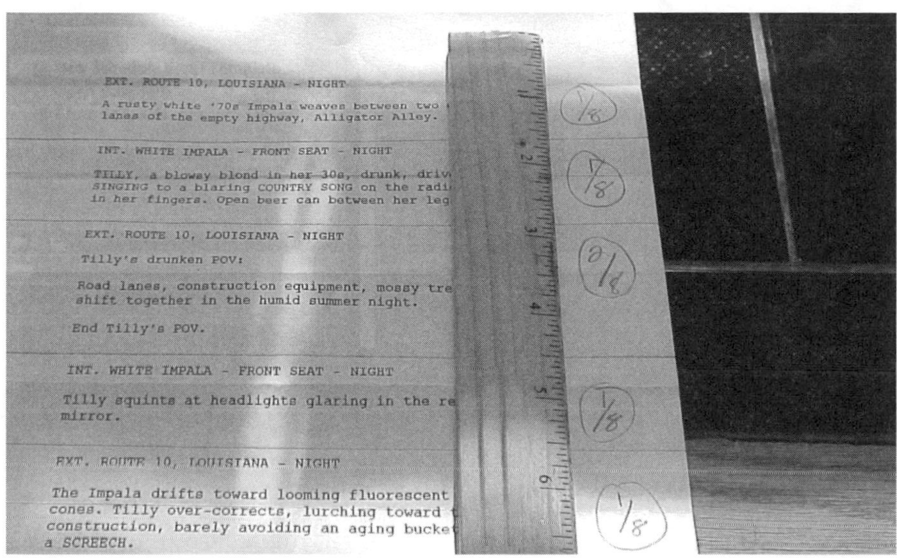

EXT. ROUTE 10, LOUISIANA - NIGHT
A rusty white '70s Impala weaves between two
lanes of the empty highway, Alligator Alley.
INT. WHITE IMPALA - FRONT SEAT - NIGHT
TILLY, a blowsy blond in her 30s, drunk, driv
SINGING to a blaring COUNTRY SONG on the radi
in her fingers. Open beer can between her leg
EXT. ROUTE 10, LOUISIANA - NIGHT
Tilly's drunken POV:
Road lanes, construction equipment, mossy tre
shift together in the humid summer night.
End Tilly's POV.
INT. WHITE IMPALA - FRONT SEAT - NIGHT
Tilly squints at headlights glaring in the re
mirror.
EXT. ROUTE 10, LOUISIANA - NIGHT
The Impala drifts toward looming fluorescent
cones. Tilly over-corrects, lurching toward
construction, barely avoiding an aging bucke
a SCREECH.
1/8
1/8
2/8
1/8
1/8


**FIG. 2.29**

One-eighth of a page is about 1 inch long

EXT. CHARACTERS GRILL – PARKING LOT – NIGHT

The parking lot of the seedy strip-mall bar is deserted, except for the rusty blue Pickup Truck, idling.

JEANETTE, 20s, leans her head out of the open window, applying red lipstick in her driver's side mirror. Impatiently, she REVS the engine.

Identify each element (Jeannette, blue pickup truck, red lipstick) assigning it to its category:

- Jeannette = Cast
- Blue truck = Vehicle
- Red lipstick = Prop

Whatever system you use, you will need to indicate every element needed for the shoot.

Rule of Thumb:

1. Start at the beginning of the scene.
2. Work one scene at a time.

3. Identify one category of elements at a time.
4. Work systematically at first to make sure you do not miss anything.

Whether working *manually* on paper or using a *tagging* function associated with a software program like Final Draft, Celtx, Movie Magic Screenwriter:

Category

1. Cast (speaking)
2. Extras
3. Props
4. Sound
5. Stunt
6. Special Effects
7. Costume/Wardrobe
8. Make-up
9. Livestock/Animals
10. Animal Handler
11. Music
12. Vehicles
13. Set Dressing
14. Greenery
15. Special Equipment
16. Notes (questions for your team)

Then go through the list again for Scene 2. Let's go through an example. Feel free to print this out from our website and participate.

**Table 2.11**

| Code | Category |
|---|---|
| Underline THICK | Cast |
| Underline SKINNY | Extras |
| Box ** | Stunt/Special Equipment |
| Circle | Vehicles |
| Circle | Props |
| ** | Special Effects |
| Circle** | Costume/Wardrobe |
| Circle** | Make-up/Hair |
| Box | Livestock/Animals |
| Box | Music/ Sound |
| Circle | Set Dressing |

Write the key on the first page of the script so that anyone looking at the script will understand how the categories are marked. 

- Mark Scene 1 by drawing a line at the end of the scene, before the next slug line (Int. or Ext.).
- Write the Scene #.
- Indicate 8th page portion, 7/8th of a page.
- Start with Category 1 – Cast. Identify each cast member with a thick underline, as per the key.

**CATEGORY #1 – Cast:** Typically, the first time a character is named in a screenplay, the NAME is CAPITALIZED.

How many characters appear in Scene #1? Five: Irma Stickle, Harv Stickle and three white-haired ladies. Lois, Celia, Hedy.

**CATEGORY #2 – Extras:** Take a look at Scene #1 in Figure 2.30 again. Are there extras in this scene? One might wonder whether Lois, Celia and Hedy are extras, but it is unusual to give extras names, and Lois has dialogue. To make sure, you could flip through the next few pages to look. As it happens, these three characters speak several lines in the upcoming pages. We will consider them as cast, not extras.

**CATEGORY #3 – Props:** Circle props in Scene #1.

Multiple golf balls, golf club.

Did questions arise? Do you imagine that Harv, teaching Irma to play golf, might have his own club? Note to ask the Director. When Irma swings her club and **misses**, there is no direct mention of her missing a golf **ball**; it's implied, so under production notes, note the need for extra golf balls. Casting: actors auditioning for Harv – can they play golf or fake it?

**CATEGORY #4 – Sound:** What sounds happen during Scene #1? According to your key, use a box to identify them.

Golf balls **MISS**, **FLIES**, **WHIZ**, **THWACK** on the head, **SAIL** through the air.

Will these sounds occur on the set? More likely to be added afterwards, in post. Make a note that the actors will need a cue to react as if they heard that sound. Mention to the AD / Director.

| | | | |
|---|---|---|---|
| Underline THICK | Cast | ** | Special Effects |
| Underline SKINNY | Extras | Circle** | Costume/Wardrobe |
| Box ** | Stunt/Special Equipment | Circle** | Makeup/Hair |
| Circle | Vehicles | Box | Livestock/Animals |
| Circle | Props | Box | Music Sound |
| | | Circle | Set Dressing |

```
FADE IN:

1    EXT. GOLF DRIVING RANGE -- DAY                          1

     Shiny Acres, Florida driving range attached to a golf   7/8
     course. Golf balls WHIZ through the air.

     Concentrating fiercely, mousy IRMA STICKLE (50s), awkward
     and new to the game, juts a hip with a wild swing of her
     club.

     She MISSES, the club FLIES and THWACKS her husband,
     overconfident HARV STICKLE, (60s) upside the head.

                          HARV
               What the!? Owwwwwww.

                          IRMA
               Are you ok? I'm sorry honey!

     Exasperated, Harv rubs his forehead.

                          HARV
               I'll show you, again.

     Harv positions Irma with her club in front of a ball,
     bends, pokes and prods her into an impossible contortion.

                          HARV (CONT'D)
               Now, just swing naturally.

     3 White Haired Ladies (70s), tan and swanky, LOIS, CELIA,
     and HEDY, in loud golf gear, approach.

                          HARV (CONT'D)
               And make it good, people are watching.

     Sweat beading on her lip, sun glaring in her eyes, Irma
     closes her eyes and fires away. The ball SAILS off.

     Irma clutches the wrenching pain in her lower back.

     Lois, the cougar of the group, gives Harv a hungry look.

                          LOIS
               Hi there.

                          HARV
               Hello ladies!
_____________________________________________________________

     INT. HAIR SALON - DAY

     The salon looks like a prison, bad lighting, ugly.
```

**FIG. 2.30**

Identify cast

Continue until you have identified each element by category — from stunts to notes, in Scene #1. The breakdown process described may seem careful and slow, but once the process is clear, start identifying elements as you read each line.

### *Identify as You Read*

With repetition, the process will become more organic, and you will identify elements as you read marking or, coding each element as you scan the text.

If you are using a *tagging* function in Final Draft, Celtx, Movie Magic Screenwriter:

- Start at the beginning of the scene;

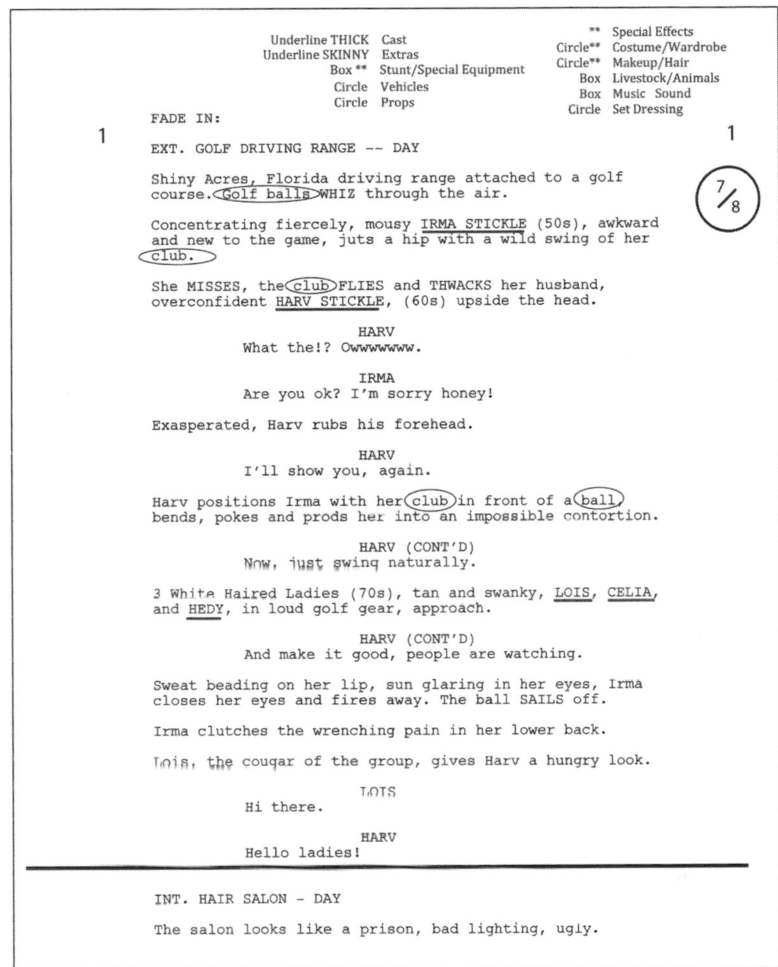

Underline THICK Cast
Underline SKINNY Extras
Box ** Stunt/Special Equipment
Circle Vehicles
Circle Props

** Special Effects
Circle** Costume/Wardrobe
Circle** Makeup/Hair
Box Livestock/Animals
Box Music Sound
Circle Set Dressing

FADE IN:

1 EXT. GOLF DRIVING RANGE -- DAY 1

Shiny Acres, Florida driving range attached to a golf course. Golf balls WHIZ through the air.

7/8

Concentrating fiercely, mousy IRMA STICKLE (50s), awkward and new to the game, juts a hip with a wild swing of her club.

She MISSES, the club FLIES and THWACKS her husband, overconfident HARV STICKLE, (60s) upside the head.

HARV
What the!? Owwwwwww.

IRMA
Are you ok? I'm sorry honey!

Exasperated, Harv rubs his forehead.

HARV
I'll show you, again.

Harv positions Irma with her club in front of a ball, bends, pokes and prods her into an impossible contortion.

HARV (CONT'D)
Now, just swing naturally.

3 White Haired Ladies (70s), tan and swanky, LOIS, CELIA, and HEDY, in loud golf gear, approach.

HARV (CONT'D)
And make it good, people are watching.

Sweat beading on her lip, sun glaring in her eyes, Irma closes her eyes and fires away. The ball SAILS off.

Irma clutches the wrenching pain in her lower back.

Lois, the cougar of the group, gives Harv a hungry look.

LOIS
Hi there.

HARV
Hello ladies!

INT. HAIR SALON - DAY

The salon looks like a prison, bad lighting, ugly.

**FIG. 2.31**

Identify props

- As you read, assign each element to its appropriate **category** by double clicking on the element (IRMA STICKLE) as you read, then click the applicable **category** (Cast Members), or drag the element over. (Your software may already identify Scene Headings, Sets and Characters with Dialogue due to formatting.)

Start with **Cast**. Read the first scene looking for **Cast**, and click on it.

Work **one** scene at a time, through each **category**, identifying every **element** in that category.

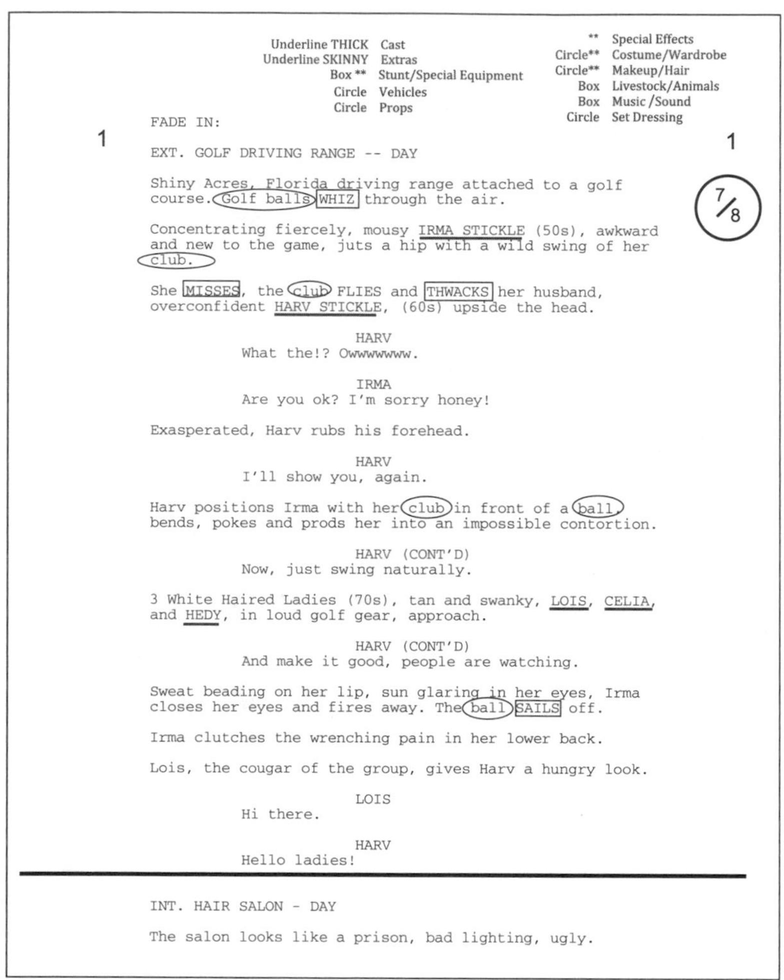

Underline THICK Cast
Underline SKINNY Extras
Box ** Stunt/Special Equipment
Circle Vehicles
Circle Props

** Special Effects
Circle** Costume/Wardrobe
Circle** Makeup/Hair
Box Livestock/Animals
Box Music /Sound
Circle Set Dressing

FADE IN:

1 EXT. GOLF DRIVING RANGE -- DAY 1

Shiny Acres, Florida driving range attached to a golf course. Golf balls WHIZ through the air.

7/8

Concentrating fiercely, mousy IRMA STICKLE (50s), awkward and new to the game, juts a hip with a wild swing of her club.

She MISSES, the club FLIES and THWACKS her husband, overconfident HARV STICKLE, (60s) upside the head.

HARV
What the!? Owwwwwww.

IRMA
Are you ok? I'm sorry honey!

Exasperated, Harv rubs his forehead.

HARV
I'll show you, again.

Harv positions Irma with her club in front of a ball, bends, pokes and prods her into an impossible contortion.

HARV (CONT'D)
Now, just swing naturally.

3 White Haired Ladies (70s), tan and swanky, LOIS, CELIA, and HEDY, in loud golf gear, approach.

HARV (CONT'D)
And make it good, people are watching.

Sweat beading on her lip, sun glaring in her eyes, Irma closes her eyes and fires away. The ball SAILS off.

Irma clutches the wrenching pain in her lower back.

Lois, the cougar of the group, gives Harv a hungry look.

LOIS
Hi there.

HARV
Hello ladies!

INT. HAIR SALON - DAY

The salon looks like a prison, bad lighting, ugly.

**FIG. 2.32**

Identify each sound

Tagging features offer an option to **tag** an element (identifying it in a certain category) once, and in certain programs, **globally** (i.e., every time the computer sees that item, prop, vehicle, costume, it is assigned to the proper category). It's a powerful feature. Try a few different approaches, and decide what you like best.

Once you have completed the tagging process, **export** the file (Dropdown: File/Export) saving it as a **.SEX** file to be imported into a scheduling program.

The pros of tagging in a program like Celtx are that you work in the native file, and if there are inconsistencies, you can fix them right there. This is particularly helpful

| | | | |
|---|---|---|---|
| Underline THICK | Cast | ** | Special Effects |
| Underline SKINNY | Extras | Circle** | Costume/Wardrobe |
| Box ** | Stunt/Special Equipment | Circle** | Makeup/Hair |
| Circle | Vehicles | Box | Livestock/Animals |
| Circle | Props | Box | Music/Sound |
| | | Circle | Set Dressing |

FADE IN:

1 EXT. GOLF DRIVING RANGE -- DAY 1

Shiny Acres, Florida driving range attached to a golf course. Golf balls WHIZ through the air.

7/8

Concentrating fiercely, mousy IRMA STICKLE (50s), awkward and new to the game, juts a hip with a wild swing of her club.

She MISSES, the club FLIES and THWACKS her husband, overconfident HARV STICKLE, (60s) upside the head.

HARV
What the!? Owwwwwww.

IRMA
Are you ok? I'm sorry honey!

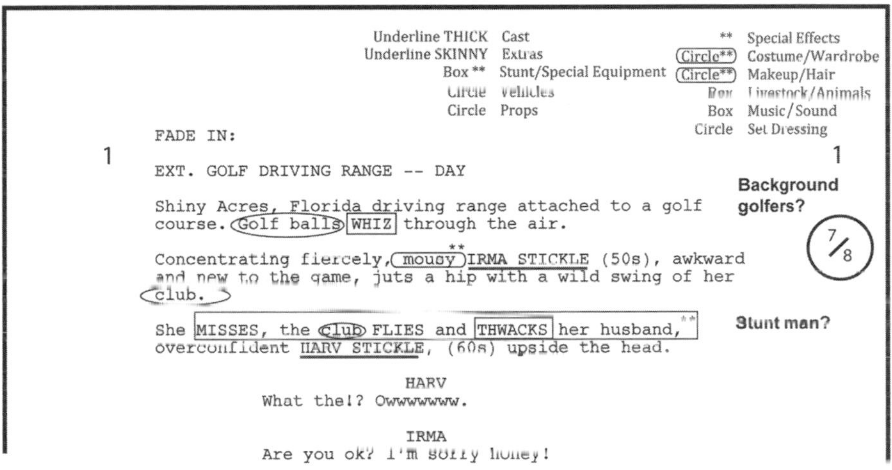

| | | | |
|---|---|---|---|
| Underline THICK | Cast | ** | Special Effects |
| Underline SKINNY | Extras | Circle** | Costume/Wardrobe |
| Box ** | Stunt/Special Equipment | Circle** | Makeup/Hair |
| Circle | Vehicles | Box | Livestock/Animals |
| Circle | Props | Box | Music/Sound |
| | | Circle | Set Dressing |

FADE IN:

1 EXT. GOLF DRIVING RANGE -- DAY 1

Background golfers?

Shiny Acres, Florida driving range attached to a golf course. Golf balls WHIZ through the air.

7/8

Concentrating fiercely, mousy IRMA STICKLE (50s), awkward and new to the game, juts a hip with a wild swing of her club.

She MISSES, the club FLIES and THWACKS her husband, overconfident HARV STICKLE, (60s) upside the head.

Stunt man?

HARV
What the!? Owwwwwww.

IRMA
Are you ok? I'm sorry honey!

**FIG. 2.33**

Identify elements as you read

for hyphenate filmmakers who are Department Head-Directors, or Department Head-Producers. The cons of tagging are that, unlike marking a script directly, you don't have a lined script once you are finished.

### Transfer Information to Breakdown Forms

Working through the script one scene at a time, identify resources, and then transfer that information to the breakdown form.

#### *Breakdown Using Scheduling Program*

If you want to *skip* the step of transferring resources onto paper breakdown sheets and instead enter the information directly into a scheduling program, that can save

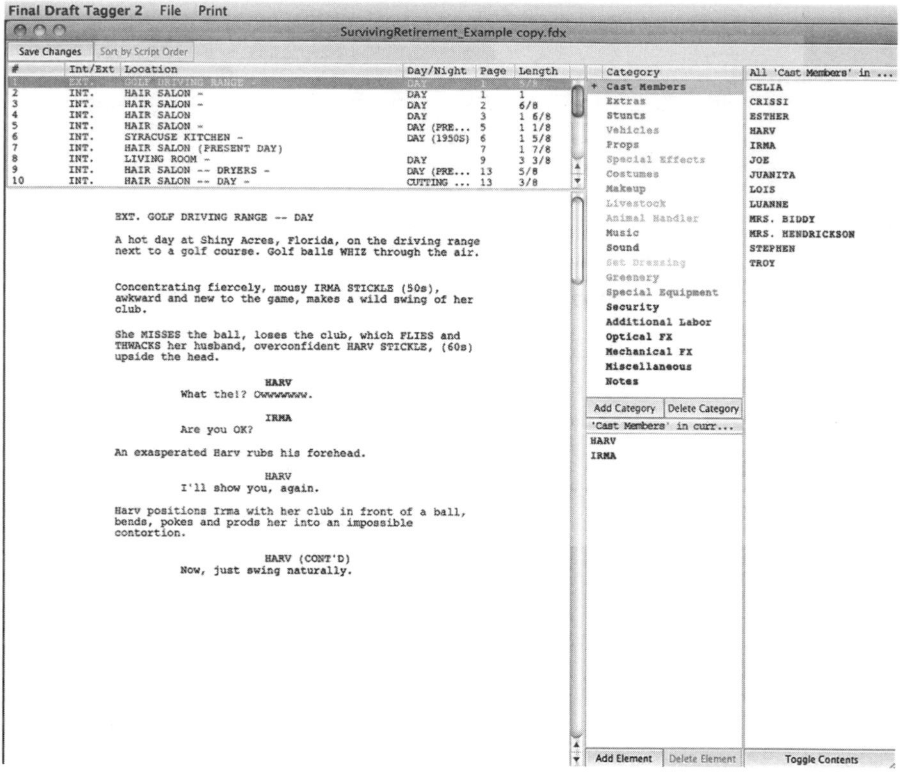

**FIG. 2.34**

Tagging programs can start the breakdown process

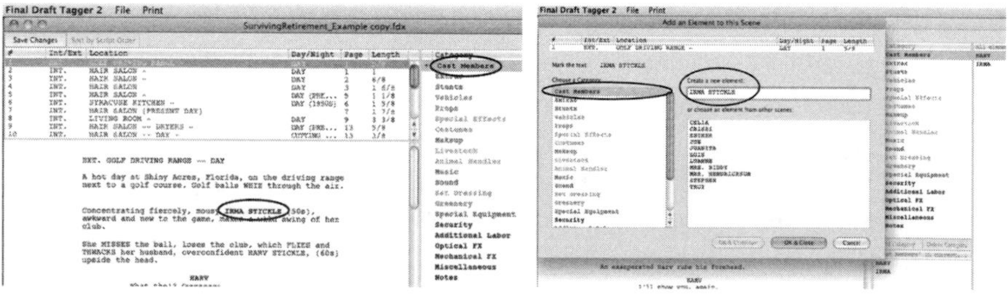

**FIG. 2.35**

Identify cast in Final Draft tagger

**FIG. 2.36**

Tag cast in Final Draft tagger

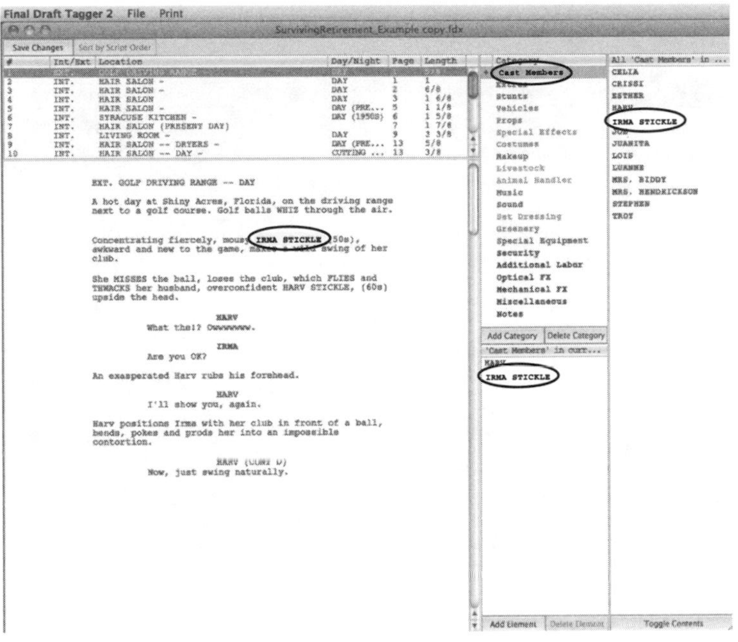


**FIG. 2.37**

Tag all elements in Final Draft tagger

time (once the script's page numbers and scene numbers are locked). We will discuss this in Chapter Three in more detail.

It is a four-part process:

1. From your screenwriting program, **export** your script as a .SEX file (**CYA**: pages **locked**, scene #s **turned on**); 
2. Open your scheduling program and start a new schedule
3. **Import** the .SEX file (this takes a couple of minutes so get a beverage);

   You land on the first breakdown sheet for Scene 1:

4. Just like the manual process, start with the first scene. Work one category at a time; **transfer** each **element** into the appropriate **category.**

Transfer information about each **element** in that scene.

The resulting breakdown sheet leaves blank category names unused in that scene, saving you ink.

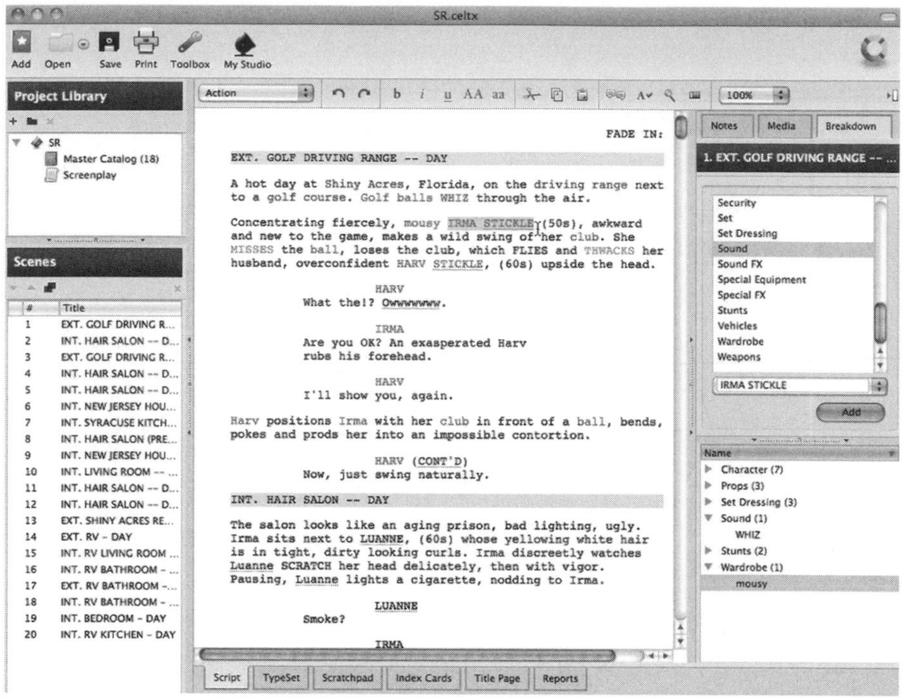

**FIG. 2.38**

Tagging all elements in Celtx

There are categories we need the Director, AD, Producer and Department Heads to help us identify regarding crew, stunts, special effects and equipment. Certain elements and categories raise questions. Document them in *production notes* then follow up.

As you go through the breakdown scene by scene, get in the habit of consciously asking yourself the questions in Table 2.13, and before long, they will emerge automatically. *Questions are good!* Whatever their title, the person breaking down the script is an easy target if something goes wrong. We are the guardians of information — the better we know the material, the easier it is to stay current on what's going on. It's important to stay current on what dramatic resources are required. When the script changes, the breakdown may have to be updated, for a couple of reasons.

Dramatic resources should be interpreted through your *question* filter, which may affect the schedule and budget.

1. Locations — when, where, permits, safety, neighbors, legality, access, power.
2. Human (cast, crew) — when, where, arrival and departure times, schedule, rules.

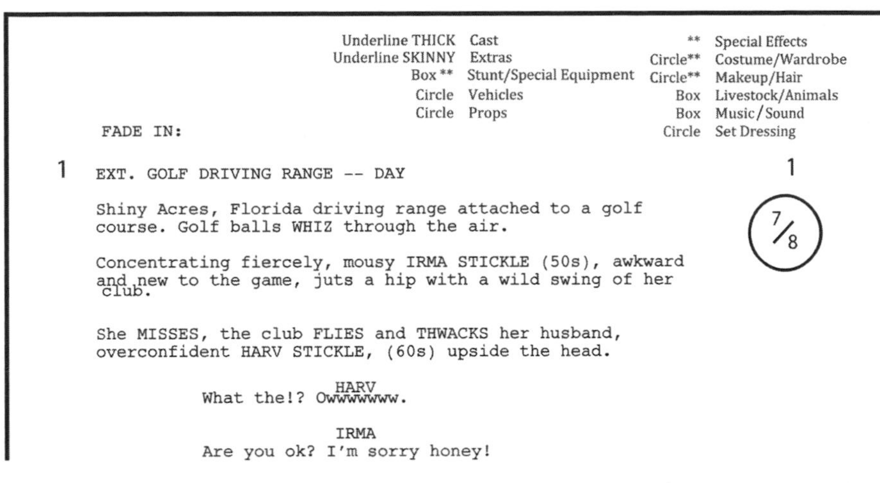
Underline THICK Cast
Underline SKINNY Extras
Box ** Stunt/Special Equipment
Circle Vehicles
Circle Props
** Special Effects
Circle** Costume/Wardrobe
Circle** Makeup/Hair
Box Livestock/Animals
Box Music/Sound
Circle Set Dressing

FADE IN:

1 EXT. GOLF DRIVING RANGE -- DAY 1

Shiny Acres, Florida driving range attached to a golf course. Golf balls WHIZ through the air.

7/8

Concentrating fiercely, mousy IRMA STICKLE (50s), awkward and new to the game, juts a hip with a wild swing of her club.

She MISSES, the club FLIES and THWACKS her husband, overconfident HARV STICKLE, (60s) upside the head.

HARV
What the!? Owwwwwww.

IRMA
Are you ok? I'm sorry honey!

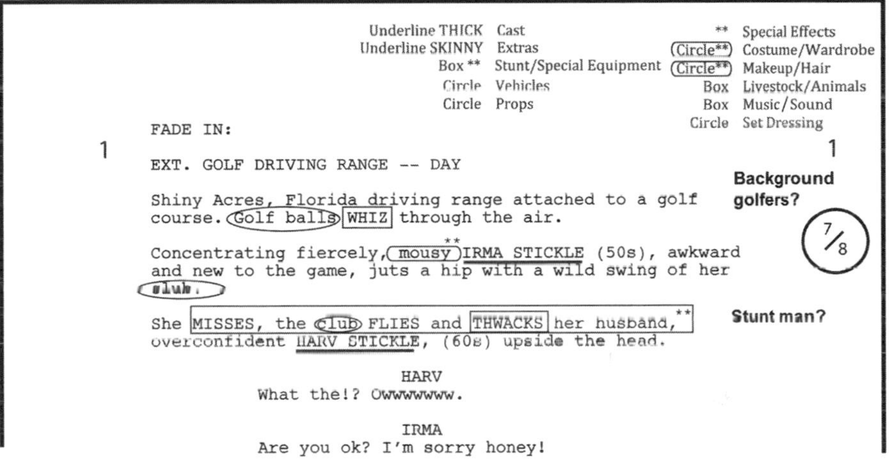
Underline THICK Cast
Underline SKINNY Extras
Box ** Stunt/Special Equipment
Circle Vehicles
Circle Props
** Special Effects
Circle** Costume/Wardrobe
Circle** Makeup/Hair
Box Livestock/Animals
Box Music/Sound
Circle Set Dressing

FADE IN:

1 EXT. GOLF DRIVING RANGE -- DAY 1



Shiny Acres, Florida driving range attached to a golf course. Golf balls WHIZ through the air.

7/8

**
Concentrating fiercely, mousy IRMA STICKLE (50s), awkward and new to the game, juts a hip with a wild swing of her club.

She MISSES, the club FLIES and THWACKS her husband,** overconfident HARV STICKLE, (60s) upside the head.



HARV
What the!? Owwwwwww.

IRMA
Are you ok? I'm sorry honey!

**FIG. 2.39**

Transfer information from each scene to a breakdown form as in Table 2.12

3. Props and set dressing – duplicates, expense, look of items, safety (firearms).
4. Vehicles, Animals – cost, availability, safety, support personnel.
5. Sounds, effects – used while shooting, inserted after the shoot during post production; what's required to pull it off successfully.

Activate your Commonsense-O-Meter – what special considerations are there when… and fill in the blanks: blizzard, assault weapons, crowds, underwater, camels, sci-fi or period pieces.

## Table 2.12

| | | | |
|---|---|---|---|
| *Color Code*<br>*Day INT – White*<br>*****Day EXT – Yellow***<br>*Night INT – Blue*<br>*Night EXT – Green*<br>(#)=Budget Category | **SCRIPT BREAKDOWN SHEET**<br>**Title:** SURVIVING RETIREMENT<br>**Production Co::** SR, LLC______ | | **Date:**<br>18_Apr_2010<br>**Script Version:**<br>WHITE |
| Breakdown Page # **1** | Set<br>Golf Driving Range | | Scene # 1 |
| Int/Ext<br>**EXT** | Day/Night<br>D | Location | Page Count<br>7/8 |
| **Scene Synopsis**<br>Harv shows Irma how to golf, he gets bonked on the bean | | | **Prepared by:**<br>Sally Forth |
| **Cast**<br>(Underline Thick)<br>**1. Irma Stickle**<br>**2. Harv Stickle** | **Extras**<br>(Underline skinny)<br>**Extras Silent Bits/Background**<br>(Underline skinny) | | **Stunts**<br>(Box**)<br>*Golf club flies up and hits Harv in head (Stunt man?)* |
| **Special Effects**<br>(* *) | **Props**<br>(circle)<br>GOLF BALLS<br>GOLF CLUB | | **Vehicles/Animals**<br>(circle) |
| **Wardrobe**<br>(circle **)<br>Mousy Irma | **Make-up/Hair**<br>(circle **)<br>Mousy Irma | | **Sound/Music**<br>(box)<br>GOLF BALLS WHIZ<br>Thwack on the head |
| **Special Equipment**<br>***<br>**Set Dressing**<br>(lime green) | **Production Notes**<br>(yellow)<br>**EXTRAS/SILENT:** Background golfers at driving range?<br>**NOTE TO ALL:**<br>**MAKE-UP/Hair:** Mousy for Florida – wrong golf clothes & shoes?<br>**SOUND:** Capture "golf noises" club swinging, balls hit. Protect boom mic from club swings and flying balls<br>**Prop:**<br>1. Multiple balls | | |
| **Director Notes**<br>Should Harv have a golf club also? | | | |

**FIG. 2.40**

New schedule

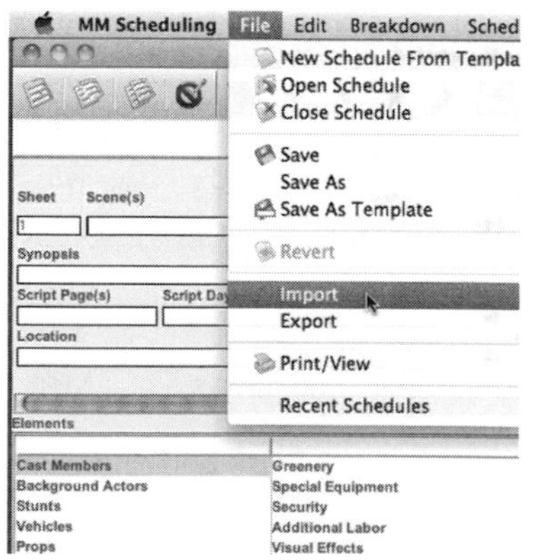


**FIG. 2.41**

Import

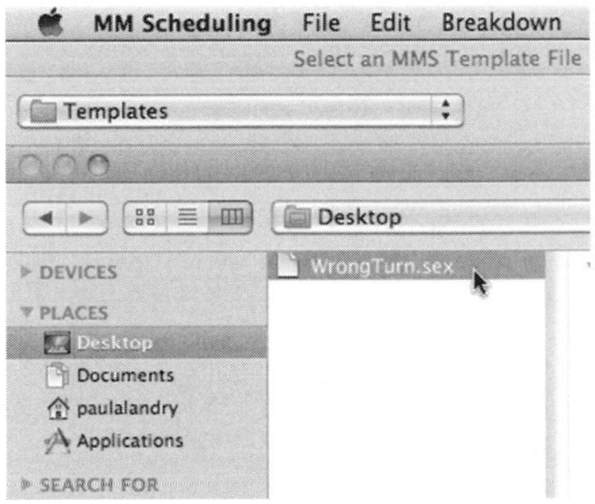


**FIG. 2.42**

Import .SEX

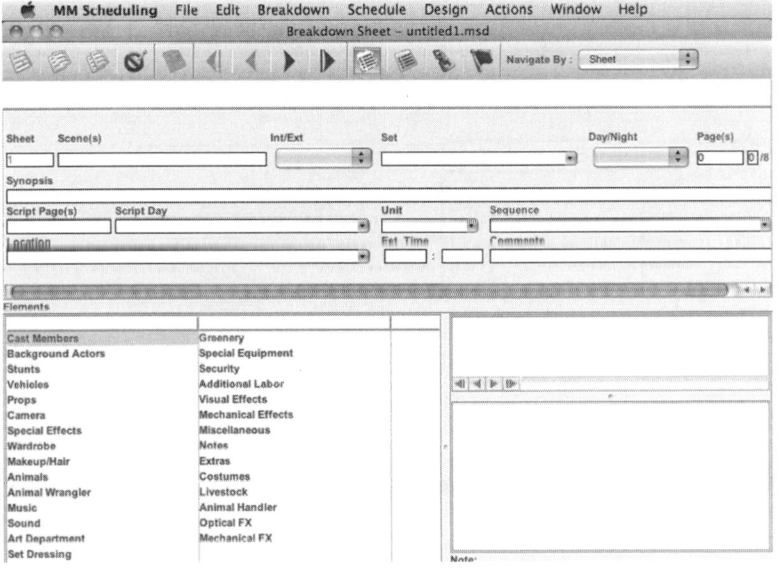


**FIG. 2.43**

Breakdown 1 for your new schedule

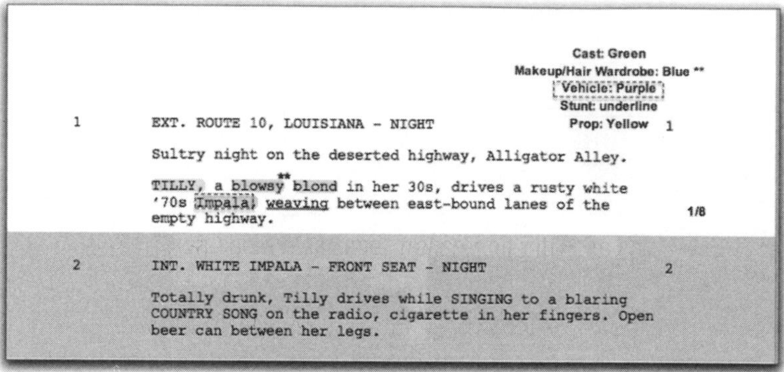

Cast: Green
Makeup/Hair Wardrobe: Blue **
Vehicle: Purple
Stunt: underline
Prop: Yellow

1 EXT. ROUTE 10, LOUISIANA - NIGHT 1

Sultry night on the deserted highway, Alligator Alley.

TILLY, a blowsy** blond in her 30s, drives a rusty white '70s Impala, weaving between east-bound lanes of the empty highway. 1/8

2 INT. WHITE IMPALA - FRONT SEAT - NIGHT 2

Totally drunk, Tilly drives while SINGING to a blaring COUNTRY SONG on the radio, cigarette in her fingers. Open beer can between her legs.

**FIG. 2.44**

Transfer information one category at a time

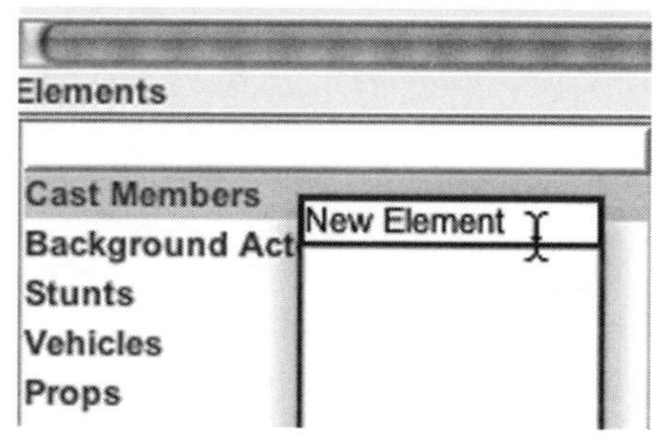


**FIG. 2.45**

Add element

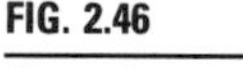

**FIG. 2.46**

Name element

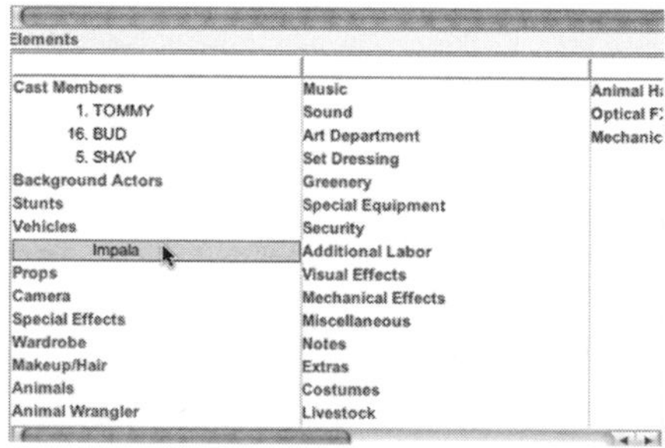


**FIG. 2.47**

Ensure that every element is added within its category

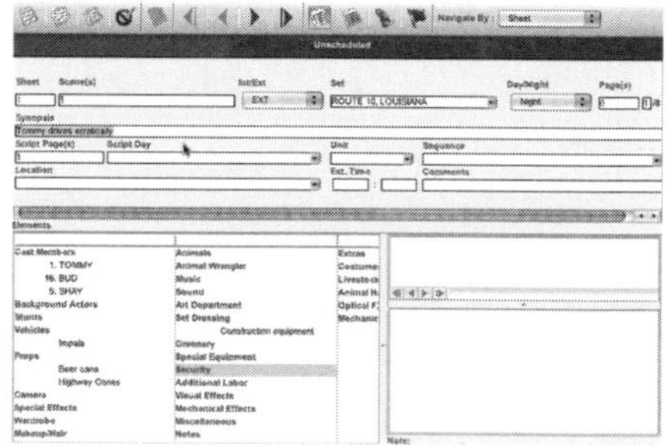

**FIG. 2.48**

Complete breakdown for that scene

Scene #: 1
Script Page: 1
Page Count: 1/8

Breakdown Sheet

Wrong Turn

Sheet #: 1
Int/Ext: EXT
Day/Night: Night
PJ Landry

Scene Description: Impala weaves on Alligator Alley
Settings: ROUTE 10, LOUISIANA
Location:
Sequence:
Script Day: N-1

| Cast Members | | |
|---|---|---|
| Tilly Stunt Double | | |
| | **Stunts**<br>IMPALA WEAVES | **Vehicles**<br>IMPALA |
| | **Wardrobe**<br>Blowsy | **Makeup/Hair**<br>Blond Tilly |
| | | |
| **Notes**<br>Road closed<br>Road deserted | | |

**FIG. 2.49**

Work through each scene one at a time, until you get to the end

**Table 2.13**

| Element | Question |
|---|---|
| • Stunts and Stunt People | • How is that done? Who does it? |
| • Vehicles, Animals, Kids | • Extra personnel, time? Safety issues? |
| • Props | • Quantity, safety issues? |
| • Make-up / Hair, Wardrobe | • Time issues? |
| • Special Effects | • Preparation, safety issues? Personnel? |

## End of Chapter Two Review

*Breaking down* a script translates the screenplay format into technical format for use in scheduling and budgeting. It's a sequential process, and the strength of the budget and schedule will only be as good as the breakdown.

The process:

1. Read script.
2. Identify resources on the script (on paper or using a computer):
   a. One scene at a time
   b. Allocate each **element** (Villain, Hero, Tan Sierra) in the script to their appropriate **category** (Props, Vehicles, Cast). This can be done on a paper copy of the script, electronic PDF of the script, or by tagging with screenwriting software.
3. Transfer information onto a breakdown sheet – manually or using a scheduling program.

*Do this in order of scenes, for every scene in the script.*

# Chapter Three

## *Organizing Resources: The Schedule*

---

**QUESTION: What are the Chances Your Team Will Exactly Follow Your First Version of a Schedule Down to the Minute?**

**ANSWER:** Two chances: slim and none. But that's okay; it serves as an essential starting point. A preliminary schedule will shift — sometimes a little, sometimes a lot.

---

Audiences attribute creativity in a movie to the Director, Writer and actors, but significant imagination goes into designing a schedule as well. The effort will be appreciated by the Producer (happy to utilize resources in a cost-efficient way), and the entire cast and crew (for creating a well-managed environment).

Scheduling is the GPS to acquiring all of the footage a Director and Editor need to make a film. This process will result in a day-by-day, and hour-by-hour timetable, for each day of your shoot, conveying to everyone involved when to do what, and where.

Scheduling and Budgeting Your Film.

## Creating a Schedule

Production scheduling has three steps:

1. Transfer information into your schedule.
2. Group like things.
3. Arrange for maximum efficiency and discuss with your team.

The breakdown process *quantifies* and *identifies* resources. Scheduling *organizes* those resources, constructing the blueprint for an actionable shoot – setting practical goals to capture needed footage. As films are usually shot out of written screenplay order, careful scheduling of principal photography is imperative so that:

- Everything needed is available;
- Necessary scenes are shot;
- Money and time are conserved by consolidating resources logically.

Film production is divided into three time divisions:

1. PREP: preproduction – planning for the shoot.
2. SHOOT: production – shooting, **AKA**: principal photography.
3. POST/WRAP: post production – editing the film.

*Production*, when the most resources are utilized (in terms of people, locations, and equipment) is the most expensive time; every moment counts. That is the primary task we are focused on in this chapter. Delays during production are costly – imagine 25 people prepped and ready to shoot a scene, then POOF: a power failure with no backup generator, yikes. Of course you'll have a backup plan (and keep breathing). Feeding everyone Hohos, Dingdongs and Twinkies can be soothing. *Pre-production* is usually organized by weeks, or lasts significantly longer than production, with lists of tasks to be accomplished in order for the shoot to take place successfully. *Post production* often lasts longer than production and is related to the complexity of the edit, amount of music and sound design, and number of special effects to be completed.

**Tools You Will Need**:

- Script (for reference);
- Completed breakdown forms:
  - Manual (production board and strips);
  - Computer (scheduling software and .SEX file).

Depending on the project, you either:

a. **Have a delivery date** – when someone expects to receive your film, because they have plans for it (distribution, festival screening, fund raising, publicity, sell online, etc.) This gives you a time target to aim for.
b. **Don't have a delivery date** – so construct your shoot in the most logical way for time- and cost-efficiency.

Either way, the process is essentially the same. Breakdown information is transferred onto a strip, and the strips are arranged in a logical order, in the computer or on a board.

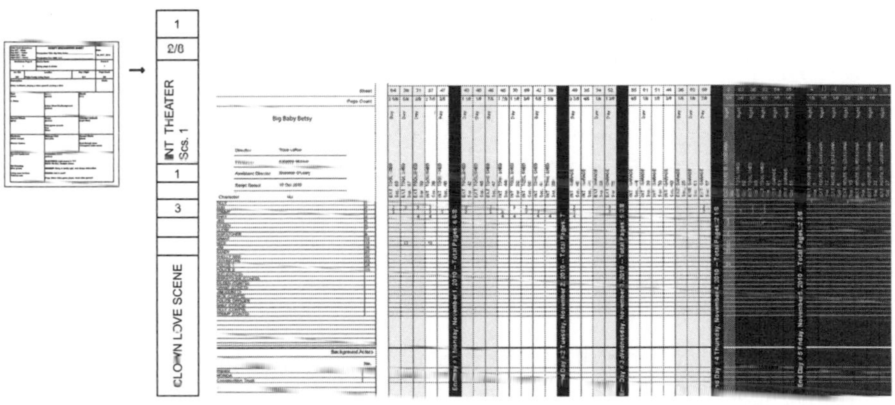


**FIG. 3.1**
One breakdown sheet = one strip

**FIG. 3.2**
Strips arranged in logical order

**FIG. 3.3**
Manual: empty production board

**FIG. 3.4**
Manual: full production board with scheduling strips

**COMPUTER APPROACH:** Scheduling software is available. Movie Magic Scheduling, Celtx, Gorilla, Showbiz, Scenios, Scenechronize, WattWenn, Filmmaker Software, Excel or other spreadsheet program like Open Office are possibilities.

These are widely available, both online and in stores that cater specifically to the film industry. The advantages of using software include time savings, ease of changes, collaboration and repurposing of information.

MANUAL APPROACH: If you schedule your project manually, you will need a production board and strips to print on. The strips are lightweight cardboard and can be moved around to create a variety of scheduling scenarios. Many DIY-ers (Do It Yourself-ers) create their own version of a board with a manila folder, cutting paper for strips. Do whatever works for you. If you are a tactile person, you might find the manual method using production board and strips helpful. As the trend is to use computers for this work, they are increasingly hard to find, but can be found in a few stores online, at FilmTV Workshops (http://filmtvworkshops.com), Ebay, and film stationery stores.

**Your System: Workflow and Consistency**

Workflow is the sequence of steps you employ to complete a task; in other words, your system.

1. Decide on the name of the project – often the title of the screenplay.
2. List key people and contact information.
3. Together with your Producer, Director or AD decide who has access, and the extent of that access. If necessary, set security parameters and passwords in your software (usually in the program "preferences").

Establish a *communication* and *update* system regarding your schedule information (if it's too early in the process, that's ok) and choose logical file naming. Strive for consistency between the file name of the screenplay, schedule and budget. Will you assign version numbers or dates to distinguish between them? Discuss with your team and make that information available to whoever needs it.

For example, on a corporate film for a hair salon, entitled *All To Get Ahead*, our team used the abbreviation "ATGA" at the front of all file names – a little shorter than the actual title.

ATGA_Script_V1 (then V2, V3, V4)
ATGA_Schedule_04MAR2009 (updated w/dates)
ATGA_Budget_09MAR2009 (updated w/dates)

(We shared information via Google Docs.)

Consistency will help you save time. Another way to save time is to safeguard your work in the computer by saving your work often, with Autosave (found in preferences) and backing up. By saving often, and saving your work on a backup drive, you safeguard the information and hardwork of that day. So if there are computer problems, you won't lose your work or information.

**FIG. 3.5**

Open Preferences in Celtx

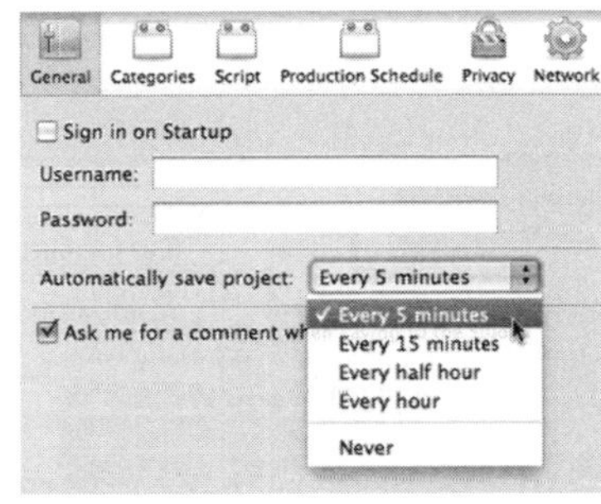


**FIG. 3.6**

Set Autosave

In Movie Magic, it looks similar.

**FIG. 3.7**

Open Preferences

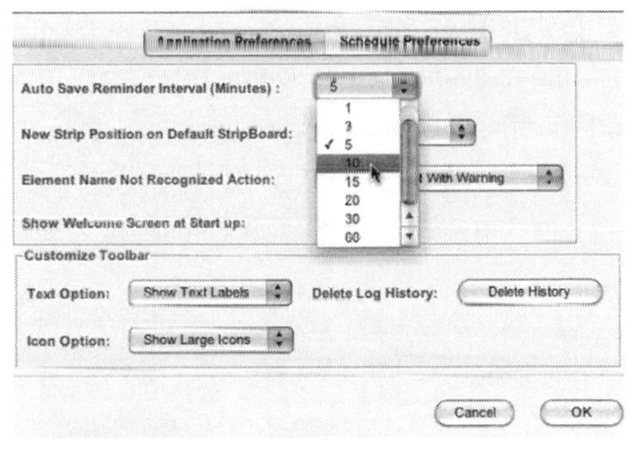


**FIG. 3.8**

Set Auto Save Reminder Interval frequently, like every 5 minutes, to safeguard your work

Decide when you will make backups (every day), and where to store them: flash drive/online.

I check that my system is in place, i.e., the strip colors conform to the colors of the breakdown sheets. This setting is found under Design/Strip Colors in Movie Magic Scheduling, but in Celtx it doesn't matter since all strips are white (for now).

**FIG. 3.9**

File menu: Design / Strip Colors

These are the standard colors, although I have seen discrepancies for night:

- **White**: INTERIOR day (white light bulbs indoors);
- **Yellow**: EXTERIOR day (yellow sunshine);
- **Blue**: INTERIOR night (blue light from TV);
- **Green** strips: EXTERIOR night (green grass at night).

Not every software permits changing these colors. In Movie Magic, you can set the colors any way you like. Click on the square that corresponds to INT and NIGHT, then double click on the color you like (I use a deep blue). Some people use a different system, so I make sure the settings work for me; I prefer INT night to be blue and EXT night green. Your choice of software will dictate these parameters.

Strip Colors

| | INT | EXT | INT/EXT | | | | |
|---|---|---|---|---|---|---|---|
| Day | 0 | 1 | 2 | 3 | 4 | 5 | 6 |
| Night | 12 | 13 | | 15 | 16 | 17 | 18 |
| | 24 | 25 | 26 | 27 | 28 | 29 | 30 |

**FIG. 3.10**

Double click on palette colors to adjust

This is also where you could add a color for an unusual or irregular element so that it sticks out – like purple for historical footage, photographs, flashbacks, flash forwards, etc. (Consistency is important. As you went through the breakdown process you may have noted inconsistencies in names – of cast, vehicles, or important props. As soon as possible, find out from the Department Head (and/or Director) what's what and who's who, as this could impact your scheduling. Is "Mrs. Pickle" the same person as "Betsy Pickle's Mom"? Maybe it's her grandmother – if so you'll need another actor. Is the "white contractor van" from scene 5 a different vehicle from "Ford Econoline Van" in scene 83? You will save time by clearing up inconsistencies as soon as possible.

An important component to workflow and consistency is organization, especially when things go crazy. So *before* things get crazy, get organized. I've found these tools helpful:

- Three ring binders for quick reference of the script, breakdown sheets, cast, crew, and vendor contact information, and many details you may want at your fingertips during the production process
- Organized by subject, separated with tabs for the various categories
- Colors, versions, etc. of the script to indicate new versions of the screenplay
- New drafts of scripts, scenes, detailed contact information.

In your computer's Internet browser, make **bookmark folders** to quickly find links that you use often, i.e., unions, film commissions, vendors, weather sites, and set up your document management system such as the one in Figure 3.3, (whether on your computer or in the cloud) with names and a structure that are easy to use.

There are many great books that cover production management more fully, and in particular it's well worth checking out books by Eve Light Honthaner, Robert Koster, Ralph Singleton, and Bastien Cleve.

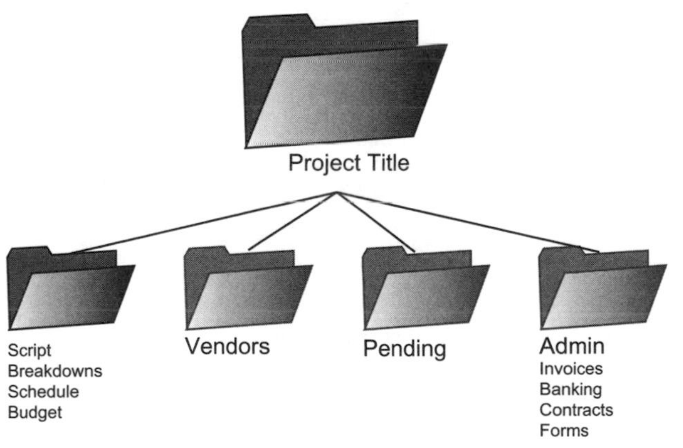


**FIG. 3.11**

Clear folder titles aid document management

The following are key points to consider when setting up a system:

- Where documents and files live;
- Naming and organizing files (by category, alphabetically);
- File Save / Autosave habits;
- Backing up computer files regularly;
- Who gets access to / can change information.

Setting up a system sooner saves time later.

## The Process: Transfer Breakdown Information into Schedule

Transfer all your breakdown information into a scheduling format; each breakdown sheet will become a strip in your schedule.

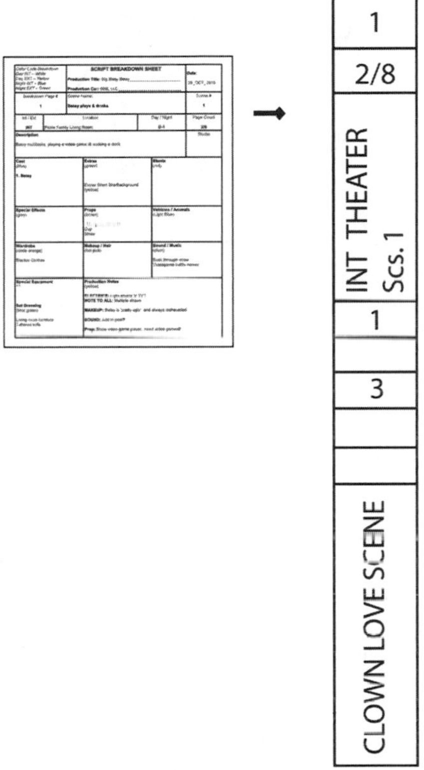


**FIG. 3.12**

Transfer each piece of information from one breakdown sheet to one strip

Arrange the strips by set, interior/exterior, day/night, then cast, to find an optimal schedule.

Color coding of schedule strips should match the breakdown sheets.

- **White** strips: INT. day (white walls inside)
- **Yellow** strips: EXT. day (sunshine)
- **Blue** strips: INT. night (blue light from TV)
- **Green** strips: EXT. night (green grass at night)

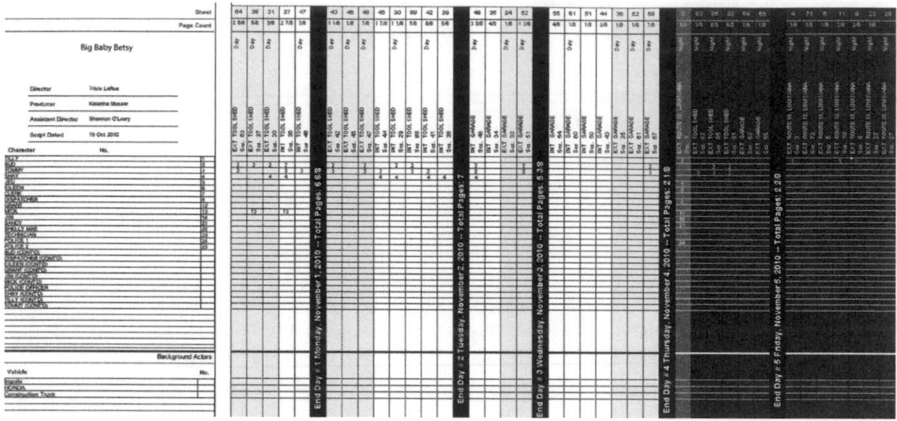


**FIG. 3.13**

Left side — header; middle to right — schedule strips

- **Black** strips: *separate* shooting days
- **Gray** strips: days off
- **Brown** strips: *personalized* alerts

You can add other colors if you like to draw attention to unusual elements.

The steps are the same, in a slightly different order, whether you're working with a computer or production board. When using a production board and strips, you will need the same number of strips colored as breakdown sheets (25 green breakdown sheets require 25 green strips, and so forth), as well as a pen to fill them in.

### Let's Go: Manual Version

A. Fill out the **header** information on your production board — film title, Producer, Director, AD, script date.

**Table 3.1**

| | **Title** |
|---|---|
| Director | Sally Forth |
| Producer | Umiko Rong |
| Assistant Director | Sindi Wardell |
| Script Dated | 04 Apr 2008 |

B. Fill in **cast** names, and assign them a **number** according to your system: meaningful ID numbers, or in order of appearance. As much as possible, we utilize abbreviations and shorthand to save room and transmit information quickly.

**Table 3.2**

| *Character* | *No.* |
|---|---|
| Queen of Diamonds | 1 |
| King of Clubs | 2 |
| Pawn | 3 |

C. **One** breakdown sheet at a time, transfer the information to a **strip** (Table 3.3) until all breakdown information has been entered.

**Table 3.3**

Breakdown Page #
Day or Night (D/N)
Interior or Exterior (INT/EXT)
Scene #
Page Count (Eighth of Page)
Location: INT. DAY Castle
Brief synopsis of scene
# assigned to the *character* in that scene
BACKGROUND ACTORS / Vehicles

**Let's Go: Computer Version**

A. Fill out the **production** information.

Open scheduling software, open a **new** schedule, name it and adjust the **preferences**. Fill out the **header** information – film title, Producer, Director, AD, script date.

Once you've filled out the relevant information, click OK.

B. **Transfer** and **verify information** to a breakdown sheet in the software, one scene at a time.

1. If you haven't done so already, **export** the script from screenwriting program as a **.SEX** file. (In your screenplay, scene numbers are on.)
2. In your scheduling program, **import .SEX file** (File / Import). Save.
   In Movie Magic, the screen opens to a breakdown sheet: the scheduling program will compute page counts, and identify scenes and number them. Alternatively open the breakdown sheet using the menu.
3. Transfer and verify essential information about the scene itself, starting with the first scene.
4. Add each element to its category and complete breakdown for each scene.

**Table 3.4**

| | | | | | | |
|---|---|---|---|---|---|---|
| | | ** STRIPS ** | | | | |
| ** HEADER SECTION ** | | | | | | |
| | | | | | | |
| **Breakdown Page No.** | | **5** | **12** | **3** | **9** | |
| **Day or Night** | | **D** | **D** | **N** | **N** | |
| **Scene** | | **5** | **12** | **3** | **9** | |
| **Page Count** | | **1/8** | **2 3/8** | **1/8** | **6/8** | |
| **Title: Checkmate** | | **INT. DAY Castle** | **EXT. DAY Moat** | **INT. NIGHT Stable** | **EXT. NIGHT Moat** | **DAY 1 - 3 3/8 PAGES** |
| **Director** | Barbara Lindsay | | | | | |
| **Producer** | Constance Trulove | | | | | |
| **Assistant Director** | Shannon McNaughton | | | | | |
| **Script Dated** | 21 April 2002 | | | | | |
| | | | | | | |
| ***Character*** | ***No.*** | | | | | |
| **Queen of Diamonds** | **1** | **1** | **1** | **1** | | |
| **King of Clubs** | **2** | | **2** | **2** | **2** | |
| **Pawn** | **3** | **3** | | **3** | **3** | |
| | | | | | | |
| **BACKGROUND ACTORS** | | **X** | | | | |
| **Vehicles** | | | | | **V** | |
| | | **Queen bosses Pawn** | **Love Scene** | **Pawn defends Queen** | **Plan to overthrow** | |

**FIG. 3.14**

Open production information

Production Info - WRONG_TURN.msd
Picture Title : A Wrong Turn
Production No. :
Company : A Wrong Turn, LLC
Director : Sally 4th
Producer : Constance Trulove
UPM : Holly Golightly
Assistant Director :
Art Director :
Set Dresser :
Script Dated :
Prepared By : Stan Dard
Timing :
Episode No. :
Misc. #1 :
Misc. #2 :
Misc. #3 :
Misc. #4 :
Cancel
OK

**FIG. 3.15**

Complete production information

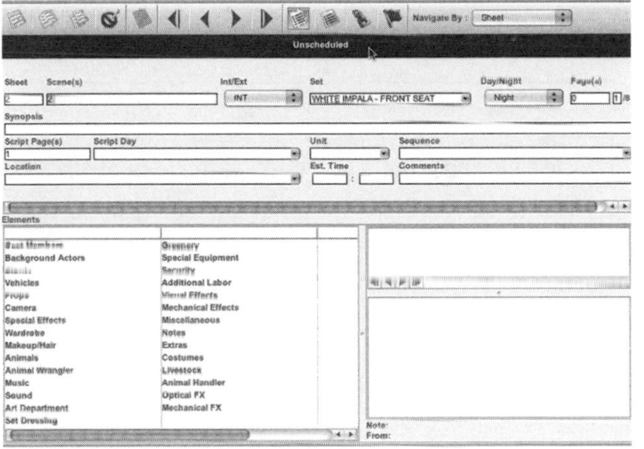


**FIG. 3.16**

Blank breakdown

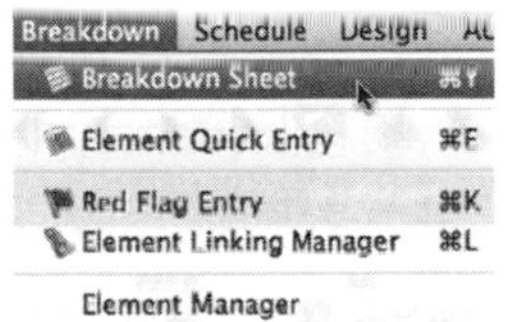


**FIG. 3.17**

Open breakdown sheet

**Table 3.5**

**Scene #** (verify)
**INT/EXT** (software may have filled in)
**Set** Location (**AKA**: Set/software may have filled in)
**Day or Night**
**Page Count** (software may have filled in)
**Brief, VIVID synopsis of scene**

The software will bring in some information, but not all. It is imperative that you work scene by scene, **verifying** that the information you marked on the script is identified in the schedule on a breakdown page (remember **CYA**: one breakdown

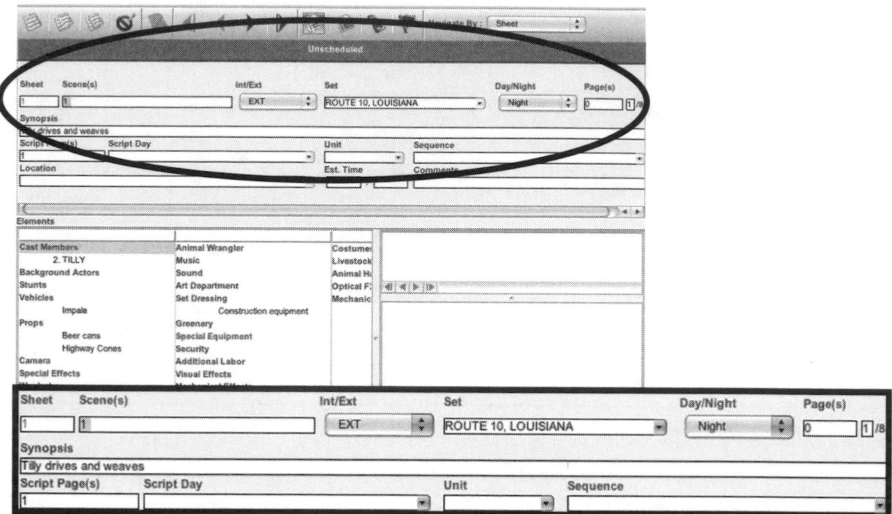


FIG. 3.18

Transfer information about the scene

sheet = one scene). This is *especially* important if you skipped the step of transferring resources onto paper breakdown sheets. Mark the script and enter the information directly into a scheduling program.

**C.** Assign cast an **ID number**.

Assign **Board ID** cast numbers in the Element Manager, according to your system.

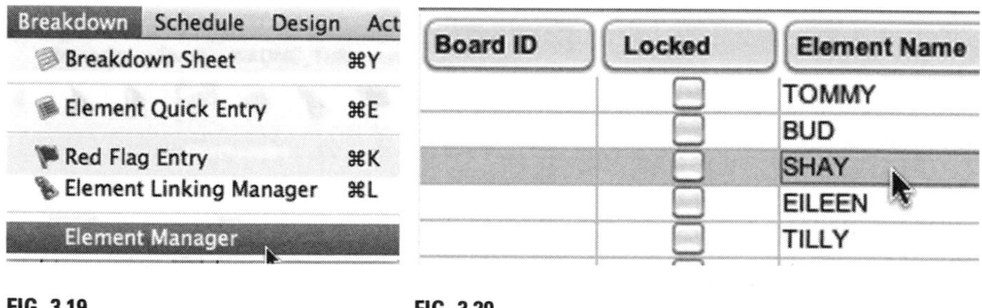


FIG. 3.19

Open Element Manager

FIG. 3.20

Double click character name

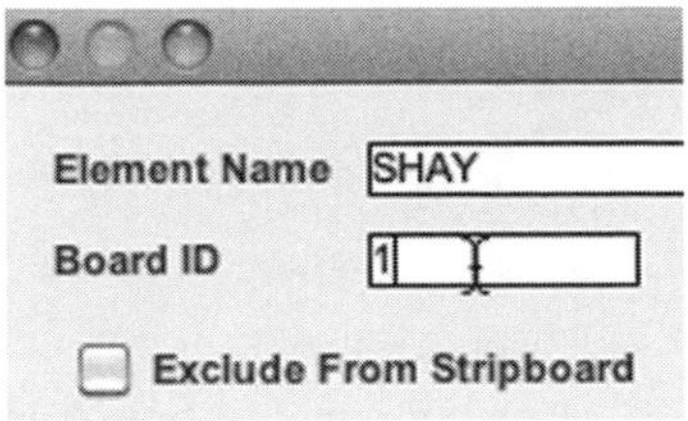

**FIG. 3.21**

Assign a Board ID# to the Element

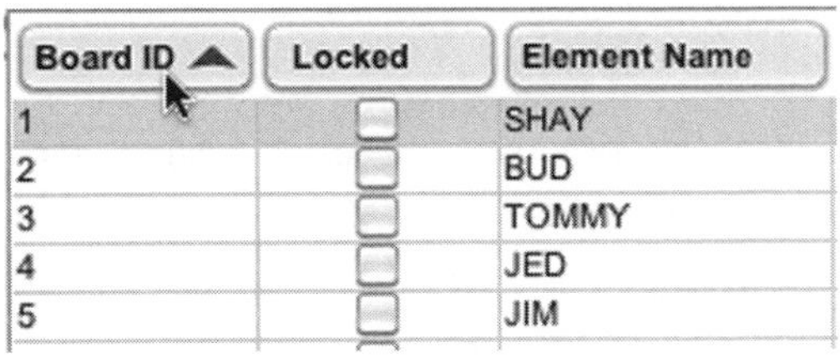

**FIG. 3.22**

Click on Board ID to list in order

## Grouping Like Things

Channel your inner slug. Productions must exercise economy in all things, so that the maximum amount of time, which often feels like precious few moments, is devoted to actually getting good footage "in the can." From a practical standpoint that translates into economy of movement. When your crew moves, it requires time and energy (**AKA**: $). Whenever possible, move the least amount the shortest distance possible.

If you were shooting in this order (see Figure 3.23), the crew would be going from inside to outside to inside, shooting night then day then night, constantly changing locations. Whew!

Look at the stripboard to group like things together. Adjust the layout as you like.

You can drag individual strips into a different order, or use sorting functions to group like things.

### Sorting by Set

The fastest way to begin organizing your schedule is to group scenes by:

1. **Set** (setting where scene occurs);
2. **Interior** / **Exterior** together;
3. **Day** together / **Night** together within each set, group.

This transforms chaos into something more manageable.

In a computer scheduling program, the initial sorting process is easy.

Add "Sort By" criteria: 1. Set; 2. IE (interior or exterior); and 3. DN (day or night), then click OK! Stripboard must be *open*.

Preproduction is a time when everything is in flux — who you will hire, where you will shoot. Grouping sets together is the first step to organizing your schedule, and, as you secure actual locations, that will allow you to refine the order. The words *set* and *location* are sometimes used interchangeably, but for our purposes SET = Scene Heading as listed in the script; for example, in INT. JOE'S HOUSE — DAY, the set would be "Joe's House." Location is the actual physical site where shooting will occur (which often isn't known in the early stages of preproduction).

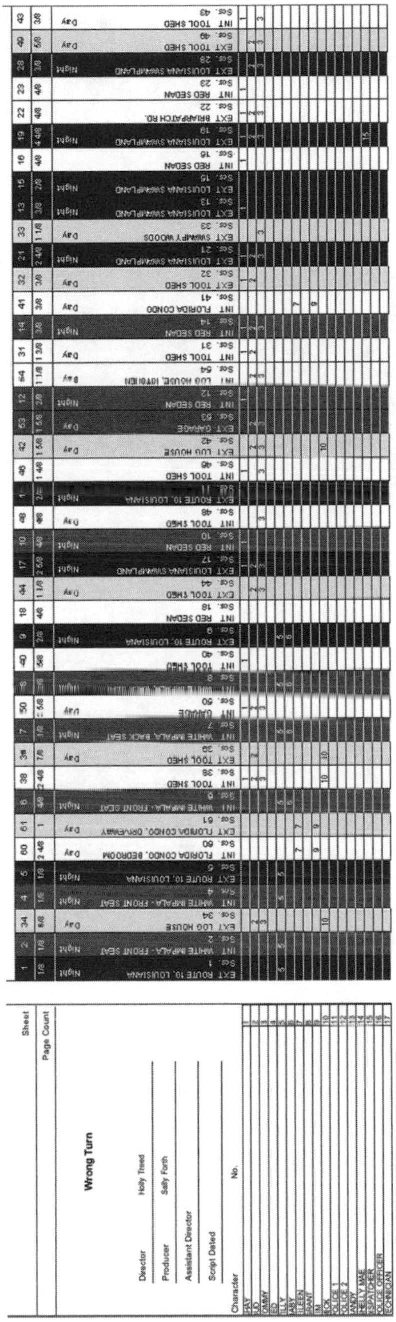

**Wrong Turn**

| | |
|---|---|
| Director | Holly Treed |
| Producer | Sally Forth |
| Assistant Director | |
| Script Dated | |

| Character | No. |
|---|---|
| HAY | 1 |
| UD | 2 |
| OMMY | 3 |
| ED | 4 |
| ILLY | 5 |
| ABY | 6 |
| ILEEN | 7 |
| RANT | 8 |
| IM | 9 |
| ICK | 10 |
| OLICE 1 | 11 |
| OLICE 2 | 12 |
| ANDY | 13 |
| HELLY MAE | 14 |
| ISPATCHER | 15 |
| OLICE OFFICER | 16 |
| ECHNICIAN | 17 |

| Sheet | Page Count | Scene | Day/Night | Cast |
|---|---|---|---|---|
| 1 | 1/8 | EXT ROUTE 10, LOUISIANA Scs. 1 | Night | 5 |
| 2 | 1/8 | INT WHITE IMPALA - FRONT SEAT Scs. 2 | Night | 5 |
| 34 | 6/8 | EXT LOG HOUSE Scs. 34 | Day | 2, 3, 10 |
| 4 | 1/8 | INT WHITE IMPALA - FRONT SEAT Scs. 4 | Night | 5 |
| 5 | 1/8 | EXT ROUTE 10, LOUISIANA Scs. 5 | Night | 5 |
| 60 | 2 4/8 | INT FLORIDA CONDO, BEDROOM Scs. 60 | Day | 7, 9 |
| 61 | 1 | EXT FLORIDA CONDO, DRIVEWAY Scs. 61 | Day | 7, 9 |
| 6 | 4/8 | INT WHITE IMPALA - FRONT SEAT Scs. 6 | Night | 5, 6 |
| 38 | 2 4/8 | INT TOOL SHED Scs. 38 | | 1, 2, 3, 10 |
| 39 | 7/8 | EXT TOOL SHED Scs. 39 | Day | 2, 10 |
| 7 | 1/8 | INT WHITE IMPALA, BACK SEAT Scs. 7 | Night | 5, 6 |
| 50 | 5/8 | INT GARAGE Scs. 50 | Day | 1, 2, 3 |
| 8 | [illegible] | INT WHITE IMPALA [illegible] Scs. 8 | Night | 5, 6 |
| 40 | 5/8 | INT TOOL SHED Scs. 40 | | 1 |
| 9 | 2/8 | EXT ROUTE 10, LOUISIANA Scs. 9 | Night | 5, 6 |
| 18 | 4/8 | INT RED SEDAN Scs. 18 | | |
| 44 | 1 1/8 | EXT TOOL SHED Scs. 44 | Day | 2, 3 |
| 17 | 2 5/8 | EXT LOUISIANA SWAMPLAND Scs. 17 | Night | 1, 2, 3 |
| 10 | 4/8 | INT RED SEDAN Scs. 10 | Night | 1 |
| 48 | 4/8 | INT TOOL SHED Scs. 48 | Day | 3 |
| 11 | 2/8 | EXT ROUTE 10, LOUISIANA Scs. 11 | Night | |
| 46 | 1 4/8 | INT TOOL SHED Scs. 46 | | 1, 3 |
| 42 | 1 5/8 | EXT LOG HOUSE Scs. 42 | Day | 2, 3, 10 |
| 53 | 1 5/8 | EXT GARAGE Scs. 53 | Day | 2, 3 |
| 12 | 2/8 | INT RED SEDAN Scs. 12 | Night | 1 |
| 54 | 1 1/8 | INT LOG HOUSE, KITCHEN Scs. 54 | Day | 2, 3 |
| 31 | 1 3/8 | INT TOOL SHED Scs. 31 | Day | 1, 2 |
| 14 | 3/8 | INT RED SEDAN Scs. 14 | Night | 1, 2, 3 |
| 41 | 3/8 | INT FLORIDA CONDO Scs. 41 | Day | 7, 9 |
| 32 | 3/8 | EXT TOOL SHED Scs. 32 | Day | 1, 2 |
| 21 | 2 4/8 | EXT LOUISIANA SWAMPLAND Scs. 21 | Night | 1, 2, 3 |
| 33 | 1 1/8 | EXT SWAMPY WOODS Scs. 33 | Day | 3 |
| 13 | 3/8 | EXT LOUISIANA SWAMPLAND Scs. 13 | Night | 1 |
| 15 | 2/8 | EXT LOUISIANA SWAMPLAND Scs. 15 | Night | |
| 16 | 4/8 | INT RED SEDAN Scs. 16 | | 1 |
| 19 | 4 4/8 | EXT LOUISIANA SWAMPLAND Scs. 19 | Night | 1, 2, 3, 15 |
| 22 | 4/8 | EXT BRIARPATCH RD. Scs. 22 | | 1, 2, 3 |
| 23 | 4/8 | INT RED SEDAN Scs. 23 | | 1 |
| 28 | 3/8 | EXT LOUISIANA SWAMPLAND Scs. 28 | Night | 2, 3 |
| 49 | 5/8 | EXT TOOL SHED Scs. 49 | Day | 2, 3 |
| 43 | 3/8 | INT TOOL SHED Scs. 43 | Day | 1, 3 |

**FIG. 3.23**

Schedule before sorting

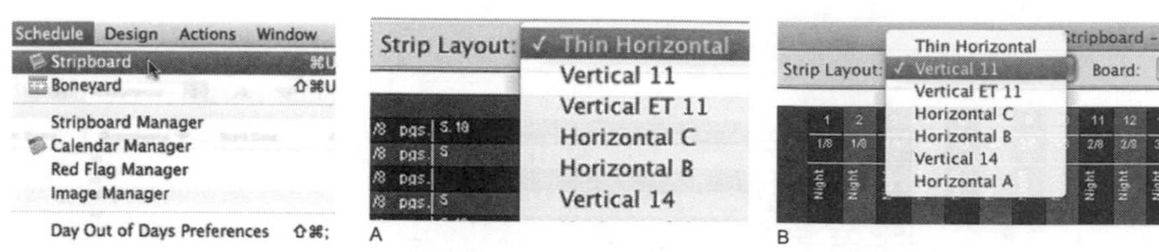


**FIG. 3.24**

Go to stripboard

**FIG. 3.25A AND B**

Adjust strip layout to a horizontal or vertical view

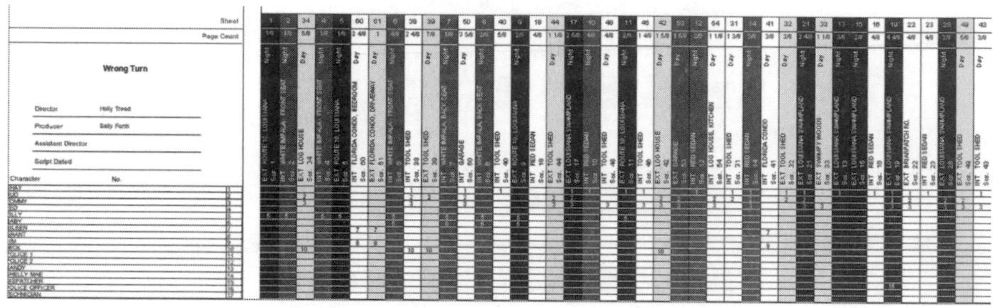


**FIG. 3.26**

Before sort

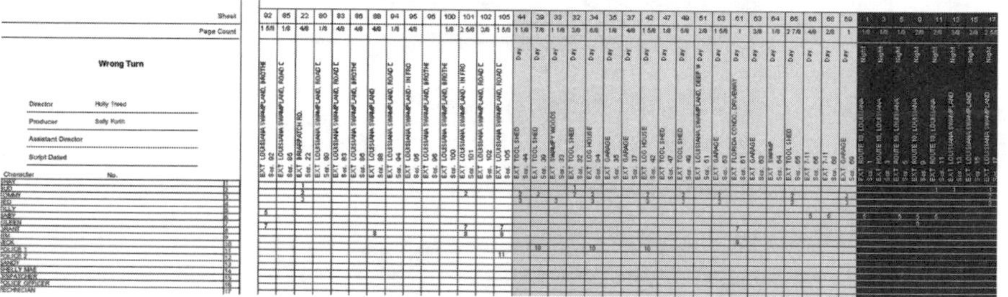


**FIG. 3.27**

After sort

**Rule of Thumb**: Weather is unpredictable; schedule *exterior* shots first, and then you can still get footage if there's a weather disruption.

**CYA**: Whenever possible, always have a back-up plan to shoot at an alternative location (**AKA:** cover set). Also, the crew can prep the interior while shooting is taking place outside.

Once sets are consolidated on your stripboard, separate each set with a *banner* – a helpful visual cue. On a production board, simply insert a black strip between each location. In your scheduling software, place your cursor on the *last* scene occurring

**FIG. 3.28**

Drop down menu: Actions / Sort

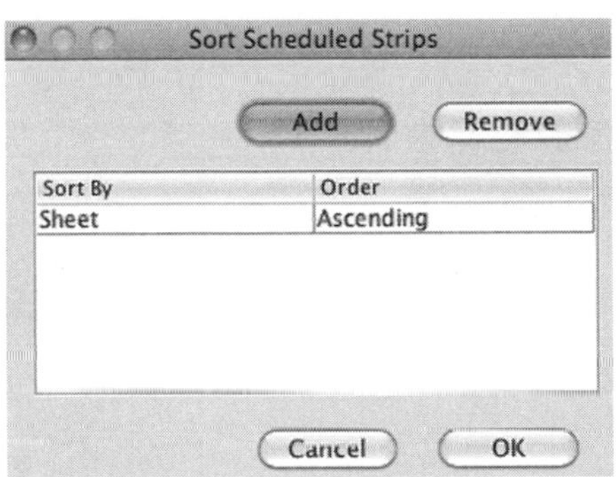


**FIG. 3.29**

Click Add

**FIG. 3.30**

Select "Sort By" criteria (Set, DN, IE)

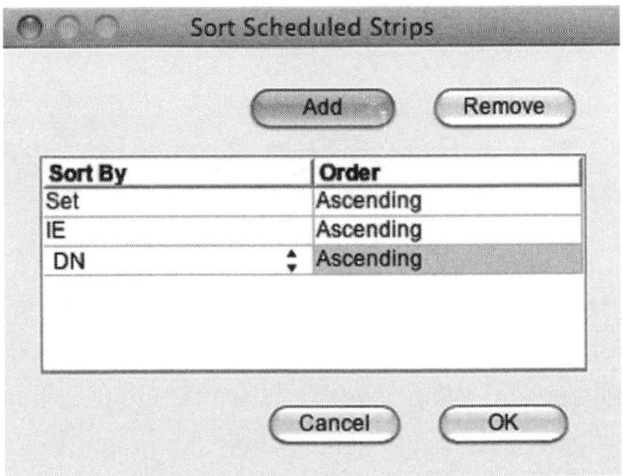


**FIG. 3.31**

Add "Sort By" criteria

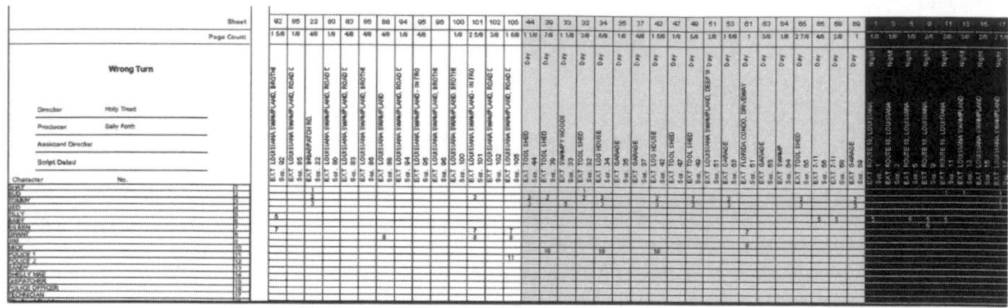

**FIG. 3.32**

After sort

on a set, then insert a text banner strip. You can leave them blank, or type something helpful to remind you.

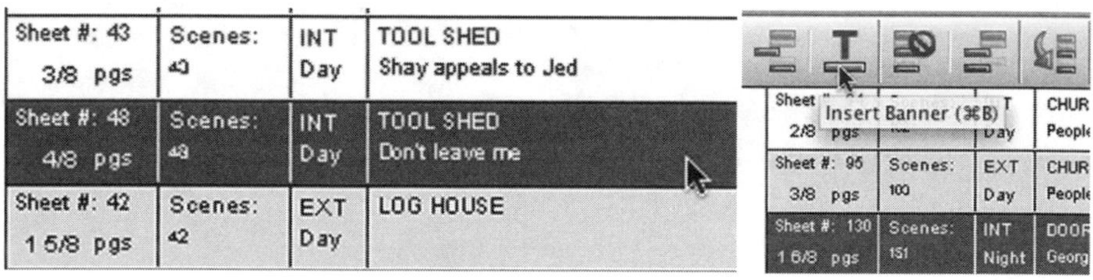


**FIG. 3.33**

Place cursor above where you want text banner

**FIG. 3.34**

Insert banner

Banner

Location Separation-Tool Shed

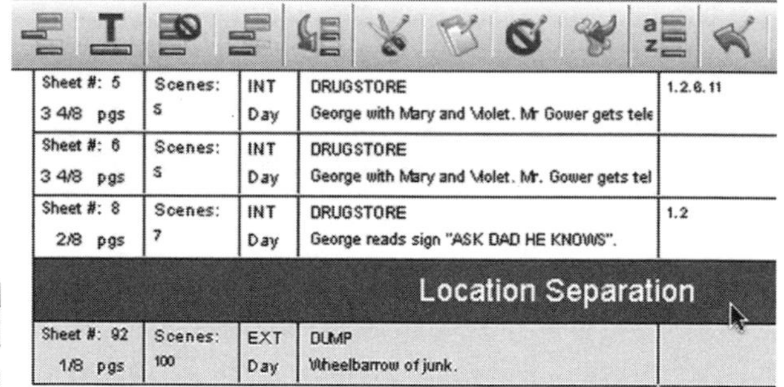


**FIG. 3.35**

Type text or leave blank

**FIG. 3.36**

Text banner

Once "1. Sets" are grouped together, and "2. Exteriors" are placed first within that set, then Interiors, consider "3. Day and Night." Alternating night to day is tough on the body and you need to schedule appropriate *turnaround / rest* time between shooting periods. While shooting one day after another, turnaround times are straightforward, i.e., a specific number of hours as mandated by guilds (12+ hours for union productions, and a humane and reasonable period on non-union productions). Switching day to night (or vice versa) is best at the end of a work week, or if possible (pending location availability) group nights together in one period, such as a week.

Discuss with your Director and AD exteriors and interiors; shooting interior night scenes during the day may save time together. Grouping night locations is one solution:

Day 1: EXT. SET 1 DAY
INT. SET 1 DAY
**Day 2: EXT. SET 2 NIGHT**
**EXT. SET 2 NIGHT**
INT. SET 2 NIGHT
INT. SET 3 NIGHT

**Cast**

As much as possible, consolidating the work schedule for each cast member is often cheaper, as you are paying the person for the shortest period of time.

Transferring breakdown information into your schedule, it appears in sequential scene order — 1, 2, 3, 4.

Once you group locations together, and have positioned exterior scenes before interior, look at which scenes your cast is in, to see if their scenes can be shifted next to one another. Characters 1–3 appear in some of these scenes.

Keeping locations together, move the actors' scenes so that they are adjacent. You can consolidate the #1 character (Queen of Diamonds), and you might also consolidate character #3 (Pawn).

The example in Table 3.8 represents the process — one strip move lines up one thing, and another thing shifts. Consolidate your locations by location, INT/EXT & DAY/NIGHT. Within those groupings, consolidate your cast. Within one day it's less important, but it becomes much more so on a day-to-day basis.

The main reason to keep your cast performances consolidated is that it's usually more cost-efficient if you are working with union actors (SAG or AFTRA). When a particular actor appears frequently throughout the entire screenplay, they will most likely be hired as *run of show*, for the entire production, so you can schedule them

**Table 3.6**

| | | | | | | | |
|---|---|---|---|---|---|---|---|
| | | Breakdown Page No. | | 1 | 2 | 3 | 4 |
| | | **Day or Night** | | **D** | **D** | **D** | **D** |
| | | **Scene** | | **1** | **2** | **3** | **4** |
| | | Page Count | | 1/8 | 2 3/8 | 1/8 | 6/8 |
| | | | | **INT. DAY Castle** | **EXT. DAY Castle-Moat** | **INT. DAY Castle** | **EXT. DAY Castle-Moat** |
| | Title: Checkmate | | | | | | |
| Director | Barbara Lindsay | | | | | | |
| Producer | Ali Trulove | | | | | | |
| Assistant Director | Tinka Stafford | | | | | | |
| Script Dated | 21 December 2002 | | | | | | |
| | | | | | | | |
| ***Character*** | | ***No.*** | | | | | |
| **Queen of Diamonds** | | **1** | | **1** | **1** | **1** | |
| **King of Clubs** | | **2** | | | **2** | | **2** |
| **Pawn** | | **3** | | **3** | **3** | | **3** |

whenever needed. The actors who appear sporadically throughout the script may prove to be more challenging, and if they are union talent, their rate will fluctuate depending on how much you can consolidate their performances.

Consolidation of actor appearances may be driven by their fee, and certain actors might get paid more than others. Here's an example of how scheduling cast can affect your budget.

The week below illustrates that Susan, character #6, will work on Monday and Friday, i.e., 2 days. She doesn't work in any other part of the project and is hired as a day player. In the following example, our first schedule attempt sets her workdays on Monday and Friday. In a union production, the actress would be paid for *all 5 days*, i.e., the entire week, rather than 2 days. On the days in between the actor is considered 'on hold' in case you need them to come in to work.

**Table 3.7**

| | | | | | | | |
|---|---|---|---|---|---|---|---|
| | | Breakdown Page No. | | 2 | 4 | 3 | 1 |
| | | Day or Night | | D | D | D | D |
| | | Scene | | 2 | 4 | 3 | 1 |
| | | Page Count | | 2 3/8 | 6/8 | 2 3/8 | 1/8 |
| | | | | EXT. DAY Castle-Moat | EXT. DAY Castle-Moat | INT. DAY Castle | INT. DAY Castle |
| | Title: Checkmate | | | | | | |
| Director | Barbara Lindsay | | | | | | |
| Producer | Ali Trulove | | | | | | |
| Assistant Director | Tinka Stafford | | | | | | |
| Script Dated | 21 December 2002 | | | | | | |
| | | | | | | | |
| *Character* | | *No.* | | | | | |
| Queen of Diamonds | | 1 | | 1 | | 1 | 1 |
| King of Clubs | | 2 | | 2 | 2 | | |
| Pawn | | 3 | | 3 | 3 | | 3 |

It is possible to save money if Susan works for 2 days rather than 5. If possible, manipulate the schedule so that her workdays are contiguous.

If cast availability is a factor on your project, start with your most important (or highest paid cast) first, and consolidate their work schedules as much as possible within each location. You do this on the production board by rearranging strips, and in the stripboard in the computer by clicking and dragging strips to different positions.

State rules for minors (anyone under 18) strictly limit their working hours, turnaround and hours on set, making it necessary to build extra time into the schedule for their scenes. Casting a minor also requires hiring extra personnel, such as a teacher, nurse, and guardian.

**Table 3.8**

| | | | | 4 | 2 | 1 | 3 |
|---|---|---|---|---|---|---|---|
| | | Breakdown Page No. | | 4 | 2 | 1 | 3 |
| | | Day or Night | | D | D | D | D |
| | | Scene | | 4 | 2 | 1 | 3 |
| | | Page Count | | 6/8 | 2 3/8 | 1/8 | 1/8 |
| | | | | EXT. DAY Castle-Moat | EXT. DAY Castle-Moat | INT. DAY Castle | INT. DAY Castle |
| | Title: Checkmate | | | | | | |
| Director | Barbara Lindsay | | | | | | |
| Producer | Ali Trulove | | | | | | |
| Assistant Director | Tinka Stafford | | | | | | |
| Script Dated | 21 December 2002 | | | | | | |
| | | | | | | | |
| *Character* | | *No.* | | | | | |
| Queen of Diamonds | | 1 | | | 1 | 1 | 1 |
| King of Clubs | | 2 | | 2 | 2 | | |
| Pawn | | 3 | | 3 | 3 | 3 | |

**Table 3.9**

| Mon | Tues | Wed | Thurs | Fri | Sat | Sun |
|---|---|---|---|---|---|---|
| 6 | | | | 6 | | |

**Table 3.10**

| Mon | Tues | Wed | Thurs | Fri | Sat | Sun |
|---|---|---|---|---|---|---|
| | | | 6 | 6 | | |

The Federal Department of Labor summarizes state laws regarding minor employment in a film, which can be found in their "Table of Child Entertainment Provisions" at http://www.dol.gov/whd/state/childentertain.htm.

Table 3.11 lists the maximum amount of time a minor can work on set. Although this table specifically pertains to California productions, it may serve as a guideline.

**Table 3.11**

| Age of Minor | Maximum Work Time on Set |
|---|---|
| 15 days—6 months | 20 minutes |
| 6 months—2 years | 2 hours |
| 2—5 years | 3 hours |
| 6—8 years | 4—6 hours |
| 9—15 years | 5—7 hours |

For more details and required paperwork, check out the Entertainment Partners download, entitled "EP Paymaster Minors", found on their website:

http://www.entertainmentpartners.com/Content/Products/Paymaster.aspx

Understanding state rules, and SAG rules (as well as other relevant unions and guilds), is important, for safety and financial reasons. Guilds and unions post many rules online, and their personnel will explain details when consulted.

The take-away from the above points there is a unique factor, whether location, cast or crew member, that is essential to the production and must be worked around. I call this a *finite resource*.

### The Most Finite Resource

Film schedules often center around one or a few resources perceived to be of utmost importance, and the most finite (finite = expensive, scarce). That may be access to a location, or the time of a particular cast or crew member, a special type of equipment, service, or related to a deal you're getting. It is entirely possible that the Producer doesn't have anything like that in mind, **CYA**: How do you know? Ask.

Once you identify this resource (usually some marketable aspect, yielding dramatic or technical results) it will act like the hub of a wheel — and a schedule will revolve around that resource. This is not an industry term, but a concept to help further refine your schedule.

*Locations* dominate scheduling because they are expensive, and we want to rent them for the least amount of time. When a star is working on your shoot, your schedule may revolve around theirs, due to expense and limited availability.

The overriding principal in organizing your schedule is to group "like" things together:

- Sets;
- Within each location – **Interior** and **Exterior** scenes;
- Within Interior or Exterior grouping – "like" times of **Day/Night**;
- Within grouped locations, and grouped times of day – *principal* actors, then minor characters.

## Arrange Schedule for Maximum Efficiency

Arranging your schedule by locations and cast works well up to a point; here are some other things to keep in mind prior to adding day breaks.

**Rule of Thumb:**

- Start the schedule with straightforward, simpler scenes (dialogue) to build confidence and chemistry;
- Remember the hub – that finite resource or constraint that dictates parts of your schedule no matter what;
- Schedule tricky scenes – stunts and action (camera cars, kids, animals, effects, choreography or equipment) – earlier in the shoot (but not on day 1) as they may need extra time;
- No unnecessary movement. Exploit the equipment setup;
- Exteriors first. Have a backup shooting plan for each day (weather) so you have cover shots;
- Give crew time to set up complicated shots and special equipment;
- Love scenes, nudity, intense emotional scenes – if possible, schedule them later in the production to build trust between key performers (nudity requires clearance from actor);
- When possible, move the shortest physical distance from one shot to the next (e.g., at a cathedral —entrance first, then the aisle, then the altar);
- Other things being equal, shoot in scene order (...32, 33, 34, 35, etc.);
- Apply logic. What makes the most sense: geography or seasonality (green summer versus snowy winter) and similar weather conditions would be grouped together;
- Ask "what could happen if?"

If you know *where* you will be shooting, there are some principles to keep your schedule as efficient as possible. Sets refer to the scene headings in a screenplay, but if you know where you will actually be shooting (locations, or shooting *sites*) and that site could serve as more than one location, group those together.

**Time:** Day or Night Inside. Night interior shots can often be filmed during the day (if there aren't windows or doorways visible), and day interiors can be shot at night if it will condense your schedule.

Use the clock – if you have a sunset scene, arrange the day of that schedule to work toward that shot.

Depending on when during the calendar year the shoot will occur, seasons have longer or shorter amounts of daylight and that may impact your schedule.

CYA: How do you know? Ask.

How long is the work week? (Monday through Friday, or Monday through Saturday?) Whether the project is union or non-union impacts the length of your work week as well as the length of the day (8, 10, 12 hours). *Local* work weeks (5 days – people have a weekend) tend to be shorter than *distant* work weeks (6 days – to get done and go home), but on low budget shoots you may not have that luxury. Weekends may be the only days you get to shoot while Monday through Friday are days off.

Once you feel that the basic order of locations and cast makes sense, insert *day breaks*. Scheduling software can automatically compute day breaks but it needs your help to verify whether they make sense.

The decision of how many pages to shoot in a day ultimately rests with the Director; however, with the help of the Director and AD we can estimate how many pages to shoot in one day on average, and then adjust for scenes that will need more, or less, time. Stationary scenes without movement, and straight dialogue (with a few actors), will take less time than scenes with complex movement or choreography (fights, dancing) interspersed with dialogue (requiring several actors).

Ask your Director/AD how many pages can be shot in a day, on average. Some scenes will need more time, but you can adjust them manually.

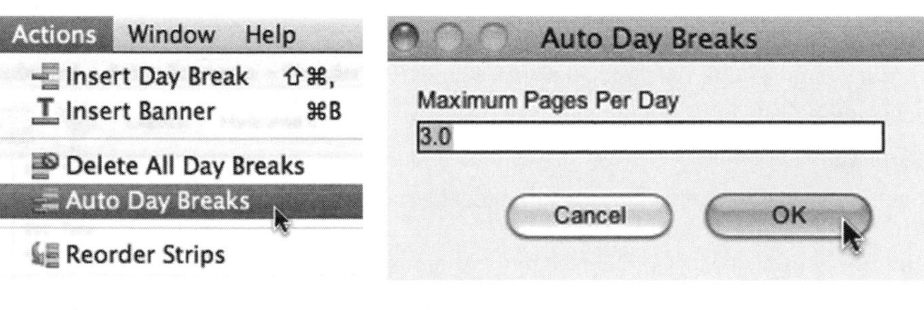


**FIG. 3.37**

Actions/Auto Day Breaks in Movie Magic

**FIG. 3.38**

Estimate maximum pages per day

Automatic Day Break sort function results in a schedule like the one in Figure 3.39. It would be great if creating a schedule were that simple, but computers need us for just this reason. Move strips or day breaks to consolidate Sets, Int./Ext., Day and Night.

Scheduled

| | | | | | |
|---|---|---|---|---|---|
| 44 | Scenes: 44 | EXT | TOOL SHED | 1 1/8 pgs. | CAST IDs: 2, 3 VEHICLE IDs: |
| 49 | Scenes: 49 | EXT | TOOL SHED | 5/8 pgs. | CAST IDs: 2, 3 VEHICLE IDs: |
| 65 | Scenes: 65 | EXT | TOOL SHED | 2 7/8 pgs. | CAST IDs: 2, 3 VEHICLE IDs: |
| 32 | Scenes: 32 | EXT | TOOL SHED | 3/8 pgs. | CAST IDs: 1, 2 VEHICLE IDs: |
| End Day # 1 Monday, November 1, 2010 -- Total Pages: 5 | | | | | |
| 39 | Scenes: 39 | EXT | TOOL SHED | 7/8 pgs. | CAST IDs: 2, 10 VEHICLE IDs: |
| 38 | Scenes: 38 | INT | TOOL SHED | 2 pgs. | CAST IDs: 1, 2, 3, 10 VEHICLE IDs: |
| 31 | Scenes: 31 | INT | TOOL SHED | 1 3/8 pgs. | CAST IDs: 1, 2 VEHICLE IDs: |
| 40 | Scenes: 40 | INT | TOOL SHED | 5/8 pgs. | CAST IDs: 1 VEHICLE IDs: |
| End Day # 2 Tuesday, November 2, 2010 -- Total Pages: 4 7/8 | | | | | |
| 43 | Scenes: 43 | INT | TOOL SHED | 3/8 pgs. | CAST IDs: 1, 3 VEHICLE IDs: |
| 46 | Scenes: 46 | INT | TOOL SHED | 1 4/8 pgs. | CAST IDs: 1, 3 VEHICLE IDs: |
| 48 | Scenes: 48 | INT | TOOL SHED | 4/8 pgs. | CAST IDs: 3 VEHICLE IDs: |
| 84 | Scenes: 84 | EXT | TOOL SHED | 2/8 pgs. | CAST IDs: 3 VEHICLE IDs: |

**FIG. 3.39**

Auto Day Breaks insert breaks without no regard for the reality of production, it is a starting point

| | | | | | |
|---|---|---|---|---|---|
| Sheet #: 38 2 pgs | Scenes: 38 | INT Day | TOOL SHED Jed & dog win Shay's trust | 1,2,3,10 | Est. Time |
| End Day # 2 Tuesday, November 10, 2010 -- Total Pages: 9 2/8 -- Est. Time: 0:00 | | | | | |
| Sheet #: 43 3/8 pgs | Scenes: 43 | INT Day | TOOL SHED Shay appeals to Jed | 1,3 | Est. Time |
| Sheet #: 48 4/8 pgs | Scenes: 48 | INT Day | TOOL SHED Don't leave me | 3 | Est. Time |
| | | | | | |
| Sheet #: 42 1 5/8 pgs | Scenes: 42 | EXT Day | LOG HOUSE | 2,3,10 | Est. Time |
| Sheet #: 34 6/8 pgs | Scenes: 34 | EXT Day | LOG HOUSE | 2,3,10 | Est. Time |
| End Day # 3 Wednesday, November 17, 2010 -- Total Pages: 3 2/8 -- Est. Time: 0:00 | | | | | |

**FIG. 3.40**

Click and drag day breaks

Days with complicated scenes result in *fewer* total pages. Days with simpler scenes, minimal movement, will yield more total pages. There is no "standard"; ultimately it is the Director's decision as to whether they can adhere to the schedule, as well as a function of budget constraints. It is possible to devote an entire day to 1/8th of a page, if there is something complex to set up and shoot; it is equally possible to schedule a day that covers nine simple pages of walk and talk.

If you know the start date of shooting, or delivery date (you can work backward), you can schedule shoot days, holidays, and days off to accommodate turnaround times, switching from day to night shoots, or vice versa. We will discuss managing the calendar later in this chapter, in the Length of Shooting Week / Day section.

**One Line Schedule**

Film scheduling programs print several reports, used for a variety of reasons: dissemination to Department Heads, cast, crew; refining the schedule in discussion with your team; working toward a shooting schedule. The ability to quickly *change* and *print* reports and schedules is one of the advantages of utilizing a computerized scheduling program, rather than a manual approach.

A scheduling stripboard holds so much information that it can be distracting. For purposes of working out the order of scenes, condensed reports can give you perspective. The *one line report* (**AKA:** one-liner) is a pared-down version of the schedule showing select information, more like a shot list.

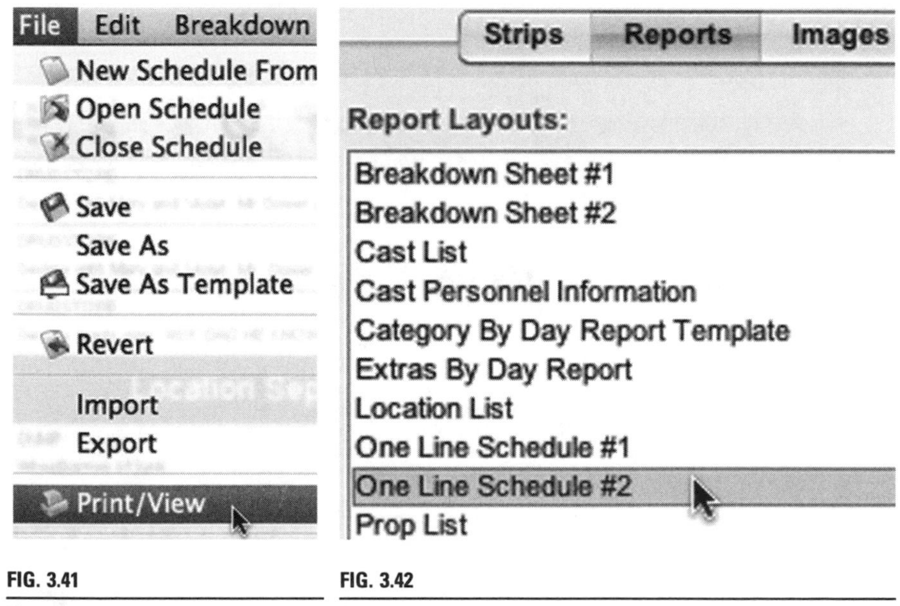


**FIG. 3.41**

View reports

**FIG. 3.42**

Select report layout

View or print these reports, customize them with day breaks or banners, and talk to your AD and Director about them; at a certain point scheduling is collaborative, and the Director needs to feel comfortable with the plan. The different formats show slightly different information.

One Line Schedule — Nov 14, 2010

| | | | | |
|---|---|---|---|---|
| Scn #: 44 | EXT | TOOL SHED<br>Jed can't listen<br>ID: 2, 3 | Day | 1 1/8 |
| Scn #: 49 | EXT | TOOL SHED<br>Shay escapes naked<br>ID: 2, 3 | Day | 5/8 |

**FIG. 3.43**

One line schedule

One Line Schedule — Nov 14, 2010

| | | | | |
|---|---|---|---|---|
| EXT | TOOL SHED | Day | Scn #: 44 | 1 1/8 |
| EXT | TOOL SHED | Day | Scn #: 49 | 5/8 |
| EXT | TOOL SHED | Day | Scn #: 65 | 2 7/8 |
| EXT | TOOL SHED | Day | Scn #: 32 | 3/8 |
| EXT | TOOL SHED | Day | Scn #: 39 | 7/8 |

**FIG. 3.44**

One line schedule – minimum view

Use reports to center in on details to help you arrange schedule order. If possible, it is preferable to shoot a longer section of the script (i.e., higher total page counts) sooner than later, other things being equal. For example, it is preferable to order the scenes as in Table 3.13 rather than Table 3.12 – more pages – earlier in the schedule.

**Table 3.12**

| I/E | Set | D/N | Scene # | Page Count |
|---|---|---|---|---|
| EXT | TOOL SHED | Day | Scn #: 44 | 1 1/8 |
| EXT | TOOL SHED | Day | Scn #: 49 | 5/8 |
| EXT | TOOL SHED | Day | Scn #: 65 | 2 7/8 |
| EXT | TOOL SHED | Day | Scn #: 32 | 3/8 |
| EXT | TOOL SHED | Day | Scn #: 39 | 7/8 |

**Table 3.13**

| I/E | Set | D/N | Scene # | Page Count |
|---|---|---|---|---|
| EXT | TOOL SHED | Day | Scn #: 65 | 2 7/8 |
| EXT | TOOL SHED | Day | Scn #: 44 | 1 1/8 |
| EXT | TOOL SHED | Day | Scn #: 39 | 7/8 |
| EXT | TOOL SHED | Day | Scn #: 49 | 5/8 |
| EXT | TOOL SHED | Day | Scn #: 32 | 3/8 |

Without the screenplay in front of us, we are merely guessing. This change in order gets a bigger section of the script shot sooner rather than later. These decisions will be affected by how many people are in each scene, complexity within the scene, the emotional trajectory overall; ultimately it is the decision of the Director and AD.

It is entirely possible that after conferring with the Director, they would like to film the scenes closer to screenplay order by scene — for dramatic build. Until you have that information, go by what makes sense from the activity in each scene of the screenplay.

**Table 3.14**

| I/E | Set | D/N | Scene # | Page Count |
|---|---|---|---|---|
| EXT | TOOL SHED | Day | Scn #: 32 | 3/8 |
| EXT | TOOL SHED | Day | Scn #: 39 | 7/8 |
| EXT | TOOL SHED | Day | Scn #: 44 | 1 1/8 |
| EXT | TOOL SHED | Day | Scn #: 49 | 5/8 |
| EXT | TOOL SHED | Day | Scn #: 65 | 2 7/8 |

**Day Out of Days**

The day out of days (AKA: DOOD, "dude") report can be customized to focus on any one particular category (vehicles, props, wardrobe) when you want to drill down, showing the schedule for each element within that category. It is a useful tool to hone in on consolidating and rearranging the schedule of actors.

The day out of days report in Figure 3.47 focuses on the schedule of the actors. This report is useful for working with SAG, during casting, as a cast budgeting tool, and for schedule problem solving. The form uses a simple code: W = Workday, SW = Start Work, H = Hold, and can be customized to your preferences.

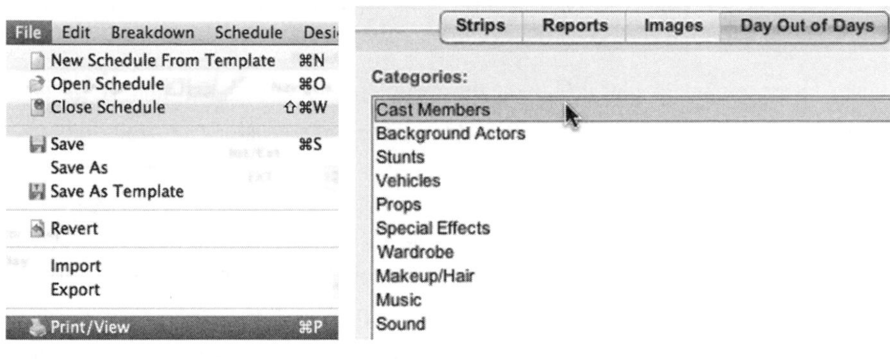


**FIG. 3.45**

View reports

**FIG. 3.46**

Select "Day Out of Days"

**Nov 13, 2010**
**11:55 PM**

**Wrong Turn**
**Day Out of Days Report for Cast Members**

**Page 1 of 4**

| Month/Day | 11/15 | 11/16 | 11/17 | 11/18 | 11/19 | 11/20 | 11/21 | 11/22 | 11/23 | 11/24 | 11/25 | 11/26 |
|---|---|---|---|---|---|---|---|---|---|---|---|---|
| Day of Week | Mon | Tue | Wed | Thu | Fri | Sat | Sun | Mon | Tue | Wed | Thu | Fri |
| Shooting Day | 1 | 2 | 3 | 4 | 5 | | | 6 | 7 | 8 | | 9 |
| 1. SHAY | | SW | W | H | W | | | H | H | W | / | W |
| 2. BUD | SW | W | W | | W | | | W | W | W | / | W |
| 3. TOMMY | SW | W | W | | W | | | W | W | W | / | W |
| 4. JED | | | | | | | | | | | / | |
| 5. TILLY | | | | SW | | | | | | W | / | |
| 6. BABY | | | | | | | | | | SW | / | |

**FIG. 3.47**

Day Out of Days

## Factors Impacting the Schedule

Every factor impacts a film schedule: the experience of your team, number of locations and distance between them (any foreign currency, customs, travel), length of script, and scope and size of production.

The most direct factors influencing any schedule relate to whether your film is a union production (i.e., it must follow strict scheduling and payment rules), how *long* the shoot will take, the number of people you are paying (and how much), how complicated or elaborate the sets, make-up, hair, art design, are extreme temperatures, and hostile environments on location. Here are some factors to consider:

- Complex scenes: how many?
- Duration of shoot;
- Number of cast involved;
- Type of genre (period pieces, futuristic pieces, musicals, 3D, effects-heavy pieces);
- Dialogue (cheaper) versus non dialogue (more time-consuming);
- Action, stunts, animals, kids, explosions, fire, water, effects (often expensive and unpredictable in terms of time and outcome).

The overriding goal, at all times, is for you to be the "Under Wonder," which means you will need to build in, to the greatest extent possible, extra time and extra money. Whatever you schedule and budget, you want the *actual results* to come in a *little under*, i.e., finish up a bit early and a little under the number you've budgeted. Exercise your caution muscle during the scheduling process — assume bad weather, that accidents may happen, and that you'll need extra time. Build in time cushions whenever possible.

### Film or Digital Format

CYA: How do you know? Ask.

Questions to ask before you start:

1. **What format are we shooting on — film or digital?** Shooting digital, HD, DVC Pro, HDV, 3D, 16 mm, Super 16, or 35 mm will impact your schedule and budget.

2. **What is the intended end-use of the film and what are the delivery requirements, if any?** Shooting film is more expensive, but is still the industry norm for exhibition in most theaters. It's not uncommon for filmmakers to shoot in a digital format, and, if necessary, for exhibition at a festival, or securing distribution, "blow up" the format to film (or reformat NTSC to PAL).

Blowing up a film is the process of *converting* one format to another. Whether the intended use of your film is for streaming on the Internet, versus projection in a movie theater, you will need the appropriate format. Discuss this with your team: Producer, AD and Director.

Film is more delicate than digital formats, and tends to be more expensive to buy and develop. Using digital formats (tapes and P2 cards) is often cheaper, as they don't require developing like film. Digital files are also native to computer formats commonly used to edit today, like Final Cut and Avid systems. When your Director is shooting on digital, they will most likely have a higher shooting ratio, since the stock is cheaper.

### Shooting Ratio and Experience

The higher the shooting ratio your Director prefers, the more time you will need, and the more $$ it will cost.

**AKA**: Shooting ratio = # of takes a Director requires for each shot. So, a "six to one" (6:1) shooting ratio means the Director will want to shoot six *separate* takes of one shot to feel comfortable that there will be sufficient footage, or coverage, of the scene. Some Directors like 10:1, others require low ratios (3:1) – it depends on them.

The experience of your Director, AD and DP, principal actors and Department Heads will absolutely impact your schedule. Experienced actors who remember their lines every time speed things along, as do prepared crew with great tools and the know – how to operate them. Vetting resumes, open communication, and clear goals will help define your original schedule and help you keep to it (you are the Under Wonder – allow for extra time whenever possible).

Experience relates not only to a job history, but also to someone's experience working with a particular format, or type of project. Inexperienced teams need more time.

**Unions and Guilds**

The decision to shoot union or not, and which ones to work with, can be confusing. Each union or guild has rules about working hours, pay rates and safety conditions. This choice has a resounding impact on your costs, paperwork and access to well-known, and therefore marketable, cast, as well as the end use of your film. Chances are good that your Producer has strong feelings on this subject either way, and as it will directly affect the schedule and budget it's best to find out sooner rather than later.

Whether to shoot union is a project-to-project decision, and often relates to hiring recognized actors, which tend to be SAG actors, or a DGA Director. Generally, the cost of making a film with union talent is higher, and the paperwork process is more complex. Your production has to find out the rules, understand and follow the rules, and sign paperwork to that effect.

The unions and guilds are separate entities, but work cooperatively. Their guidelines are detailed in their Basic Agreement (or MBA, Minimum Basic Agreement), either posted online or you can get a copy from the union. It is helpful to check out the websites, and speak to reps — SAG first, then DGA, IATSE, and WGA (if applicable) — to understand the rules; preferably, as far in advance as possible. The SAG agreements (which often drive the process) are specific about the film length, duration of the shoot, budget range, and end use.

Your schedule details must abide by their guidelines (length of shooting day, arrangement of the days, hours worked, holiday, turnaround time between shooting days, meal penalty) to understand the rules, and what can happen (penalties and fines) if rules are broken.

Parameters for pay rates, hours and general flexibility are tied directly to the anticipated budget *range* of the production (i.e., low budget, modified low budget, or ultra low budget), and the *type* of film it is (i.e., training, experimental, or student).

The minimum budget range is $50,000, except for the SAG New Media Agreement, created for distribution online and in mobile formats. The ranges in Table 3.15 correspond to low budget production ranges according to SAG.

**Table 3.15**

| Budget Minimum | Maximum Budget |
|---|---|
| Short film | <$50,000 |
| Ultra low | <$200,000 |
| Modified low | <$625,000 |
| Low budget | $2,500,000 |

The unions have rules that overlap and intersect and can seem confusing. If you don't know whether the production you are working on will become a union project, concentrate on assembling the most logical schedule possible, then collaborate with your team to adjust it as needed.

Screen Actors Guild: www.SAG.org www.SagIndie.org

Directors Guild: www.DGA.org

International Alliance of Theatrical Stage Employees:

www.iatse-intl.org/home.html

Writers Guild: www.WGA.org

International Cinematographers Guild: www.cameraguild.com

International Brotherhood of Teamsters: www.teamster.org

American Federation of Musicians: www.AFM.com

Different states have different rules regarding unions; your state may have a collective bargaining agreement with the union, or perhaps it is a "right-to-work" state. Areas with high populations, or developed film industries, tend to have more potential cast and crew options, whether union talent or not. Often, the matter goes back to two issues: budget range and project goal. Thorough online research, as well as talking with other local filmmakers, production accountants, entertainment attorneys and film commissioners can help steer you toward the right decision for your project when you are ready. (More about unions in Chapter 4.)

Right-to-work states include: Alabama, Arizona, Arkansas, Florida, Georgia, Idaho, Iowa, Kansas, Louisiana, Mississippi, Nebraska, Nevada, North Carolina, North Dakota, Oklahoma, South Carolina, South Dakota, Tennessee, Texas, Utah, Virginia, and Wyoming.



**Locations**

*Location incentive programs* are popular in the United States and in many other regions around the world. Film incentive programs were created to draw production to an area, creating jobs, and spurring spending in a state or city.

These programs typically offer deals (no sales tax, or free location permits) or financing in the form of refundable tax credits, or tax rebates, to productions based on very specific conditions — from budget ranges to numbers of local hires. The rules change, and there is an application process (it's not a sure thing for every applicant), but these programs are driving *where* projects are made. To stay abreast of news about details and (frequent) updates, read up in the trades like *Variety* & *Hollywood Reporter*, *Movie Maker* and *IndieWire*, and be aware that the terminology is not standardized, so ask lots of questions. Locations are an important component of film-making; however, you can create a schedule even if you do not know exactly where you are shooting. Most regions have websites detailing the specifics of their program; start at the Association of Film Commissioners International, www.afci.org.

If your production is working with a location manager, ask about: using one location site for multiple sets, access to electric, size of doorways, and proximity of parking — as you may need to build in a little more time to accommodate certain conditions specific to every location.

*Travel can be expensive*. Movement of any kind on a set, and between sets and locations, incurs costs and often extends your schedule, which incurs costs. Traveling expenses, whether for transportation, lodging, or fuel, per diem, all add up. It's not just the people moving from one place; often it is also the equipment. Once everyone arrives, they must be housed and fed.

Proximity of your crew and cast to the shooting sites, the sites to each other, and access to them, will all impact your schedule. If the production is traveling outside of the home country, additional time and costs will be incurred for things like lodging, currency exchange, recovery from jet lag, homeland security issues, acquiring visas, lost passports, translation, and so forth. This is an issue where it just depends on your film; hiring key local crew may be a more time- and cost-efficient option than transporting everyone working on your film.

**Length of Shooting Week / Day**

Unions shoots dictate specifically the length of the shooting week and the day based on where the shoot is, and what type of project, so if you are working on a union project, find the rules and stick to them. For certain productions, a 13-hour day might be ideal; you have to weigh that against the possibility of burn out.

There are different rules for Minors (anyone under 18) — state laws apply whether you are shooting a union picture or not. Permits, limited working hours, the presence of guardians, teachers, and any other support personnel are subject to labor laws on a state-by-state basis. For specific information, see the Table of Child Entertainment

Provisions: http://www.dol.gov/whd/state/childentertain.htm. SAG details provisions for minor performers if you are shooting SAG film.

Many indie filmmakers shoot when their team is "available," which can spread a production over weeks or months when principles are free. The longer the shooting is stretched out (say 30 days of shooting done over 2 months versus 30 days spread over weekends over the course of an entire year), the more this will impact motivation, memory of the project, and closeness as a group. However, there are several examples of films that were successful using this strategy, like *Open Water*. Each project is unique and will be driven by the goals of the core team – you, the Producer, Director, and AD.

A grueling schedule without any days off is not likely to yield the best results – energy will flag, and as people get tired and irritable conflicts will arise. For union productions, strict adherence must be paid to schedule parameters to avoid incurring additional expenses for overtime pay, meal penalties, and turnaround times.

Figures 3.48 through 3.50 illustrate how to manage your calendar, and adjust the parameters of the work week (which can be helpful even if you don't know the exact shoot dates).

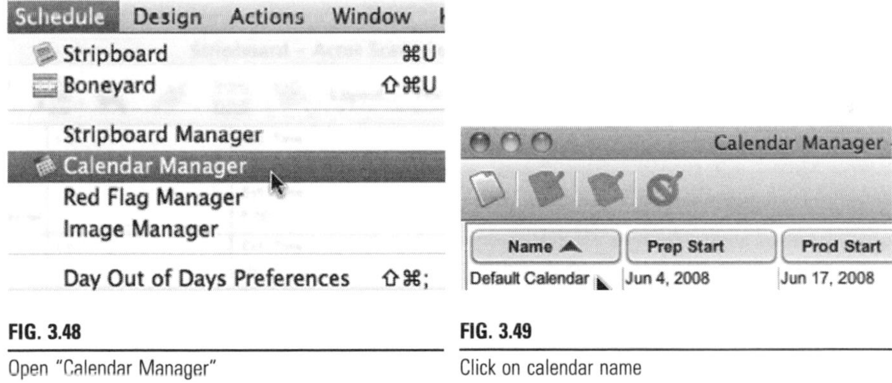


**FIG. 3.48**

Open "Calendar Manager"

**FIG. 3.49**

Click on calendar name

Name the calendar logically as in Figure 3.50 (e.g., 5- or 6-day week, season, start date, etc. – whatever makes sense), add days off and holidays, and try out different dates for the start of prep and prod, and for the end of shoot and post.

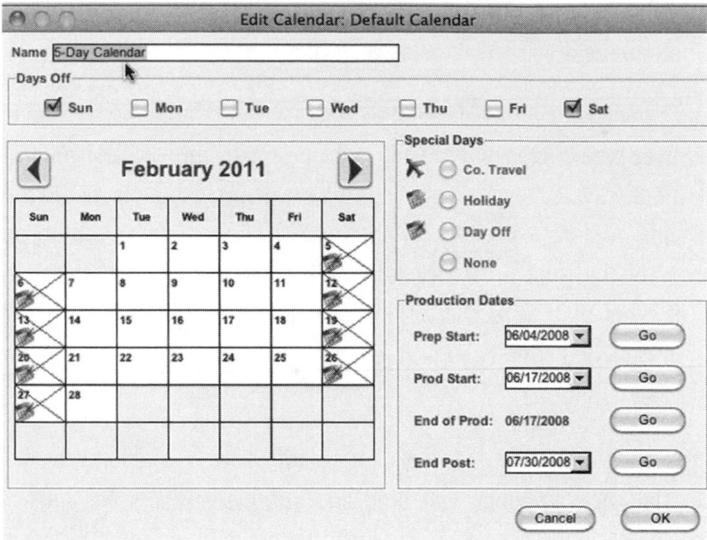


**FIG. 3.50**

Adjust calendar parameters

# Sample Schedules

## Short Doc. Film

Scheduled

| | | | | | |
|---|---|---|---|---|---|
| Sheet #: 8<br>4/8 pgs | Scenes:<br>8 | EXT | Cranston RI Backyard<br>Grandchildren stories | Day | 4.5.6 |
| Sheet #: 2<br>1 7/8 pgs | Scenes:<br>2 | EXT | Cranston RI Backyard<br>Life living with Larry | Day | 2.3 |
| Sheet #: 3<br>3 5/8 pgs | Scenes:<br>3 | INT | Music Studio<br>Larry play favorite songs | Day | 1 |
| Sheet #: 4<br>2 1/8 pgs | Scenes:<br>4 | INT | Larry living room<br>Larry reminisce-lots of stories | Day | 1 |
| End Day # 1 Monday, November 22, 2010 -- Total Pages: 8 1/8 | | | | | |
| Sheet #: 6<br>1 2/8 pgs | Scenes:<br>6 | INT | Senior Center<br>Performance live at Senior Center | Day | 1 |
| Sheet #: 5<br>5/8 pgs | Scenes:<br>5 | INT | Back Street Bar<br>Favorite watering hole | Day | 1.9 |
| Sheet #: 1<br>3 4/8 pgs | Scenes:<br>1 | INT | Music Studio<br>Stills & Stories | Day | 1.2.6 |
| Sheet #: 9<br>1 pgs | Scenes:<br>9 | INT | Music Studio<br>Kathleen's radio show | Day | 6 |
| End Day # 2 Tuesday, November 23, 2010 -- Total Pages: 6 3/8 | | | | | |
| Sheet #: 7<br>3/8 pgs | Scenes:<br>7 | INT | Music Studio<br>Techie aspects | Day | 1.2 |
| Sheet #: 10<br>6/8 pgs | Scenes:<br>10 | INT | Music Studio<br>Sing AlonFamily g | Day | 1.2.3.4.5.6 |
| End Day # 3 Wednesday, November 24, 2010 -- Total Pages: 1 1/8 | | | | | |
| The end | | | | | |

**FIG. 3.51**

Short doc. schedule, shot in DV, 15 min. long

## Student Short Film

### Scheduled

| | | | | |
|---|---|---|---|---|
| Sheet #: 2<br>3/8 pgs | Scenes:<br>2 | EXT<br>Day | APARTMENT PARKING LOT<br>Krissy ignored | 1 |
| Sheet #: 1<br>5/8 pgs | Scenes:<br>1 | INT<br>Day | MESSY APARTMENT - LIVING ROOM<br>Krissy dresses for work | 1 |
| Sheet #: 4<br>5/8 pgs | Scenes:<br>4 | INT<br>Night | OFFICE BUILDING<br>Thinking cap | 1 |
| Sheet #: 3<br>3/8 pgs | Scenes:<br>3 | EXT<br>Night | OFFICE BUILDING<br>Krissy's late to second job | 1 |
| Total: 1 Day Shoot | | | | |

**FIG. 3.52**

One-day shoot: student short, HDV, 2 min.

## Webisode

### Scheduled

| | | | | | |
|---|---|---|---|---|---|
| Sheet #: 8<br>2/8 pgs | Scenes:<br>8 | EXT<br>Day | Car<br>Hmmm, coffee | 3 | Est. Time |
| Sheet #: 5<br>3/8 pgs | Scenes:<br>5 | EXT<br>Day | Car<br>Hi there | 2.3 | Est. Time |
| Sheet #: 6<br>2/8 pgs | Scenes:<br>6 | EXT<br>Day | Car<br>Do you see what I see | 2.3 | Est. Time |
| Sheet #: 9<br>3/8 pgs | Scenes:<br>9 | EXT<br>Day | Car<br>Closer look | 2.3 | Est. Time |
| Sheet #: 7<br>7/8 pgs | Scenes:<br>7 | EXT<br>Day | Car<br>Don't misunderstand | 1.2.3 | Est. Time |
| Sheet #: 10<br>4/8 pgs | Scenes:<br>10 | INT<br>Day | Car<br>Happy couple | 2.3 | Est. Time |
| Sheet #: 1<br>2/8 pgs | Scenes:<br>1 | INT<br>Day | Web Browser<br>Cursor appears & types | 1 | Est. Time |
| Sheet #: 2<br>3/8 pgs | Scenes:<br>2 | INT<br>Day | Landing Page<br>Cursor Looking for Love | 1 | Est. Time |
| Sheet #: 3<br>1/8 pgs | Scenes:<br>3 | INT<br>Day | Warning Page<br>I agree | 1 | Est. Time |
| Sheet #: 4<br>4/8 pgs | Scenes:<br>4 | INT<br>Day | Love Post<br>Scroll words | 1 | Est. Time |
| One Fine Day: Two Camera Setup: 23_June_2009 | | | | | |

**FIG. 3.53**

Branded DV webisode, 2.5 min.

## Corporate Video

| Scheduled | | | | | | |
|---|---|---|---|---|---|---|
| 1 | 1 | EXT | Subway Entrance | Day | 2/8 pgs. | 2 |
| 2 | 2 | EXT | 11 Wall-Entry | Day | 2/8 pgs. | 1.3.4.5.6 |
| 4 | 4 | INT | 50th Floor - Lobby | Day | 2/8 pgs. | 1.2.3.4.5.6 |
| 10 | 10 | INT | 50th Floor - Conference Room | Day | 7/8 pgs. | 1.2.3.4.5.6 |
| 3 | 3 | INT | 50th Floor - Conference Room | Day | 5/8 pgs. | 2.4.6 |
| 7 | 7 | EXT | 11 Wall-Entry | Night | 3/8 pgs. | 1.2 |
| End Day # 1 Monday, June 14, 2010 -- Total Pages: 2 5/8 | | | | | | |
| 8 | 8 | INT | President's Office | Day | 4/8 pgs. | 1 |
| 5 | 5 | INT | Main Lobby - East Window | Day | 3/8 pgs. | 2 |
| 6 | 6 | INT | Cafeteria | Day | 1/8 pgs. | 2.3.4.6 |
| 9 | 9 | INT | 44th Floor - Corp Fin Cubicals | Day | 2/8 pgs. | 7.8 |
| End Day # 2 Tuesday, June 15, 2010 -- Total Pages: 1 2/8 | | | | | | |
| Finis | | | | | | |

**FIG. 3.54**

Corporate industrial video, HDV, 4.5 min.

## TV Commercial

| Scheduled | | | | | | |
|---|---|---|---|---|---|---|
| 1 | 1 | EXT | Main Street | Day | 1/8 pgs. | 1 |
| 6 | 4 | EXT | Grove Park-Picnic | Day | 2/8 pgs. | 1 |
| End Day # 1 Saturday, May 29, 2010 -- Total Pages: 3/8 | | | | | | |
| 7 | 5 | EXT | Church | Day | 1/8 pgs. | 1 |
| 8 | 6 | EXT | Farmer's Market | Day | 1/8 pgs. | 1 |
| End Day # 2 Sunday, May 30, 2010 -- Total Pages: 2/8 | | | | | | |
| 10 | 8 | EXT | Rally | Day | 1/8 pgs. | 1 |
| 11 | 10 | INT | Arthur Day High School | Day | 1/8 pgs. | 1 |
| 9 | 7 | INT | Studio | Day | 1/8 pgs. | 1 |
| 3 | 3A | All | PHotos | Photo | 1/8 pgs. | |
| 4 | 3B | All | PHotos | Photo | 1/8 pgs. | |
| 5 | 3C | All | PHotos | Photo | 1/8 pgs. | |
| 2 | 2 | All | Stock Footage | Stock | 1/8 pgs. | |
| End Day # 3 Monday, May 31, 2010 -- Total Pages: 7/8 | | | | | | |
| Finis | | | | | | |

**FIG. 3.55**

Television commercial spot, 30-second, DVC Pro

## Feature

| Scheduled | | | | | | |
|---|---|---|---|---|---|---|
| 12 | 12 | EXT | Tiny Grocery Store | Day | 4/8 pgs. | 1, 8 |
| 16 | 16 | EXT | Tiny Grocery Store | Day | 1 5/8 pgs. | 1, 2 |
| 36 | 36 | EXT | Tiny Grocery Store | Day | 4/8 pgs. | 1 |
| 53 | 53 | EXT | Tiny Grocery Store | Day | 1 2/8 pgs. | 1, 9, 11 |
| 67 | 67 | EXT | Tiny Grocery Store | Day | 1 2/8 pgs. | 1, 9 |
| **End Day # 1 Monday, February 7, 2011 -- Total Pages: 5 1/8** | | | | | | |
| 66 | 66 | EXT | Tiny Grocery Store | Day | 2 3/8 pgs. | 1, 2 |
| 13 | 13 | INT | Tiny Grocery Store - Bathroom | Day | 6/8 pgs. | 1, 11 |
| 14 | 14 | INT | Tiny Grocery Store | Day | 5/8 pgs. | 1, 8, 11 |
| 37 | 37 | INT | Tiny Grocery Store | Day | 7/8 pgs. | 1, 8, 15, 16 |
| **End Day # 2 Tuesday, February 8, 2011 -- Total Pages: 4 5/8** | | | | | | |
| 38 | 38 | INT | Tiny Grocery Store | Day | 1 7/8 pgs. | 1, 2, 8 |
| 15 | 15 | INT | Tiny Grocery Store - Meat Station | Day | 1 4/8 pgs. | 1, 11 |
| 68 | 68 | INT | Tiny Grocery Store - Meat Station | Day | 6/8 pgs. | 1, 5 |
| 43 | 43 | EXT | Cafe | Day | 1 5/8 pgs. | 1, 13 |
| 28 | 28 | EXT | Gas Station | Day | 6/8 pgs. | 1, 2, 4, 14, 15, 16 |
| **End Day # 3 Wednesday, February 9, 2011 -- Total Pages: 6 4/8** | | | | | | |
| 29 | 29 | EXT | Neighborhood Convenient Store | Day | 1 1/8 pgs. | 1, 2, 4 |
| 46 | 46 | EXT | Downtown - Street | Day | 6/8 pgs. | 1, 2, 20 |
| 47 | 47 | EXT | Downtown Street - Water Dispensing M | Day | 1 7/8 pgs. | 1, 2, 4, 10 |
| 54 | 54 | EXT | Downtown - Street | Day | 1 1/8 pgs. | 1, 5, 9 |
| 57 | 57 | EXT | Downtown Street - Taco Truck Stand | Day | 2/8 pgs. | 1, 5, 17 |
| **End Day # 4 Thursday, February 10, 2011 -- Total Pages: 5 1/8** | | | | | | |
| 25 | 25 | EXT | May's House | Day | 6/8 pgs. | 1, 8 |
| 2 | 2 | INT | May's House - Hallway | Day | 2/8 pgs. | 1 |
| 63 | 63 | INT | May's House - Living Room | Day | 2 6/8 pgs. | 1, 8 |
| 40 | 40 | INT | May's House - Kitchen | Day | 6/8 pgs. | 1, 11 |
| 11 | 11 | INT | May's House - Bathroom | Day | 5/8 pgs. | 1, 8 |
| 39 | 39 | INT | May's House - Bathroom | Day | 1/8 pgs. | 1 |
| **End Day # 5 Friday, February 11, 2011 -- Total Pages: 5 2/8** | | | | | | |
| 50 | 50 | INT | May's House | Night | 2/8 pgs. | 1, 2 |
| 10 | 10 | INT | May's House - Bathroom | Night | 3/8 pgs. | 1, 8 |
| 1 | 1 | INT | May's House - Bathroom | Night | 2/8 pgs. | 1 |
| 51 | 51 | INT | May's House - Bedroom | Night | 2 5/8 pgs. | 1, 2 |
| 59 | 59 | INT | May's House - Bedroom | Night | 2 6/8 pgs. | 1, 5, 11 |
| 45 | 45 | INT | May's House - Living Room | Night | 2 2/8 pgs. | 1, 8, 11 |
| **End Day # 6 Saturday, February 12, 2011 -- Total Pages: 8 4/8** | | | | | | |
| DAY OFF | | | | | | |
| 7 | 7 | INT | Inga's House - Bedroom | Night | 2/8 pgs. | 4, 6, 9 |
| 6 | 6 | INT | Inga's House - Bedroom | Night | 1 6/8 pgs. | 1, 2, 3, 4, 6, 7, 9 |
| 8 | 8 | INT | Inga's House - Bedroom | Night | 5/8 pgs. | 1, 2, 3, 4, 6, 7, 9 |
| 74 | 74 | INT | Inga's House - Bedroom | Night | 1 4/8 pgs. | 1, 2, 3, 4, 5, 6, 9 |
| 76 | 76 | INT | Inga's House - Bedroom | Night | 2/8 pgs. | 1, 2, 3, 4, 6, 9 |
| 78 | 78 | INT | Inga's House - Bedroom | Night | 1 pgs. | 1, 2, 3, 4, 5, 6, 9 |
| 75 | 75 | INT | Inga's House - Hallway | Night | 1/8 pgs. | 5 |
| 77 | 77 | INT | Inga's House - Hallway | Night | 2/8 pgs. | 5 |
| **End Day # 7 Monday, February 14, 2011 -- Total Pages: 5 6/8** | | | | | | |
| 44 | 44 | EXT | Bus stop | Night | 1/8 pgs. | 1 |
| 34 | 34 | EXT | Bus stop | Night | 5/8 pgs. | 1, 4 |
| | | | | | | |
| 3 | 3 | EXT | Downtown - Street | Night | 2 pgs. | 1, 2, 3, 10 |
| 5 | 5 | EXT | Downtown - Street | Night | 6/8 pgs. | 1, 2, 3, 6, 7 |
| 9 | 9 | EXT | Downtown - Street | Night | 2 3/8 pgs. | 1, 2, 3, 4, 6, 7, 9 |
| **End Day # 8 Tuesday, February 15, 2011 -- Total Pages: 5 7/8** | | | | | | |
| 49 | 49 | EXT | Downtown - Street | Night | 2 1/8 pgs. | 1, 2, 6 |
| 58 | 58 | EXT | Downtown - Street | Night | 2 7/8 pgs. | 1, 5, 17, 21, 22 |
| **End Day # 9 Wednesday, February 16, 2011 -- Total Pages: 5** | | | | | | |
| 33 | 33 | EXT | College Apartment - back yard | Night | 2 4/8 pgs. | 1, 4, 13 |
| 31 | 31 | INT | College Apartment | Night | 5/8 pgs. | 1, 2, 4, 19 |
| 32 | 32 | INT | College Apartment - Kitchen | Night | 2 pgs. | 1, 2, 13, 19 |
| **End Day # 10 Thursday, February 17, 2011 -- Total Pages: 5 1/8** | | | | | | |
| 24 | 24 | EXT | Rose's House | Night | 1/8 pgs. | 1 |
| 69 | 69 | EXT | Roach Coach | Night | 1 1/8 pgs. | 1, 5 |
| 4 | 4 | INT | Neighborhood Convenient Store | Night | 6/8 pgs. | 1, 2, 3, 6, 7 |
| 70 | 70 | EXT | Auto shop | Night | 5/8 pgs. | 1, 5 |
| 71 | 71 | INT | Auto shop | Night | 7/8 pgs. | 1, 5 |

**FIG. 3.56**

Narrative feature film schedule, 35 mm, 90 min.

| | | | | | | |
|---|---|---|---|---|---|---|
| End Day # 11 Friday, February 18, 2011 -- Total Pages: 3 4/8 | | | | | | |
| 2 DAYS OFF SAT / SUN | | | | | | |
| 73 | 73 | INT | Camaro | Day | 1 6/8 pgs. | 1, 5 |
| 72 | 72 | INT | Camaro | Night | 4 7/8 pgs. | 1, 5 |
| End Day # 12 Monday, February 21, 2011 -- Total Pages: 6 5/8 | | | | | | |
| 48 | 48 | EXT | Park | Day | 1 pgs. | 1, 2, 6 |
| 27 | 27 | EXT | 7-11 - Parking Lot | Day | 2 1/8 pgs. | 1, 2, 4 |
| 42 | 42 | EXT | Bus stop | Day | 1/8 pgs. | 1 |
| 65 | 65 | EXT | Bus stop | Day | 1 2/8 pgs. | 1, 4 |
| 30 | 30 | INT | Cesar's Bedroom | Day | 2 4/8 pgs. | 1, 2, 3 |
| 41 | 41 | INT | Bus | Day | 2/8 pgs. | 1 |
| End Day # 13 Tuesday, February 22, 2011 -- Total Pages: 7 2/8 | | | | | | |
| 35 | 35 | EXT | Downtown - Street | Day | 1 7/8 pgs. | 1, 2 |
| 79 | 79 | EXT | Downtown Street | Day | 1 2/8 pgs. | 1, 2 |
| 19 | 19 | EXT | Downtown - Street | Day | 2 6/8 pgs. | 1, 2, 6, 7 |
| 60 | 60 | EXT | Downtown - Street | Day | 6/8 pgs. | 1, 6, 7 |
| End Day # 14 Wednesday, February 23, 2011 -- Total Pages: 6 5/8 | | | | | | |
| 21 | 21 | EXT | Park | Day | 2 pgs. | 1, 12 |
| 26 | 26 | EXT | Park | Day | 1 3/8 pgs. | 1, 2 |
| 62 | 62 | EXT | Park | Day | 1 pgs. | 1, 6 |
| 61 | 61 | EXT | Rocco's House | Day | 1 pgs. | 1, 6, 7 |
| End Day # 15 Thursday, February 24, 2011 -- Total Pages: 5 3/8 | | | | | | |
| 52 | 52 | EXT | Tax Office | Day | 1 5/8 pgs. | 1, 5 |
| 55 | 55 | EXT | Tax Office | Day | 2 1/8 pgs. | 1, 5 |
| 64 | 64 | EXT | Tax Office | Day | 1 pgs. | 1, 18 |
| 20 | 20 | INT | Tax Office | Day | 1 pgs. | 1, 2, 18 |
| End Day # 16 Friday, February 25, 2011 -- Total Pages: 5 6/8 | | | | | | |
| 17 | 17 | INT | Thrift Store | | 2 2/8 pgs. | 1, 2 |
| 56 | 56 | INT | Thrift Store | Day | 1 pgs. | 1, 2 |
| 18 | 18 | INT | Thrift Store - Cash Register | Day | 1/8 pgs. | 1, 2 |
| 23 | 23 | INT | Rose's house - Bedroom | | 7/8 pgs. | 1, 12 |
| 22 | 24, 25 | INT | Rose's house - living room | Day | 5/8 pgs. | 1, 12 |
| End Day # 17 Saturday, February 26, 2011 -- Total Pages: 4 7/8 | | | | | | |

**FIG. 3.56**

(Continued)

## End of Chapter Three Review

Scheduling has three steps:

1. **Transfer information into your schedule.**
   A. Fill out production information, title, key team members.
   B. One breakdown sheet at a time, *transfer* all info into schedule and *verify* consistency of information.
   C. Assign cast ID numbers.
2. **Group like things.**
   A. By Set, Int/Ext, Day/Night.
   B. By Cast – major characters, then minor characters.
   C. By the most finite resource (special equipment, star with limited availability).
3. **Arrange for maximum efficiency for your production.**
   A. Start schedule with two "easier" days.
   B. Exteriors first.
   C. Move shortest physical distance.
   D. Separate locations with a banner as a visual cue.
   E. Look at reports (day out of days, one-liner, for troubleshooting).
   F. Follow up: consult your team, to establish how many pages to get each day, and discuss how to improve and refine your work.

Scheduling is a process that will continue to be shaped with new information: specific locations, cast and crew. The decision to shoot union or non-union will significantly influence your schedule, as will the format of the film and its end use.

# Chapter Four

## *Pricing Resources: The Budget*

---

**QUESTION: "How Much Do I Owe You?" – Clark Griswold (Chevy Chase)**

**ANSWER:** "How much you got?" – Mechanic *VACATION*

---

Film budgets come in a wide variety of sizes, from no-lo, to micro, to millions. Initial expectations come from the Producer – with *some* idea of what to spend, or *none*. With some idea, you are backing into a range; without any, you are building it up from scratch. Start with the information you have and work from there.

Budgeting is a three-stage process:

1. **Identify** and **obtain** prices (from multiple sources) for: equipment (shoot); union rates (cast and crew); film commissions and studios (locations); post facilities; and include what you already know and money spent or committed so far. Build an initial budget at full price.
2. **Negotiate** potential deals and refine budget with input from your team. Amend budget with deals.
3. **Lock in** your deals with signed contracts (employment contracts, location contracts, permits). Create alternate versions of the budget to find savings.

An initial budget is a starting point, to be revised and reshaped. Once a final figure is established, the budget is *locked*: that's the number to stay under. Money may shift between accounts, but that total is not to be exceeded.

## Budget Components

A film budget is composed of two main ingredients, divided by an invisible line. These two main ingredients are creative costs **Above the Line** (like research and development in traditional business), and the cost of making the script – **Below the Line** costs (similar to manufacturing expenses).

**Table 4.1**

| **Above the Line** | *Creative Costs* | **Producer, Director, Script, Cast** |
|---|---|---|
| **Below the Line** | *Manufacturing Costs* | Everything else:<br>**Production** (Shoot and Prep.)<br>**+Post Production** (Edit, Wrap)<br>**+Other** (Insurance, Legal Fees) |
| **Total** | **Above the Line**<br>**+ Below the Line**<br>**= Cost to make film** | |

Above the Line costs *start* the process. An idea is transformed into a script; a Producer drives the process; a Director visualizes the film; and cast members realize the roles.

Below the Line costs are driven by the script:

> **Production**: shooting expenses – sets, construction, wardrobe, props, materials, electricity, locations, crew.
>
> **Post:** editing sound and picture, completion.
>
> **Other** contractual costs related to the entire project.

As shown in the budget summary Topsheet in Figure 4.1, the header at the very top provides essential information about the production.

Referring to Above the Line as "creative" costs does not imply that people working Below the Line are not artists. All film production workers marry technical and imaginative abilities. The successful completion of a film depends upon the entire cast and crew utilizing all of their skills.

*The "line" is a Hollywood artifact to organize costs and is not set in concrete. An essential creative component could be moved from below to above the line, if considered to be a major factor in the development of the project.*

FILM TITLE
Producer
Director
Line Producer

Date
Format
Length
Locations

| Acct No. | Category Description | Page | Total |
|---|---|---|---|
| 1100 | Screenplay | 1 | $25 |
| 1200 | Producers | 1 | 0 |
| 1300 | Directors | 1 | 100 |
| 1400 | Cast | 1 | 175 |
| | **TOTAL ABOVE THE LINE** | | **300** |
| | | | |
| 2100 | Production Staff | 2 | 125 |
| 2200 | Extras | 2 | 25 |
| 2300 | Sets | 2 | 350 |
| 2400 | Props | 3 | 50 |
| 2500 | Costumes | 3 | 175 |
| 2600 | Make-up & Hair | 3 | 200 |
| 2700 | Electrical | 4 | 1,500 |
| 2800 | Camera | 4 | 350 |
| 2900 | Sound | 4 | 350 |
| 3000 | Film/Video Stock | 5 | 100 |
| 3100 | Locations/Catering/Transport | 5 | 400 |
| | **TOTAL BTL PRODUCTION** | | **3,625** |
| | | | |
| 4000 | Editing | 6 | 2,500 |
| 4100 | Sound & Music | 6 | 150 |
| 4200 | Lab & Duplication | 6 | 3,500 |
| | **TOTAL BTL POST** | | **6,150** |
| | | | |
| 5000 | Insurance | 7 | 2,500 |
| 5200 | Legal | 7 | 175 |
| 5300 | Publicity | 7 | 2,500 |
| 5400 | General & Administrative | 7 | 350 |
| | **TOTAL BTL OTHER** | | **5,525** |
| | | | |
| | Total Above the Line | | $300 |
| | | | |
| | Production | | 3,625 |
| | + Post | | 6,150 |
| | + Other | | 5,525 |
| | = Total Below the Line | | 15,300 |
| | | | |
| | Above the Line + Below the Line = | | 15,600 |
| | + Contingency (10% of ATL + BTL) = | | 1,560 |
| | **= GRAND TOTAL** | | **$17,160** |

**FIG. 4.1**

Above the Line creative costs appear at the top; Below the Line script costs follow, with a total at the bottom

## Construction

Budgets are constructed in layers, with the financial plan as a whole condensed on the Topsheet – a 1–2 page summary showing broadly *how much* a film will cost, and *where* money is to be spent. Each successive layer, i.e. Account, Detail, 4th Level, contains more specific details.

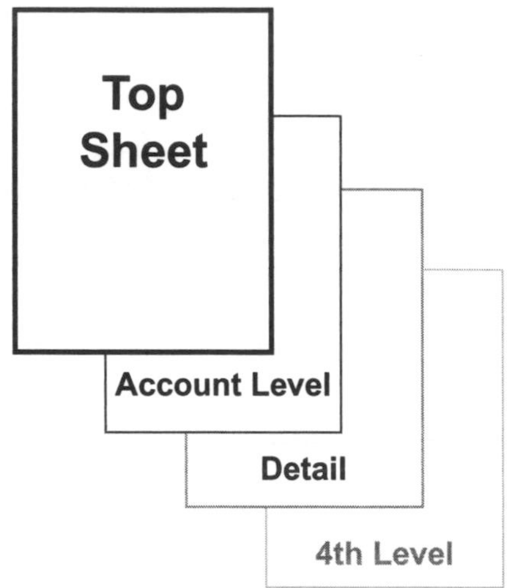


**FIG. 4.2**

A budget consists of layers

"TAD4" is one way to remember the structure:

> **Topsheet** on top summarizes all categories: made up of several **A**ccounts: broadly describing types of expenses, made up of all the **D**etails: specific sub-accounts – people, rates, equipment, with a **4th** Level: home for extra information (if needed).

The **Topsheet** (**AKA:** Top Level or Summary) of the budget is typically shown to potential investors who don't necessarily want every detail.

Most budgets are several pages long; this multi-layered structure works like a zoom lens, allowing you to work at different perspectives inside and throughout on an as-needed basis. The **Topsheet** is like an Establishing Shot (the big picture), the **Account Level** a Medium Shot (who and what's involved), and the **Detail Level** is a Close Up (to input data for calculations). A **4th Level** would serve as an Extreme Close Up.

For example, on this Topsheet (Table 4.2) for an ultra-low budget music video shot in one day on DV format, $500 is budgeted for the category of "Wardrobe, Make-up & Hair."

Drilling down to the Account Level (Table 4.3) reveals more information, for example, how that $500 will be allocated specifically. For this film, all Department Heads

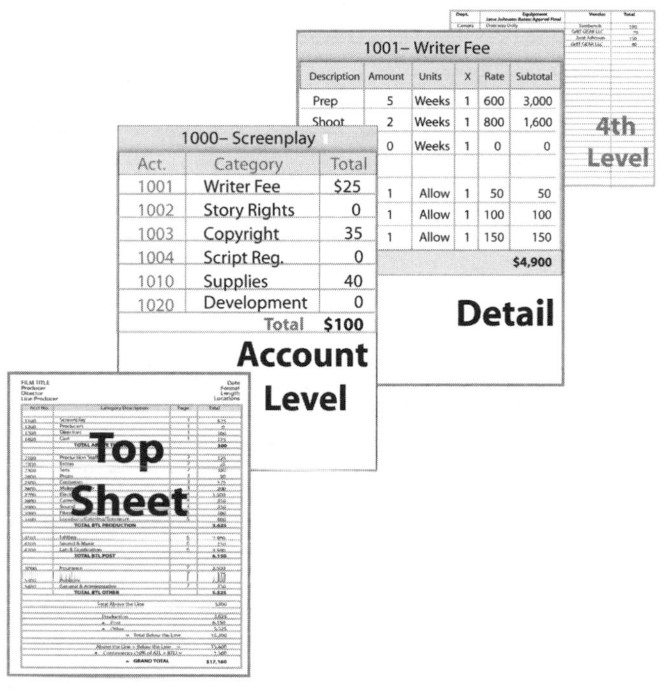

1001– Writer Fee
Description Amount Units X Rate Subtotal
Prep 5 Weeks 1 600 3,000
Shoot 2 Weeks 1 800 1,600
0 Weeks 1 0 0
1 Allow 1 50 50
1 Allow 1 100 100
1 Allow 1 150 150
$4,900
Detail
4th Level
1000– Screenplay
Act. Category Total
1001 Writer Fee $25
1002 Story Rights 0
1003 Copyright 35
1004 Script Reg. 0
1010 Supplies 40
1020 Development 0
Total $100
Account Level
Top Sheet


FIG. 4.3

Budget construction shows data at the level of information required, on an as-needed basis

were paid the same – $200. The Account Level illustrates how one position is compensated *compared with others*, or people compared with equipment and expendables, but it does not show all of the particulars.

Drilling down to the Detail Level (Table 4.4) shows how each dollar will be spent. The Head Hair Stylist is to be paid for prep and shoot time, and for the use of his kit.

Budgeting software created specifically for filmmaking uses this layered approach to: integrate with other programs in their software suite; to help you *work* in the budget; and for accounting purposes. When creating a budget on paper, or in Excel, you need only the Topsheet and Detail Level information, as shown in Figure 4.4.

**Presentation**

Budgets are private documents. Financiers, bankers, attorneys, sales agents, distributors, investors, insurance companies, and stakeholders (who may be partners or team members) may see the Topsheet, but are not interested in every line item. Producers work with the entire budget and see it all. Key crew, like Department Heads, may be intimately familiar with the budget for *their* department, but none

**Table 4.2**

| Title | | Format |
|---|---|---|
| Producer | | Length |
| Director | | Date |
| | | |
| **Acct #** | **Category Description** | **Total** |
| 1000 | Story & Screenplay | 250 |
| 1200 | Producer | 350 |
| 1300 | Direction | 800 |
| 1400 | Cast | 1,750 |
| | **Total Above the Line** | **3,150** |
| 2000 | Production Staff | 2,250 |
| 2100 | Props | 500 |
| 2200 | **Wardrobe, Make-up & Hair** | **500** |
| 2300 | Camera, Sound & Electrical | 1,500 |
| 2400 | Locations, Food, Transport | 1,200 |
| 2500 | **Total Production** | **5,950** |
| 3000 | Editing | 800 |
| 3100 | Sound & Music | 250 |
| | **Total Post Production** | **1,050** |
| 4000 | Insurance & Legal | 750 |
| | **Total Other** | **500** |
| | **Total Below the Line** | **7,500** |
| | A/L + B/L = | 10,650 |
| | Contingency (10%) | 1065 |
| | **Grand Total** | **$11,715** |

**Table 4.3**

| **2200 Wardrobe, Make-up & Hair** | | |
|---|---|---|
| **Acct. No.** | **Account Description** | **Total** |
| 2201 | Head Make-up Artist | 200 |
| **2202** | **Head Hair Stylist** | **200** |
| 2203 | Make-up Supplies | 75 |
| 2204 | Hair Supplies | 25 |
| 2205 | Wigs | 0 |
| | **Total** | **500** |

other. A printed budget displays the Topsheet and Detail Levels only, and suppresses accounts that are not utilized.

There are two reasons that budgets are not handed out, like candy, to everyone:

1. Crew and cast working on a film will be sensitive to what others are being paid, and any perks that they themselves are NOT receiving. Pay disparities

**Table 4.4**

| 2202 – Head Hair Stylist | | | | | |
|---|---|---|---|---|---|
| **Description** | **Amount** | **Units** | **X** | **Rate** | **Subtotal** |
| Prep | 1 | Days | 1 | 50.00 | 50.00 |
| Shoot | 1 | Days | 1 | 150.00 | 150.00 |
| Kit/Equipment Rental | 1 | Allow | 1 | 50.00 | 50.00 |
| GRAND TOTAL | | | | | $200.00 |

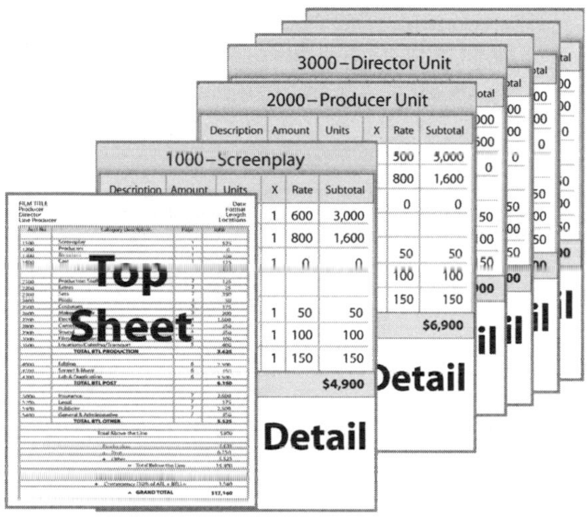


**FIG. 4.4**

Budget print-outs contain Topsheet and Detail Levels

(no matter what the logical reason) create tension. It is not advisable to give the budget to everyone on the project.

2. Distributors, Sales Agents, Producers' Reps and Producers themselves, i.e. anyone involved with the sales or licensing of the film, may want to keep the budget private. It can affect the *perceived* value of the film, and ultimately the price that buyers, or licensees, will pay for the right to exploit it. Exceptions include the "Under-$15,000-Movie" used as marketing (*Paranormal Activity, The Blair Witch Project, Mariachi*). Your team must decide: let the film speak for itself, or tell everyone your budget as a marketing hook. If revenue is your goal, consider allowing the film to speak for itself, with the budget remaining quiet.

The reality of certain indie feature success stories is that actual production budgets were made for mere thousands, but once a distributor or studio licensed or purchased

**Table 4.5** Topsheet

Topsheet

| **Title** | **Producer** | | | **Length** | | |
|---|---|---|---|---|---|---|
| **Format** | **Director** | | | **Shoot days** | | |
| | | | | | | |
| **Acct #** | **Category Description** | | | | | **Total** |
| 1000 | Story and Rights | | | | | $410 |
| 1100 | Producers | | | | | 100 |
| 1200 | Directors | | | | | 250 |
| 1300 | Cast | | | | | 280 |
| | **Total Above the Line** | | | | | **1,040** |
| | | | | | | |
| 1400 | Production Staff | | | | | 140 |
| 1500 | Production Film & Lab | | | | | 144 |
| 1600 | Camera & Sound | | | | | 825 |
| 1700 | Make-up & Hairdressing | | | | | 150 |
| 1800 | Sets & Props | | | | | 525 |
| 1900 | Set Lighting | | | | | 625 |
| 2000 | Locations & Food | | | | | 6,240 |
| | **Total Production** | | | | | **8,649** |
| 3000 | Editing & Music | | | | | 6,900 |
| 3200 | Post Production Film & Lab | | | | | 3,575 |
| | **Total Post Production** | | | | | **10,475** |
| 4000 | Insurance & Legal | | | | | 2,030 |
| 5000 | Publicity & Misc. | | | | | 25 |
| | **Total Other** | | | | | 2,055 |
| | **Total Below the Line** | | | | | **21,179** |
| | | | | | | |
| | **GRAND TOTAL: ATL + BTL** | | | | | **$22,219** |

the film, they spent hundreds of thousands to enhance it in post, for release into theaters or other distribution.

A full budget for presentation purposes, to work with your team members who require all the specifics, includes the Topsheet and Detail Level, as in Tables 4.5 and 4.6.

### Calculation

Budgets are constructed on a *grid* (Table 4.7), demonstrating what specifically is budgeted for (the vertical axis), and how totals are calculated (the horizontal axis).

**Table 4.6** Detail Level

Detail Level

| Acct # | Description | Amount | Unit | X | Rate | Subtotal |
|---|---|---|---|---|---|---|
| 1001 | Writer Fee | 1 | Allow | 1 | 250 | 250 |
| 1004 | Copyright | 1 | Allow | 1 | 35 | 35 |
| 1010 | Supplies | 1 | Allow | 1 | 125 | 125 |
| | **Total 1000** | | | | | **410** |
| 1101 | Executive Producer | 1 | Allow | 1 | 75 | 75 |
| 1102 | Producer | 1 | Allow | 1 | 25 | 25 |
| | **Total 1100** | | | | | **100** |
| 1201 | 1st Unit Director | 1 | Weeks | 5 | 50 | 250 |
| | **Total 1200** | | | | | **250** |
| 1301 | Principal Players | 3 | Weeks | 2 | 40 | 240 |
| 1302 | Day Players | 4 | Days | 2 | 5 | 40 |
| | **Total 1300** | | | | | **280** |
| 1401 | Unit Production Manager | 1 | Allow | 1 | 35 | 35 |
| 1402 | Production Office Coordinator | 1 | Allow | 1 | 35 | 35 |
| 1403 | 1st Assistant Director | 1 | Allow | 1 | 35 | 35 |
| 1404 | Location Manager | 1 | Allow | 1 | 35 | 35 |
| | **Total 1400** | | | | | **140** |
| 1501 | Tape Stock (DV tapes) | 12 | Tapes | 1 | 12 | 144 |
| | **Total 1500** | | | | | **144** |
| 1601 | Director of Photography | 1 | Weeks | 4 | 25 | 100 |
| 1602 | Camera Operator | 1 | Weeks | 3 | 25 | 75 |
| 1603 | Purchases | 1 | Allow | 1 | 75 | 75 |
| 1604 | Rentals | 1 | Allow | 1 | 575 | 575 |
| | **Total 1600** | | | | | **825** |
| 1701 | Key Make-up Artist | 1 | Weeks | 5 | 15 | 75 |
| 1702 | Head Hair Stylist | 1 | Weeks | 5 | 15 | 75 |
| | **Total 1700** | | | | | **150** |
| 1801 | Key Prop Master | 1 | Weeks | 5 | 15 | 75 |
| 1851 | Sets & Props Purchases | 1 | Allow | 1 | 345 | 345 |
| 1852 | Sets & Props Rentals | 1 | Allow | 1 | 180 | 105 |
| | **Total 1800** | | | | | **525** |
| 1901 | Lighting Kit | 1 | Allow | 1 | 450 | 450 |
| 1902 | Expendables | 1 | Allow | 1 | 175 | 175 |
| | **Total 1900** | | | | | **625** |
| 2001 | Location Fee | 5 | Days | 12 | 50 | 3,000 |
| 2010 | Production Catering/Kraft Svces | 24 | Meals | 30 | 4.5 | 3,240 |
| | **Total 2000** | | | | | **6,240** |
| 3001 | Editor Fee | 1 | Allow | 1 | 3,500 | 3,500 |
| 3002 | Edit Bay Rental | 1 | Allow | 1 | 150 | 150 |
| 3010 | Composer Fees | 1 | Allow | 1 | 250 | 250 |
| 3025 | Song Licensing | 2 | Allow | 1 | 1,500 | 3,000 |
| | **Total 3000** | | | | | **6,900** |
| 3201 | Post Finishing & 3 DVDs | 1 | Allow | 1 | 3,575 | 3,575 |
| | **Total 3200** | | | | | **3,575** |
| 4001 | Insurance (3-week shoot) | 1 | Allow | 1 | 1,500 | 1,500 |
| 4050 | Legal Fees | 1 | Allow | 1 | 530 | 530 |
| | **Total 4000** | | | | | **2,030** |
| 5001 | Publicity: Web Hosting & Domain | 1 | Allow | 1 | 25 | 25 |
| | **Total 5000** | | | | | **25** |

**Table 4.7**

| | **Horizontal Axis Is The Equation** | | | | |
|---|---|---|---|---|---|
| **Vertical** | | | | | |
| **Axis** | | | | | |
| **Lists** | | | | | |
| **Each** | | | | | |
| **Budget** | | | | | |
| **Item** | | | | | |

On the horizontal axis, there are five equation components (Table 4.8).

**Table 4.8**

| | **1** | **2** | **3*** | **4** | **5** |
|---|---|---|---|---|---|
| **Description** | **Amount** | **Units** | **X** | **Rate** | **Subtotal** |
| **of line item *(prep time, shoot time, wrap time, kit rental)*** | **Number** of **units** to be worked ***(time usually)*** | **Type *(days, weeks, hours – allow for flat rate)*** | **"Times" Number of that item described *(people, equipment, 1 or 2 grips, 4 or 5 C-stands)*** | **$ to be paid per unit *(for 1 day, or 1 week or flat rate)*** | **Multiply Amount by X by Rate = Subtotal** |
| **Item** | **AMOUNT of** | **UNITS** | **X** | **Rate =** | **Subtotal** |
| **Prop Wand** | **1** | **Allow** | **10** | **50.00** | **$500.00** |

* X is a multiplier that stands for the mathematical symbol "times." If you are renting one prop – a wand – the X column is 1, confirming the rental of one wand. Change X to 2, in order to double the calculation (saving you the trouble of entering this line two separate times, or 10 times, 50 times, etc.), for as many of one identical item to be obtained for the same terms. *The X default is 1 unless you change it.*

To calculate the Head Hair Stylist's wages for **prep** time, see Table 4.9a.

**Table 4.9a**

| **2202 – Head Hair Stylist** | | | | | |
|---|---|---|---|---|---|
| **Description** | **Amount** | **Units** | **X** | **Rate** | **Subtotal** |
| **Prep** | **3** | **Days** | **1** | **1.00** | **3.00** |
| Shoot | 2 | Weeks | 1 | 2.00 | 4.00 |
| Kit Rental | 1 | Allow | 1 | 2.00 | 2.00 |
| | **3 Days X** | | **1 Stylist X** | **$1.00 per day =** | **$3.00** |

To calculate the Head Hair Stylist's total wages for **shoot** time, see Table 4.9b.

**Table 4.9b**

| 2202 – Head Hair Stylist | | | | | |
|---|---|---|---|---|---|
| **Description** | **Amount** | **Units** | **X** | **Rate** | **Subtotal** |
| Prep | 3 | Days | 1 | 1.00 | 3.00 |
| **Shoot** | **2** | **Weeks** | **1** | **2.00** | **4.00** |
| Kit Rental | 1 | Allow | 1 | 2.00 | 2.00 |
| | **2 Weeks X** | | **1 Stylist X** | **$2.00 per Week =** | **$4.00** |

The Head Hair Stylist will be paid for the use of his **kit**, at a flat rate (Table 4.9c).

**Table 4.9c**

| 2202 – Head Hair Stylist | | | | | |
|---|---|---|---|---|---|
| **Description** | **Amount** | **Units** | **X** | **Rate** | **Subtotal** |
| Prep | 3 | Days | 1 | 1.00 | 3.00 |
| Shoot | 2 | Weeks | 1 | 2.00 | 4.00 |
| **Kit Rental** | **1** | **Allow** | **1** | **2.00** | **2.00** |
| | **1 Kit Allowed X** | | **1 Stylist X** | **$2.00 flat rate =** | **$2.00** |

The total line is at the bottom of the entire wage for this crew member (Table 4.9d).

**Table 4.9d**

| 2202 – Head Hair Stylist | | | | | |
|---|---|---|---|---|---|
| **Description** | **Amount** | **Units** | **X** | **Rate** | **Subtotal** |
| Prep | 3 | Day | 1 | 1.00 | **3.00** |
| Shoot | 2 | Week | 1 | 2.00 | **+ 4.00** |
| Kit Rental | 1 | Allow | 1 | 2.00 | **+ 2.00** |
| **GRAND TOTAL** | | | | | **= $10.00** |

There are two ways to pay cast and crew, which are shown at the Detail Level:

- Paying a **flat rate** – all the work to be completed by a certain person on the project, as defined by the total amount of time agreed upon.
- Paying connected to **time increments** – daily/weekly/hourly rates, paid to a certain person hired to do tasks in the scheduled time.

**Table 4.10a** Pay by flat rate – one price

| Description | Amount | Units | X | Rate | Subtotal |
|---|---|---|---|---|---|
| Prep/Shoot/Wrap | 1 | Allow | 1 | 5,250 | 5,250 |

**Table 4.10b** Pay by time increment – weekly, daily, or hourly rate

| Description | Amount | Units | X | Rate | Subtotal |
|---|---|---|---|---|---|
| Prep | 3 | Weeks | 1 | 500 | 1,500 |
| Shoot | 5 | Week | 1 | 700 | 3,500 |
| Wrap | 2 | Days | 1 | 125 | 250 |
| | | | | | 5,250 |

When paying based on time increments, there are three basic stages, which may be repeated if the project is divided up into local and distant locations:

1. **Prep** (Preproduction, *planning* stage)
2. **Shoot** (Principal Photography) and
3. **Wrap** (Post Production, *after* shoot)

When paying weekly, it is customary to pay higher fees for shoot time (compared with prep or wrap) when the work is the most complex and demanding, and higher fees for *distant* work in all categories (compared with local).

Not all positions are hired for the same duration. Fewer people are needed for wrap (returning equipment, paying bills), and/or prep time (rehearsals, art dept., buying items for the shoot like wardrobe, props); some work during shoot only.

Include and negotiate for personal items used in the shoot – budget permitting, e.g. computer, or equipment/kit/box rental. This information is entered at the Detail Level.

The following example (Table 4.11) illustrates paying by time in weekly increments.

Film budgeting software generates totals (spreadsheets like Excel will too, if set up correctly). Budgeting on paper requires a calculator, pencils and erasers.

*Account numbers* connect the data together.

**Table 4.11**

| Description | Amount | Units | X | Rate | Subtotal |
|---|---|---|---|---|---|
| Prep Local | 2 | Weeks | 1 | 1,000 | 2,000.00 |
| Shoot Local | 1 | Weeks | 1 | 1,500 | 1,500.00 |
| Wrap Local | 0 | Weeks | 1 | 0 | 0 |
| | | | | | |
| Prep Distant | 2 | Weeks | 1 | 1,250 | 2,500.00 |
| Shoot Distant | 1 | Weeks | 1 | 2,000 | 2,000.00 |
| Wrap Distant | 1 | Weeks | 1 | 1,250 | 1,250.00 |
| | | | | | |
| Kit/Equipment Rental | 8 | Weeks | 1 | 50 | 400.00 |
| Supplies/Materials | | | | | |
| **Total Wages** | | | | | **9,650.00** |
| | | | | | |
| FICA | 6.2% | | 1 | 9,650 | 598.30 |
| FUI | 0.8% | | 1 | 9,650 | 77.20 |
| SUI | 5% | | 1 | 9,650 | 482.50 |
| Workmen's Comp | 3.98% | | 1 | 9,650 | 384.070 |
| Payroll Service Fee | 0.5% | | 1 | 9,650 | 48.25 |
| Medicare | 1.45% | | 1 | 9,650 | 139.93 |
| Overtime Allow | 12% | | 1 | 9,650 | 1,158.00 |
| Miscellaneous | | | | | |
| Guild Fees | | | | | |
| Car Allowance | | | | | |
| Total Fringes | | | | | 2,888.25 |
| **GRAND TOTAL** | | | | | **12,538.25** |

## Account Numbers

Elements in a film budget are assigned account numbers; to easily locate information, group similar types of expenses, and for accounting purposes. There are several standard systems, so use the one that works for you and your team.

The first two digits refer to the broad category. In the example in Table 4.12a, the column on the left lists an account number. Any number that starts with "11" (1101, 1102, 1103, etc.) contributes a line item to that category total: 1100–1199 = Story & Screenplay.

Account 1100 totals $100; drill down to the **Account** Level to see accounts # 1101–1106 – the elements that comprise 1100 Story & Screenplay (Table 4.12b).

**Table 4.12a**

| Account | Category Description | Total |
|---|---|---|
| **1100** | Story & Screenplay | $100 |
| **1200** | Continuity | 0 |
| **1300** | Producer's Unit | 50 |
| **1400** | Director's Unit | 50 |
| **1500** | Talent (**AKA**: Cast) | 50 |
| | **Total Above the Line** | **250** |

**Table 4.12b**

| Account # | Account Description | Total |
|---|---|---|
| 1101 | Story Rights Purchase | 10 |
| 1102 | Writers' Fees | 50 |
| 1104 | Research | 25 |
| 1105 | Typing | 0 |
| 1106 | Duplication | 15 |
| | **Total 1100** | **$100** |

Use only what you need; if you need more accounts, add them to the category that makes the most sense. *Budgeting software will print out only the account items used, and you can always delete accounts not used if you are working on paper or in Excel.*

If you needed to add a technical expert versed in details about the script subject (dressage trainer, firefighter, spy, master gardener, neurologist), add an additional account inside 1100 Story & Screenplay. The new account must start with an "11" (because 1100 is the overall number for Story & Screenplay) and not duplicate a number already in use. 1150 could be your new account "Technical Experts."

**Table 4.13**

| Account # | Account Description | Total |
|---|---|---|
| 1101 | Story Rights Purchase | 10 |
| 1102 | Writers' Fees | 50 |
| 1104 | Research | 25 |
| 1105 | Typing | 0 |
| 1106 | Duplication | 15 |
| 1150 | Technical Experts | 100 |
| | **Total 1100** | **$200** |

One common aspect of any budget numbering system is that the categories use *large* numbers – numbers with lots of room between them – to hold as many line items as are needed, and to make it easy to add new accounts.

Budgeting software offers templates with a variety of numbering conventions, associated with specific studios, financing entities, distributors, or production companies. Templates include many categories determined by the size and complexity of a project. You can alter an existing template, or design your own.

Budgets are customizable. You might need new line items, limited only by your common sense and imagination: Creature & Mechanical Effects, Scuba Gear, Marine Units, Military Equipment, Armory, Stages, Translators, Internet Synergy, Product Placement, Screenings, Aerial Units, Blue Screen Units, Translators, Home Rentals, Trailers, Entourage.

Table 4.14 illustrates one commonly used numbering system.

**Table 4.14**

| | | |
|---|---|---|
| 1100 | STORY, RIGHTS, CONTINUITY | |
| 1200 | PRODUCERS' UNIT | |
| 1300 | DIRECTOR | |
| 1400 | CAST | |
| 1900 | FRINGE BENEFITS | |
| 1999 | Total Fringes | |
| | **Total Above the Line** | |
| | | |
| 2000 | PRODUCTION STAFF | |
| 2100 | EXTRA TALENT | |
| 2200 | SET DESIGN | |
| 2300 | SET CONSTRUCTION | |
| 2400 | SET STRIKING | |
| 2500 | SET OPERATIONS | |
| 2600 | SPECIAL EFFECTS | |
| 2700 | SET DRESSING | |
| 2800 | PROPERTY | |
| 2900 | WARDROBE | |
| 3000 | PICTURE VEHICLES & ANIMALS | |
| 3100 | MAKE-UP & HAIRDRESSING | |
| 3200 | LIGHTING | |
| 3300 | CAMERA | |
| 3400 | PRODUCTION SOUND | |
| 3500 | TRANSPORTATION | |
| 3600 | LOCATION | |
| 3700 | PRODUCTION FILM & LAB | |
| 3800 | VIDEO TAPE: PRODUCTION | |
| 4000 | SECOND UNIT | |
| 4100 | TESTS | |
| 4200 | STAGE RENTAL | |
| 4399 | Total Fringes | |
| | **Total Below The Line Production** | |
| | | |
| 4400 | VISUAL EFFECTS | |
| 4500 | EDITING | |
| 4600 | MUSIC | |
| 4700 | POST PRODUCTION SOUND | |
| 4800 | POST PROD FILM & LAB | |
| 5299 | Total Fringes | |
| | **Total Below The Line Post** | |
| | | |
| 6500 | PUBLICITY | |
| 6700 | INSURANCE & LEGAL | |
| 6800 | GENERAL EXPENSE | |
| 7499 | Total Fringes | |
| | **Total Below The Line Other** | |

## Backing into a Number

A common scenario is backing into a number, when the Producer has an idea of what they think (or hope) the film can be made for, and can raise.

**CYA**: How do you know? Ask.

- How much money do they already *have*?
- How much can they realistically *raise*?
- What are the likely funding *sources*?
- Where do they *expect* this project to go?
- Where do they *hope* this project will go?
- Distribution and Marketing plans?
- Film festival plans?

Nine times out of ten, if you don't have an actual number to work toward, you might have a range. Whether or not you're making a union film, you can use those budgetary definitions as guidelines. Feature film budgets under $10,209,000 are some variation on the "low budget" spectrum. Above that and you're officially out of low budget territory. For the major studios, the concept of low budget can stretch up and into the $50 million dollar range and beyond, but for our purposes:

**Rule of Thumb**: Below $10.2 million = low budget.

This parameter comes from union agreements (if you are not making a union film it doesn't matter); union rules change, so this is subject to change. *Union rates are updated (periodically, sometimes yearly), as are budget definitions.* If the thought of a budget up and into the millions makes you laugh, you're not alone. Film budgets *under* a million bucks are more common than not; every completed film represents a significant investment of energy and time, no matter what cash was spent to make it. Building your scheduling and budgeting muscles will stretch any penny, pound, yen or euro that your production can find.

**Rule of Thumb: Pay scales** — how much people get paid depends on the size of the budget. Bigger budgets = higher rates, and vice versa. This is true for union and non-union. Table 4.15 illustrates budget ranges compared with union pay scales, in $US.

Once your team has weighed the pros and cons of a union production, start budgeting.

**Table 4.15**

| Budget Minimum | Budget Maximum | DGA | SAG | WGA | IATSE | Teamsters |
|---|---|---|---|---|---|---|
| | $35,000 | | Student | | | |
| $50,000 | 200,000 | Level 1A | Ultra Low | Tier 1 Independent Low Budget | Ultra Low | Sideletter 7 |
| 200,000 | 500,000 | Level 1A | Modified Low | Tier 1 Independent Low Budget | Ultra Low | Sideletter 7 |
| 500,000 | 625,000 | Level 1B | Modified Low | Tier 2 Independent Low Budget | Ultra Low | Sideletter 7 |
| 625,000 | 725,000 | Level 1B | Modified Low w/ Background Actor Incentive OR Low Budget | Tier 2 Independent Low Budget | Ultra Low | Sideletter 7 |
| 725,000 | 937,500 | Level 1B | Modified Low Budget w/ Diversity Incentive OR Low Budget | Tier 2 Independent Low Budget | Ultra Low | Sideletter 7 |
| 937,500 | 1,030,000 | Level 1B | Low Budget | Tier 2 Independent Low Budget | Ultra Low | Sideletter 7 |
| 1,030,000 | 1,500,000 | Level 2 | Low Budget | Tier 2 Independent Low Budget | Ultra Low | Sideletter 7 |
| 1,500,000 | 2,500,000 | Level 2 | Low Budget | Basic Agt Low Budget | Tier 1 Low | Sideletter 7 |
| 2,500,000 | 2,570,000 | Level 2 | Low Budget w/Diversity Incentive OR Basic Agreement | Basic Agt Low Budget | Tier 1 Low | Sideletter 7 |
| 2,570,000 | 3,605,000 | Level 3 | Low Budget w/Diversity Incentive OR Basic Agreement | Basic Agt Low Budget | Tier 1 Low | Sideletter 7 |
| 3,605,000 | 3,904,000 | Level 4a | Low Budget w/Diversity Incentive OR Basic Agreement | Basic Agt Low Budget | Tier 1 Low | Sideletter 7 |
| 3,904,000 | 5,000,000 | Level 4a | Basic Agreement | Basic Agt Low Budget | Tier 1 Low | Sideletter 7 |
| 5,000,000 | 5,150,000 | Level 4a | Basic Agreement | Basic Agt Low Budget | Tier 2 Low | Sideletter 7 |
| 5,150,000 | 7,000,000 | Level 4b | Basic Agreement | Basic Agreement | Tier 2 Low | Sideletter 7 |
| 7,000,000 | 8,000,000 | Level 4c | Basic Agreement | Basic Agreement | Tier 2 Low | Basic Agreement |
| 8,000,000 | 9,500,000 | Level 4c | Basic Agreement | Basic Agreement | Tier 3 Low | Basic Agreement |
| 9,500,000 | 10,209,000 | Basic Agreement | Basic Agreement | Basic Agreement | Tier 3 Low | Basic Agreement |
| 10,209,000 | 12,000,000 | | | | Tier 3 Low | |

## Price Resources

Budgeting is a three-step process:

**Step 1.** Identify and obtain prices and rates

**Step 2.** Negotiate prices and rates

**Step 3.** Lock in prices and rates

**Step 1. Identify and obtain prices** for: locations, key crew and cast, equipment. Vet candidates and present the information to your team. With this information, build a preliminary budget at full price.

**Step 2. Negotiate**. With team input and your first, second, and third choices, contact and negotiate potential deals with crew and vendors. Refine budget with this information.

**Step 3. Lock in** with contracts and written agreements once you and your team have made final choices of locations, people and vendors.

*FYI:* After a Producer's vision, the imagination of a Director impacts every aspect of a film. If there is no Director yet attached to the project, that is the first step: it will inform everything that follows.

Start by gathering information. Vendors want business; crew and actors want work. There's a lot of free information available that requires only your time and energy to ferret it out. Plan to shop around for rates, prices, services, wages; ask if there are any deals available, and tell people about your project. A firm *start date* will bring out the best deals available.



### Step 1: Identify and Obtain Prices

Start with your team. What key figures, if any, do they know? If they are thinking of specific people, locations, rates, vendors, equipment, services, get that information first. Then get information from other sources. Ask everyone: What did you pay? How much do things cost, and who gave you the best rates? Contact companies, and filmmakers you admire, to find out what deals they made. For references, ask what it's like to work with them: Are they prepared? On time? Responsive to the Director?

With team input, build a *preliminary* budget at *full* price by plugging in the rates of the team's collective first choice of A-List crew, cast, and equipment into your budget.

CYA: Gathering information is time-consuming. Keep your resources organized and handy for future use. Also, keep records of deals offered, responses, and how decisions were made; a paper trail is vital if something goes amiss.

**Price Identifying Resources**

**Film commissions:**

AFCI.org (location-based information, worldwide)

**Film Communities:**

Massify.com
TriggerStreet.com
ShootingPeople.org
IFP
Women Make Movies, DCTV
WIFT
Film Find
AIVF
Local Production Guides

**Trade Magazines:**

*Variety Magazine* and website
*The Hollywood Reporter* and website
*Movie Maker Magazine*
*IndieWire*
*DV Magazine*
*VideoMaker*
*American Cinematographer*
*Post Magazine*
*Real Screen*
*Screen International*

**Cast, Crew Equipment Databases and Help Wanted:**

Trade magazines classifieds
Backstage.com and magazine
Mandy.com
Media-match.com
CrewNet.com
ProductionHub.com
Craigslist.org
Motionographer (animators)
Mediabistro.com (writers)
Film school job boards (cast, crew, extras)
NY411.com, NYPG
LA411.com
Chitown411.com (Chicago)
Filmaka.com
Crewster.com
Crew Connection (they'll find crew for you)
(Local TV Stations recommend camera and sound crew)
Hollywood Creative Directory – HCDonline.com Hollywood Blue Book
*Producer's Masterguide*
*Creative Handbook*
Breakdownservices.com
LAcasting.com
NYCastings.com
Castitblog.com
Central Casting
I-actor on SAG
IMDB Pro

*Where* in the world are you working? Start soliciting rates and fees for suitable locations, key people and equipment; you want to avoid transporting the entire cast and crew, if at all possible. Using location-based production incentives will drive this process.

#### *Locations*

Identify and obtain prices from multiple sources, so you have options. What does the script call for? Start with recommendations from your team and look for locations appropriate for the sets in your script. (Start with film commissions, many offer image databases; begin with a location scout who is familiar with the area.) To minimize costs, consider:

- shooting interiors locally, to minimize travel;
- locations that can serve multiple sets; and
- the type of exterior settings in the story (desert, blue collar suburb) closest to you.

Price local sound stages, or look into shooting in controlled spaces if it suits the story. Weigh security, a controlled atmosphere and convenience, against price. Before you decide it is too expensive, find out what is available. Once you know where you are shooting, obtain rates and availability of the key people who will drive the production process, i.e. Department Heads.

#### *Key Crew*

Weigh the benefits of hiring *locally* or *transporting* key cast and crew, or a mix. Movement incurs expense – balance that against the look required by the screenplay. Draft and post email help-wanted ads for key Department Heads.

Director, AD, DP/Camera Operator, Location Manager or Scout, Art Director or Production Designer, Casting Director and Department Heads are usually identified first. Often, your team will drive the hiring process. Directors have strong feelings about who they want to work with, particularly the 1st Assistant Director, DP, and Editor.

Look at reels, call references, and chat with candidates via phone to find out their rates – present the best choices to your team. **CYA**: The lower your budget, the more important it is to check references and have backup folks to call if someone bails. Mention the union status of the project in the ad, and if a union or guild member wants to apply, the consequences are on them. Find as many potential candidates as possible.

*In the indie world of multi-talented multitaskers, peripheral equipment and abilities are often welcome, for example a car, digital camera or video camera, an aptitude on Facebook, or the ability to tweet on Twitter during a shoot.* Contact references; ask what it's like to work with this person. Are they prepared? On time? Responsive to the Director? Find out availability.

If you are budgeting a non-union shoot and do not know what to pay the crew, but want to be fair, establish a tiered system, where Department Heads will be paid the same rate. Pay their assistants a certain percent (5–20%) less, and *their* assistants a percentage (25–40%). Often there is a "going rate" in an area: a range based on a certain level of experience.

#### *Cast*

Working with a Casting Director can save time, if you can afford it. They will need a *synopsis* of the story, and cast *breakdowns* for key characters: role, physical description, age range, pertinent dramatic information, any special abilities required. Request resumes and headshots. Mention the union status of the project in the ad, and post them online and in trades. Prepare *sides* for the casting call – portions of the scene that an actor appears in – so they will have dialogue to read in the audition. Using abundant casting resources online can save time.

Actors are drawn to an exciting project, good roles, and a talented Producer and Director. List notable credits. Key roles will set the look and tone of the entire cast. If you have identified a Casting Director, begin working with them. If a guild or union actor wants to work on your non-union project, it's their choice.

Advantages of working with a Casting Director include time savings, as well as a knowledge of agents, actors and rates. They understand how to streamline the audition process, and union and guild rules.

#### *Equipment*

##### *Post production services*

When shooting film, does your team have a relationship with a lab? If not, contact labs convenient to your Director and team, and solicit bids for needed services.

When shooting digital, you may need post lab services for effects shots, format conversion, sweetening or color correction. Once you find your Editor, they will have input. Post production facilities will sometimes invest their services in a film for an ownership interest and credits (upfront discounted or free services in exchange for an equity interest in the film).

The format you shoot on and finish on may be different, and will be important information to discuss with your lab and post production vendor.

*Equipment rental houses*

Many of your crew will have their own gear, but you still need to identify and contact the rental houses for rate sheets on camera, sound, lighting gear, props, film or tape stock, and expendables so you know you're getting the best deal. The lowest price is not always the best deal – consider service, after hours service, or help if something isn't working or needs replacing, flexibility on terms, and stuff thrown in for free.

Get as much information in a price quote as possible – a detailed rate sheet or catalog, weekly rates, weekend rates, daily rates. What defines a weekly rental? Is it Mon–Fri (5 days), or can you pick up the gear Saturday before that Monday and return it the following Sunday (9 days)? Are there any student or low budget discounts?

**Step 2: Negotiate**

With your team's input, contact first choices first in order, then second choices in order, etc. See what kind of flexibility the crew, cast, or vendor has – are they willing to make some kind of deal with you? Be straightforward about your budget and financing, start dates (firm or not), the project and people involved.

Once a company or person quotes a price, it's common to counter-offer with a lower price (50% lower might seem insulting, so start with 25–30% lower). Be forthright and polite, let them know you appreciate their consideration; they may come up with an alternative. The best deal is when both sides get to "yes."

Make notes about the deals (e.g. kit thrown in for free, or deferred pay). Present the options to your team and collectively make decisions. Then *refine your budget*, by creating a new version with this deal information. (So now you have a full price version and a deal version.)

### Step 3: Lock in Your Deals

Seal the deal with deal memos and written agreements, i.e. contracts. Open accounts with vendors (find out what the process is regarding deposits, credit card on file, insurance limits). Gather necessary contact information and distribute the essential paperwork, and establish communication channels.

It is not unusual for things to be in flux for a time. If there is uncertainty about prices, availability, and location access, let potential vendors or crew know about this. Also let them know if you are waiting to hear about another obligation before you can commit to them.

## Factors Impacting the Budget

Every factor pertaining to a film, aside from dialogue, impacts the budget. Talk is the only thing cheap in filmmaking. Many questions will have been answered during scheduling, but if not, it's time to make decisions before you can move forward:

- Type of project;
- Existing plans regarding locations;
- Pay, no pay, union or not;
- Length and format of the project;
- Has the Director signed off on the schedule;
- What specific resources, if any, have already been identified?
- Scale / scope (two characters talking in a room is cheaper than shooting *Gone With The Wind* meets *Star Wars* at sea)

The length of principal photography has the biggest impact on a budget. During production, the biggest quantity, and the most expensive resources, are utilized.

Budget inflators:

- Stunts, action, choreography;
- Pyrotechnics: fire, explosions;
- Specific weather effects, shooting at night, outside;
- Destruction of anything: property, cars, buildings;
- Planes, trains, boats, cars, buses, traffic accidents;
- Children, animals, numerous quantities of people, or any specific thing;
- Elaborate sets, special effects, period piece, sci-fi;
- New untested machinery (like the mechanical shark in the first *Jaws* movie).

All of the above require sufficient time to block, rehearse, set up, storyboard, shoot, troubleshoot; and require equipment or safety personnel that adds costs.

**Type of Project**

Discuss with the Producer what the goal is, or the intended end use of the film, as these things will inform the budget. With the rise in new and changing distribution platforms, there are more options than ever before. Goals may include profitability, fund-raising, gaining experience and exposure, winning festivals and contests, securing a distribution, meeting new filmmakers or finding more work. Clear goals focus the energy.

***Short Forms: Web distribution***

*Type*: Short film

*Purpose*: Gain exposure, enter film festivals and contests, build your reel and gain experience, earn money through syndication or ad revenue

*Budget*: Parameters come from the Producer

*Type*: Short film as trailer: as a teaser to find funds and partners, create a longer film based on this one

*Purpose*: Gain exposure, enter film festivals and contests, build reel and gain experience

*Budget*: Parameters come from the Producer

*Type*: Short "Work for hire" – you've been hired to create specific content for someone else for a specific reason, for promotional, personal, gift, fund-raising, or advertising uses

*Purpose*: Get paid, build your reel and gain experience

*Budget*: Parameters come from the client

*Type*: Short as pilot (test tape)

*Purpose*: Creating a template for series of films or shows based on this one – whether for distribution as webisode or mobisode, Vook, game, app, or other online or mobile distribution, or TV product – based on these characters and situations. You plan to use this to find funds, distribution, or partners to create a series, pitch and sell the concept

*Budget*: Parameters come from the Producer, network liaison, industry norm, distributors

***Spec Television & Internet TV***

*Type*: 30 second to 2 minute commercial, ½ hour or 1-hour long pilot for television – whether community access, leased access, online portals, or a specific channel for pitching as a template for a series of shows based on these characters and situations

*Purpose*: To raise funds and find distribution and partners to create an ongoing series

*Budget*: Parameters come from the Producer

*Type*: 30-second to 2-minute commercial, corporate video, or music video for pitching (whether to an ad agency, corporation, band, or other potential client) to sell, or as a template based on these characters and situations

*Purpose*: You plan to use this to get hired to create something similar or gain exposure, enter contests, build your reel and gain experience

*Budget*: Parameters come from the Producer

#### *Long-form Programming*

*Type*: Specific long-form film (over ½ hour up to 90 minutes) whether feature-length narrative film or doc, movie of the week, or mini series.

*Purpose*: Exposure, enter film festivals and contests, build your reel and gain experience, earn money from release on DVD, TV and online, to license or sell all rights to a distributor, and make money and build feature credits, and hope for theatrical release

*Budget*: Parameters come from your team or research as to what budget ranges similar films have been created for. Information about budget ranges can come from speaking with distributors, or research in trade magazines such as *Variety, The Hollywood Reporter, MovieMaker, IndieWire, IMDB, Box Office Mojo, The Numbers, Screen International, Video Maker, Real Screen, Rentrak, The Wrap* and from filmmakers.



### Locations and Incentives

Where are you shooting? There are several concerns. Traveling, housing, and feeding cast and crew is more expensive than local shooting. Shooting on location may be less expensive than using a sound stage, however, sound stages offer the advantage of a controlled, secure environment. If you anticipate budgeting a film well over $50,000, you may consider applying for location-based production incentives.

Have any specific location resources for the film already been identified (for example, City Hall, actor's mom's house, etc.)? This information should go into your budget first, if these are firm commitments. *Where* a script is set will determine what kind of look you need from your locations. Ideally, you can double up a few sets at one location to economize movement.

Moving incurs expense; the farther away you have to move, even a small crew, the more expensive. Flying is generally more expensive than driving, and then the decision of hiring locally or transporting your cast and crew arises. Discuss with your team the requirements of the script: Are the locations exotic? Does the story take place abroad? Can the locations be in your home state or city, distant regions, or in a variety of locations? Can you cheat North Carolina for Florida? Typically, the audience will not know whether a scene was shot at a retirement community in Shiny Acres, FL or someplace else.

As of this writing, most states in the U.S., and many overseas territories, have film production incentives. I have heard financiers say that they wouldn't even *consider* financing a film that isn't using incentives. The purpose of them is to bring production to an area, hire their workers, and use their locations, hotels and services. In return (if you are spending enough), perks range from free locations, permits and security personnel, and no sales tax, to a chunk of the budget paid back to the production (after navigating the process, which varies from place to place).

There are different rules, terminology and applications for each incentive, which are constantly changing because these programs are tied into local and regional governments. As taxpayers, the economy, and political interests shift, so too do these programs. Each area has a maximum to spend annually, so if you don't get in line for this year, you may get in the queue to wait for next year. Just because you apply, doesn't mean you're in. For most states, there is a minimum required to be spent on very specific types of local expenses, whether crew salaries, facilities or equipment.

Applying for a production incentive makes sense if it *fits* your film *in terms of your budget* (over $50,000 + waiting time), hiring local folks and vendors, extra paperwork, and waiting for approval with no guarantee. States require minimum local expenditures ranging from $20,000 and up (often that is only part of a larger budget). If you don't want to wait, or follow specific rules, or your production doesn't meet the guidelines, skip it.

In addition to regionally based programs like state, parish, city or province-based incentives, there are federal-level programs worldwide. The purpose of these programs is to grow the native industry, more so than to help you make your film. If a particular foreign location is perfect for the project, and won't impede progress, it is worth checking out; however, you may have to partner with a native Producer or production company, and it will add additional time and paperwork to the production process (as it will include visa applications, immunizations, currency exchange, etc.). Film commissions play a pivotal role in these programs, and are a good first point of inquiry.

Table 4.16 lists minimum local expenditures by U.S. state programs, as of 2011.

Unlike other financing, incentives are "free" money; the production gives up very little in exchange for the funding. However, there must be a fit between film and incentive. To stay up to date, check the Entertainment Partners and Film Commission websites (Table 4.17).

**Union, Guilds, and Wages**

The union/guild versus non-union/guild issue is a chicken and egg situation that goes back to money, then time. Shooting union (insert the word "/guild" every time you see union) is more expensive (required minimum pay scales and benefit fringe payments), and more complicated than non-union: there is more paperwork, restrictive rules, requirements, layers of oversight (that's not always a bad thing). If you shoot non-union, your film may lack recognized (i.e., marketable) actors.

The unions and guilds are separate entities, but cooperate through collective bargaining. Speak to union reps to understand the rules, as far in advance as possible. Most unions have low budget and new media agreements to assist independent Producers to hire qualified crew and cast for their budget range, but the maxim of more time, money and paperwork still holds. Pay scales and working hours are established by unions, and are set by the anticipated budget size (with bigger budgets, people are paid more), and the *type* of film it is (training, experimental, student).

Rules of Thumb:

- Union rules are *location*-based.
- You do not have to use union talent; it's not against the law. You can become a SAG signatory, and not use other unions.

Factors Impacting the Budget

**Table 4.16**

| State | Minimum Local Expenditures |
|---|---|
| Alabama | $500,000 |
| Alaska | $100,000 |
| Arizona | $250,000 |
| Arkansas | ≥$50,000 |
| California | $1m minimum for features, $500k MOW, mini series. 75% of total budget or 75% of production days in CA |
| Colorado | $100,000 |
| Connecticut | $100,000 |
| District of Columbia | $250,000 |
| Florida | $100,000 |
| Georgia | $500,000 |
| Hawaii | $200,000 |
| Idaho | $200,000 |
| Illinois | $50,000 <30 minutes |
| | >$100,000 for productions ≥30 minutes |
| Indiana | Features and TV $100,000; |
| | digital media, music video, commercials, training, marketing or communications productions: ≥$50,000 |
| Kentucky | $500,000 feature film<br>$200,000 commercial, and<br>$50,000 for a documentary |
| Louisiana | >$300,000 |
| Maine | $75,000 |
| Maryland | $500,000 |
| Massachusetts | $50,000 |
| Michigan | $50,000 |
| Minnesota | $200,000 docs<br>$50,000 music videos |
| Mississippi | $20,000 |
| Missouri | $50,000 if <30 minutes and $100,000 if >30 minutes |
| Montana | No minimum |
| New Mexico | No minimum |
| New York | Must use qualified production facility, budgets under $15 m |
| North Carolina | $250,000 |
| Ohio | >$300,000 |
| Oklahoma | Minimum budget $50,000, local spend ≥$25,000 |

(*Continued*)

**Table 4.16** (Continued)

| State | Minimum Local Expenditures |
|---|---|
| Oregon | local filmmaker = ≥$75,000, non local $750,000 |
| Pennsylvania | ≥60% of the budget |
| Puerto Rico | $1,000,000 features, short films = $100,000 |
| Rhode Island | $300,000 |
| South Carolina | $1,000,000 |
| Tennessee | $500,000 headquartered outside the state, and $150,000 if within |
| Texas | $250,000 |
| Utah | $1,000,000 |
| Washington | $500,000 features, TV = $300,000 |
| West Virginia | $25,000 |
| Wisconsin | $50,000 |
| Wyoming | $200,00 |

- If you use *one* union, that doesn't mean you have to use *all* of them.
- Once you are signatory with a particular union for a film, you must *fill all the positions covered by that union with union members.* (So, you become signatory to the DGA – you can hire a DGA Director, and you must also hire a DGA UPM and AD. Hire an IATSE DP, then all the BTL positions will be IATSE.)
- If you're shooting in or near a dense metropolitan area in the U.S. you can find a qualified crew base, both union and non.
- Union members are not supposed to work on non-union projects, but the responsibility is on them – they will be fined (if busted).

*What to pay people?* Start with what you know. Is anyone already attached to your project, like a principal actor or Director? What deal was made – was it verbal or written? If the star will be paid $5 million, this is not a micro budget film. If this is the Producer's first feature, the budget probably won't be millions.

When building a budget *from scratch*, a contradiction arises. Wage scales are tied to the budget range. A film shot for $500,000 pays different rates to cast and crew than a film made for $2 million, $12 m, or $70 m. On top of payment for services rendered, there may be additional fees for benefits and residuals – how to decide what to pay? The union/guild payment hierarchy is logical – Department Heads earn a certain amount, 2nds make a little less, 3rds a little less. For example, in a Tier I production

**Table 4.17**

| Association of Film Commissioners Int'l www.afci.org | |
|---|---|
| Alabama www.alabamafilm.org | Montana www.montanafilm.com |
| Alaska www.alaskafilmgroup.org | Nebraska www.filmnebraska.org |
| Arizona www.azcommerce.com/film | Nevada www.nevadafilm.com |
| Arkansas | New Hampshire www.nh.gov/film |
| http://www.arkansasedc.com/arkansas-film-commission.aspx | New Jersey www.njfilm.org |
| California www.film.ca.gov | New Mexico www.nmfilm.com |
| Colorado | New York www.nylovesfilm.com |
| www.coloradofilm.org/locationcolorado-filmincentives.htm | North Carolina www.ncfilm.com |
| Connecticut www.ctfilm.com | North Dakota www.ndtourism.com |
| Delaware | Ohio www.clevelandfilm.com |
| www.dedo.delaware.gov/filmoffice/default.shtml | www.filmcincinnati.com |
| District of Columbia www.film.dc.gov | www.filmcolumbus.com |
| Florida www.filminflorida.com | Oklahoma www.oklahomafilm.org |
| Georgia www.filmgeorgia.org | Oregon www.oregonfilm.org |
| Hawaii www.hawaiifilmoffice.com | Pennsylvania www.filminpa.com |
| Idaho www.filmidaho.com | Puerto Rico www.puertoricofilm.com |
| Illinois www.filmillinois.state.il.us | Rhode Island www.film.ri.gov |
| Indiana www.in.gov/film | South Carolina www.FilmSC.com |
| Iowa www.filmiowa.com | South Dakota www.filmsd.com |
| Kansas www.filmkansas.com | Tennessee www.film.tennessee.gov/film.htm |
| Kentucky www.kyfilmoffice.com | Texas www.governor.state.tx.us/film |
| Louisiana www.lafilm.org | Utah www.film.utah.gov |
| Maine www.filminmaine.com | Vermont www.vermontfilm.com |
| Maryland www.marylandfilm.org | Virginia www.film.virginia.org |
| Massachusetts www.mafilm.org | Washington www.filmwashington.com |
| Michigan www.michigan.gov/filmoffice | West Virginia www.wvfilm.com |
| Minnesota www.mnfilmandtv.org | Wisconsin www.filmwisconsin.net |
| Mississippi www.filmmississippi.org | Wyoming www.filmwyoming.com |
| Missouri www.mofilm.org | |

(total budget \$1.5–\$5 m), IATSE minimum pay scale for key crew (Department Heads) is \$21.99 / hour – that's for Key Grip, Key Greens, Key Costumer; the 2nd in all those departments will be paid \$19.86, and 3rd will be paid \$17.74 (plus payroll taxes and union fringes for everyone). Moving up in the union literally means moving up the pay scale ladder.

This structure can be applied to *non-union* films as well. Pay keys the same, 2nds the same (a little less than keys), and so on. Add payroll taxes. When in doubt, use the lowest tier for all pay rates as a reference to build your budget, discounted slightly – by 10–20%. Find out state law regarding minimum wages and overtime where you will be shooting.

Rules of micro to low budget and indie filmmaking include: not to buy if you can rent, don't rent if you can borrow, and, if possible, exchange credits or deferred salary or profit points for salary upfront. Whatever budget you have, spending it wisely is key. How to do that is not always obvious. Perhaps your Producer hopes to shoot a no-budget project, without paying anyone a wage or paying for equipment.

*No-budget Film*

Unfortunately, no-budget doesn't mean free. Scripts will need to be printed, tapes and expendables have to come from somewhere, and it is necessary to feed people as well as you can. Insurance is crucial, in case of an accident. If we could see into the future, we would have played that winning lottery number by now! Shoots can be unpredictable. When you seek crew and cast for a no-budget film, be clear in order to manage expectations.

**Rule of Thumb**: No matter what the budget, *feed* people well and keep them safe. 

Variations on the theme of free:

1. *Will work for the 3 Fs, for:*
   - free;
   - food;
   - finished film, finito.

   The meals and copy experience is a way to network, gain experience, and build a reel. The production doesn't provide anything but meals, beverage, and film copy, so the cast or crew won't get paid, or reimbursed for expenses, no per diem, and they won't share in future film profits, if any. State this clearly. If possible, reimburse people for transport, or actors for dry cleaning expenses when they wear their own clothing. An unspoken understanding is that you will recommend or hire this person, if possible, for future paid work.
2. *Free friends with benefits*. There are many variations on this – call everyone you know and ask them to pitch in for a credit and copy of the completed film. Crew and cast may receive *deferred* pay (**AKA**: payment later) or a share

in net profits. Among friends and colleagues, a common deal is "I will work on your film for free and you work on mine."

3. *For free (but not on my own dime).* None of the cast or crew receives a wage for their services, but are reimbursed for select expenses (you spell these out clearly upfront), such as their travel, tolls, cell phone usage during the shoot, expendables, wardrobe cleaning for actors.

When cast/crew work for free, depending where you live, you are lucky if they:

- Show up;
- Know their job;
- Can do their job;
- Do a good job.

Particularly on free and micro budget projects, scout and arrange for backup, in case people don't show up. Most filmmakers are hard working, but it's important to **CYA:** have *backup folks* to call!

Now that you have a schedule, you know the number of actors, extras, vehicles and locations you will need — in addition to specific props and set dressing — and can research prices. Consult with your Director and AD to find out what size of crew will be needed. Department heads will also help you find prices, and equipment vendors are happy to provide rates. *For the latest union/guild pay rates all in one place,* The Entertainment Partners Paymaster Rate Guide, Showbiz & Gorilla *are published annually.*

**Crew UP**: Ask your team which crew positions to seek first, check the wording of the search ads, and where to place them. Feature-length films typically need at least a Director, 1st and 2nd AD, PM, and a production office coordinator. Other members of the crew might include: 1st and 2nd Assistant Camera Operator/Driver, Key Grip and Driver, Key Gaffers, Dolly Grip, Electrician/Grip, Key Make-up, Wardrobe and Hair, Sound Recorder and Boom Operator, Art Director, Prop Master, Editor and Assistant Editor, Sound Editor, three to four PAs, Production Accountant, Craft Service, Script Supervisor, Still Photographer, Painter, Carpenter, and Operator of the honey wagon. On nimble productions, one person might hold two or more of these positions. Shorts generally need fewer people. Be sure to request resume and credits, references, links to a reel, equipment or kit list and price (is it insured?), whether the person has a car, and availability.

SAG is typically a first stop. It's important to understand how they work, so contact them. It is possible (but not easy) to find Financial Core union members with hybrid status, working both union and non-union. If you live near big urban areas or areas with developed film centers, it is possible to find great non-union crew.

Also, remember that the projected budget range of your film (as shown in Table 4.15 on page 134) impacts whether you can afford union.

The following union websites are a first stop:

*Writers:* www.wga.org / www.wgaeast.org

*Actors and performers:* www.sag.org / www.sagindie.org / www.aftra.org

*Directors, ADs, UPMs (Location Managers on the East Coast)*: www.DGA.org

*Technicians, Craftspeople and Crew* (IATSE **AKA:** IA – most BTL crew): www.iatse-intl.org
As signatory you have a choice to be a "one-off," making just one film under this agreement (which is probable), or a "term" deal, committing to three films.

*Transportation, Animals and their Wranglers, Catering (Location Managers on the West Coast)*:

www.teamster.org

*Musicians:* www.afm.org

Tables 4.18–4.20 show some sample rates as a reference. Consult the union to obtain the latest prices and most up-to-date information. Unless noted, they are hourly rates.



### Project Length and Format

#### *Length*

The longer your project, the more expensive it is. More pages = more time on screen. More time on screen = more shooting time, which incurs expense. Due to growing distribution formats and improvements in technology, it is difficult to calculate an exact "per minute" formula, although you could calculate averages.

*For example*:

$70,000,000 feature film; 100 min. long = on average,
$700,000 spent per completed production minute

**Table 4.18**

| IATSE Rates | Up to $5m | $5m–$8.5m | $5m–$8.5m | $5m–$8.5m | $8.5m–$12m | $8.5m–$12m | $8.5m–$12m |
|---|---|---|---|---|---|---|---|
| Film Budget Range | **Tier 1** | **Tier 2 2011** | **Tier 2 2012** | **Tier 2 2013** | **Tier 3 2011** | **Tier 3 2012** | **Tier 3 2013** |
| Director of Photography | STN | STN | STN | STN | STN | STN | STN |
| Camera Operator | STN | 41.73 | 42.56 | 43.84 | 43.94 | 44.82 | 46.16 |
| Digital Imaging Technician | STN | 41.73 | 42.56 | 43.84 | 43.94 | 44.82 | 46.16 |
| 1st Asst. Camera | Key | 36.22 | 36.94 | 38.05 | 38.12 | 38.88 | 40.05 |
| 2nd Asst. Camera | 2nd | 27.75 | 28.31 | 29.15 | 29.2 | 29.78 | 30.68 |
| Still Photographer | STN | 41.73 | 42.56 | 43.84 | 43.94 | 44.82 | 46.16 |
| Film Loader | 3rd | 23.71 | 24.18 | 24.91 | 24.96 | 25.46 | 26.22 |
| Camera Utility | Key | 28.93 | 29.51 | 30.4 | 30.45 | 31.06 | 31.99 |
| Digital Utility | 2nd | 24.98 | 25.48 | 26.24 | 26.31 | 26.84 | 27.64 |
| Key Grip | Key | 28.93 | 29.51 | 30.4 | 30.45 | 31.06 | 31.99 |
| Best Boy Grip | 2nd | 26.16 | 26.68 | 27.48 | 27.55 | 28.10 | 28.94 |
| Company Grip | 3rd | 24.97 | 25.47 | 26.23 | 26.31 | 26.84 | 27.64 |
| Dolly Grip | 2nd | 27.1 | 27.64 | 28.37 | 28.54 | 29.11 | 29.98 |
| Chief Lighting Technician | Key | 28.93 | 29.51 | 30.4 | 30.45 | 31.06 | 31.99 |
| Best Boy Electric | 2nd | 26.16 | 26.68 | 27.48 | 27.55 | 28.10 | 28.94 |
| Lighting Technician | 3rd | 24.98 | 25.48 | 26.24 | 26.31 | 26.84 | 27.64 |
| Rigger Gaffer | Key | 27.13 | 27.67 | 28.51 | 28.56 | 29.13 | 30 |
| Art Director (weekly – on call) | STN | 2,274.23 | 2,319.72 | 2,389.31 | 2,436.69 | 2,485.42 | 2,559.99 |
| Lead Person | 2nd | 24.89 | 25.39 | 26.15 | 26.33 | 26.86 | 26.67 |
| Swing Gang | 3rd | 23.86 | 24.34 | 25.06 | 25.12 | 25.62 | 26.39 |
| Production Painter | 2nd | 31.81 | 32.45 | 33.41 | 33.49 | 34.16 | 35.19 |
| Set Painter | 3rd | 27.69 | 28.24 | 29.09 | 29.14 | 29.72 | 30.62 |
| Set Designer | Key | 30.76 | 31.38 | 32.32 | 32.37 | 33.02 | 34.00 |
| Scenic Artist | STN | STN | STN | STN | STN | STN | STN |
| Construction Coordinator | STN | STN | STN | STN | STN | STN | STN |
| Propmaker Foreman | Key | 29.34 | 29.93 | 30.82 | 30.90 | 31.52 | 32.46 |
| Propmaker | 3rd | 25.55 | 26.06 | 26.85 | 26.89 | 27.43 | 28.26 |
| Gang Boss | 2nd | | | | | | |
| Special Effects Foreman | STN | STN | STN | STN | STN | STN | STN |
| Asst. Special Effects | STN | STN | STN | STN | STN | STN | STN |
| Set Decorator | STN | STN | STN | STN | STN | STN | STN |
| Prop Master | Key | 28.93 | 29.51 | 30.4 | 30.45 | 31.06 | 31.99 |
| Asst. Prop Master | 2nd | 25.55 | 26.06 | 26.85 | 26.89 | 27.43 | 28.26 |

(*Continued*)

**Table 4.18** (Continued)

| | | | | | | | |
|---|---|---|---|---|---|---|---|
| Key Greens | 2nd | 26.16 | 26.68 | 26.84 | 27.55 | 28.10 | 28.93 |
| Marine Dept. Coordinator | STN | 25.55 | 26.06 | 26.15 | 29.9 | 30.50 | 28.26 |
| Boat Handlers | STN | 24.89 | 25.39 | 26.15 | 26.33 | 26.86 | 26.67 |
| On Set Picture Cars & Boats | STN | 24.89 | 25.39 | 27.38 | 26.33 | 26.86 | 26.67 |
| Costume Designer | STN | STN | STN | STN | STN | STN | STN |
| Key Costumer | Key | 28.93 | 29.51 | 30.4 | 30.45 | 31.06 | 31.99 |
| First Set Costumer | 2nd | 26.16 | 26.68 | 27.48 | 27.44 | 27.99 | 28.94 |
| Costumer | 3rd | 24.98 | 25.48 | 26.24 | 26.31 | 26.84 | 27.64 |
| Key Make-up Artist | Key | 33.26 | 33.93 | 34.94 | 35.03 | 35.73 | 36.8 |
| Asst. Make-up Artist | 2nd | 28.28 | 28.85 | 29.71 | 29.77 | 30.37 | 31.27 |
| Key Hair Stylist | Key | 28.93 | 29.51 | 30.4 | 30.45 | 31.06 | 31.99 |
| Asst. Hair Stylist | 2nd | 25.73 | 26.24 | 2703 | 27.09 | 27.63 | 28.46 |
| Sound Mixer | STN | 46.6 | 47.53 | 48.96 | 49.02 | 50.00 | 51.5 |
| Boom Operator | 2nd | 31.42 | 32.05 | 33.01 | 33.07 | 33.73 | 34.75 |
| Utility Sound Technician | 3rd | 30.08 | 30.68 | 31.6 | 31.63 | 32.26 | 33.23 |
| Video Assist (record) | Key | 28.93 | 29.51 | 30.4 | 30.45 | 31.06 | 31.99 |
| Script Supervisor | Key | 29.16 | 29.74 | 30.64 | 30.68 | 31.29 | 33.23 |
| First Aid / Medic | 2nd | 26.16 | 26.68 | 27.48 | 27.55 | 28.10 | 28.94 |
| Craft Services | 2nd | 26.16 | 26.68 | 27.48 | 27.55 | 28.10 | 28.94 |
| Craft Utility | 3rd | 24.98 | 25.48 | 20.24 | 20.31 | 20.04 | 27.04 |
| Editor (weekly – on call) | STN | 2,756.63 | 2,811.77 | 2,896.12 | 2,901.72 | 2,959.75 | 3,048.54 |
| **Sound Editors | STN | 1,986.10 | 2,025.82 | 2,086.60 | 2,039.20 | 2,079.98 | 2,142.39 |
| **Music Editors | STN | 1,986.10 | 2,025.82 | 2,086.60 | 2,039.20 | 2,079.98 | 2,142.39 |
| Asst. Editor (45 hr/wk) | Key | 1,601.47 | 1,633.50 | 1,682.50 | 1,686.19 | 1,719.91 | 1,771.51 |
| Apprentice Editor (40hr/wk) | 3rd | 832.47 | 849.50 | 875.03 | 876.72 | 894.25 | 921.09 |
| *POC | 2nd | STN | STN | STN | STN | STN | STN |
| *APOC | 3rd | STN | STN | STN | STN | STN | STN |
| *Art Dept. Coordinator | 2nd | STN | STN | STN | STN | STN | STN |
| *Production Accountant | Key | STN | STN | STN | STN | STN | STN |
| *Asst. Production Accountant | 2nd | STN | STN | STN | STN | STN | STN |
| Story Analyst | Key | STN | STN | STN | STN | STN | STN |
| Location Manager (On call) | STN | STN | STN | STN | STN | STN | STN |
| Assistant Location Manager | STN | STN | STN | STN | STN | STN | STN |
| All Others | STN | STN | STN | STN | STN | STN | STN |

Figures for LA and "Production Cities": Chicago, Cleveland, Detroit, Orlando, San Francisco, St. Louis, NYC, Washington DC
STN = Subject to Negotiation – these rates shall be greater than "key" rates
One-off rates – for one production

**Table 4.19** Outside of "Production cities": Chicago, Cleveland, Detroit, Orlando, San Francisco, St. Louis, NYC, Washington DC

| TIER I up to $5m | | | |
|---|---|---|---|
| **IATSE** | **2011** | **2012** | **2013** |
| Key | $21.99 | $22.43 | $23.10 |
| 2nd | $19.86 | $20.26 | $20.87 |
| 3rd | $17.74 | $18.09 | $18.63 |
| | | | |
| Fringes | Tier 1 | Tier 2 | Tier 3 |
| Administration Fees | 1% | 2% | 2% |
| Pension RSP | 4% | 4% | 5% |
| Health & Welfare | 3% | 4% | 4% |
| Vacation Pay | 3% | 4% | 5% |
| **Total** | **11%** | **14%** | **16%** |
| First 8 hours are straight time (plus payroll taxes, plus fringes). Work hours over 8 on the first five days of the work week and on a sixth work day are time and a half. Double time paid after 14 hours on first six work days of work week and all hours worked on a seventh day in a work week, or on a designated holiday. Hours worked beyond 15 any day are paid triple time. | | | |

$100,000 digital feature film; 90 min. long = on average, $1,111 spent per completed production minute

Cable programming, whether an infomercial, on leased access, or from basic to premium, can cost from $20 a minute (man on street, talking heads, game show, amateur cooking show) to $500,000 a minute for an HBO extravaganza show like *Rome*. The vision of the Producer and the Director for the length of the film should approximate the script length (i.e., 90 pages = 90 minutes). If not, what's the plan?

### *Format*

Upon choosing a format with your team, consider the end use, crew experience, and access to equipment. The format that the film will be shot on, and then delivered on, will impact your budget. If you have a delivery date and a list of delivery requirements (from a distributor, broadcaster or other entity) follow those to the letter. Film stock and equipment are more expensive than video; film requires a bigger crew, more lights, and a more expensive post production process. The two points of format to consider are the format you capture the image on (film, tape, P2 cards, DV, HD) and the format the film is completed on. Widespread popularity of the many affordable

**Table 4.20**

| IATSE | |
|---|---|
| Meal penalty | $7.50 |
| 2nd meal penalty | $10.00 |
| 3rd and succeeding | $12.50 |
| Per diem | |
| Breakfast | $8.50 |
| Lunch | $13.00 |
| Dinner | $29.00 |

| DGA Members | Minimum Wages | | | | |
|---|---|---|---|---|---|
| **Director** | High Budget (over $9.5m) | Shorts & Docs | | | |
| Weekly Salary | $16,184 | $11,650 | | | |
| Guaranteed Prep | 2 weeks | 2 days | | | |
| Guaranteed Employment | 10 weeks | 1 wk + 1 day | | | |
| Guaranteed Cutting Allowance | 1 week | 0 | | | |
| Compensation for Days Worked beyond Guarantee | 3,237 | 2,312 | | | |
| Daily Employment Where Permitted | 4,046 | 2,890 | | | |
| | **UPM** | **1ST AD** | **KEY 2ND AD** | **2ND 2ND AD** | **ADDL (3RD) 2ND ASST** |
| Weekly Salary (LOCATION) | $4,620 | $4,393 | $2,944 | $2,779 | $1,690 |
| Weekly Salary (distant) | 6,470 | 6,143 | 4113 | 3884 | 2873 |
| Weekly Production Fee, Studio | 1,001 | 814 | 621 | 0 | 0 |
| Weekly Production Fee, Location | 1,193 | 1,001 | 814 | 0 | 0 |
| Daily Employment Salary, Studio | 1,155 | 1,098 | 736 | 695 | 423 |
| Daily Employment Salary, Location | 1,618 | 1,536 | 1028 | 971 | 593 |
| Daily Employment Production Fee Studio/Location | 250/290 | 240/250 | 155/204 | 0/0 | 0/0 |

*(Continued)*

nonlinear editing systems, such as Avid, Final Cut, Adobe, iMovie and Sony, enable a Director and a Freelance Editor, with the latter's computer, to work together more quickly and cheaply than if the entire process were conducted at a post facility.

Offline editing is the practice of duplicating the original footage on film or tape in order to store and protect the original. It has historically been done this way due to

**Table 4.20** (Continued)

| **WGA:** Screenplay purchase minimums | |
|---|---|
| Low Budget ($5m or less) | |
| Original Screenplay | $42,088 |
| Non-original Screenplay | 34,251 |
| Story or Treatment | 20,554 |
| Original Story or Treatment | 28,382 |
| | |
| High Budget (above $5m) | |
| Original Screenplay | 86,156 |
| Non-original Screenplay | 70,489 |
| Story or Treatment | 31,332 |
| Original Story or Treatment | 47,000 |

(*Continued*)

the fragility of film and tape stock. After online editing, the original film or tape media can be conformed, or "onlined," in the online editing stage. The *beauty* of editing digital files on a computer is infinite choice, and the *curse* of editing digital files is copious footage and infinite choice. On a nonlinear system, the Editor can jump to any part of the project, rather than working in order. Typically, original footage is digitized into the computer. The Editor and Director are then free to work with all the options to create the final cut. Nonlinear editing offers the possibility of editing the entire film without touching the original. Table 4.21 illustrates some common workflows.

**Table 4.20** (Continued)

| TEAMSTERS | | |
|---|---|---|
| Occupation Code | Classification | **Hourly rate** |
| 3500 | Transportation Coordinator | None |
| 3501 | 1st On Production Driver Gang Boss Hired | $35.58 |
| 3502 | All Other Gang Bosses (except ace). Code Nos. 3551 and 3581 | 32.39 |
| 3511 | Drivers of automobiles, station wagons, minivans (9 or fewer passengers) and motorcycles | 17.51 |
| 3518 | Drivers of automobiles, station wagons, minivans (9 or fewer passengers) and motorcycles who regularly worked for the Producer in ace. Code No. 3511 throughout the term of the 2001 Agreement. | 24.81 |
| 3512 | Drivers of other vehicles which require a Class C license to operate – crew cabs, pick-up trucks, lot tractors (shop mules or hooties), 5-ton trucks – and condors | 26.29 |
| 3513 | Hyphenate Driver I Craftsperson | 28.68 |
| 3520 | Drivers of vehicles requiring a Class B license, including operators of maxivans (10 or more passengers), buses (excluding forty (40) passenger buses), dump trucks, 5-ton crew cabs, crew cabs towing trailers less than 6,000 lbs. off the lot, forklifts (excluding pettibone forklifts), skip loaders, water trucks and motor homes, but excluding 10-ton trucks | 28.68 |
| 3521 | Drivers of forty (40) passenger buses, 10-ton trucks, and pettibone forklifts and drivers of vehicles requiring a Class A license, including vehicles towing trailers over 6,000 lbs. and operators of cranes, back hoes, bulldozers, heavy duty tractors and honey wagons | 30.92 |
| 3523 | Camera Car Driver | 35.38 |
| 3524 | Production Van Driver/Operator | 36.32 |
| 3525 | Stunt and/or Blind Driver | None |
| 3526 | Chapman Crane Op | 35.58 |
| 3531 | Automotive Service Person | 17.51 |
| 3532 | Automotive Service Person working regularly for Producer | 24.81 |
| 3543 | Dispatcher | 32.39 |
| 3550 | Ramrod | None |
| 3551 | Wrangler Gang Boss | 32.54 |
| 3561 | Wrangler | 30.09 |
| 3562 | Driver/Wrangler | 30.92 |
| 3563 | Wrangler (Pick Up) | 45.38 |
| 3565 | Wrangler (Braider) | 38.03 |
| 3571 | Trainer (Domestic Livestock) | None |
| 3573 | Trainer (S Table) | 41.65 |
| 3575 | Wild Animal Trainers | 41.65 |
| 3576 | Wild Animal Handlers | 36.14 |
| 3581 | Automotive Gang Boss | 35.58 |
| 3591 | Automotive Mechanic | 32.61 |
| 3592 | Dog Trainer | 36.14 |
| 3593 | Dog Handler | 30.09 |
| | | |
| Minimum call, 8 hrs, after 8 and/or 40 hours Time + 1/2 | | |

(*Continued*)

**Table 4.20** (Continued)

| **SAG Theatrical Minimums** | |
|---|---|
| **Day Performers** | **Per Day** |
| Performer | 809 |
| Stunt Performer | 809 |
| Stunt Coordinator (employed at less than "flat deal" minimum) | 809 |
| Airplane Pilot (Studio) | 1,081 |
| Airplane Pilot (Location) | 1,406 |
| | |
| **Weekly Performers** | **Per Week** |
| Performer | 2,808 |
| Stunt Performer | 3,015 |
| Stunt Coordinator (employed at less than "flat deal" minimum) | 3,015 |
| Airplane Pilot (Studio) | 3,015 |
| Airplane Pilot (Location) | 927 |
| | |
| **Multiple Picture Performers** | **Per Week** |
| Performer | 2,808 |
| | |
| **Background Actors** | **Per Day** |
| Schedule X | 139 |
| Special Ability | 149 |
| Stand-Ins | 154 |
| Swimmers / Skaters | 322 |
| | |
| **Singers** | **Per Day** |
| Solo and Duo | 875 |
| Groups 3–8 | 768 |
| Groups 9+ | 670 |
| | |
| **Stunt Performers (Employed Under Term Contracts)** | |
| 10 to 19 Weeks Guaranteed (per week) | 2,409 |
| 20 Weeks or More Guaranteed (per week) | 2,006 |
| | |
| **Dancers** | |
| *Daily Rates* | |
| Solo/Duo | 809 |
| 3–8 | 709 |
| 9+ | 619 |
| Rehearsal | 475 |
| | |
| **Stunt Coordinators – Theatrical – Flat Deal** | |
| Per Week | 4,650 |
| Per Day | 1258 |
| | |
| SAG New Media | Subject to negotiation |
| Ultra Low | Budgets <200,000 (500K with deferrals) |
| All SAG performers except Stunt Coordinators | 100/day |
| Stunt Coordinators | K1, K2, or K3 |
| SAG Pension and Health 15.3% | |

**Table 4.21**

|  | Film Shoot, Film Edit Film Master | Film Shoot, Digital Edit, Film Master | Film Shoot, Digital Edit, Digital Master | Film Shoot, Film Edit, Digital Master | Digital Shoot, Digital Edit, Digital Master |
|---|---|---|---|---|---|
| | Film shoot | Film shoot | Film shoot | Film shoot | Digital shoot |
| | Process negative | Process negative | Process negative | Process negative | Capture footage into edit system |
| | Sort and choose takes, print takes | Sort and choose takes | Sort and choose takes | Sort and choose takes, print takes | Offline edit, graphic effects |
| | Workprint (dailies or rushes) synced with audio and screened/logged | Telecine – transfer selected takes to tape | Telecine – transfer selected takes to tape | Workprint (dailies or rushes) synced with audio and screened/logged | EDL – Edit Decision List |
| | Workprint edited, approved, negative pull list created | Digital offline editing | Digital offline editing | Workprint edited, approved, negative pull list created | Online editing |
| | Cut negative | EDL – Edit Decision List | EDL – Edit Decision List | Cut negative | |
| | Color timing<br>Printing to answer print, print elements, release print | Pull and cut negative | Online editing, color correction | Telecine – transfer selected takes to tape<br>Online edit (assembly, titles, dissolves)<br>Video master and dupe | |
| | | Color timing printing lab, printing elements, release print | | **Or:**<br>Film opticals<br>Color timing<br>Lab processing<br>Answer print<br>Telecine transfer film to tape | |

## Building a Budget

Start with what you know:

- Based on your schedule, X shooting days
  - Prep time for preproduction (+3–4 times production)
  - Post production time (+3–4 times production)
- Where you will be shooting? If you are applying to use an incentive program, find out if there is a required budget form.
- Union/Non-union? Combination? Unsure – see next question.
- Backing the budget into a number, a range, or no idea?
- Planned use of film
- Experience of team (more time + more $ for less experienced)
- Costs incurred on project so far? (even unpaid projects)
  - Script / Story rights / Writer
  - Cost to create schedule and budget
- Director attached to project? Y/N
  - Other crew or cast already attached to the project –their fees, payment expectations? (cast, key crew, equipment, locations)
- Firm delivery date, and delivery requirements.

Using the same principles, you can build your budget with pencil and paper, Excel, or other spreadsheet programs.

**Setup**

The header of your topsheet will identify the film.

| | |
|---|---|
| **Project Title:** | **Holidays:** |
| **Script Dated:** | **Travel Days:** |
| **Budget Dated:** | **Producer** |
| **Start Date:** | **Director:** |
| **Finish Date:** | **Location(s):** |
| **Total Days:** | **Union(s):** |
| **Post Weeks:** | **Prepared By:** |

In budgeting software, select a template, name it and save it. All of the templates can be changed as you like. The Superbudget Template created by Bob Koster, a budgeting rockstar, is so thorough that you are unlikely to overlook anything. On the flip side, the Academic Template offers basic essentials. If working on paper, grab blank budgets and a pencil.

Identify title, team, script version, date, and other information in File/Print Setup.

Click OK, and SAVE.

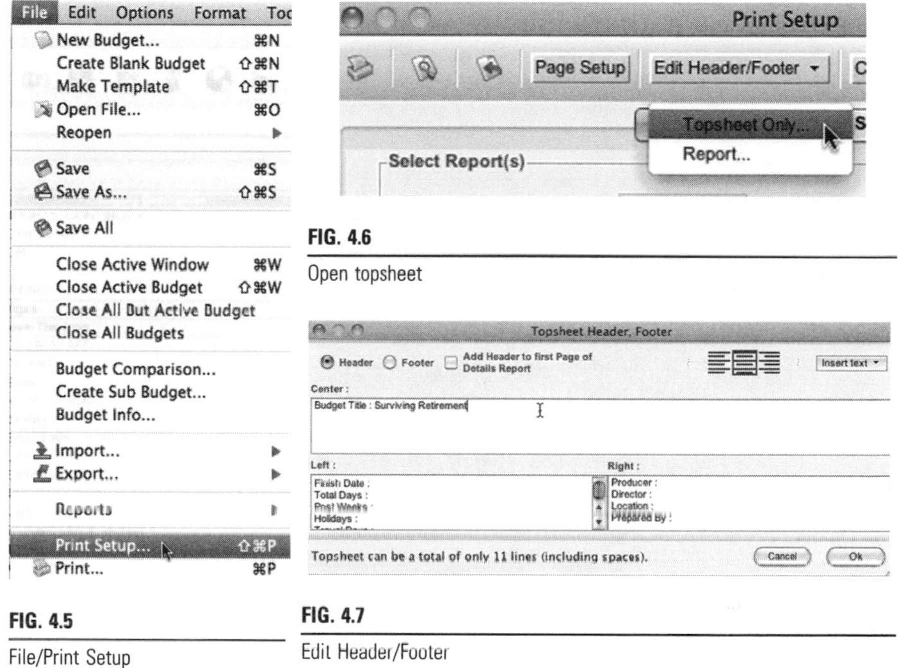


**FIG. 4.6**

Open topsheet

**FIG. 4.5**

File/Print Setup

**FIG. 4.7**

Edit Header/Footer

*Setup Globals*

These are shortcuts used frequently for time and rates (length of shoot, prep, wrap, work hours, pay scales). Changing a figure once in Globals automatically updates the budget, so you don't have to manually change it for each cast or crew.

**FIG. 4.8**

Setup Globals

Assign a "Name" and "Calculation" to Globals you will use often, i.e., the length of the total shoot (S), or segments of the shoot (locally or distant).

**Table 4.22**

| Name | Description | Calculation | Units | Dec | VALUE |
|---|---|---|---|---|---|
| *Abbreviation* | *Brief description* | *=formula or quantity* | *W=Weeks H=Hours* | *Decimals* | *Automatically calculated* |
| **SL** | Shoot Local | 3 | Weeks | 2 | 0 |
| **SD** | Shoot Distant | 2 | Weeks | 2 | 0 |
| **S** | **Shoot Total** | **=SL+SD** | Weeks | 2 | 0 |

An example of Globals: at the Detail Level, in "Amount" type in the name abbreviation. "S" will fill in the amount for total shoot.

| Description | Amount | Units | X | Rate | Subtotal |
|---|---|---|---|---|---|
| Prep | 1 | Week | 1 | 400 | 400 |
| **Shoot** | **=S** | Weeks | 1 | 500 | 500 |

*Setup Fringes*

Shortcuts for taxes, payroll fees, union or guild-specific payments.

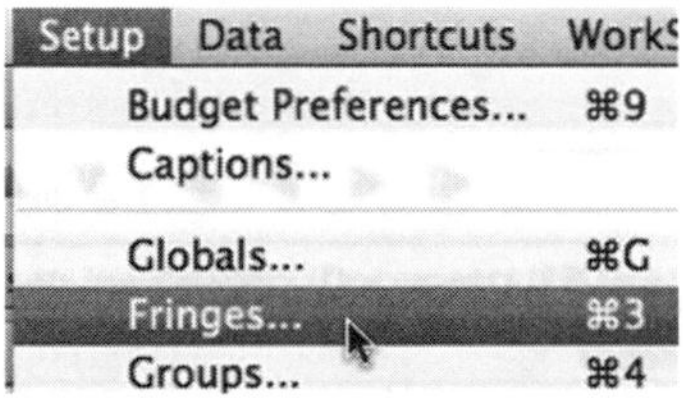

Setup Data Shortcuts WorkS

Budget Preferences... ⌘9

Captions...

Globals... ⌘G

Fringes... ⌘3

Groups... ⌘4

**FIG. 4.9**

Fringes calculate benefits and taxes

On top "Fringe Benefits by Percentage" are paid as a percent of wages.

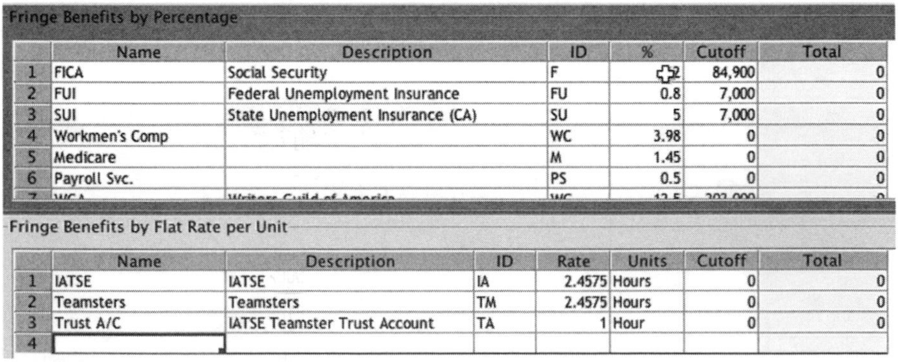

Fringe Benefits by Percentage

| | Name | Description | ID | % | Cutoff | Total |
|---|---|---|---|---|---|---|
| 1 | FICA | Social Security | F | [illegible]2 | 84,900 | 0 |
| 2 | FUI | Federal Unemployment Insurance | FU | 0.8 | 7,000 | 0 |
| 3 | SUI | State Unemployment Insurance (CA) | SU | 5 | 7,000 | 0 |
| 4 | Workmen's Comp | | WC | 3.98 | 0 | 0 |
| 5 | Medicare | | M | 1.45 | 0 | 0 |
| 6 | Payroll Svc. | | PS | 0.5 | 0 | 0 |
| 7 | [illegible] | [illegible] | [illegible] | [illegible] | [illegible] | [illegible] |

Fringe Benefits by Flat Rate per Unit

| | Name | Description | ID | Rate | Units | Cutoff | Total |
|---|---|---|---|---|---|---|---|
| 1 | IATSE | IATSE | IA | 2.4575 | Hours | 0 | 0 |
| 2 | Teamsters | Teamsters | TM | 2.4575 | Hours | 0 | 0 |
| 3 | Trust A/C | IATSE Teamster Trust Account | TA | 1 | Hour | 0 | 0 |
| 4 | | | | | | | |

**FIG. 4.10**

Fringes calculate as a % of wages, or a flat rate per hour

"Fringe Benefits by Flat Rate per Unit" is a specific payment amount connected to a specific unit — hours worked, days, etc. Once set up, fringes are applied at the Detail Level.

**FIG. 4.11**

Select the lines for applicable fringes

Click on fringes (for a Writer, WGA and Payroll).

| | Ind. | Description | Amo... | Units | X | Rate | Subt |
|---|---|---|---|---|---|---|---|
| 2 | | | 0 | | 1 | 0 | |
| 3 | | WGA-Rates Low Budget | 1 | | 1 | 0 | |
| 4 | ▸ | Treatments | 0 | | 1 | 0 | |
| 5 | ▸ | First Draft | 1 | Allow | 1 | 32,505 | 3 |
| 6 | ▸ | Second Draft | 0 | | 1 | 0 | |
| 7 | ▸ | Final Draft | 1 | Allow | 1 | 9,000 | |

View/Apply Fringes – AFunl

| | | | | |
|---|---|---|---|---|
| ☐ FICA | 0 | ☐ FUI | 0 | ☐ SUI |
| ☐ Medicare | 0 | ■ Payroll Svc. | 208 | ■ WGA |
| ☐ Vacation/Holi | 0 | ☐ SAG | 0 | ☐ Overtime |
| ☐ IATSE | 0 | ☐ TEAMSTERS | 0 | ☐ TRUST A/C |
| ■ Payroll Taxes | 6226 | | | |

**FIG. 4.12**

Apply relevant fringes (WGA Writer, WGA and Payroll)

Click "Make Fringe" and close. The program will add the appropriate fringes.

*Setup Units*

Shortcuts that establish the length of shooting week, day, or other units.

Once Units are set up at the Detail Level, type "A" for Allow, "W" for Week, "D" for Day, which are the default units in most budgeting programs. You can add more if you like.

| Description | Amount | Units | X | Rate | Subtotal |
|---|---|---|---|---|---|
| Prep | 1 | Week | 1 | 400 | 400 |
| Shoot | 1 | Day | 1 | 500 | 500 |
| Kit | 1 | Allow | 1 | 10 | 10 |

Change numbers in Units where necessary to generate the proper calculation. Is a work day 8 hours? (Unlikely in production, 10–13 is more likely). Week = days you

**FIG. 4.13**

Units calculate appropriate length of day, week, etc.

will work in the week (5 or 6), × hours in a day. With a 12-hour work day, a 6-day work week will equal 12 (hours) × 6 (days) = 72 hours. Flip it around if you are doing a weekend shoot: 2-day weeks, 13 hours per day = 2 × 11 = 22 work hours.

When creating a budget manually or in Excel, include the fringe amounts and a key for Units at the top for quick reference.

Set up one account, then copy and paste to use again. Table 4.23a shows an account for a non-union member paid at a flat rate.

**Table 4.23a**

| 1601-AD | Amount | Unit | X | Rates | Subtotal |
|---|---|---|---|---|---|
| *Non-DGA* | | | | | |
| *Polly Hasenfeffer* | 1 | Allow | 1 | 75,000 | 75,000 |
| | | | | | |
| Computer Rental | 1 | Allow | 1 | | |
| Computer Supplies | 1 | Allow | 1 | | |
| Car Allowance | 13 | Allow | 1 | 250 | 250 |
| **Total** | | | | | **75,250** |

Apply fringes (taxes). For a union crew member paid weekly or daily, see Table 4.23b.

Table 4.23c shows an example of a non-union crew member paid weekly or daily.

Apply fringes (taxes).

**Table 4.23b**

| 1601-AD | Amount | Unit | X | Rates | Subtotal |
|---|---|---|---|---|---|
| *DGA:* | | | | | |
| Polly Anna | | | | | |
| Prep Local | 5 | Weeks | 1 | 5,000 | 25,000 |
| Shoot Local | 3 | Weeks | 1 | 5,000 | 15,000 |
| Wrap Local | 2 | Weeks | 1 | 5,000 | 10,000 |
| | | | | | |
| Prep Distant | 4 | Weeks | 1 | 5,000 | 20,000 |
| Shoot Distant | 2 | Weeks | 1 | 5,000 | 10,000 |
| Wrap Distant | 1 | Week | 1 | 5,000 | 5,000 |
| | | | | | |
| Production Fee – Local | 3 | Weeks | 1 | 800 | 2,400 |
| Production Fee – Dist | 2 | Weeks | 1 | 900 | 1,800 |
| Severance | 0 | Flat | 1 | 5,000 | 0 |
| | | | | | |
| Overtime | 10 | % | 0 | | |
| Computer Rental | 1 | Allow | 1 | 250 | 250 |
| Computer Supplies | 1 | Allow | 1 | 50 | 50 |
| Car Allowance | 5 | Weeks | 1 | 250 | 1,250 |
| **Total** | | | | | **90,750** |

**Table 4.23c**

| 1601-AD | | | | | |
|---|---|---|---|---|---|
| | **Amount** | **Unit** | **X** | **Rates** | **Subtotal** |
| *Non-DGA:* | | | | | |
| *Polly Wahnnercracker* | | | | | |
| Prep Local | 5 | Weeks | 1 | 5,000 | 25,000 |
| Shoot Local | 3 | Weeks | 1 | 4,000 | 12,000 |
| Wrap Local | 2 | Weeks | 1 | 0 | 0 |
| Prep Distant | 4 | Weeks | 1 | 200 | 800 |
| Shoot Distant | 2 | Weeks | 1 | 100 | 200 |
| Wrap Distant | 1 | Week | 1 | 250 | 250 |
| Overtime | 10 | % | 0 | | |
| Computer Rental | 1 | Allow | 1 | 100 | 100 |
| Computer Supplies | 1 | Allow | 1 | 50 | 50 |
| Car Allowance | 5 | Weeks | 1 | 250 | 1,250 |
| **Total** | | | | | **39,650** |

Copy by clicking on the upper left corner. Paste information at the Detail Level.

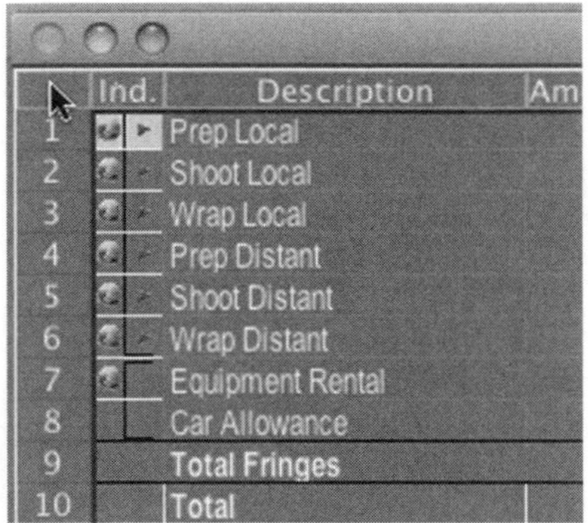


**FIG. 4.14**

Copy/Paste at the Detail Level. Click on the upper left-hand cell above Number "1"; click Edit/Copy

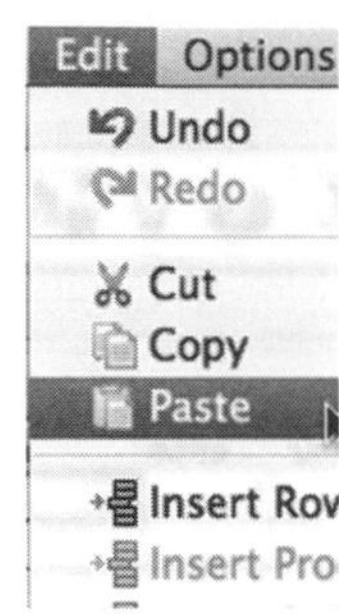


**FIG. 4.15**

Click Edit/Paste. Alter as needed

**Above the Line: Creative and Development Costs**

Above the Line categories include development costs – initial ingredients the Producer thinks will make a great project – a story and script, Writer, Director and cast. Find out if the Producer promised any of the Above the Line team a portion of the film's profits (**AKA**: backend).

In the employment contract, in addition to noting the salaries for these people, and their duties, you would define those profits, or points (1 point = 1%) that will be due to them. This profit participation may be called *net points* or *defined proceeds*, and is distributed after other expenses are paid. To promise *gross points* means payment before expenses are paid, and this is not advised. With some exceptions, Below the Line workers do not share in the profits. The number of points – or participation in future profits – cannot be predicted ahead of time, as there is no way to know if there will be profits, so this is not included in the budget.

The Producer who initiated this project likely spent money building a development package – script or story idea, Director, lead actor – and/or likely made deals with these parties, so start with the information you have and input figures into the budget that were already paid out, or promised.

On films that are passion projects, e.g. first features, many of the ATL players may be paid nothing upfront, and contract to receive a portion of a film's profits.

We will work in a sequential way through categories in order of their account number.

*1100 Story, Rights, Continuity*

Screenplay and story rights are a key Above the Line cost, and run from 2–10% of a film's budget. A production must own the motion picture rights to the story of the film. You could pay one person for the idea and another to transform that idea into a script.

Enter data at the Detail Level. The Writer could be paid a flat rate (Table 4.24a).

**Table 4.24a**

| Description | Amount | Units | X | Rate | Subtotal |
|---|---|---|---|---|---|
| Flat Rate | 1 | Allow | 1 | 500 | 500 |

Alternatively, the Writer could be paid for incremental versions of the script (Table 4.24b).

**Table 4.24b**

| | Amount | Unit | X | Rate | Subtotal |
|---|---|---|---|---|---|
| First Draft | 1 | Allow | 1 | 32,505 | 32,505 |
| Final Draft | 1 | Allow | 1 | 9,000 | 9,000 |
| Polish | 1 | Allow | 1 | 1,000 | 1,000 |
| Total | | | | | 42,505 |

A Producer might *option* a script, like a "lease to buy," controlling the property for a small down payment (5% of the purchase price), for a limited time (1–2 years) until purchasing the property outright (pay the other 95%).

**Table 4.24c**

| | Amount | Unit | X | Rate | Subtotal |
|---|---|---|---|---|---|
| Option Price | 1 | Allow | 1 | 150 | 30 |
| Purchase Price | 1 | Allow | 1 | 300 | 300 |

*Copyright registration* offers legal proof if someone infringes; it costs $35 at the U.S. Copyright Office (www.ECO.gov). Do it again if the story changes significantly. The cost to clear the script legally is included in legal expenses.

Fringes applied include payroll taxes, and WGA members receive guild fringes (12.5%).

**FIG. 4.16**

Apply fringes as required

| | | | | | | | | | | | |
|---|---|---|---|---|---|---|---|---|---|---|---|
| ■ | FICA | 6.2% | ■ | FUI | 0.8% | ■ | SUI | 5% | ■ | Workmen's | 3.98% |
| ■ | Medicare | 1.45% | ■ | Payroll Svc. | 0.5% | □ | WGA | 12.5% | □ | DGA | 13.25% |
| □ | Vacation/H | 7.719% | ○ | IATSE | $2.46/Hour | □ | SAG | 13.15% | ○ | Teamsters | $2.46/Hour |
| □ | Overtime | 0% | □ | State Sales | 8.25% | ○ | Trust A/C | $1.00/Hour | | | |

Total : 0 FICA,FUI,SUI,Workmen's Comp,Medicare,Payroll Svc.

**FIG. 4.17**

Payroll taxes and payroll service (if you are using one) are commonly added to Writer's pay; WGA Writers also receive WGA fringes

Check with your Producer if anything has been paid for the story rights or Script Writer. The production will need to prove ownership of the rights if it is to be sold or distributed (unless it is in the public domain). Even if acquired for $1 (paid by check), *get it in writing*. Whether an original idea, or a derivative work (based on something else), the production must procure the rights from the copyright holder. (For more info, check out *The Pocket Lawyer for Filmmakers, A Legal Toolkit for Independent Producers*, Focal Press — it makes a great gift!)

With non-WGA Writers, it's a matter of negotiation. WGA salaries correspond to the budget size and the nature of the material (Table 4.25).

*1200 Producers' Unit*

Most films have several Producers, and it is hard to know by the credits exactly who did what. In filmmaking, Producer credits are flexible; their duties are less clearly defined than other positions. Producer credits *may* go to people actually working on the film, or contributing in another way, i.e., finding financing, key personnel, or a location.

The number of people in this category relates to the size and scale of the project. It's common for low budget features to have an Executive Producer, Producer, Co-Producer, Associate Producer and Producer Assistants Above the Line, while Below the Line, you might have a Line Producer and/or UPM, Production Office Coordinator/ Production Secretary, Assistant Production Coordinator, and a few Production Assistants staffing the office. It really depends. Many films start off with a core

**Table 4.25**

<table>
<tr><th colspan="2">WGA Theatrical Rates</th><th colspan="2">Low Budget (under $5m)</th><th colspan="2">High Budget ($5m and up)</th></tr>
<tr><td colspan="2">Original Screenplay + Treatment</td><td colspan="2">$62,642</td><td colspan="2">$117,602</td></tr>
<tr><td colspan="2">Treatment</td><td colspan="2">28,382</td><td colspan="2">47,000</td></tr>
<tr><td colspan="2">Screenplay 1st Draft</td><td colspan="2">24,668</td><td colspan="2">47,000</td></tr>
<tr><td colspan="2">Screenplay Final Draft</td><td colspan="2">9,592</td><td colspan="2">23,602</td></tr>
<tr><td colspan="2">Rewrite</td><td colspan="2">20,554</td><td colspan="2">31,334</td></tr>
<tr><td colspan="2">Polish</td><td colspan="2">10,283</td><td colspan="2">47,000</td></tr>
<tr><td colspan="6">Other WGA Rates</td></tr>
<tr><td colspan="3">Week to Week Employment (film)</td><td colspan="3">5,098 / wk</td></tr>
<tr><td colspan="3">Commercial/Industrial Short Form</td><td colspan="3">600 / day</td></tr>
<tr><td colspan="3">Commercial/Industrial Long Form</td><td colspan="3">2500 / day</td></tr>
<tr><td colspan="3">Narration</td><td colspan="2">957 / 2 min or less</td><td>3,388 2-5 minutes</td></tr>
<tr><td colspan="3">Network Prime Time (30 min or less)</td><td colspan="2">Story 4,165</td><td>Teleplay 10,115</td></tr>
<tr><td colspan="3">New Media; Dramatic</td><td colspan="2">662 / 2 min or less</td><td>331 each add'l min</td></tr>
<tr><td colspan="3">New Media: Comedy, Variety, Daytime</td><td colspan="2">386 / 2 min or less</td><td>193 each add'l minute</td></tr>
<tr><td colspan="6">1100 Story, Rights, Continuity Account Numbers.</td></tr>
<tr><td>1102</td><td>RESEARCH</td><td colspan="4">Books, interviews, materials, consulting experts</td></tr>
<tr><td>1107</td><td>SECRETARY & TYPISTS</td><td colspan="4">You may need this for transcription, or to help the Writer</td></tr>
<tr><td>1108</td><td>DUPLICATION & PRINTING</td><td colspan="4">$0.05 per page, printer toner, brads, etc.</td></tr>
<tr><td>1109</td><td>SCRIPT TIMING</td><td colspan="4">Script supervisor times the reading of the script aloud so the resulting script isn't too long, or short</td></tr>
<tr><td>1117</td><td>RENTALS</td><td colspan="4" rowspan="4">Providing living and travel while writing, or to work with team</td></tr>
<tr><td>1151</td><td>AIRFARES</td></tr>
<tr><td>1154</td><td>LIVING EXPENSES</td></tr>
<tr><td>1155</td><td>AUTO/TAXIS/LIMOS</td></tr>
<tr><td>1185</td><td>OTHER COSTS</td><td colspan="4">Miscellaneous charges, reimbursements, shipping</td></tr>
<tr><td>1199</td><td>WGA FRINGE BENEFITS</td><td colspan="4">(14.5%) For WGA members</td></tr>
</table>

crew (Producer, LP) and as things heat up, hire more people. The PM or LP relies heavily on the Production Office Coordinator, to keep on top of paperwork and the million details in the production office.

Producers' fees may be paid as a flat rate, or weekly, and often receive profit participation. The Producer may also want initial out-of-pocket costs included in the budget for reimbursement in *Development* expenses (research, travel, legal) (Table 4.26).

**Table 4.26**

| | | |
|---|---|---|
| 1201 | EXECUTIVE PRODUCER | The big one – the fewer the better for exclusivity. Provides a significant contribution, financing, access to financing, securing rights |
| 1202 | PRODUCERS | There may be several – some are hands on, some are not. Paid flat rate with profit participation |
| 1203 | LINE PRODUCER | Breaks down script, creates schedule and budget, and oversees them, as well as hiring, union and location matters |
| 1204 | ASSOCIATE PRODUCER | Often acts as Post Production Supervisor – herding the film through the winding process of post, or used as a contractual incentive |
| 1208 | LEGAL & AUDITING | A script clearance firm goes over the script, then provides information needed to minimize the production's legal risks and satisfy insurance requirements |

On a recent Hollywood $70m thriller, the EP received $2.5m, one Producer $850,000, and the Producer/Writer $3.3m (for producing and writing). On low budget features, the Producers may fund the picture themselves, and build very modest salaries of $10,000 into the budget just hoping to recoup that, get the film made, and earn net profits.

An Executive Producer finds the *money*, the Producer acts as the *parent* to the film, and everyone supports this effort. The Line Producer manages the *budget* and *schedule* – a position found in Production Staff (2000).

The Executive Producer and Producer may be paid a flat rate (as it is difficult to quantify their time), or weekly. They usually receive a profit participation (not included in the budget).

**Table 4.27**

| Description | Amount | Units | X | Rate | Subtotal |
|---|---|---|---|---|---|
| Prep/Shoot/Wrap | 1 | Allow | 1 | 5,000 | 5,000 |

Producer's support staff (secretary) are typically paid weekly or daily.

| Description | Amount | Units | X | Rate | Subtotal |
|---|---|---|---|---|---|
| Prep | 3 | Weeks | 1 | 500 | 1,500 |
| Shoot | 1 | Week | 2 | 600 | 1,200 |
| Wrap | 4 | Days | 1 | 100 | 400 |

*FYI:* When multiple Producers are involved in a production, let cast and crew know which person has the last word.

Trade organizations representing Producers include: The Alliance of Motion Picture & Television Producers (www.AMPTP.org); the entertainment industry's collective bargaining representative; and the PGA (Producer's Guild of America, www.producersguild.org).

Regardless of affiliation, Producers negotiate their rate on a per-project basis; there is no standard.

*1300 Director's Unit*

Spurred by the imagination of the Producer, the Director (**AKA**: 1st Unit Director) realizes the script through a visual and audio plan — through casting, choice of locations, camera placement, lighting, artistic choices, and pacing. Inspired by the Producer's vision, with the blueprint of the script as a guide the Director works to create the finished film as seen in his or her mind's eye, and works toward that end.

The *Director's unit* is led by the 1st Unit Director, and may include a 2nd Unit Director (who can double as Stunt Coordinator), and a choreographer for dancing or fights, if needed.

At the Detail Level, design the Director's account carefully so you can copy/paste to reuse it as a template again for any member of the DGA. This position may be paid as a one-price flat rate or weekly on features, and daily on short projects. *FYI: If a crew or cast member is paid at a flat rate, it does not mean they must be paid in one big check; it will be split throughout the project.* If paying weekly, there are different rates for prep, shoot or wrap. On a non-union picture, the rate is a matter for negotiation. Experience is important — every Director wants that important first feature directing credit.

1201 - 1st Unit Director

| Description | Amount | Units | X | Rate | Subtotal |
|---|---|---|---|---|---|
| Non-DGA: FLAT RATE for All | 1 | Allow | 0 | 55,000 | 0 |
| | 1 | | 0 | 0 | 0 |
| Non-DGA: | 1 | | 0 | 0 | 0 |
| Prep Local | 5 | Weeks | 1 | 3,500 | 17,500 |
| Shoot Local | =SL | Weeks | 1 | 4,500 | 13,500 |
| Wrap Local | 0 | Weeks | 1 | 4,000 | 0 |
| Prep Distant | 4 | Weeks | 1 | 4,000 | 16,000 |
| Shoot Distant | =SD | Weeks | 1 | 5,000 | 10,000 |
| Wrap Distant | 0 | Weeks | 1 | 5,000 | 0 |
| | 1 | | 0 | 0 | 0 |

**FIG. 4.18**

Non-DGA Directors are typically paid under scale

DGA members, like other guild members, are paid according to minimum rates tied to the film's budget (called *scale*) and must be paid at least scale or higher. In-demand Directors may request higher rates and perks. Additional expenses are itemized at the bottom, if they apply. Most Directors will expect a profit participation.

| DGA: | 1 | | 0 | 0 | 0 |
|---|---|---|---|---|---|
| Prep Local | 0 | Weeks | 0 | 5,000 | 0 |
| Shoot Local | =SL | Weeks | 0 | 5,000 | 0 |
| Wrap Local | 0 | Weeks | 0 | 5,000 | 0 |
| Prep Distant | 0 | Weeks | 0 | 6,000 | 0 |
| Shoot Distant | =SD | Weeks | 0 | 6,000 | 0 |
| Wrap Distant | 0 | Weeks | 0 | 6,000 | 0 |
| Production Fee - Local | =SL | Weeks | 0 | 723 | 0 |
| Production Fee - Distant | =SD | Weeks | 0 | 863 | 0 |
| Severance | 0 | Flat | 0 | 5,000 | 0 |
| | 0 | | 0 | 0 | 0 |
| Kit Rental | 0 | Weeks | 1 | 0 | 0 |
| Supplies & Materials | 0 | Weeks | 1 | 0 | 0 |
| Car Allowance | 0 | Weeks | 1 | 0 | 0 |
| Per Diem | 0 | Days | 1 | 0 | 0 |
| **Total** | | | | | **$0** |

**FIG. 4.19**

The DGA has specific rates based on the budget of the film with regards to rates, travel, and fringes

Check DGA for the most up-to-date rates (www.dga.org).

**Level 1 & 2**: Budget ≤ $2,570,000. Pay is "subject to negotiation" (DGA)

**Level 3**: $2,570,000 ≤ $3,605,000. Pay $75,000 for minimum guarantee of 13 weeks

**Level 4A:** $3,605,000 ≤ $7 million. Pay is 75% of scale and **Level 4B** – $7–9 m pay is 90% of scale

**Over $9.5m** – per Basic Agreement

Many Directors work through a *Loan Out* corporation – you hire the Director's Loan Out company, and that company provides the Director's services. Primarily done for tax reasons, the Loan Out will be responsible for paying payroll taxes, while you will be responsible for paying DGA fees (if hiring a DGA member). The IRS has been examining the use of Loan Outs in recent years, but that's not your problem.

If your team doesn't have a Director yet, start there first. Talented Directors will attract talented actors and crew. Discuss with your team the type of Director you need. Your Director is a critical team member from whom everything else follows: the look and tone of the story, pacing, lighting, and marketability.

**Table 4.28**

| | |
|---|---|
| Weekly Salary | $12,138 |
| Guaranteed Preparation | 2 Weeks |
| Guaranteed Employment | 10 Weeks |
| Guaranteed Cutting Allowance | 1 Week |
| Days Worked Beyond Guarantee | $2,428 |
| Daily Employment Where Permitted | $3,035 |

Make sure to apply relevant fringes (Payroll taxes + DGA fees for DGA members)

| | |
|---|---|
| Non DGA Industrial/Corporate | 1,500–3,500/day |
| Non DGA Feature | 10,000 |
| DGA Network Prime Time | 23,118 (½ hr) |
| DGA Network Prime Time | 39,258 (1 hr) |
| DGA Daily Employment | 4,128/day for ½ hr show |
| DGA Daily Employment | 3,272/day for 1 hr show |

Criteria for hiring a Director:

- Experience shooting this genre of film, in equivalent budget range;
- Tells a story well; footage looks great;
- Prepared, organized, reliable, good with actors, and a clear communicator.

*1400 Cast*

Cast rates vary widely, depending on the union status of the cast member and demand. From the scheduling process, you know how many cast members, and how often, you will need them. Print the *Day Out of Days Report for Cast Members* (AKA: DooD).

**12:13 AM** **Day Out of Days Report for Cast Members**

| Month/Day | 02/07 | 02/08 | 02/09 | 02/10 | 02/11 | 02/12 | 02/13 | 02/14 |
|---|---|---|---|---|---|---|---|---|
| Day of Week | Mon | Tue | Wed | Thu | Fri | Sat | Sun | Mon |
| Shooting Day | 1 | 2 | 3 | 4 | 5 | 6 | | 7 |
| 1. Claude | SW | W | W | W | W | W | | W |

**FIG. 4.20**

The *Day Out of Days Cast Report* helps indicate which cast should be hired for the duration of the entire shoot, as day or weekly players

Key talent may be hired at a flat rate (Table 4.25) as *run of show* (AKA: series, allow), available to show up any time they are needed. This is usually more expensive than hiring someone on a weekly or daily basis. The run of show actor is essentially standing by, even when not on set, so they cannot take other work.

To increase the marketability of your film, consult a casting Director (and tell everyone you know) if you are looking for a cameo (or just voice-over) by a star. This person would probably be hired for the *shortest* time possible, and if they like the project may work for SAG scale. Beware the cost of perks; personal chefs, private trailer, etc. all add up (Fig. 4.22).

| 1301 - Principal Players | | | | | |
|---|---|---|---|---|---|
| Description | Amount | Units | X | Rate | Subtotal |
| All Cast NON-SAG | 1 | | 1 | 0 | 0 |
| | 1 | | 1 | 0 | 0 |
| 3101-01 Lead #1 | 1 | | 1 | 0 | 0 |
| #1 Claude | 1 | | 1 | 0 | 0 |
| Jonny Chen (Non-SAG) | 1 | Allow | 1 | 4,500 | 4,500 |
| | 1 | | 1 | 0 | 0 |
| 3101-02 Lead #2 | 1 | | 1 | 0 | 0 |
| #2 Tina | 1 | | 1 | 0 | 0 |
| Trixe LaRue | 1 | Allow | 1 | 4,000 | 4,000 |
| | 1 | | 1 | 0 | 0 |
| 3101-03 Supporting #3 | 0 | | 0 | 0 | 0 |
| #3 Stanley | 1 | | 1 | 0 | 0 |
| Don Bean | 2 | Weeks | 1 | 700 | 1,400 |

**FIG. 4.21**

Lines at the Detail Level may be used to indicate other key information about cast or crew. Cast often require prep time, but do not need wrap time after shooting unless they need to dub lines for the post production process

Don't assume the production cannot afford a particular cast-related resource until you have done a little research. Also, if your project appeals to a specific niche audience or has a social appeal, stars may make themselves available to the production and take SAG scale. Lead actors often work through a Loan Out corporation – you pay the Loan Out corporation for that person's services and the Loan Out corporation pays the federal and state taxes. You pay SAG or AFTRA fringes if applicable.

SAG performers are categorized as full members in good standing (call SAG) or financial core (hybrid union and non-union status). The cast portion of the budget includes all related expenses (Table 4.29).

*1900 Fringes*

Fringes come in two types: payroll taxes, and Union/Guild payments. Payroll taxes are both federal, and state, paid out as a percent of a worker's pay (that's why they are called *payroll taxes*).

| 1302 - Day Players | | | | |
|---|---|---|---|---|
| Description | Amount | Units | X | Rate |
| Day Player 1 | 1 | | 0 | 0 |
| 1302-01 Day #1 | 1 | | 1 | 0 |
| #1 Louie's Mom | 1 | | 1 | 0 |
| Ima Celebrityo | 1 | Day | 1 | 35,000 |
| SAG: Financial Core | 1 | | 1 | 0 |
| | 1 | | 1 | 0 |
| Patricia's Ima's Trailer | 1 | Allow | 1 | 1,300 |
| Hair/Makeup | 1 | Allow | 1 | 1,800 |
| Assistant | 1 | Allow | 1 | 800 |
| Personal Chef | 1 | Allow | 1 | 650 |
| Misc. Expenses | 1 | Allow | 1 | 250 |
| Dog food for Kiki | 1 | Allow | 1 | 125 |

**FIG. 4.22**

Celebrity cast members may require additional expenses unrelated to their performance

Loan Out companies (which a Director or talent may work through) are not required to pay payroll taxes.

Everyone who is *not* working through a Loan Out company (i.e., most of the crew and cast) is required to pay:

**FICA** SS = Social Security: 6.2% of the employee's salary up to a maximum of $106,800. Once an employee earns over $106,800, the employer stops contributing SS

**FICA** MEDI = Medicare: 1.45% of the employee's salary, with no maximum.

**FUI** = Federal Unemployment Insurance: 0.8% up to a maximum of $7,000. The employer must pay FUI if the worker's total wages equal $1,500 or more during any quarter of the year, and/or if they employed one worker for 20 weeks of the year.

**SUI** = State Unemployment: rates depend on laws of that state.

**WC** = Worker's Compensation (**AKA**: Workman's Comp) provides wage replacement and medical benefits for employees who are injured in the course of employment. It ranges from 4–7%, based on laws in that state, and varies whether or not projects contain dangerous situations (stunts, special effects). If the production's insurance policy for the production covers this, you need not apply it. There's no cut-off; it must continue to be paid regardless of employee earnings.

When your film uses a payroll service (great idea), they will charge you a fee as a percentage of payroll, such as 0.5%, or as a per-check fee.

**Table 4.29**

| | | |
|---|---|---|
| 1401 | LEAD 1 | Stars sell tickets, which is why their salaries can be so extreme. Stars require working through their agent (10% will be added on top of salary). Unknown actors may work for SAG scale wages, deferred pay, share in the profits, minimum wage, or "subject to negotiation" for new media |
| | | |
| 1402 | LEAD 2 | |
| 1403 | LEAD 3, etc. | |
| 1404 | WEEKLY SUPPORTING | Actors working 4 days or more, hired on a weekly basis |
| 1405 | WEEKLY/DAY PLAYERS | Actors working 3 days or less. Local/non union will save money |
| 1406 | STUNT COORDINATOR | **AKA:** Stunt Gaffer. Experienced Stunt Coordinator can plan the best looking and safest stunt; there are specialties relating to the materials or skills (fire, water, falling, vehicles) required for the stunts. Start with this person for pricing all of the equipment and people needed for stunt work |
| 1407 | STUNTS & ADJUSTMENTS | Stunt people are paid as actors and given pay bumps: "adjustments" based on the difficulty and dangerousness of the stunt |
| 1408 | LOOPING | **AKA:** ADR (Automatic Dialogue Replacement) where the actor performs their lines for audio only |
| 1409 | VOICE-OVERS | Audio narration recorded |
| 1410 | FORCED CALLS | SAG actors are required to take a 12-hour consecutive Rest Period (Turnaround), and violation of either daily or weekly rest period is known as a "forced call". The penalty is one day's pay or $950. |
| 1413 | CASTING DIRECTOR | Helps find and audition cast; they know agents, actors, rates. Prep day $200–1,000, and casting day $400–1,500 depending on # roles |
| 1414 | CASTING DIRECTOR ASSISTANTS | Assisting Casting Director |
| 1415 | CASTING EXPENSES | Casting office, use of a computer, video camera. Extras cast by separate company specializing in extras |
| 1416 | STUNT PURCHASES/ RENTALS | Stunts typically require rigging, wire, pads, small exploding squibs for bullets, blood bags or fake blood-filled capsules; fire stunts require gloves, hoods, special clothing, oxygen tank, flammable gel, mortar and prima chord for explosions |
| 1441 | LEAD 1 TRAVEL AND LIVING | May include car rental, limos, hotel and accommodations, per diem (a certain amount of $ "per day" for whatever – food, gum, newspapers), and the array of expenses allocated to transport and care for the Above the Line personnel. This category requires clear parameters and monitoring, or can be used to build up a budget |
| 1442 | LEAD 2 TRAVEL AND LIVING | |
| 1443 | LEAD 3 TRAVEL AND LIVING | |
| 1451 | AIRFARES | Union rules may require first class |
| 1454 | LIVING EXPENSES | Accommodations or per diem |

In Movie Magic Budgeting (and many other budgeting-specific software programs), you can set up a total fringes line as in Table 4.30, where the computer keeps track of the total number of fringes, making it easier for accounting purposes. In this example, the total includes all the Above the Line fringes, like WGA, SAG, WGA payments, and payroll-related fees.

**Table 4.30**

| Act No | Description | Amount | Units | X | Rate | Subtotal | Total |
|---|---|---|---|---|---|---|---|
| 1999 | Total Fringes | 20.94% | | | | | |
| | FICA-SS | 6.2% | | | | | |
| | FICA-MEDI | 1.45% | | | | | |
| | FUI | 0.8% | | | | | |
| | SUI: (STATE) | 8.6% | | | | | |
| | WC: (STATE) | 3.89% | | | | | |

Union/Guild fringes are mandated by corresponding organizations and are subject to change when guilds or unions update their agreements. Above the Line fringes include:

WGA 12.5%
DGA 13.25%
SAG 15.3%

Below the Line fringes include:

DGA 13.25%
IATSE $2.16 per hour
IATSE and Teamsters Trust Account $1.00 per hour
Possibly AFM (30%) for musicians working on your score
SAG 15.3% looping, singers

You can add lines for overtime and state sales tax, vacation and holiday pay as is customary (if you think you will need them), in addition to standard payroll taxes.

**Below the Line: Production**

We will work in a sequential way through categories in the order of their account number. Readers are encouraged to consider the Locations (3600) section of the budget early in planning process, as that will inform many other Below the Line figures. Just as many decisions about film production stem from the choice of Director, the same is true for locations. *Where* you will shoot will determine other factors of the project, for example who is hired, who is transported to a specific place, applying for local production incentives, available crew base. Once you know where (country, region, state, city) you want to shoot, pricing Below the Line costs is a straightforward process.

*2000 Production Staff*

Production staff consists of the folks managing the production office and overall logistics: wardens of the schedule and budget, hiring and making sure people get paid. Big productions might use a large production staff in addition to a Line Producer, while smaller productions may have a lean production staff.

Historically, a studio, with many films in various stages of progress, had a Production Manager overseeing one production, among many. Today, that position is more likely to bear the title Production Executive. Whether you employ a PM to manage the entire production, and a Line Producer (non-union) to manage every "line" of the budget, and a PM or UPM (DGA) (overseeing a second unit), depends on the budget, and complexity of the production. Small films need just one UPM, and possibly no Line Producer — in which case all management of the schedule and budget falls under the domain of the UPM.

Together the PM (overseeing office staff) and the 1st Assistant Director (the Director's right hand overseeing the set) drive progress on the film on a day-to-day basis, keep everyone informed, make sure equipment is available, and that people are where they're supposed to be. On behalf of the Producer and Director, these two make many hiring decisions and are often the front lines of information.

Compact crews may just include one AD, then add another for a complex day to handle paperwork, oversee actor preparation, and work with background actors. Complex productions might utilize a 2nd 2nd AD and/or 3rd AD hired for cumbersome situations, like moving large groups, to supervise PAs (Production Assistants).

Whatever you call them, and however their duties are divided, one of the LP, PM, or UPM is a chief keeper of the budget and schedule. They need lots of prep, all shoot, and maximum wrap time to open and set up the office, and effectively close it out after meeting all billing, invoicing, returns, etc. at the end of the project. Inexperienced crew need two to three times prep as shoot time, experienced crew can get away with less. The right arm of this person is usually the Production Coordinator, maintaining order in the office.

For example, let's assume the production will use a Production Manager who is a DGA member. Set this account up carefully and you can copy/paste it to other DGA crew accounts. The account might look like the example in Table 4.32.

Whether in a scheduling program, Excel or on paper, you can insert information so you don't have to look elsewhere for it, for example the location of the hire (NY

**Table 4.31**

| | | |
|---|---|---|
| 2001 | LINE PRODUCER | Keeps film on schedule and budget. Manages entire production, if working alone, spearheads prep, may break down script, and manage schedule and budget throughout; reports to Producer. Logistical leader, $2,200–7,000/wk |
| 2002 | PRODUCTION MANAGER | If working without LP, fulfills Line Producer duties. If working with LP, reports to LP to maintain budget and schedule, (DGA) $2,000–6,500/wk |
| 2003 | UNIT PRODUCTION MANAGER | PM may require support, or this person may oversee a 2nd Unit (DGA) |
| 2004 | FIRST ASSISTANT DIRECTOR | Front line of on-set information and safety, runs the set on behalf of Director, $4,400–6,200/wk |
| 2005 | SECOND ASSISTANT DIRECTOR | As the 1st AD is to the Director, the 2nd AD is to the 1st AD. Wrangles paperwork. Stands in for 1st AD if they have to leave set, $3,000–4,100/wk |
| 2007 | 3RD ASSISTANT DIRECTOR | (**AKA**: "2nd 2nd AD" ) When necessary, $2,700–3,900/wk |
| 2008 | SCRIPT SUPERVISOR | Guards continuity within a film, usually by taking lots of pictures, (IATSE) $29–32/hr |
| 2009 | LOCATION MANAGER | Researches, scouts, manages locations, (Teamsters) $1,400–2,000/wk |
| 2010 | ASST LOCATION MANAGER | Assists location manager as needed, (Teamsters) $1,200–1,400/wk |
| 2011 | PRODUCTION COORDINATOR | (**AKA**: POC – Production Office Coordinator) Wrangles paperwork and safety training, keeps records. Works prep, shoot, wrap, (IATSE) $1,250–1,350 |
| 2012 | ASST OFFICE COORDINATOR/ SECRETARY | Assists POC as needed, $860–920/wk |
| 2013 | PA-OFFICE STAFF ASSISTANTS | Assist office with anything and everything, $75–200/day |
| 2014 | PA-SET STAFF ASSISTANTS | Assist set with anything and everything, $75–200/day |
| 2015 | PRODUCTION ACCOUNTANT | May be hired as a firm or individual, (IATSE) $1,900–2,100/wk |
| 2016 | ASST PRODUCTION ACCOUNTANTS | Assist the production accountant, (IATSE) $28–31/hr |
| 2050 | SAFETY OFFICER | Crew member videotapes rehearsals and safety meetings |
| 2085 | OTHER COSTS | Production office supplies, purchases and rentals |

Hire), rate and union status – it's a matter of personal taste. DGA members require production fees (weekly bonus paid when camera rolls) and severance (1 week of pay upon completion of assignment), while non-DGA members do not. Computer rental and supplies are a good investment.

A non-union version of this account might look like the example in Table 4.33.

**Table 4.32**

| 2001 – PRODUCTION MANAGER | | | | | |
|---|---|---|---|---|---|
| | **Amount** | **Unit** | **X** | **Rates** | **Subtotal** |
| DGA: | | | | | |
| NY Hire | | | | | |
| *$5,000-wk, 6 day wks* | | | | | |
| Prep Local | 5 | Weeks | 1 | 5,000 | 25,000 |
| Shoot Local | 3 | Weeks | 1 | 5,000 | 15,000 |
| Wrap Local | 2 | Weeks | 1 | 5,000 | 10,000 |
| | | | | | |
| Prep Distant | 4 | Weeks | 1 | 6,000 | 24,000 |
| Shoot Distant | 2 | Weeks | 1 | 6,000 | 12,000 |
| Wrap Distant | 1 | Week | 1 | 6,000 | 6,000 |
| | | | | | |
| Production Fee – Local | 3 | Weeks | 1 | 723 | 2,169 |
| Production Fee – Distant | 2 | Weeks | 1 | 863 | 1,726 |
| Severance | 1 | Flat | 1 | 5,000 | 5,000 |
| **SUBTOTAL** | | | | | **100,895** |
| | | | | | |
| Computer Rental | 1 | Allow | 1 | 500 | 500 |
| Computer Supplies | 1 | Allow | 1 | 250 | 250 |
| Car Allowance | 5 | Weeks | 1 | 250 | 1,250 |
| | | | | | |
| **Total Fringes** | | | | | **31,253** |
| **Total** | | | | | **134,148** |

Table 4.34 shows non-union rates for production office staff.

*2100 Extra Talent*

*Extras*: If you are using casting assistance, ask for their help in this area as well. Costs in this category include actors without lines, stand-ins, general background to fill out the screen, transportation for them, meals, wardrobe fittings, interviews and overtime (Table 4.35) Extras (**AKA**: background or atmosphere) may be paid daily, weekly, or as a flat rate, are usually paid minimum wage, or close to it and must also be fed. Communicating with large groups of people tends to be difficult, so don't expect days with large groups of extras to move as quickly as days without them. (Under severe budget constraints, shoot somewhere lots of people congregate). As a rule, extras do not speak, and are directed by an AD, rather than the Director.

**Table 4.33**

| 2001 – PRODUCTION MANAGER | | | | | |
|---|---|---|---|---|---|
| | **Amount** | **Unit** | **X** | **Rates** | **Subtotal** |
| Non-DGA: | | | | | |
| NY Hire | | | | | |
| *$4,000-wk, 6 day wks* | | | | | |
| Prep Local | 5 | Weeks | 1 | 4,000 | 20,000 |
| Shoot Local | 3 | Weeks | 1 | 4,000 | 12,000 |
| Wrap Local | 2 | Weeks | 1 | 4,000 | 8,000 |
| | | | | | |
| Prep Distant | 4 | Weeks | 1 | 5,000 | 20,000 |
| Shoot Distant | 2 | Weeks | 1 | 5,000 | 10,000 |
| Wrap Distant | 1 | Week | 1 | 5,000 | 5,000 |
| | | | | | |
| **SUBTOTAL** | | | | | **75,000** |
| | | | | | |
| Computer Rental | 1 | Allow | 1 | 500 | 500 |
| Computer Supplies | 1 | Allow | 1 | 250 | 250 |
| Car Allowance | 5 | Weeks | 1 | 250 | 1,250 |
| | | | | | |
| **Total Fringes** | | | | | **9,504** |
| **Total** | | | | | **86,504** |

**Table 4.34**

| | **Budget Ranges** | | |
|---|---|---|---|
| | **$1m or less** | **$1m to $6m** | **$6m or more** |
| Line Producer | $2,200/wk | $3,200/wk | $5,000/wk |
| Production Supervisor | 1,500/wk | 2,000/wk | 2,800/wk |
| Production Secretary | 700/wk | 800/wk | 900/wk |
| PA in office or on set | 8/hr | 9/hr | 10/hr |

*2200 Set Design*

Working in tandem with the Director, the *Production Designer* and *Art Director* make sure that every detail an audience sees in a film looks authentic, through careful choice of every color, fabric, and accessory (Table 4.36). This department needs lots of prep time and shoot time but little wrap. Most of these positions are IATSE.

**Table 4.35**

| | | |
|---|---|---|
| 2101 | STAND-INS | An actor who stands in for a principal actor, looks roughly the same, $154/day |
| 2102 | GUILD EXTRAS | Hired to look like a certain type, $139/day |
| 2103 | NON UNION EXTRAS | Hired to look like a certain type, $75–125/day or 10/hr |
| 2110 | EXTRAS CASTING COORDINATOR | Oversees extras, $600–750/wk |
| 2155 | ATMOSPHERE CARS | This includes cars driven by extras to fill out a scene, or parked cars |

**Table 4.36**

| | | |
|---|---|---|
| 2201 | PRODUCTION DESIGNER | Adds considerable production value, by the choice of settings and design, paid weekly $2,500 + ($7,000/wk big budget studio films) |
| 2202 | ART DIRECTOR | Productions may have one or both Production Designer and Art Director, $1,800–2,500 (7,000/wk big budget studio films) |
| 2203 | ASSISTANT ART DIRECTOR | Assists the Art Designer, $600–1,800/wkly |
| 2204 | SET DESIGNERS | Create drawings and renderings as previs to discuss and plan all design, $33/hr |
| 2207 | ILLUSTRATOR | In addition to a set designer, an illustrator may be hired to assist with story boarding and creating artistic, $25–33/hr |
| 2211 | GRAPHICS DESIGNER | Designs sets and props for a film, either with drawings or renderings, under request of Director and Production Designer, $25–33/hr |
| 2213 | ART DEPT COORDINATOR | Renting, buying, inventory, care for design materials, $982–1,100/wkly |
| 2216 | PURCHASES | Research and materials |
| 2217 | COMPUTER/BOX RENTALS | Computer, art kit and materials rented for the use of the art department |
| 2218 | ART DEPT RENTALS | May include special equipment, or computers |
| 2280 | PRINTING/XEROX/ PHOTO DEV | Lots of printing and copying to collect and plan design |
| 2285 | OTHER COSTS | Miscellaneous items that will be required |

*2300 Set Construction and Strike*

Many films don't use sets, because they do all their shooting on location. However, if the production requires a secure, indoor space, with specific sets that cannot be found on location, or need to be used over and over throughout the shoot, it may make sense to budget for them. When planning sets, consider construction, storage, striking them down, proper disposal, and an area to work on and transport materials. Seek more than one bid so you have options. Substantial prep is needed, as well as shoot and wrap time to return, dismantle and dispose of sets.

You can farm out the construction job – retain a company who will do the whole thing and charge you on their payroll. Or you can hire the positions shown in Table 4.37 and carry them on your payroll.

**Table 4.37**

| | | |
|---|---|---|
| 2301 | CONSTRUCTION LABOR | Workers building the set, subcontracted by the Construction Coordinator |
| 2302 | CONSTRUCTION COORDINATOR | Gang boss, hires team, oversees construction. Fee subject to negotiation, $2,000–2,400/wk |
| 2303 | CONSTRUCTION FOREMAN | Answers to coordinator, $25–27/hr |
| 2304 | SCENIC ARTIST | Specializes in painting. Fee subject to negotiation |
| 2307 | BACKINGS | Large backdrops or photographs to add atmosphere to a set |
| 2308 | GREENS | Plants and greenery, alive or plastic, Greensperson $26–28/hr |
| 2309 | SCAFFOLDING | Like any building, scaffolding might be needed to work on set construction |
| 2310 | FIRST AID | Medic to deal with any accidents on set, $350–400/day nurse, EMT, fire officer $550/day and up |
| 2316 | PURCHASES | Construction materials, wood, nails, etc. |
| 2317 | BOX RENTALS | Rent equipment or special tools as required |
| 2318 | EQUIPMENT RENTALS | Rollers, rigging, hoists, hardware, assemblies, harnesses, slings, clamps, trolleys |
| 2321 | SIGNS AND GRAPHICS | When constructing a town or business, you will need corresponding signage |
| 2322 | SETUP/CONSTRUCT OTHER DEPT | If you are outsourcing the entire construction job and you get a package bid, then you do not need to break it down – put that entire fee here |
| 2376 | WAREHOUSE RENTAL | The crew will need a space to build, work on and store sets |
| 2385 | OTHER COSTS | A miscellaneous category |
| 2398 | LOSS & DAMAGE | Insurance and the cost to replace or repair damaged items |

Waste disposal and construction striking may require renting a dumpster, or additional payment for hazardous or flammable materials. States and cities have different rules, so check with your film commission, or the studio where you are renting space.

### *2500 Set Operations*

Set operations consist of grips shading and manipulating light made by the electricians; the caterers and craft services workers feeding everyone; and the various technicians and artists working on set to keep everything set up and running smoothly (Table 4.38).

**Table 4.38**

| 2501 | FIRST COMPANY GRIP | (**AKA:** Key Grip) Runs grip team, needs prep tie, production, some wrap, \$29–32/hr |
|---|---|---|
| 2502 | SECOND COMPANY GRIP | (**AKA:** Best Boy Grip) Assists the Key Grip as needed, \$26–29/hr |
| 2503 | DOLLY GRIP | Operates dolly smoothly (rolling camera around on wheels), \$28–29/hr |
| 2505 | OTHER COMPANY GRIPS | Set up C-stands, apple boxes and sandbags, \$26–27/hr |
| 2507 | SET PAINTER | On the spot painter, fix any paint damage, \$28–30/hr |
| 2508 | STANDBY CARPENTER | On the spot carpenter handyman, \$28–30/hr |
| 2509 | RIGGING CREW | Prepares and rigs set ahead of the shooting crew, \$800–1,000/wk per person |
| 2510 | OTHER LABOR | Extra folks to help set up, carry, move and control all of the gear, \$20–25/hr |
| 2511 | CRAFT SERVICE LABOR | Folks in charge of feeding everyone, \$26–28/hr |
| 2512 | CRAFT SERVICE PURCHASES | The food, plates, supplies, snacks, soda, water, for cast and crew |
| 2516 | PURCHASES | Sandbags, clips, screws, knives, gloves, tape, adhesives, chalk — you name it |
| 2517 | BOX RENTALS | Clamps, stands and grip equipment, and disposable gear a grip owns |
| 2518 | EQUIPMENT RENTALS | Grip equipment |
| 2519 | CRANES | Crane needs a special operator and driver |
| 2585 | OTHER COSTS | Miscellaneous costs |
| 2598 | LOSS & DAMAGE | Insurance and the cost to replace or repair damaged items |

A 1-ton grip truck costs about \$175 per day (a 2-ton truck \$300), plus mileage, fuel, prep and loading charge. The bigger the truck, the more gear you can transport, but the higher the per-day charge. Additional and specialized equipment costs more, and the Key Grip will guide you as to what required is.

***2600 Special Effects***

The *special effects* industry is growing quickly, and is becoming increasingly specialized, depending on the type of effect you are looking for. The most important thing if you are working on an effects-heavy film, or a film with one really dramatic, make or break effect, is that the F/X Supervisor is experienced in this type of effect, and knows which effects houses will nail it. References from crew and post people are important.

This is a category that can be expanded as needed for your project (Table 4.39). This section is specifically for mechanical effects, like fire, smoke, pyrotechnics, explosions, weather effects (rain birds, snow throwers, foggers, ritters for wind), firearms (squibs for fake bullets), as well as electronic effects, like stuff breaking and shattering (balsa wood and harmless sugar glass). You will need adequate time for preparation and safety, as well as to rehearse with the actors and stunt people.

CGI effects (**AKA**: computer generated imagery) are in post production, as 4400 Visual Effects, but all effects require planning during preproduction for seamless integration into the film.

**Table 4.39**

| | | |
|---|---|---|
| 2601 | F/X SUPERVISOR | (**AKA**: Keyman) Requires adequate time to prepare and plan with post house, and to solicit bids, $1,200–1,800/wk (big budget films 45/hr) |
| 2603 | COMPANY F/X TECHNICIANS | All of crafts people executing effects, $800–1,200/wk |
| 2616 | PURCHASES | Runs the gambit from green to blue screen material, squibs, paints and silicone, to foam, resins, clay, and more |
| 2618 | EQUIPMENT RENTALS | Equipment to create the effects |

***2700 Set Dressing***

The *set dressing* (**AKA**: decoration) department (Table 4.40) works closely with the construction and props department under the Production Designer and Director to guarantee a specific look. Regular meetings during prep and production help to eliminate dual efforts between the set and prop departments. Once the Production Designer and Art Director are hired they will want input on who is chosen as Set Decorator. Ample prep is required, as is shoot, and a small amount of wrap, kit or computer rental, and occasionally a line item for research. The planning required can be as intense as the 800 + sets dressed over the *Harry Potter* series, or as simple as using existing furnishings at the location for a film like *The Celebration*.

It is important to clearly denote which items are to be procured as either props *or* set dressing to eliminate any confusion. The actor uses props to act with (grabbing, throwing), but set dressing is used passively (sit or lay on furniture). A good example of this is in the movie *Signs*. A baseball bat is mounted on the wall in the living room as a symbol of past glories. It appears as set dressing, but then Joaquin Phoenix grabs the bat to defend his family and beats up an alien. That baseball bat is a prop, while the rack it is mounted to the wall on is set dressing.

Your Director may not need a storyboard artist for the entire shoot (or the budget might not allow it). However, it can be worthwhile to hire an artist just for storyboarding tricky scenes, stunts, or as a means of saving expensive shoot time.

**Table 4.40**

| | | |
|---|---|---|
| 2701 | SET DECORATOR | Coordinates appropriate set dressing for production design. Subject to negotiation, $1,300–2,000/wk |
| 2703 | LEAD PERSON | Set Decorator crew = Swing Gang – led by the Lead Person, $25–28/hr |
| 2704 | ADDITIONAL SET DRESS LABOR | Elaborates sets, fast load ins and outs need extra time and people, $24–26/hr |
| 2705 | DRAPERY, CARPETING, FIXTURES | A Draper hangs window curtains, and anything that hangs or drapes, $25–28/hr |
| 2712 | MANUFACTURING - MATERIALS | Glue, scissors, nail guns, thread, sewing materials |
| 2716 | PURCHASES | Fabric and carpet, etc. |
| 2718 | RENTALS | Sewing and upholstery machines, scaffolding |
| 2776 | WAREHOUSE RENTAL | Storage during hiatus between shoots |
| 2785 | OTHER COSTS | Miscellaneous line item for anything that doesn't fit neatly into the other categories |
| 2798 | LOSS & DAMAGE | Insurance and the cost to replace or repair damaged items |

### *2800 Property*

The *prop* department works with the art department selecting specific objects, decoration and furnishings that add to the look of a film. Led by the *Property Master*, the prop department requires prep, wrap and a small amount of wrap time to return or sell props.

Chairs, beds and tables aren't considered props when an actor uses them in a typical fashion, but when they are thrown, smashed, or handled with emotional intent to convey meaning, they are props. The Property Master and the art department coordinate their efforts within the vision of the Director and Production Designer. Crew in this department requires plenty of prep time, shoot time, and wrap to return rented props.

**Table 4.41**

| | | |
|---|---|---|
| 2801 | PROPERTY MASTER | Researches, seeks and rents props, $29–32/hr |
| 2802 | ASST PROP MASTER | Helps the Prop Master, inventories and cares for props, $26–29/hr |
| 2803 | ADDITIONAL PROP LABOR | Extra help, $24–26/hr |
| 2812 | MANUFACTURED PROPS | If the Prop Master can't find what they want it may be cheaper to make it |
| 2816 | PURCHASES | Props and things to create, and repair props |
| 2818 | RENTALS | Props expected to stay intact and that can be returned |
| 2820 | WEAPONS EXPERT | A state-licensed crew member with powder and explosives license, $1,500–3,000/wk |
| 2821 | GUNS & WEAPONS | Must possess the proper pistol license for handguns or assault weapons |
| 2898 | LOSS & DAMAGE | Insurance and the cost to replace or repair damaged items |

*2900 Wardrobe*

The work of the wardrobe department is more obvious in historical or period films (*Coco Before Chanel, Jane Eyre, Marie Antoinette*), futuristic films, or highly stylized movies where fashion is a key part of the story (*Black Swan, The Young Victoria, Alice, Sex and the City*), than in typical contemporary film. It is common to procure duplicate pieces for lead actors in case of damage, or to have one outfit as clean and pressed, then the identical outfit as the dirty, wrinkled version if it appears in different scenes.

Without adequate preparation and plenty of staff during a shoot, the wardrobe department can slow everyone down, through no fault of their own. Supervising dressing, jewelry and accessories, including outerwear and uniforms, for many people in a short amount of time requires adequate numbers of people to do the job, and duplicates of clothing close at hand so as not to delay expensive shoot time.

**Table 4.42**

| | | |
|---|---|---|
| 2901 | COSTUME DESIGNER | Curates the visual style of clothing selected and approved for all cast. Subject to negotiation, $1,500–2,400/wk |
| 2902 | ASST COSTUME DESIGNERS | Assist Costume Designer with research, purchases, return wardrobe, $29–32/hr |
| 2903 | WARDROBE SUPERVISOR | Keeps inventory of clothing, assists wardrobe dept, $26–29/hr |
| 2905 | SET COSTUMERS | Assist as needed, $25–27/hr |
| 2908 | ALTERATIONS & REPAIRS | A seamstress or tailor will be needed to mend, sew, and tailor, $23–25/hr |
| 2909 | CLEANING & DYEING | 24-hour nearby access and speedy turnaround are key. $50–750/day depending on how big the cast, and damage to clothes |
| 2916 | PURCHASES | Clothing and accessory purchases |
| 2918 | RENTALS | Sewing machines, steamers, hangers, thread, needles, steamers |
| 2976 | WARDROBE SHOP RENTAL | Racks, hangers |
| 2985 | OTHER COSTS | Storage, digital cameras to take lots of pictures for continuity |
| 2998 | LOSS & DAMAGE | Insurance and the cost to replace or repair damaged items |

*3000 Picture Vehicles and Animals*

Picture vehicles and animals may seem like unusual bedfellows, but they are both types of non-human characters appearing on camera.

Films often show actors driving, and to get those images, we need a picture car or any scooter, truck, car, motorcycle, tank, wagon, in front of a camera. Generally the actor is not operating any vehicle. A tow dolly or trailer may be attached to the vehicle (possibly with a crane arm) for a bird's-eye view. Low budget camera cars may consist of two people shooting from a motorcycle (one driving, one shooting) in front of an actor who actually is driving. This is dangerous and not recommended, but it works at a pinch. Shooting from the back or front seat is possible but doesn't provide much room.

**Table 4.43**

| | | |
|---|---|---|
| 3007 | PICTURE CAR RENTALS | Moving or non-moving, being depicted in the film frame or any vehicles associated with moving the camera ($750–1,500 wk) and hire driver as well, similar rate |
| 3010 | MISC VEHICLE RENTALS | Like Extras, but for cars ($75–450/vehicle) |
| 3011 | REPAIRS/ MODIFICATIONS | Cosmetic changes to cars |
| 3050 | ANIMAL ACTORS | Animal (you will need a wrangler, and/or trainer), transportation |

Animals from different facilities cannot be housed together; they must be protected from equipment, sharp objects, and electricity, and protected from local wild and domesticated animals. There are strict rules regarding work hours and care. The American Humane Society (which issues the official "No Animals Were Harmed"® end-credit) will vet your script (pun intended). They require notification of animal handler names, veterinarian, and types of sets, locations and environmental conditions the animal will be subjected to.

Animal actors and wranglers are part of the Teamsters union. Wranglers are paid anywhere from $31–46 per hour, and animal rates vary up into the thousands depending on rarity and difficulty to train. You might pay $5,000–25,000 per day for the animal during shoot time, and half that during prep and training. Bugs are priced in hundreds or thousands, livestock cost $200 per head per day, trained horses $400 and up, dogs $200 per day, and primates $1,000–5,000 per day.

#### *3100 Make-Up and Hairdressing*

Make-up artists are one of the last touch points an actor has before they are on set. Women generally take from an hour to several hours for make-up and hair, and men generally less, depending on how elaborate the requirements for the film. Make-up and hair need some prep time, and shoot time, but no wrap. High definition has made the work of make-up and hair dressing even more challenging, as we see every pore, detail and hair in greater detail than ever before.

**Table 4.44**

| | | |
|---|---|---|
| 3101 | KEY MAKE-UP ARTIST | Perfects the actors' faces and moods, \$34–36/hr (big budget films \$60/hr) |
| 3102 | ASSISTANT MAKE-UP | Allows adequate budgeting for assistants, \$28–30/hr (big budget films \$50/hr) |
| 3103 | ADDITIONAL MAKE-UP LABOR | Extra make-up stylists may be necessary for heavy days, \$22–27/hr |
| 3105 | PROSTHETICS | Appliances and masks to drastically change features, \$28–30/hr |
| 3111 | KEY HAIR STYLIST | Styles, cuts and dyes hair, \$29–32/hr (big budget films \$60/hr) |
| 3112 | ASSISTANT HAIR STYLIST | Allows adequate budgeting for assistants, \$26–28/hr (big budget films \$50/hr) |
| 3113 | ADDITIONAL HAIR LABOR | Extra hair stylists may be necessary for heavy days, \$20–24/hr |
| 3114 | WIGS & HAIRPIECES | Change actors' appearance, match a stunt double or body double |
| 3116 | PURCHASES | Flat or curling irons, blow dryers, brushes, airbrush make-up systems, product |

*3200 Lighting*

The movie business didn't exist before lights and electricity, and the *electric* department (Table 4.45) creates and maintains lighting on the set, and handles related safety issues. This department creates the light which the other departments use the DP and Director use it like paint on a canvas, the actors move in and through it, and the grips shade, alter and diffuse it. The lighting department creates and utilizes power sources during shooting, and requires adequate prep, shoot and enough wrap to return and account for all equipment.

Not everyone working in the lighting department will be a licensed electrician, but they should understand watts, volts, candle power, color temperature, weights, beam angles, floods, spots, amperage load, outlets, circuit breakers, live cables, fire codes, whether to tie into a building's existing power, and where to rent a generator.

Working with, and around, electricity requires careful planning and is dangerous. Weather conditions and sprinkler systems add to the risk of shock or electrocution in the event of an accident. Electrical staff may be members of IATSE and/or IBEW (International Brotherhood of Electrical Workers).

*3300 Camera*

The camera department (Table 4.46) is led by the DP, who implements the Director's vision through lighting, choice of lens, and camera movement. This department needs adequate time to choose format, due to rapid changes in digital, high definition, and

**Table 4.45**

| | | |
|---|---|---|
| 3201 | CHIEF LIGHTING TECHNICIAN | (**AKA**: Gaffer) heading up the electric dept. DP will have strong opinions about who should hold this important job. Renting their kit will save money, $29–32/hr (big budget films $38/hr) |
| 3202 | BEST BOY | The second electrician, $26–28/hr (big budget films $34/hr) |
| 3203 | GENERATOR OPERATOR | Generator is used on locations without power. Rented with a driver/operator (2nd Company Grip) and driver/operator ($250–300/day) on top of that.The Best Boy may drive and operate it, or an operator will be hired specifically for this task |
| 3204 | LIGHTING LABOR | Set up and move lights safely, $25–29/hr |
| 3206 | RIGGING GAFFER | Pre-rigging and striking is a way to prep a set before the crew arrives, then break it down when they're done, saving expensive shoot time, $25–29/hr |
| 3207 | RIGGING/STRIKE | |
| 3209 | GLOBES/GELS | Tools of the trade to color and diffuse light |
| 3211 | GENERATORS | Price range from $350–$1,000/day, based on the amperage power. Add fuel charge ($100–300 day) and transport |
| 3216 | PURCHASES | Lighting expendables, muslin, battens, marker sprays, fuses and wires |
| 3218 | EQUIPMENT RENTALS | The Chief Lighting Technician will advise on how big a grip package to rent |
| 3219 | LIGHTING PACKAGE | |
| 3220 | STAGE PACKAGE | If you rent a studio space and use their lighting equipment |
| 3285 | OTHER COSTS | Miscellaneous extra equipment, riggings, dimmers |
| 3298 | LOSS & DAMAGE | Insurance and the cost to replace or repair damaged items |

3D formats. The DP should be experienced and comfortable in the format on which the Director wants to shoot.

### *3400 Production Sound*

Great sound contributes to high production value and makes a good film better. Poor sound can make a beautiful looking film painful to watch. Even if your camera picks up sound, you may want a separate sound recording made. The better the sound you get during shoot time, the less you have to do to "fix it in post" or do ADR (automatic dialogue replacement, **AKA:** looping) re-recording actors' lines (Table 4.47).

### *3500 Transportation*

Almost everything in a film needs to be moved at some point – equipment, sets, wardrobe, actors, Director – and the transportation team needs time to plan and obtain the right vehicles for the job. During principal photography, when time is of the essence, this is of critical importance: resources and people must arrive where, and when, they are needed. In addition to budgeting for vehicles, don't forget gas,

**Table 4.46**

| 3301 | DIRECTOR OF PHOTOGRAPHY | (**AKA:** Cinematographer, DP, or DoP [in the U.K.]) generates the Director's vision by specific technical choices: use of a certain camera, film stock, lighting, cameras, lens, camera motion and direction. The Director will certainly want to choose the DP. The DP. is paid subject to negotiation, and may be paid from $500–3,500 per day, highest paid position in Camera dept |
|---|---|---|
| 3302 | CAMERA OPERATOR | Operates the camera, pans, tilts, or handheld movements, $42–46/hr |
| 3304 | STEADICAM OPERATOR | Enables smooth camera movement through attachment of the device onto the operator, $800/day and up |
| 3305 | FIRST ASSISTANT CAMERA | Pulls the focus for the camera, maintains camera reports of good takes, $36–39/hr |
| 3306 | ADDITIONAL CAMERA ASSTS | If required, load film magazines, label film cans, tape, log takes, operate slate (**AKA:** film clapper), $28–30/hr |
| 3307 | CAMERA LOADERS | Load and unload the film properly, and guarantee its safety, $24–26/hr |
| 3308 | STILL PHOTOGRAPHER | Takes pictures of everything on set, $42–46/hr |
| 3316 | PURCHASES | Tape, filters, marking pens, pressurized air, static free wipes, black bags, for example |
| 3318 | EQUIPMENT RENTALS | Additional and specialty cameras |
| 3319 | STEADICAM RENTALS | You need to rent the Steadicam in addition to hiring someone to operate it ($800–1,500/day) |
| 3320 | CAMERA PACKAGE | Panavision, Red Camera, Arriflex, Moviecam, Canon, Sony. Varies widely: $300–2,500 per day depending on format, lenses, supplies, add ons |
| 3385 | OTHER COSTS | Miscellaneous items not specifically mentioned, related to camera gear |
| 3398 | LOSS & DAMAGE | Insurance and the cost to replace or repair damaged items |

**Table 4.47**

| 3401 | SOUND MIXER | Leads the sound team, $47–50/hr |
|---|---|---|
| 3402 | BOOM OPERATOR | Holds the mic on a pole (boom) (hopefully out of the shot), $31–34/hr |
| 3403 | CABLE PERSON | Moves cable out of the way and keeps boom operator safe, $27–31/hr |
| 3410 | DAILIES SOUND TRANSFER | Transfer of sound with time code for editing and synching with picture |
| 3416 | PURCHASES | Tapes and other expendables required by the Sound Mixer |
| 3418 | EQUIPMENT RENTALS | Digital audio tape recorder, booms, mixer unit, mics + tapes, $300–600/day |
| 3420 | SOUND PACKAGE | |
| 3422 | WALKIE TALKIES | Communication for crew working on set to communicate |
| 3498 | LOSS & DAMAGE | Insurance and the cost to replace or repair damaged items |

oil, tolls, parking, and security (Table 4.48). Drivers must have the appropriate class of license for the size and type of the truck.

Transportation is the Teamsters union. The size of the budget will dictate the number, variety, and size of vehicles in your project – anything from honeywagons (trucks with both toilets and dressing rooms) to individual motor homes for your star.

**Table 4.48**

| | | |
|---|---|---|
| 3501 | COORDINATOR | The Transportation Coordinator heads it up, and this person should come on as early as possible. An expert in logistics, this person hires drivers and selects appropriate vehicles. Subject to negotiation, $375/day, $2,500–3,000/wk |
| 3502 | CAPTAIN | A driver supervising other drivers, $36/hr, $1,400–2,500/wk |
| 3504 | LOCATION DRIVERS | As many as necessary, varies by type of vehicle, $18–38/hr, $900–1,800/wk |
| 3516 | PURCHASES | On camera rigged, painted, or modified in some way |
| 3519 | LOCATION RENTALS | Production vehicles to carry gear, people, sets |
| 3520 | SELF-DRIVE VEHICLES | Rental cars for use of key team members on distant shoot, $300–450/wk |
| 3544 | GASOLINE & OIL | Rising and unpredictable, so reinforce this number, and when you are shooting in another state, call around to compare rates as compared to your area |
| 3546 | REPAIRS & MAINTENANCE | If you can swing it, a mechanic is great to have around too |
| 3547 | PARKING/ PERMITS/TAXIS | Depending on where you will shoot, these costs can be substantial |
| 3553 | MEAL ALLOWANCE | Meal allowance while on the road |
| 3585 | OTHER COSTS | Miscellaneous costs |
| 3598 | LOSS & DAMAGE | Insurance and the cost to replace or repair damaged items |

Camera cars $250–600/day

Wardrobe minivan $360/wk

Production van $300–450/day

Honeywagon $450/day, $2,250/wk

Utility truck $1,000–1,500/wk

Water truck $2,000 + /wk

Calculate mileage, gas, parking, maintenance, driver wages and vehicle expenses.

*3600 Location*

Filming "on location" is the norm, and productions use sound stages for music videos, TV, commercials, or for a particular use in a film, such as elaborate sets, the need for quiet or privacy, rigging or special effects shot requirements. Production incentives require specific paperwork and rules, such as hiring local vendors, stages, talent, or crew. They vary from state to state. Ultimately, travel incurs expense, so that fundamental decision about where to shoot, who and what to bring (shipping equipment can be expensive, and not every location has the same quality and quantity of vendors for gear) will substantially impact your budget (Table 4.49).

The fundamental questions upfront are:

- Where will you go?
- Who from your team should travel?
- Who does not need to travel?

Combining sets at one location will save you travel time and money. Utilize film commission websites and online resources like Reel Scout (www.reel-scout.com). Tell everyone about the film, and the type of locations you seek. Access to a great, affordable (or free) location may be worth a (tiny) role in a film, or an *Associate Producer credit.* A location scout can assist you in this process. Once you have chosen a region (state or city) which looks appropriate for the project, pricing Below the Line costs is a straightforward process. Work systematically through each line item.

*3700 Production Film and Lab*

Like so many other things in film production, seek referrals. These charges will take place only during production, for raw stock, developing, printing and dailies; other stock and lab costs belong to Editorial and post production. The DP, with input from the Director and Producer, selects the stock, amount and brand. You can save money by buying short ends, long ends, re-cans (always test film stock no matter where you get it), or 16 mm versus 35 mm (Table 4.50).

*3800 Video Tape: Production*

If you are shooting digitally, stock is covered in the previous account; however, there are specialty areas of videotape that the production may require (Table 4.51).

*4000 Second Unit*

When your production can send an independent unit out to shoot stunts, inserts, cutaways, or establishing shots, and does not need cast members, the Director, or sound. It's an efficient way to double up shoot time, having two teams work at the same time. Simultaneous shooting of an additional unit creates time and cost

**Table 4.49**

| | | |
|---|---|---|
| 3601 | AIRFARES | Certain guild crew members require first class airfare and flight insurance, $150–1,500/RT |
| 3604 | LIVING EXPENSES | On location your team needs a place to stay and per diem money for sundries. Unions stipulate specific meal and per diems for their members |
| 3606 | SCOUTING/SURVEY COSTS | Photos, working with a local rental car company. Vary widely |
| 3607 | LOCATION SITE RENTAL FEES | Whatever the owner and you agree upon — there are no standard rates |
| 3609 | COURTESY PAYMENTS | Gratuities to keep the cameras rolling |
| 3613 | SHIPPING – FEDEX, FREIGHT | Shipping expenses including equipment, wardrobe, props |
| 3614 | SHIPPING – CUSTOMS, TAXES | Shipping tariffs, taxes, and customs charges |
| 3620 | CATERED MEALS | Food ($9–20/meal) + chef/driver, cook/driver (may be one person), $15–30/hr |
| 3621 | CATERER HELPERS | Staff to serve, cook and clean up food and dining area |
| 3622 | CRAFT SERVICE | Snacks, drinks available between meals (varies $20–250/day) |
| 3624 | WATER | |
| 3630 | SECURITY SERVICES | Guards to watch over equipment, wardrobe, vehicles |
| 3631 | POLICE & FIREMEN | As required by local regulations, $20–35/hr |
| 3632 | MISC LOCAL EMPLOYEES | Locals can provide you with good information faster |
| 3640 | PRODUCTION OFFICE RENTAL | Production office space |
| 3641 | XEROX RENTAL & SUPPLIES | Copiers, paper, printers, toner, phone service |
| 3642 | TELEPHONE | |
| 3643 | MOBILE TELEPHONES | |
| 3646 | OFFICE PURCHASES | |
| 3647 | OFFICE EQUIPMENT RENTALS | |
| 3698 | LOSS & DAMAGE | Insurance and the cost to replace or repair damaged items |

efficiencies. Hire a company that specializes in second unit work, paying for just a day or so of film, or per foot. Or send your own second unit crew.

***4100 Tests***

To determine whether a certain look, actor, film stock, or set dressing is right, the team may want to run make-up, wardrobe, camera or screen tests to verify their choice before committing to a specific effect, equipment, stock, style, look or person.

**Table 4.50**

| 3702 | NEGATIVE FILM | Raw stock for film (priced by foot or roll) and digital, priced by tape or solid state component, memory stick or P2 card |
|---|---|---|
| 3704 | NEGATIVE DEVELOP | Processing is priced by foot, and 16 mm is cheaper than 35 mm |
| 3705 | PRINT DAILIES | The workprint, lab's price per foot. Shooting on anything besides P2 cards or memory stick, the format will have to be transferred to a digital format |
| 3729 | LAB PROCESSING | |
| 3785 | OTHER COSTS | Miscellaneous prices related to buying and testing stock |

**Table 4.51**

| 3809 | VIDEO PLAYBACK | When a television or computer screen prop or set dressing must play images that will look correct on camera |
|---|---|---|
| 3815 | TELEPROMPTER | Used to aid actors by showing their lines |

*4200 Stages*

Renting facilities such as sound stages may be essential if you require controlled environment. Indies may be able to get away with using an empty warehouse (*Reservoir Dogs*), while a production company working with a studio may be required to use the studio's facilities, equipment, personnel, and commissary. Understand exactly what costs the production will be responsible for. You do not want to pay for duplicate equipment; schedule studio time at the end of principal photography, after you have returned non-studio rental equipment to vendors.

**Table 4.52**

| 4202 | SOUND STAGES | Usually, the facility will require you to use their equipment. Priced by day |
|---|---|---|
| 4250 | TRASH REMOVAL | The facility will bill you for proper trash removal |
| 4285 | OTHER COSTS | Storage fees, additional personnel on hand, overtime, security |

*4399 Total Fringes (Below the Line Production)*

Union/Guild fringes are mandated by corresponding organization and are subject to change when guilds or unions update their agreements (Table 4.53). Below the Line fringes include:

- DGA 13.25%
- SAG 15.3%
- IATSE $2.46 per hour
- Teamsters $2.46 per hour
- Teamsters IATSE and Teamsters Trust Account $1.00 per hour.

Add lines for overtime and state sales tax, vacation and holiday pay as is customary (if you think you will need them), in addition to standard payroll taxes.

**Table 4.53**

| Act No | Description | Amount | Units | X | Rate | Subtotal | Total |
|---|---|---|---|---|---|---|---|
| 4399 | Total Fringes | | | | | | |
| | FICA-SS | 6.2% | | | | | |
| | FICA-MEDI | 1.45% | | | | | |
| | FUI | 0.8% | | | | | |
| | SUI: (STATE) | 8.6% | | | | | |
| | WC: (STATE) | 3.89% | | | | | |

**Below the Line: Post Production**

Post means "after," so post production is what supposedly happens *after* shooting. However, planning for post production happens *early* in the preproduction process; your Editor and post facilities have a big impact on the completed film, and the editing process begins during principal photography, as soon as there is footage to edit.

Hire a *post production supervisor*, or assign these duties to an Associate Producer. This person will serve as a liaison, project manager and facilitator. Post production could be very complex and expensive, with multiple editors and offshore effects teams; it depends on whether the end film is to be effects-laden, hit song- and music-driven, or relatively streamlined if the editing department is one person using Final Cut nearby.

Advances in technology offer increased options in post production, so it's important to understand exactly what has to happen and in what order, and what the Editor or lab requires to do their job.

A good Editor makes magic on a daily basis, and starts at the beginning of production. *If you pay only four people in your crew, let it be the Editor, the caterer, the Sound Person, and the DP.* An Assistant Editor logs and tracks footage to help the Editor do their job better. (Motion Picture Editors Guild is part of IATSE.)

Depending on your budget, you may hire a *Music Supervisor* or *Music Producer*, who will find a *composer* to write an original score (with the Director's approval), buy music from a music library, or track down the cost of using pre-existing songs.

If you have a distribution deal in place, it is important to get the delivery requirements as soon as possible, for production, and also get them in the hands of the post production supervisor. This information will be needed to make sure you complete all the final deliverables, on whatever format on aspect ratio is required.

CGI effects (**AKA:** computer generated imagery) may include green or blue screen (so you can key out those wild colors and add any background), composites and matte shots (creating vivid backgrounds by combining parts of different images, sometimes overlaid additional hand drawn or computer images), rotoscoping and extensive previsualization (**AKA:** previs) to make sure the effects are well planned. The more numerous and elaborate the effects, the more expensive and larger this category will be — it might swell to include animators, models, special computer programs, matte painters, compositors, or motion capture technology.

Without a distribution deal, the completed format of your project depends on the Producer's intended end use. Budget for sound sweetening and color correction in local labs to get the film as clear sounding and good looking as possible prior to making copies for festival and competition entries, as the competition is fierce.

*4400 Visual Effects*

A 1-hour conversation with effects folks prior to production can save thousands of dollars and tons of time in post, so start asking around as early as possible to find the right people and company for the production. Effects can be outsourced as a complete package, depending on their amount and complexity; it is important to solicit several bids for the sake of comparison. There is a wide variety of effects: optical, animation, models, previs programs, painting backgrounds, motion graphics. This is a rapidly growing part of the film industry; expand or condense this section as is necessary for the type of film you are making (Table 4.54).

**Table 4.54**

| | | |
|---|---|---|
| 4402 | SPECIAL VISUAL EFFECTS | From animators to render stations, programmers, webmasters, character designers and modelers, compositors and the myriad of optical effects, expand or contract this category as needed. Effects are priced as flat package, hourly or weekly depending on the technology and vendor |
| 4499 | FRINGE BENEFITS & PR TAXES | At this time, there isn't a guild specifically for visual effects artists. Add payroll taxes for each employee (unless outsourcing the work) and add fringes for IATSE Editors |

*4501 Editing*

A film is written three times (at least). The first time when the script is created by the Writer, the second when the Director creates the vision for it through shooting, and the third when the Editor interprets both story and footage during the edit process. Depending on whether you shoot on film or video, the processes or duties may be slightly different. The Editor is as important a creative force on a film as the DP and Director, and begins work during production.

Editing choices: hire an Editor with their own equipment (mobile and cheapest); hire an Editor and rent a space; or engage a post production facility (convenient but expensive). Most editing is done in the computer, then the film is output to the desired format.

**Table 4.55**

| | | |
|---|---|---|
| 4501 | EDITORS | Start during production, screen dailies, select footage, assemble rough cut $2,400–2,900/wk (big budget films $6,000–8,000/wk) |
| 4502 | ASSISTANT EDITORS | Log and organize footage, the Editor's right-hand person, $1,400–1,650/wk |
| 4503 | LOOPING EDITOR & ASST | Edit ADR tracks, $1,400–1,650/wk |
| 4504 | MUSIC EFFECTS EDITOR & ASST | Create music track, confirm sync, prep music cue sheets. Music Editor: $1,700–2,500 wk. Asst $1,400–1,650/wk |
| 4505 | SOUND EFFECTS EDITOR & ASST | Suggest and source sound effects, supervise foley sessions, synch effects to picture ("Pre-Lay" in video). Editor: $1,700–2,500 wk, $300–450/day; Asst: $1,400–1,650/wk |
| 4509 | CODING | On film, to keep workprint and sound print in sync, after the film is cut |
| 4510 | PROJECTION | Whatever we pay to rent the space used to project dailies, screen tests |
| 4511 | MUSIC EFX - PURCHASES/RENTALS | Costs for temporary "temp" track while working on a project or music effects |
| 4515 | EDIT EQUIPMENT/ SUPPLIES | Software, hardware as required, shipping if editing on location, costs for drives for extra memory ($250–1,500), benches, supplies |
| 4516 | FILM SHIPPING & MESSENGERS | Shipping and messenger costs, for dailies, prints, or paperwork during editing |
| 4517 | POST PRODUCTION SUPERVISOR | Oversees and coordinates post process and vendors, $1,500–3,500/wk |
| 4520 | CGI & DIGITAL EFFECTS | Creation of computer effects and graphics, varies depending on complexity. Effects can be outsourced for cost savings, then incorporated by an Editor. Obtain multiple bids, consult your Editor. Priced by effect, at an hourly rate, $25–150/hr |
| 4530 | ELECTRONIC EDITING SYSTEMS | Avid or Final Cut systems $2,500–6,500/wk, edit bay rental, editing space. Costs vary widely, $250–2,500 /wk depending on where you edit, whether you use your Editor's equipment, a well-equipped post house, and how long it takes, $250–2,500/wk |
| 4536 | FILM TO TAPE TRANSFERS | Priced by the foot 0.12–.50/foot, or hourly ($650 + /hr High Def, $385/hr NTSC Digital Video), plus cost of tape stock |
| 4541 | DUBS | Dub prices depend on the format and quantity, DVDs $12–25 |
| 4551 | TRAVEL & LIVING EXPENSES | Housing and transporting editing team if necessary |
| 4585 | OTHER COSTS | Miscellaneous, from OT, to client services |

*4600 Music*

There are several options: create an original score, license pre-recorded music from a music library and pay needledrop fees per usage, buy royalty-free music (one song or a collection at a flat rate), or license existing recorded songs (can be expensive and time-consuming). The Producer, Director and Editor will feel strongly about the film's music. Start looking for a composer during prep.

Many composers create the entire score with a synthesizer from a home studio with samples that closely approximate a live score. It is cost prohibitive to hire live musicians, but even a few live tracks over a synthesizer create a vivid effect. You can get a package deal for the entire music score, at a flat rate. The composer will produce and record everything, presenting you with finished tracks, and you avoid having to deal with AFM (musicians' union). A flat rate feature score might range from $20,000 to $75,000, depending on the composer, length of the film and nature of the music programming.

**Table 4.56**

| | | |
|---|---|---|
| 4601 | MUSICIANS | Live musicians, AFM rates ($260–300/session + $130–200/session for doubling). Contractor who hires musicians, $775–800/session |
| 4602 | COMPOSERS-LYRICISTS | Screen edited film, "spot" where music will go, compose and record music. Prices range from $20 k and up to $1 m for composing celebrities. |
| 4603 | ARRANGERS-ORCHESTRATORS | Chosen by composer. Take composer's idea and arrange or orchestrate music as required. Charge per page, $30–75/pg |
| 4604 | COPYISTS | Chosen by composer. Charge per page, $30–75/pg |
| 4608 | SINGERS | Covered under SAG and AFTRA (Solo and Duo, $875/day) |
| 4614 | SCORING CREW & FACILITY | Recording facility, midi and programming fees, room rates, tuning, setup, $150–350/hr, negotiate day rate, "lock-out" for less than hourly. Engineers, $1,200–2,000/day. Scoring stage and mixdown, $1,200–1,900/day |
| 4615 | TRAVEL & LIVING | Housing and transporting composer if necessary |
| 4617 | INSTRUMENT RENTALS | Paid to Doublers (saxophone who plays clarinet for example) |
| 4618 | CARTAGE | Fee to bring big instruments to session: harp, bass, cello, percussion, pianos |
| 4646 | MUSIC RIGHTS | May include mechanical, publishing, synch rights |
| 4695 | STUDIO CHARGES | Administrative costs, contractors |

Music rights are complex; you may need permission from the publisher, composer, performer and/or record label. Sync rights are required to synchronize music to visuals, and a license to reproduce a record in a film is a "master use" license. With any non-original music score that is not royalty-free, start with ASCAP, BMI and an entertainment lawyer.

*4700 Post Production Sound*

In addition to music, sound consists of the recorded dialogue from production, creating and adding sound effects (foley), and recording dialogue (ADR or Looping) or narration for clear sound. No matter how lovely the images, or how amazing the music, if the audience cannot understand the dialogue, an important aspect of the film is lost.

**Table 4.57**

| | | |
|---|---|---|
| 4703 | TRANSFER COSTS | Transfer sound from the original format, and/or DAT recording to editing format. Priced per foot, $0.35–0.45/ft (depending on format) |
| 4706 | SOUND PACKAGE | ADR, foley and mix. Record dialogue for clearer sound, requires bringing back actors. Foley artists find appropriate sound effects or create them. Foley stages $300–450/hr, Foley artists $375–500/day |
| 4709 | MIX | (**AKA:** Dub) Pre-dub, $200–400/hr. Final dub – mixed to stereo sound all effects and music, $350–800/hr. Sound sweetening, priced hourly, $200–500/hr. Layering dialogue tracks and music to create depth, mixed in time to picture. Cost varies, $1,000–4,000/day or hourly depending on the service |
| 4710 | M&E | M&E (music and effect) tracks, plus dialogue |
| 4717 | RENTALS | Stage rental and equipment foley, costs vary depending on where the sound work is done. Recording studios charge by day ($1,200–5,000), or work stations and pre-dub by the hour ($150–500/hr) |
| 4785 | OTHER COSTS | Create temp dubs for previews |
| 4790 | SOUND PROCESS LICENSE FEES | Dolby licensing, noise reduction, surround and stereo ($10,000 per feature) |

*4800 Post Production Film and Lab*

Once a film has been completely edited in the computer, i.e., the picture, sound, dialogue, effects, dissolves, fades, titles, music, and color, and has been sound sweetened, a key decision to be made (usually during preproduction) is on what format the film will be output. There are many formats, from DVD to output for digital cinema projection, 35 mm, digibeta or DVCcam, which may be required for broadcasting. Solicit bids from different labs depending on the plans for the film. If you are working with a distribution company, they will provide you with explicit instructions and lists of all delivery requirements such as run time, technical formats, documentation, and required marketing materials (Table 4.58).

*5299 Total Fringes (Below the Line Post Production)*

Fringes for post production include all payroll taxes to employees working in post production (Table 4.59).

**Table 4.58**

| | | |
|---|---|---|
| 4810 | STOCK FOOTAGE | License pre-existing clips, priced by second, varies widely depending on how long a clip you use, how historic or iconic it is, the source (studio or stock footage library) and the film's ultimate distribution. Additional cost for research, locating the footage you need, and converting it to the proper format |
| 4819 | PRINTS & REPRINTS | A series of prints is created depending on final delivery format of project. Priced by foot |
| | | Print to film requires an answer print ($0.95–$1.09/ft), composite, show print, Interpositive, Internegative ($0.93–.99/ft) until a final answer print |
| 4820 | SOUND NEGATIVE-DEVELOP | Usually a flat rate, $7,000–10,000 |
| 4826 | ANSWER PRINT/ PROTECT MASTERS | Lab combines cut negative, coloring code, optical soundtrack, optical effects and titles, repeated until film is perfect. Answer print (1.00–1.15/ft) or flat rate |
| 4827 | OPTICAL MFG | Optical effects created – fades, dissolves, titles, head and end credits. Convert sound tape to optical track to marry w/picture |
| 4828 | MISC LAB COSTS | Timing and color correction, additional prints |
| 4830 | NEGATIVE CUTTING | Film: negative and effects cut and conformed by negative cutter based on EDL (edit decision list). Digital: if shot on tape, master edited online, using EDL, creates new master |
| 4840 | VIDEO CASSETTES | Creation of video masters |
| 4885 | OTHER COSTS | Rush charges, overtime |

**Table 4.59**

| Act No | Description | Amount | Units | X | Rate | Subtotal | Total |
|---|---|---|---|---|---|---|---|
| 1999 | Total Fringes | | | | | | |
| | FICA-SS | 6.2% | | | | | |
| | FICA-MEDI | 1.45% | | | | | |
| | FUI | 0.8% | | | | | |
| | SUI: (STATE) | 8.6% | | | | | |
| | WC: (STATE) | 3.89% | | | | | |



Union/guild fringes include IATSE payments for Picture and Sound Editors, their assistants, and foley artists, AFM and SAG if applicable.

Below the Line fringes include:

DGA 13.25%

IATSE $2.46 per hour

IATSE and Teamsters Trust Account $1.00 per hour

Possibly AFM (30%) for musicians working on your score

SAG 15.3% looping, singers

You can add lines for overtime and state sales tax, vacation and holiday pay as is customary (if you think you will need them), in addition to standard payroll taxes.

**Below the Line: Other Expenses**

*Other* expenses (Table 4.60) are those that apply to the production as a whole (insurance and legal costs), the future of the production (publicity and marketing), financing, and miscellaneous costs that do not fit easily into one particular category. These types of expenses are calculated as "contractual", a certain percent based on the entire budget.

*Publicity* costs include everything paid for to the end of getting the film out there – postcards, premiums, website, festival and market and contest applications. Publicity is just as important as making the film itself. Plan marketing that fits with the project from prep, allocate a robust budget, and get someone working on this from the outset.

Stacey Parks' *Inside Guide to Independent Film Distribution* (Focal Press), and Jon Reiss' *Think Outside the Box Office* (jonreiss.com) offer great tips in this arena.

*Insurance* may be purchased for the duration of the shoot (if it's a short-term production), as is common on features; or a year-long policy (e.g., annual Producer's insurance policy, or production DICE: Documentary, Industrial, Commercial, Educational) may be more practical for documentarians, longer-term projects, or a company with a series of projects over a year.

Filmmakers think "I can't afford insurance," but you can't afford to get sued either, right? *General liability, employer liability, auto* and *workmen's comp*, at the minimum, will help you sleep better at night. The upfront cost is relatively small compared with catastrophic damages in the case of a lawsuit, severe injuries or death.

*Legal costs* range from 3–10% of the total budget, depending on the source of your material, amount of legal contracts and advice needed, and help with understanding and negotiating a distribution contract.

**Table 4.60**

| | | |
|---|---|---|
| 6500 | PUBLICITY | Everything from posters to festival attendance costs, trailer creation |
| 6700 | INSURANCE & LEGAL | Insurance (3–6%). Legal fees (3–10%), contracts, script clearance, title registration |
| 6800 | GENERAL EXPENSE | Administrative, business license, MPAA rating (2,500 + features, $750 shorts) |

## Sample Budgets

**Table 4.61**

| **Industrial Film: Salon & Make-up Demo** | **Title: Tempt-Tress** | | |
|---|---|---|---|
| **Shoot: 1 day** | **Producer: Sally Forth** | | |
| **Prep: 3 days** | **Budget date: 8/1/2010** | | |
| **Post: 6 days** | SCRIPT DATE: 7/23/2010 V3_TT | | |
| **Product demo** | Budget prep: Constance Lai | | |
| | | | |
| **ABOVE THE LINE** | **Qty** | **Rate** | **Total cost** |
| Writer | 1 | 500 | $500 |
| Producer | 1 | 900 | 900 |
| Director | 1 | 800 | 800 |
| Models | 5 | 500 | 2500 |
| **TOTAL ABOVE THE LINE** | | | **4,700** |
| | | | |
| **BELOW THE LINE** | | | |
| **PRODUCTION** | **Qty** | **Rate** | **Total cost** |
| Production Manager | 2 | 700 | 1400 |
| Cameras (includes gear/personnel) | 2 | 1,500 | 3000 |
| Gaffer | 1 | 600 | 600 |
| Grip | 1 | 200 | 200 |
| 2 Production Assistants | 2 | 150 | 300 |
| Key Hair | 1 | 700 | 700 |
| Key Make-up | 2 | 500 | 1000 |
| Sound | 1 | 300 | 300 |
| Lighting Equipment Rental | 1 | 350 | 350 |
| Transportation of Gear and Equipment | 1 | 100 | 100 |
| Tape Stock | 4 | 20 | 80 |
| Catering | 18 | 20 | 360 |
| **PRODUCTION TOTAL** | | | **8,390** |
| | | | |
| **POST PRODUCTION** | | | |
| Editing (includes high end graphics, logging and editing) | 8 | 1,500 | 12,000 |
| 1 Music Composer | 1 | 1,700 | 1,700 |
| 1 Voice-over Session | 2 | 250 | 500 |
| 1 Voice-over Talent | 1 | 1,000 | 1,000 |
| DVD Authoring | 1 | 1,000 | 1,000 |
| **POST PRODUCTION TOTAL** | | | **16,200** |
| | | | |
| Total Above the Line | | | 4,700 |
| Total Below the Line | | | 24,590 |
| ***Subtotal*** | | | ***$29,290*** |
| Contingency | | | $2,929.00 |
| **GRAND TOTAL** | | | **$32,219.00** |

Tables 4.62 and 4.63 show examples from micro budget films. On bigger, more expensive productions, additional categories would be included.

**Table 4.62** No-budget 2.5-minute web video

| Account Numbers | Category | Total |
|---|---|---|
| **Above The Line** | | |
| **1100** | Story & Screenplay | 10 |
| **1300** | Producer | 25 |
| **1400** | Direction | 25 |
| **1500** | Cast | 45 |
| | **Total ATL** | **105** |
| | | |
| **Below The Line** | | |
| **2000** | Production Staff | 15 |
| **2100** | Extra Talent | 55 |
| **2200** | Sets | 10 |
| **2300** | Props | 15 |
| **2400** | Wardrobe, Make-up/Hair | 25 |
| **2500** | Electrical | 12 |
| **2600** | Camera | 25 |
| **2700** | Sound | 25 |
| **2800** | Locations/Food | 150 |
| | **Total Production** | **332** |
| | | |
| **4000** | Editing | 25 |
| **4100** | Music | 15 |
| | **Total Post** | **40** |
| | **Total ATL** | **105** |
| | Production | 332 |
| | Post | 40 |
| | **Total BTL** | **372** |
| | **Grand Total** | 477 |

**Table 4.63** Micro-budget HDV video pilot (5 min.)

| **Title: All** | **Shoot: 2-day** | **6-day prep, 6-day post** |
|---|---|---|
| A Film by | Sally Forth | |
| **Account Numbers** | **Category** | **Total** |
| **1100** | Story & Screenplay | 100 |
| **1200** | Continuity | 0 |
| **1300** | Producer | 50 |
| **1400** | Direction | 50 |
| **1500** | Cast | 100 |
| | **Total Above the Line** | **300** |
| | | |
| **2000** | Production Staff | 100 |
| **2100** | Extra Talent | 25 |
| **2200** | Sets | 50 |
| **2300** | Props | 50 |
| **2400** | Wardrobe, Make-up/Hair | 50 |
| **2500** | Electrical | 50 |
| **2600** | Camera | 50 |
| **2700** | Sound | 50 |
| **2800** | Locations | 150 |
| **2900** | Film and Lab | 75 |
| **3000** | Visual Effects | 50 |
| | **Total Production** | **700** |
| **4000** | Editing | 50 |
| **4100** | Music | 15 |
| **4200** | Post Sound | 25 |
| **4300** | Post Graphic | 35 |
| **4400** | Hard Drive | 25 |
| | **Total Post Production** | **150** |
| **5000** | Publicity | 10 |
| **6000** | Insurance | 5 |
| **7000** | General Expenses | 15 |
| | **Total Other** | **30** |
| | | |
| | **Total Above the Line** | **300** |
| | Production | 700 |
| | + Post Production | 150 |
| | + Other | 30 |
| | **= Total Below the Line** | **880** |
| | | |
| | A/L + B/L = | 1,180 |
| | Contingency (10%) | 118 |
| | **Grand Total** | **1,298** |

**Table 4.64** $1m SAG indie low budget feature/red camera

| | **Above the Line** | |
|---|---|---|
| 100 | Line Producer | 10,000.00 |
| 200 | Director | 15,600.00 |
| **300** | ***Cast*** | |
| 310 | Principal Cast | 39,861.00 |
| 320 | Supporting Cast | 4,170.00 |
| 330 | Stunt Coordinator | 3,036.00 |
| 340 | Agents' Fees | 3,986.10 |
| 350 | SAG fringes | 7,573.59 |
| 360 | Casting | 7,000.00 |
| 370 | Cast Travel | 1,000.00 |
| 380 | Cast Insurance | 0.00 |
| 399 | Misc | 750.00 |
| **400** | ***Production staff*** | |
| 410 | Production Manager | 14,400.00 |
| 420 | Production Coordinator | 8,550.00 |
| 430 | First AD | 10,800.00 |
| 440 | Key 2nd AD | 6,120.00 |
| 450 | APOC/Office PA | 3,600.00 |
| 460 | Set PAs | 23,280.00 |
| 470 | Interns | 0.00 |
| 480 | Script Supervisor | 6,112.50 |
| 490 | Production Accountant | 21,100.00 |
| | **Total ATL** | **186,939.19** |
| | **BTL: Production** | |
| **500** | ***Production Staff*** | |
| 510 | 2nd 2nd AD | 4,800.00 |
| **600** | ***Camera*** | |
| 610 | Director of Photography | 10,087.50 |
| 620 | 1st AC | 7,037.50 |
| 630 | 2nd AC | 5,842.50 |
| 640 | Steadicam | 4,000.00 |
| 650 | Camera Rentals | 56,860.00 |
| 660 | Expendables | 1,000.00 |
| 670 | Loss and Damage | 500.00 |

(*Continued*)

**Table 4.64** (Continued)

| **700** | ***Production Sound*** | |
|---|---|---|
| 710 | Sound Mixer | 7,437.50 |
| 720 | Boom Operator | 4,862.50 |
| 730 | Purchases | 1,000.00 |
| 740 | Sound Package | 7,500.00 |
| 750 | Comtek | 950.00 |
| 760 | Walkie Talkies | 1,500.00 |
| 770 | Loss and Damage | 750.00 |
| **800** | ***Art Dept*** | |
| 810 | Production Designer | 13,200.00 |
| 820 | Art Director | 9,500.00 |
| 830 | Leadman | 4,000.00 |
| 840 | PD Purchases | 45,000.00 |
| **900** | ***Set Decoration*** | |
| 910 | Set Decorator | 6,000.00 |
| 920 | Set Decorator #2 | 7,000.00 |
| 930 | Set Decoration Purchases | 0.00 |
| **1000** | ***Props*** | |
| 1010 | Property Master | 5,250.00 |
| 1020 | Payment to Assistant | 1,600.00 |
| 1030 | Prop Purchases | 2,400.00 |
| 1040 | Specialty Props | 4,500.00 |
| 1050 | Loss and Damage | 1,000.00 |
| 1060 | Additionals | 10,000.00 |
| **1200** | ***Make-up & Hair*** | |
| 1210 | Key Make-up Artist | 6,917.50 |
| 1220 | Key Hair | 5,972.50 |
| 1230 | Asst Hair and Make-up | 480.00 |
| 1240 | Purchases | 1,000.00 |
| **1300** | ***Wardrobe*** | |
| 1310 | Costume Designer | 12,000.00 |
| 1320 | Wardrobe Supervisor | 6,662.50 |
| 1340 | Wardrobe Assistant | 0.00 |
| 1350 | Purchases | 9,500.00 |
| 1360 | Loss and Damage | 0.00 |

(*Continued*)

**Table 4.64** (Continued)

| | | |
|---|---|---|
| **1400** | ***Grip and Electric*** | |
| 1410 | Key Grip | 7,437.50 |
| 1420 | Best Boy Grip | 6,737.50 |
| 1430 | Grips | 11,015.00 |
| 1440 | Gaffer | 7,837.50 |
| 1450 | Best Boy Electric | 6,562.50 |
| 1460 | Electric | 5,507.50 |
| 1470 | Purchases | 4,500.00 |
| 1480 | Rentals | 36,000.00 |
| 1490 | Loss and Damage | 1,000.00 |
| **1500** | ***Transportation*** | |
| 1510 | Production/Mini | 2,905.00 |
| 1520 | Stop Truck | 2,745.00 |
| 1530 | Art Cube | 4,392.00 |
| 1540 | Art Mini Van | 3,992.00 |
| 1550 | Camera/Sound Cargo | 1,995.00 |
| 1560 | 15 PAX #1 | 2,994.00 |
| 1570 | 15 PAX #2 | 2,495.00 |
| 1580 | Unit Cube | 2,745.00 |
| 1590 | Gas and Oil | 9,000.00 |
| 1600 | Parking | 6,000.00 |
| 1800 | Taxis | 300.00 |
| 2000 | MTA Passes | 608.00 |
| 2010 | Tolls | 1,500.00 |
| 2020 | Generator | 8,000.00 |
| 2030 | Parking Tickets | 1,150.00 |
| **3000** | ***Location /Set*** | |
| 3010 | Location Manager | 7,750.00 |
| 3020 | Location Scout | 5,000.00 |
| 3030 | Parking Coordinator | 1,920.00 |
| 3040 | Site Rentals Fees and Permits | 85,000.00 |
| 3050 | Courtesy Payments | 500.00 |
| 3060 | Loss and Damages | 1,000.00 |
| 3070 | Meals | 31,800.00 |
| 3080 | Craft Service Purchases | 3,600.00 |
| 3090 | Unit Supplies | 2,500.00 |

(*Continued*)

**Table 4.64** (Continued)

| | | |
|---|---|---|
| **4000** | **Office Supplies** | 3,500.00 |
| 4010 | Telephone/Pagers | 3,000.00 |
| 4020 | Shipping | 500.00 |
| 4030 | Production Office | 2,500.00 |
| **5000** | ***Production Film & Lab*** | |
| 5010 | Film Stock | 0.00 |
| 5020 | Daily Prints | 0.00 |
| 5030 | Dailies out to HDCAM Video | 1,350.00 |
| 5040 | HDCam Tape Stock | 0.00 |
| 5050 | DVCam Tape Stock | 0.00 |
| 6010 | Production Payroll Fringe | 44,302.30 |
| | **Total Production** | **597,750.80** |
| ***7000*** | ***BTL: Post*** | |
| 7010 | *Editorial* | |
| 7020 | Film Editor | 19,500.00 |
| 7030 | Suite Rental | 5,100.00 |
| 7040 | Film Supervisor | 4,250.00 |
| 7050 | *Music* | |
| 7060 | Composer | 10,000.00 |
| 7070 | Music Rights | 15,000.00 |
| 8000 | *Post Production Sound* | |
| 8010 | Sound Package and Mix | 34,900.00 |
| 8020 | *Post Production Film* | |
| 8030 | Color Correction | 15,045.00 |
| 8040 | Post Fringes | |
| 8050 | Fringes (19%) | 3,705.00 |
| | **Total Post** | **107,500.00** |
| **9100** | ***BTL: Other*** | |
| 9200 | *Legal Accounting* | |
| 9300 | Production Legal | 5,000.00 |
| 9400 | Insurance | 8,506.00 |
| 9520 | Media Storage | 10,000.00 |
| 9999 | Contingency @ 10% | 91,589.20 |
| | **Total Other** | **115,095.20** |
| | **Total Budget** | **1,007,485.19** |

## End of Chapter Four Review

Budgeting is a three-stage process:

1. **Identify** and **obtain prices** from multiple sources starting with what you already know, generally in this order:
   a. Locations
   b. Key Crew (with their equipment)
   c. Cast
   d. Vendors: Equipment, Services
      Build a preliminary budget at full price.
2. **Negotiate** potential deals and present data to Producer and Director. Refine your budget.
3. **Lock in** your deals with signed contracts.

A film budget is composed of two main ingredients: initial creative costs **Above the Line**, and **Below the Line** costs of making the script.

Budgets are organized in *layers*, starting with a *Topsheet* which summarizes all the categories. Each category is made up of several *Accounts*, which broadly describe the type of expenses, made up of the *Detail Level* specific sub-accounts – people, rates, equipment – which is where we input most of the data. *Account numbers* connect and organize the data.

Budgets are constructed on a grid, where the *vertical* axis lists each budget item, and the *horizontal* axis is the equation for each budget item, i.e., the amount to be worked × units × # of needed item × rate = subtotal.

Crew and cast may be paid a *flat rate* (Allow) or by *time* period, prep, shoot, wrap, on a weekly, daily, or hourly rate.

Union members add fringes and standard taxes (FICA, SUI, FUI, Worker's Comp) to their wages. Some guild and union pay scales are connected to the film's budget level. Non-union members are typically paid taxes on top of their wages, and are paid per negotiation.

Many factors will impact the budget, including the:

- Producer's budget range (or no idea);
- Type of project;

- Existing plans regarding locations, cast, crew;
- Pay, no pay/union or not;
- Length, format and destination of the project;
- Intended use of location and incentive funding.

To set up your budget, select a template and establish your numbering system. Add production information, globals, fringes and units. Build your first account and copy/paste/alter it as needed.

# Chapter Five
## *Helpful Scheduling and Budgeting Tips*

*"Help me! Help meeeeeeeee!"*

**The Fly (1958)**

---

## Gaining Experience

Experience is something you only get by performing a task multiple times. In addition to creating several schedules and budgets to build that experience, strengthen your budget and schedule with these tips:

1. Run through different scenarios;
2. Ask for help and advice;
3. Look at the numbers;
4. Create a picture of your schedule and budget.

### 1. Run through Different Scenarios

*Scheduling*

Look at the big picture, and then look at small, detailed pictures.

Save your draft. Back it up. Reopen, and do a Save As: name the file logically (*Title_Version #_6Days*); look at the stripboard anew. Mix it up, and take a fresh look for potential discovery (*don't take deleted scenes out of the boneyard).* Try scenarios with longer or shorter days, e.g., 5- vs. 6-day weeks, all-weekend shoots, etc.

Shift the stripboard view from "Horizontal" to "Vertical". Examine individual Day out of Days Reports for sets, cast, props, vehicles, locations, to study them for potential consolidation.

*Budgeting*

Create *budget groups* and compare them with each other. Save your draft. Back it up. Reopen, and do a Save As: name the file logically (version _). Create *versions* of budgets and compare them, considering the variables where you have some flexibility.

### 2. Ask for Help and Advice

Start with the AD, Director and Producer. As you add Department Heads, ask for their insight on specific issues regarding personnel and equipment. Cutting people and equipment might seem savvy and indeed lower the budget, but the conditions created may cause the work to become more difficult, or take longer.

If your team is inexperienced, find advisors working in production management, such as UPMs or Line Producers, who, in exchange for an invitation to the wrap party, or credit, will answer the occasional question. These might include local filmmakers you know or have met online in online film communities, people whose films you've seen and liked, instructors, authors of IndieWire and MovieMaker film articles, members of WIFT, IFP, Yahoo groups, and Meetup Groups, and people you have met through social media.

### 3. Look at the Numbers

*Scheduling*

12 hour work day

−1.5 hour for meals (two meal breaks @ ½ hour each + time getting to/from)

= 10.5 hours left

−1.5 hour to set up lighting (or more)

= 9 hours left

−1 hour break down/secure gear

= 8 hours left

−1 hour for miscellaneous (or more), such as:

- production meeting
- wardrobe/hair/make-up/art (retouches after takes and meals)
- the "concern" of the day (drama, dispute, insurance claim, late arrival)
- paperwork (filling out/handing in time sheets, call sheets, petty cash, receipts)

= 7 hours (or much less) to work toward capturing desired footage.

That's a day with no major crisis or weather interruptions.

You also need to subtract time spent communicating, rehearsing, and blocking, which will vary depending on the complexity of the scene, lighting design, and camera movements. Working with animals, children and stunts, elaborate costumes and make-up, crowds, and working at night, or in extreme temperatures or weather, will take three to four times longer — so an 8–9 hour day is now 2–3 hours of potential actual shooting time. Yikes! Only a fraction of your total hours will be spent "making the day", getting scheduled script pages into video (even if all the equipment is working and operated perfectly). Each new camera setup takes time — to move lights, and equipment, and to set up. Each new "take" requires time, communication, blocking, set up, and mental and physical reset. Moving to a different location takes time.

How to account for the 20 minutes and $50 spent wheedling and bribing the pan flute player in Times Square who insists upon playing (accompanied by a boombox) right next to where you are shooting?

Once a shooting schedule is created, the Director and AD are guardians of the schedule (as is each cast and crew member, more informally). With your team, make up and discuss a *daily timetable*, hour by hour, to see where you can borrow or save time.

*Budgeting*

It is natural to desire as much artistic, and technical, variety in a film as possible, such as actors of all ages, sizes and abilities, helicopter and underwater shots, stunts, puppets, animatronics, celebrities, miniatures, pyrotechnics, crane shots, or a 78-piece marching band. Low budgets pose a challenge to natural artistic inclinations.

If a budget is extremely tight, ask the Director and Department Heads what their top two wishes are, and how those would impact the finished product. Let everyone make their case and pitch in to identify how they could make it happen, e.g., calling in favors, friends, etc. Research rates and deals that might be made and potential budget account shifts. (If we come under budget on our stunts on shoot day 4, we'll put that cash toward a helicopter shot. (*After* making sure the needed footage isn't available in a stock film library.))

With this information, create a version of the budget with the *top two* requests of the Director and Department Heads, and have a meeting with your team to discuss possible strategies to fulfill such wishes. It may be worth seeking additional financing, writing a grant, or seeking a (corporate) partner who could assist with this fulfillment.



**4. Create a Picture of your Schedule and Budget**

*Scheduling*

When you have a schedule and budget that you think is workable, put it in pictures. As filmmakers, sometimes it is easier to conceptualize an image. Time allocation in a typical 12-hour day schedule might look one way, with a complex day allocated differently.

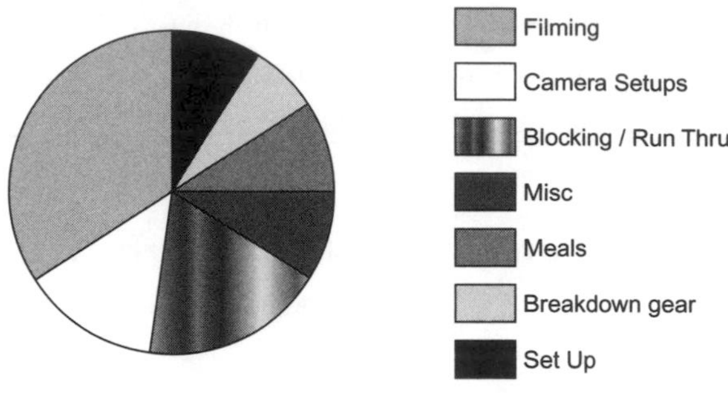


**FIG. 5.1**

Another way to look at your schedule

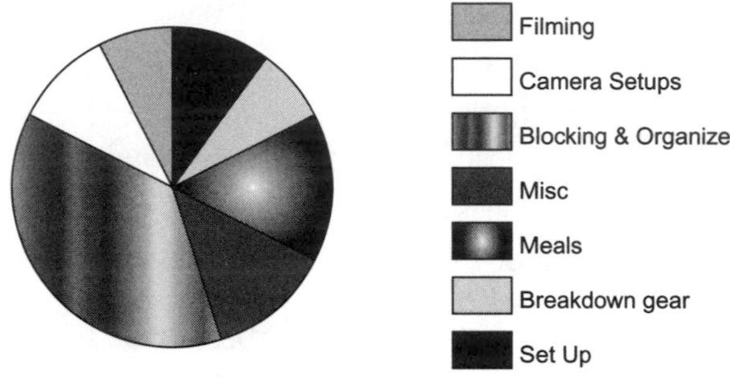


**FIG. 5.2**

Complex days require more blocking and organizing

Preproduction time is relatively cheap compared with shoot time, so take advantage of it by organizing and analyzing the shoot with your team to find potential time savings. A timeline, whether online, in Excel or scheduling software, or on paper, is a great way to keep duties top of mind. Create a list of critical tasks to be completed, and on top list time segments — in days, or weeks, or months. Shading indicates who will head up those tasks. Tables 5.1 and 5.2 show example timelines for a documentary and a feature, respectively.

Once a timeline has been established, actionable checklists help everyone stay on track.

*Budget Proportions*

Do the budget proportions make sense for the goals and experience of your team? The bigger the budget, the higher the Above the Line costs. As budgets descend from lower millions, to hundreds of thousands and below, Above the Line costs

**Table 5.1**

| Documentary Timeline | | | | | | | | | | | | | | | |
|---|---|---|---|---|---|---|---|---|---|---|---|---|---|---|---|
| **Dev & Prep** Weeks | 1 | 2 | 3 | 4 | 5 | 6 | 7 | 8 | 9 | 10 | 11 | 12 | 13 | 14 | 15 |
| Write/refine treatment | | | | | | | | | | | | | | | |
| Create budget | | | | | | | | | | | | | | | |
| Create timeline | | | | | | | | | | | | | | | |
| Research grants/funding | | | | | | | | | | | | | | | |
| Research story points | | | | | | | | | | | | | | | |
| Scout subjects | | | | | | | | | | | | | | | |
| Scout shooting sites | | | | | | | | | | | | | | | |
| Fiscal sponsorship apps | | | | | | | | | | | | | | | |
| Initial grant applications | | | | | | | | | | | | | | | |
| Secure accounting | | | | | | | | | | | | | | | |
| Fundraising | | | | | | | | | | | | | | | |
| Business entity formation | | | | | | | | | | | | | | | |
| Secure legal rep. | | | | | | | | | | | | | | | |
| Create, finalize legal docs | | | | | | | | | | | | | | | |
| Pre-interviews | | | | | | | | | | | | | | | |
| Music research | | | | | | | | | | | | | | | |
| Research post grants | | | | | | | | | | | | | | | |
| Marketing and sales strategy | | | | | | | | | | | | | | | |
| Secure PR firm | | | | | | | | | | | | | | | |
| Festival research/plan | | | | | | | | | | | | | | | |
| Marketing materials | | | | | | | | | | | | | | | |
| Research markets | | | | | | | | | | | | | | | |
| **Shoot & Post** Weeks | 1 | 2 | 3 | 4 | 5 | 6 | 7 | 8 | 9 | 10 | 11 | 12 | 13 | 14 | 15 |
| Hire DP, crew and Editor | | | | | | | | | | | | | | | |
| Procure equipment | | | | | | | | | | | | | | | |
| Insurance and permits | | | | | | | | | | | | | | | |
| Secure editing | | | | | | | | | | | | | | | |
| Principal photography | | | | | | | | | | | | | | | |
| Rough cut edit | | | | | | | | | | | | | | | |
| Test screening | | | | | | | | | | | | | | | |
| Final cut | | | | | | | | | | | | | | | |
| Mix/color correction | | | | | | | | | | | | | | | |
| Transfer | | | | | | | | | | | | | | | |
| Deliverables | | | | | | | | | | | | | | | |
| DVD design/authoring | | | | | | | | | | | | | | | |
| Cast and crew screening | | | | | | | | | | | | | | | |
| Wrap up production | | | | | | | | | | | | | | | |
| Implement marketing | | | | | | | | | | | | | | | |

**Table 5.2**

| Feature Timeline | | | | | | | | | | | | | |
|---|---|---|---|---|---|---|---|---|---|---|---|---|---|
| **Development** | Month | **J** | **F** | **M** | **A** | **M** | **JN** | **JL** | **A** | **S** | **O** | **N** | **D** |
| Identify story or script, secure rights, hire writer | | | | | | | | | | | | | |
| Create initial schedule and budget | | | | | | | | | | | | | |
| Create project timeline | | | | | | | | | | | | | |
| Screenplay first draft | | | | | | | | | | | | | |
| Order copyright and title reports | | | | | | | | | | | | | |
| Financing strategy, sales agents, distributors | | | | | | | | | | | | | |
| Scout producing partners/Cast/Key crew | | | | | | | | | | | | | |
| Scout locations and production incentives | | | | | | | | | | | | | |
| Create biz plan / investment memo / proposal | | | | | | | | | | | | | |
| Seek financing | | | | | | | | | | | | | |
| Prepare contracts for Above the Line personnel | | | | | | | | | | | | | |
| **Preproduction:** *financing secured* | | | | | | | | | | | | | |
| Screenplay second draft | | | | | | | | | | | | | |
| Secure accounting | | | | | | | | | | | | | |
| Trigger funding | | | | | | | | | | | | | |
| Setup production office and form business entity | | | | | | | | | | | | | |
| Secure legal representation: contracts | | | | | | | | | | | | | |
| Insurance | | | | | | | | | | | | | |
| Union paperwork | | | | | | | | | | | | | |
| Hire DP, key crew, Editor, composer | | | | | | | | | | | | | |
| Update schedule and budget | | | | | | | | | | | | | |
| Locations: secure | | | | | | | | | | | | | |
| Secure main vendors: equipment, editing, post | | | | | | | | | | | | | |
| Casting and rehearsals | | | | | | | | | | | | | |
| Hiring all crew | | | | | | | | | | | | | |
| Marketing and sales strategy, festival and market plan | | | | | | | | | | | | | |
| Script locked | | | | | | | | | | | | | |
| Create marketing materials / press kit / Secure PR firm | | | | | | | | | | | | | |
| Production schedule locked | | | | | | | | | | | | | |
| Equipment, props, costumes secured | | | | | | | | | | | | | |
| Release forms/permits/executed contracts | | | | | | | | | | | | | |
| Budget locked | | | | | | | | | | | | | |
| **Production** | Month | **J** | **F** | **M** | **A** | **M** | **JN** | **JL** | **A** | **S** | **O** | **N** | **D** |
| Principal photography | | | | | | | | | | | | | |
| Begin edit | | | | | | | | | | | | | |
| **Post Production** | Month | **J** | **F** | **M** | **A** | **M** | **JN** | **JL** | **A** | **S** | **O** | **N** | **D** |
| Festival paperwork, marketing and press kit | | | | | | | | | | | | | |
| Wrap up production materials | | | | | | | | | | | | | |
| Post timeline finalized | | | | | | | | | | | | | |
| Rough cut edit | | | | | | | | | | | | | |
| Fine cut | | | | | | | | | | | | | |
| Sound cut | | | | | | | | | | | | | |
| Begin music composing | | | | | | | | | | | | | |
| Music score recording | | | | | | | | | | | | | |
| Music (additional) priced and cleared | | | | | | | | | | | | | |
| Sound edit and mix | | | | | | | | | | | | | |
| Transfer to optical track | | | | | | | | | | | | | |
| Negative cut | | | | | | | | | | | | | |
| Timing, sweetening, prints | | | | | | | | | | | | | |
| Compile deliverables | | | | | | | | | | | | | |
| Screenings and DVD authoring | | | | | | | | | | | | | |

shrink in proportion to other sections, while the portion allocated to post production will grow. Many expenses in post are hard costs (facilities and lab) and cannot be deferred, or exchanged for credits or profits. Production costs depend on the willingness of cast and crew to defer pay, or share in profits in lieu of payment upfront.

In a perfect world, the *majority* of any budget should be seen on screen, [**AKA:** in **production values**,] whatever the Producer considers that to be – a star, great sets and props, or amazing locations. The quest for production value is one reason that every budget is one-of-a-kind. For low budget films without recognizable stars that means most of the budget is Below the Line. What *is* paid for during production should yield double the results on screen, i.e., for every $25 spent, $50 worth of value should appear in the film.

Casting a star, even in a cameo role, will raise Above the Line costs, and Below the Line costs as well. It may be worth it if the star greatly increases salability of the film: 50% (Above the Line) / 50% (Below the Line) on big budget studio films is not uncommon. In most cases, it's difficult to hire pricey actors without the Below the Line infrastructure (trailers, entourage, agent's fee) to support them, although you may be able to cast a known star for Voice Over, brief walk-on scene or in some other time-efficient way. Extensive CGI will require the post production part of the budget to go up. Bottom line, if you have a budget with 90% Above the Line, and 10% Below the Line, something is amiss.

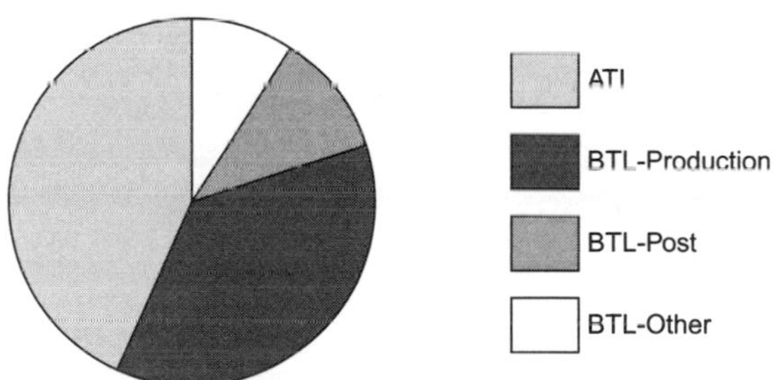


**FIG. 5.3**

On a $75 million studio film, almost half is spent on ATL (Above the Line) expenses

A **Rule of Thumb** (for low budget to micro budget projects) is to allocate at least 70% of your funding Below the Line, so your financial plan yields production value at every level possible. For example, if the Producer of your project gives you a low budget range figure to back into, allowing 30% for Above and 70% for Below the Line, is a practical place to start.

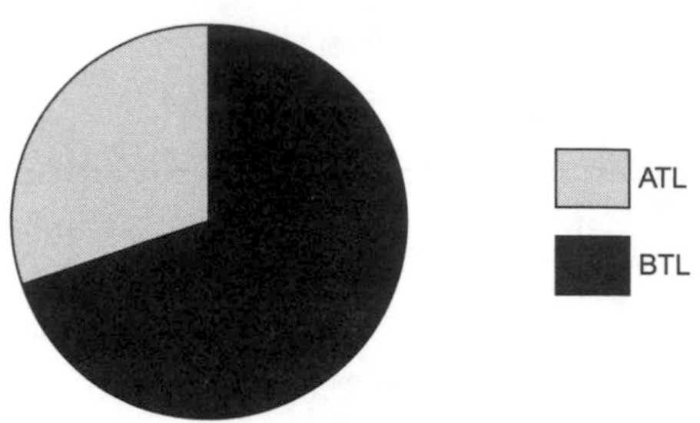


**FIG. 5.4**

Know *where* the largest part of your budget is allocated and *why*

In practical terms, that will give you a general idea of where and how you will spend resources. Use a calculator to see how the money would be divided in rough terms.

**Table 5.3**

| Total Film Budget | 30% Above the Line | 70% Below the Line |
|---|---|---|
| $100 | $30 | $70 |
| $1,000 | $300 | $700 |
| $10,000 | $7,000 | $3,000 |
| $100,000 | $70,000 | $30,000 |
| $1,000,000 | $700,000 | $300,000 |
| $10,000,000 | $7,000,000 | $3,000,000 |

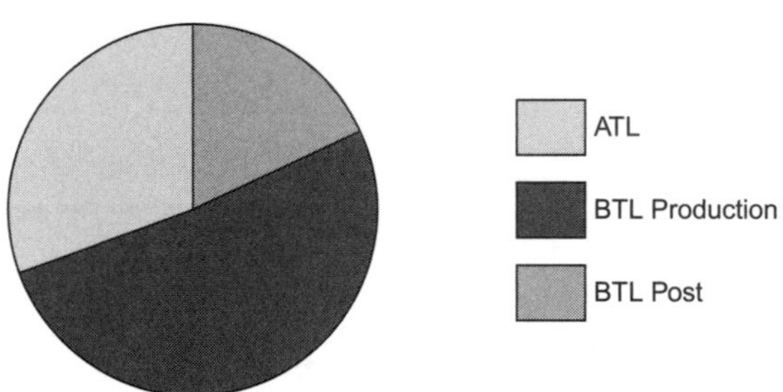


**FIG. 5.5**

Bigger budgets spend a larger proportion on Above the Line costs. This $5 million feature example isn't high compared with many Hollywood films, but is a significant budget for an indie filmmaker

For example, if a total locked budget is $10,000, and the Director requests a crane that will cost $9,000 to rent, there is homework to be done. Is there a vendor (company or individual) that owns this equipment and might rent it (and operate it) on the cheap? How expensive will the insurance and transport be? Are you working with a vendor who might be able to help you? Ask everyone you know, and put out notices

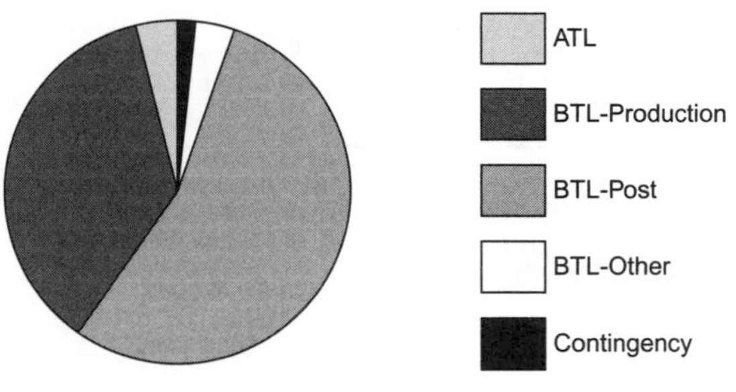


**FIG. 5.6**

Digital features made for under $20,000 spend the least amount possible on ATL expenses

to that effect on film boards and online. Might this person take a credit, or small acting cameo, or a promotional plug in exchange for the use of the equipment? Is similar, or older, equipment available that can approximate the effect? At the end of the day, if the production cannot afford the equipment, the Director has to evaluate what it was about the shot that they most desired — height, movement, scale — and decide if shooting from above on a balcony, using some other equipment, might approximate the effect.

Using appropriate budget proportions as a guide, you will immediately notice if things are wandering off course. For example, if you have $1,000 to make a digital short film, you will need as much of that money to be spent Below the Line as possible, for tapes, props, locations, food, etc. So 70% ($700) of that $1,000 is spent Below the Line and 30% ($300) is spent Above the Line, maybe to pay for copies of the script, transporting the ATL team. With a budget that size, better to forgo any ATL costs at all, and use the money for post or marketing.

Whatever the budget proportions are, it's your job to know *why* they are like this, and to make a best efforts decision with your team as to how they can yield the best film possible.

*Marketing*

For those who plan DIY robust marketing plans and want to make sure money is available, you may slice the budget as shown in Table 5.4.

This planning ensures that you can pull off publicity and marketing plans with an appropriate budget to do so. It requires discipline to leave that part of the budget untouched.

**Table 5.4**

| Marketing 50% | Film Budget 50% |
|---|---|
| Merchandise, web presence, DVD copies, street teams, posters, postcards, festival market entries, screenings | 15% Above the Line<br>35% Below the Line |
| In the case of a total budget of $500,000 | |
| $250,000 is the marketing budget | $250,000 is the film budget (with $75,000 of that ATL and $175,000 of that BTL) |

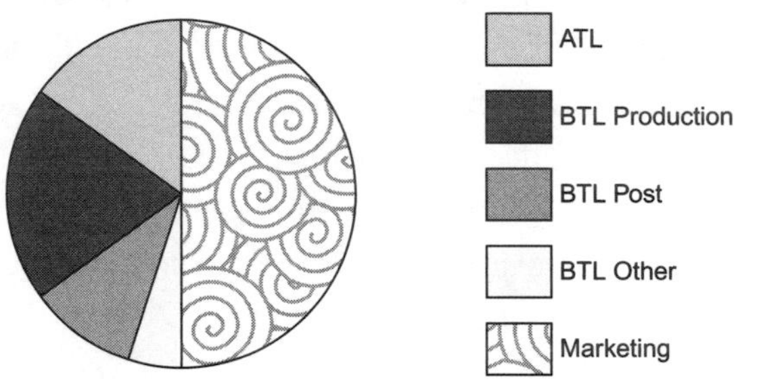


**FIG. 5.7**

A robust marketing budget that is equal to the total production cost ensures that you will still have money to market the film when it is completed. This may cover a website, screeners, festival entries, etc.

## Evolution of the Schedule and Budget

Once you've created the initial schedule and budget, new information will affect them. The schedule will go through at least four major iterations:

1. **Preliminary**: Input from Producer. Once the location and season are pinpointed, it's time to shoot (check historical weather forecasts). This preliminary schedule will evolve as the Director, AD and other key crew are identified.
2. **Fortified**: Create a schedule that will pump up the budget, with longer weeks (6 versus 5), and longer hours (14 versus 13). This approach is one way to inflate a schedule for the sole purpose of reinforcing the budget. Most likely, you won't work the full 12 or 13 hours, and that saving can be applied elsewhere. Often, on complex days, it's easier to complete a long day than to break it down and set up again. However, it is safer to plan that the complex day will require overtime, *and* extend into another day, which may also require OT.
3. **Comparison:** Create a 6-day week versus a 5-day one; weekday schedule versus weekends (non-union); 11-hour day versus 12-hour (12 vs. 13, etc.); completion before key specific festival due dates or other target date. Alternate easy and difficult weeks to avoid burnout.
4. Can you take advantage of **3-day weekends**? The team must be open to this idea. Slow seasons may yield equipment deals and crew looking to pick up a gig, though year-end holidays are a tough sell.

**Table 5.5**

| | |
|---|---|
| December | New Year's Day |
| January | Birthday of Martin Luther King, Jr. |
| February | Washington's birthday |
| May (end) | Memorial Day |
| July 4 | Independence Day |
| September (start) | Labor Day |
| October | Columbus Day |
| November | Veterans Day |
| November | Thanksgiving Day |
| December | Christmas Day |

The budget should go through at least four major iterations:

1. **Preliminary budget**: Once you get numbers, create a *full price* budget (the real cost of doing the film). This budget could be used to raise financing, or as your springboard. Research the going rates in your area, and if you don't know, use union rates as a guide.
2. **Perfect world**: Create a perfect world version, including the first choice of cast and crew. Add a robust marketing budget and great equipment, as well as ample time to utilize it. This budget could be used to raise initial financing, or defend an expensive request (underwater cameras and cameraman, tanks, cranes, star voice over).

3a. **Practical**: Create a practical version with *deals* (favors called in, deferrals by key crew and cast stakeholders in the film, etc.). This budget is not used for fundraising (except in the case of lo-no budget projects or docs). A good tool to use is to bring in partners. Include at least 1 of the top 2 requests made by Department Heads. A *cost plus* version of the budget is created by building a profit (usually 10–15%) into each line item; this is commonly used in corporate videos, commercials, and music videos.

3b. Or. . .**No Matter What**: A hell or high-water budget. You and your team are just going to do it, on a specific start date. Not everyone will need this version, but it can serve as powerful motivation for partners, crew and cast willing to work for credit and experience.

Your Producer may request budget *portions* (e.g., to make one stunt or major scene, to *prove the concept*) as a trailer budget to convey the idea to funders, or development budget, post production budget, effects budget, local versus distant budget.

4. **Final Approved Budget**: This is what the Producer signs off on, and once *locked*, must not be exceeded.

### The Team

Once your preliminary schedule and budget are completed, go over them in detail with your team. The Producer, AD and Director, DP, Production Designer and Production Accountant bring a unique perspective that helps you find time, and monetary savings.

The collaborative nature of filmmaking sometimes creates conflict, particularly on small budget indie films where crew and cast may be responsible for multiple duties.

What will help alleviate tension is that you stay organized, and everyone knows who is in charge and what their duties are. With your core team, commit to a schedule, and establish a budget for each department that Department Heads should be prepared to stick with.

No matter what you call them, you need someone in charge of key areas. These are usually Department Heads trained in a particular skill or craft, but in the DIY film environment, if you want to get a film made, do it with the resources you can muster. You will at least need someone in charge of:

- *Finances*: Raising money, controlling money, paying people, maintaining the budget and schedule (combination of Producer, LP, Accountant);
- *Visuals* (led by the Director): Encompassing the Art dept, props, sets and locations, combined with the "look of actor" (hair/makeup, wardrobe);
- *Safety and Security* (usually the AD), running the set, providing an optimal and safe environment to shoot;
- *Camera and Sound*: Format, operations, equipment (On lo-no projects, hiring one person to handle camera and sound is not uncommon; ***however***, that's a big responsibility to carry and crappy sound will kill a great picture);
- *Food and Shelter*: Quality and quantity of meals, access to facilities: bathrooms, dressing rooms, parking, subway stop. Crew and cast often frame their working experience in terms of the quality of food on a shoot (I'm not kidding). (LP, Production Office Coordinator, Catering);
- *Electricity, Rigging, Shading*: lights and power;
- Establishing a *website*, and your social media and online presence, as early as possible. (Producer of Marketing and Distribution).

**Priorities, Prices and Deal Making**

You are the newest overlooked superhero, the *Under Wonder*. Your plans are completed just under the maximum time, and a little under budget. Fortify the budget in categories like travel, stunts and safety; there's a good case to be made for all of them. It's not "padding" — you are adding reinforcement where necessary.

While building your crew, seek to hire the best, smartest people. Tune into the other person's WIFM channel (What's In it For Me). Is there something you can do for them? Just ask, nicely. The worst someone can say is no. Everything is negotiable. Really. Put yourself in the other person's shoes and find out what they need/want:

- Credits, money, access to equipment?
- Experience, to build skills, move up within their field, or into a different aspect of production?
- Relationships, networking?
- Support and help with their projects?
- To find an agent, get into a union?
- To travel?
- Are they excited about working on this subject, script, other crew and cast?

*Priorities*

Budgeting forces you, and everyone in your team, to make decisions and prioritize. Of the many details in a budget, how do you decide which equipment, prop, location, or line item is more important than another? Examining 90 script pages, 90 breakdown sheets, and a budget that runs 70 pages long may seem overwhelming, so take it back to the story. This is a good exercise to do with your team – what is the core value in this script? If you can establish this, it will focus your budget. The reality of modern filmmaking is that everyone on your team must expand their creative abilities, by owning their portion of the budget make an amazing film with whatever is available.

Start with genre; discuss where the money should be directed. Of course you want the best possible crew and equipment, the most talented actors, and ideal locations. But every production, even *Avatar*, comes to a point where they have to pick and chose highest priority expenses. No movie has unlimited resources.

What is the most important facet of your film? A comedy had better be funny – how is money spent for funny? Madcap pranks, physical comedy (requiring a stunt coordinator), an unlikely location, gags, or props? More than likely, funny comes from the writing and the actors, and that's where the money should be prioritized, as opposed to travel, expensive sets, etc. Thorough casting sessions to find up-and-coming comedians and rehearsal time to foster chemistry may be time and money well invested.

If the film is a coming-of-age story about a young girl and her dog, then the money should be spent to get the right child actor (and support system including welfare worker or teacher, or parent/guardian), as well as a dog with sufficient training and a brilliant wrangler. The magic of the story is likely to come from preparation of both, and the chemistry between them. What makes a convincing fantasy? Props, costumes, and make-up. For a drama, the actors and story are key, as well as the climactic scene, any love scene, and the chemistry. This exercise will assist with the brainstorming necessary to prioritize certain budget line items over others.

It is useful to compare where your film fits into the overall industry landscape. The 10 genres in Table 5.6 are the most profitable to date, for all films of all budgets.

**Table 5.6**

| Genre | Characteristics |
|---|---|
| Comedy | Funny, writing, talent |
| Adventure | Locations, sets, dashing believable hero(ine) |
| Drama | Authenticity: locations, costumes, actors |
| Action | Stunts, hero and villain charisma |
| Thriller/Suspense | Special effects, sets |
| Romantic Comedy | Funny, chemistry, wardrobe |
| Horror | Special effects, make-up |
| Documentary | Vividly told, insider view |
| Musical | Choreography |
| Black Comedy | Funny and dark writing, talent |

Table 5.7 the top most profitable indie films (comparing grosses to budget).

**Table 5.7**

| Genre | Title |
|---|---|
| Horror | *Paranormal Activity* |
| Doc | *Tarnation* |
| Action | *Mad Max* |
| Doc | *Super Size Me* |
| Horror | *The Blair Witch Project* |
| Horror | *Night of the Living Dead* |
| Drama | *Rocky* |
| Horror | *Halloween* |
| Coming of age | *American Graffiti* |
| Comedy | *Clerks* |

It is interesting to survey the following list: the lowest budget films to make $1 million at the box office. None relies on lavish effects. The bedrock is writing, performance and directing, which comes back to preparation and prioritizing.

*El Mariachi*

*Paranormal Activity*

*Slacker*

*In the Company of Men*

*The Brothers McMullen*

*Deep Throat*

*Clerks*

*Gabriela*

*Super Size Me*

*Pi*

***Prices***

Using a bidding process is one way to gather competitive prices. Once key crew creates a list of exactly what they will need for the production, identify relevant vendors and submit a request for competitive bids to each vendor. Let them know you're looking for the best bid. It's a straightforward way to let the market compete for your business. We know that the lowest price is not always the best deal. Your funders may want to know why you didn't select the lowest price, so keep notes on why and how decisions were made.

***Deal making 101***

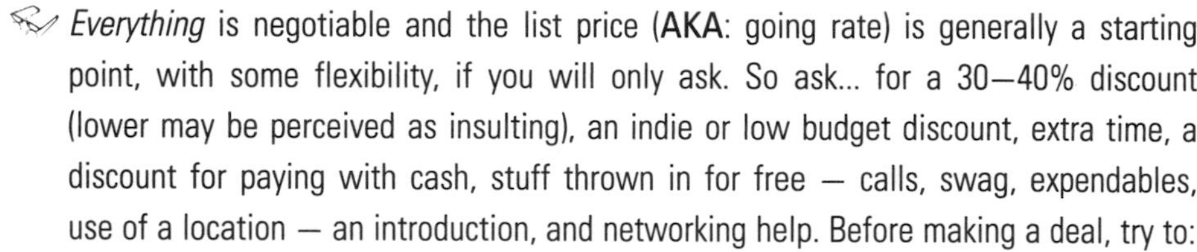

*Everything* is negotiable and the list price (**AKA**: going rate) is generally a starting point, with some flexibility, if you will only ask. So ask... for a 30–40% discount (lower may be perceived as insulting), an indie or low budget discount, extra time, a discount for paying with cash, stuff thrown in for free – calls, swag, expendables, use of a location – an introduction, and networking help. Before making a deal, try to:

- borrow;
- barter: product placement, exchange advertising;
- haggle and offer credits.

*Talk with other filmmakers*: where did they get the best deals? *Build relationships*: return calls and emails, and let vendors know when they didn't get the gig. Nobody likes to be kept hanging, so this will build up your karma credits and reputation.

*Start an account* with a vendor. That way if you get in a bind, and have established a relationship with them, they may stretch a little to help you if something comes up.

*Repay favors*: write online reviews; send thank you notes, small gifts, and invitations to screenings or wrap parties; put links on your website; sing the praises of everyone who lends a hand. Referrals equal money.

When you think of *product placement*, the *i-Robot* Audi automobiles, *E.T's* Reese's Pieces, *Up in The Air* (American Airlines, Hertz), James Bond, or any of the franchise films come to mind. In the low budget spectrum (particularly without a theatrical or TV distribution deal), you are more likely to obtain a free product (or temporary use of a product) in exchange for showing the business in a favorable or neutral manner.

There are companies that specialize in product placement, matching up products to filmmakers, and a benefit of that is the company has done the legal work (clearances) and know exactly how you can use the product. With a small budget, why would an advertiser be interested in appearing in a film? Chances are, without a well-known celebrity, a distribution deal in place, or a really powerful hook, they won't, but you never know.

Films with niche audiences, or topical subject matter, are more likely to find success in this arena. (Of course the company will want to see the synopsis.)

- Main setting of the movie takes place in a certain type of business location;
- Faith-based material;
- Documentaries focusing on specific philanthropic, medical or health issues, or hot button social issues (gun control, bullying, tanorexia);
- Material based on a particular product, sport, activity, food or beverage.

Start locally by approaching a business owner who may let you use something for free, feed you, or give you make-up, clothing or props, a location, or a place to hold the wrap party — use your imagination. For no-lo budgets, it's unlikely the company will give you cash, or advertise for you in return for you showing their stuff in your film, but you never know, so ask. If you are not sure whom to contact at a big company, start with the media and public relations department.

There are trade publications for nearly every aspect of the entertainment business and you can check *Product Placement News* (www.productplacement.biz) for trends in product placement and the branded entertainment business.



### Changes During Shooting

The best way to see into the future is to imagine it early on, while there's time to prepare. Channel your inner paranoia, and play Chicken Little, asking yourself what could go wrong, as many times and in as many ways possible. When the sky falls, where is it likely to land? Plan for the worst, to push for the best.

What will we do if:

- it rains?
- the power goes out?
- there's a barking dog next door?
- someone's late?
- equipment is missing, or damaged?
- the location is locked, with no way to access?
- the insurance certificate didn't come in time?
- there's no tape or film stock?
- there's a serious accident, or someone is sick?

Keep this list nearby while going through the schedule, and make backup plans, and collaborate with the AD. You are the primary advocate for the film's schedule and budget. Ask your team how you can find more time, money, security, equipment, generators, backup locations, just in case — you want to have some options. "How are we going to tackle. . ."

## Safety and Insurance

There's no price on safety. OK that's a lie, there's an exact price on safety and that's how we purchase insurance. No-lo filmmakers sometimes skirt insurance (unless forced to by location owners, vendors or funders), relying on luck, but it's a dangerous game and not worth it. Contact a broker who handles production insurance, and they will find the best rates from a variety of insurance providers.

But what about our no-lo $20,000 feature – "we don't need insurance, we can't afford it." At least get a *quote* to cover your people (liability and workers' comp) and equipment, and E&O insurance to CYA and for the audiovisual content in the film – that will speed the transaction along when distributors come calling. *Don't be embarrassed to ask lots of questions about insurance – it is confusing.*

You can buy insurance for the duration of a shoot (short-term production); or a year-long policy (annual Producer's insurance policy, or production DICE: Documentary, Industrial, Commercial, Educational) is more practical for documentarians, longer-term projects, or a company with a series of projects over a year.

In the film's budget, insurance is a *contractual* cost, calculated as a percent of the total budget (2–4%), and is based on the length of the film, and its content (i.e., stunts, pyrotechnics and explosions, animals, kids, vehicles, firearms, fights, boats, aircraft, live gangster rap music scenes, a piece of equipment worth $350,000+, scaffolding; will increase the price of the insurance). The more dangerous the content of the script, the more people and equipment you need, the more valuable your props and locations (if you are shooting in the White House – your insurance costs will be higher than if you are shooting in Aunt Maisy's garage), the longer your shoot, and the higher the cost of your policy.

The *premium* is what you pay for insurance upfront, the *deductible* is what you will need to pay in case of a claim (something happens and you need to use the insurance) before the insurance company kicks in and starts paying up to the limits established on your policy.

*Comprehensive General Liability* provides protection in case of losses due to bodily injury, or property damage, caused by the insured's employees or agents, as a result of filming. Location owners require proof of this if you're shooting on their property; governmental agencies usually require it for shooting on public property, or to obtain film permits.

*Workers' Compensation* and *Employer's Liability* provide coverage for medical, disability or death benefits to any cast, crew or office employee (paid or unpaid) who becomes ill, or is injured, working on the film. If you are hiring cast and crew as independent contractors (often LLCs, Loan-Out corporations), they are supposed to carry their own workman's comp. Find out who is and isn't covered, and what the procedures are in the event of an injury or incident.

*Equipment, Props, Sets* and *Wardrobe Insurance* covers loss and damage to *rented* equipment, e.g., camera, sound, lighting, and miscellaneous rented equipment, e.g., props, sets, and wardrobes from all vendors.

Most rental companies require proof — a certificate of insurance, with their company added to it — before they will rent you their gear. They usually insist upon a credit card for a deposit as well, in case the equipment is destroyed. Some vendors offer *floater policies* (you ride on their insurance for an extra fee) but these are more expensive than if you procure the insurance yourself. Owned equipment requires a separate policy.

The equipment folks usually request the following:

- You add their company as Additional Insured to your policy
- You add their company to be named as Additional Loss Payee to your policy
- Your insurance provides adequate coverage (they'll tell you the limits)
- You fax/email them the certificate, call to confirm receipt

Hiring crew with their own insured equipment is a plus because they take good care of it.

*Errors and Omissions* insurance protects you from claims about film content involving violation of personal rights, libel, or slander (important for documentary makers), and is usually required for distribution. An entertainment attorney specializing in legal clearances will review the script or story, origins, characters, names, locations, and similarity to real events or people. E&O protects you in case your title violates a third-party trademark, against accidental failure to obtain consent, lawsuits alleging copyright infringment, plagiarism, defamation or degrading of people or products.

*Auto* (hired and non-owned): liability covers injury to third parties, or damage to property caused by vehicles rented for the production. The physical damage part of the policy provides coverage for damage to the vehicles themselves.

You can also purchase insurance to cover the negative, film and videotape loss, principal cast (requires completion of a health questionnaire and a physical), aircraft, animals, boats, office contents, foreign production, adverse weather, additional insureds, jewelry, fine art (on location), illness, bereavement, and kidnapping and ransom.

*Third-Party Property Damage* covers loss, damage to, or destruction of property of others, including loss of use of that property in your care, custody or control.

*Guild Travel Accident* insurance is required by guilds and unions, and can be extended to non-union cast and crew as well.

Shop around. Non-profits and film-related trade organizations like WIFT, IFP, Fractured Atlas, and Shooting People, have relationships with insurers and may provide discounted deals for members. Local film commissions, trades, and other filmmakers are great resources for insurance — ask lots of questions. How fast can you get coverage? Is there a person available after hours (often when indies are shooting)? The upfront cost is small compared with catastrophic damages in the case of a lawsuit, severe injuries, or death.

## Publicity and Marketing

You will need a paper and an electronic press kit to relate the "story" of the film to distributors, festivals, press and fans, quickly and easily. Much of this can be generated for free. Start as early as possible, or hire someone to create and gather the following materials:

- News hooks to make it easy for journalists to write about you;
- Synopsis, list of credits;
- Bios of key cast and crew;
- Production stills;
- Key art and great graphics pertaining to the story, logo;
- Trailers and teasers, provocative clips from the film;
- Canned videotaped "interviews" where your publicity folks ask the questions and your filmmakers answer them on camera;
- Transcribed version of the above;
- Website, Facebook page, presence on film communities, YouTube page;
- Genre, estimated length of completed film, anticipated rating;
- Sell Sheet (poster on the front, synopsis and bios on the back – once you have team and cast attached).

Budget for promotion: whether all Do-It-Yourself or not, planning your festival or your marketing and distribution strategy, budget early on.

Go to *Festivals* to compete and win prizes, and attract the attention of distributors. There are many, but only the biggest ones (Cannes, Tribeca, Toronto, Sundance, Berlin, Rotterdam, Venice, Locarno, San Sebastian, Karlovy Vary, Los Angeles Film Fest) attract distributor attention. Pick and choose which to apply to; there are thousands, and if you get in, try to go. Many festivals that charge submission fees will give you a break if you submit early. It's important for your PMD (Producer of Distribution and Marketing) to understand that the world premiere is valuable, so do your best to get that at the biggest festival possible, because you only get one. Festivals are inundated with submissions, so a personal recommendation from someone connected with the festival can give your project a boost in the crowd. Ask everyone you know, and their friends, who might know someone in contact with a festival programmer. Withoutabox.com is a one-stop shop for fests.

*Film market* attendance is more expensive than festival attendance (if you register). A budget for festival or market attendance would include travel and lodging, registration fees, one-sheets, screeners, postcards, and business cards. Markets are a forum for buying and selling films. Contracting with a Producer's rep or sales agent eliminates the need for a member of your team to attend, as the rep or agent will be there on your behalf. A Producer's rep seeks U.S. distribution and helps find a foreign sales agent for international rights; they charge upfront or take a percentage of the deal (10–35%). Independent sales reps license the film on your behalf domestically and internationally, earning a percentage of the deal (10–35%). A sales agency may focus on U.S. and/or domestic, and often requires a down payment, earning a percentage (15–40%) of deals they make, after recouping their expenses. For more info, check out Stacey Parks' *Inside Guide to Independent Film Distribution* (Focal Press). Film markets include Cannes, AFM, Tokyo, Toronto, MIP-TV, MIP-Com, Berlin, and NATPE.

*Marketing and publicity*: Marketing is the campaign you *pay* for, such as placements of ads in various media, while publicity is the act of activating *free* buzz and word of mouth about a film through interviews, press releases, publicity stunts, and appearances. You will need to cut multiple trailers and teasers – to post on your website social media and for use in ancillary elements like apps, contests, games, features, mobisodes, and webisodes. You can find editors who specialize in this, or build it into your editing budget.

*Premiums*: Anything you give out that has the name of the film and the website (pencils, shirts, caps, bracelets, temporary tattoos, jewelry, mugs, rubber bananas, etc).

*Online presence*: At the outset of preproduction, you will need someone to build your website, and establish a social media presence. Tech-savvy PAs or interns may be able to save you money in this arena.

## Distribution Expenses

Plan your distribution and marketing activities from the start, and budget accordingly.

If you are planning on applying for a movie rating by the MPAA Classification and Ratings Administration (CARA), it is based on the budget of the film; do not assume you will receive the rating you expect. www.filmratings.com/filmRatings_Cara/#/resources/

If the Producer wishes for that unmistakable Dolby sound, and the corresponding logo, that begins with your post production facility – get a quote for price and licensing fees.

E&O insurance is an important one for distribution purposes, so get a quote from your provider when you shop around for production insurance. While some distributors or sales agents might pick this cost up for you, there's no guarantee, and the downside is that you may have problems getting it when you most need it. (This is the same with title registration.) To obtain Errors and Omissions insurance, you must get a Script Clearance Report, usually from an attorney who specializes in this field. The point of the report is to minimize legal exposure by checking names of people, locations, businesses, product names, schools, organizations, film clips, photographs, books, works of art, props and anything else that may have been copyrighted by another person or corporation.

Also for E&O insurance, you will need, a title report (search), and title opinion (lawyer approval of the search and results), based on prior use of your proposed title, similarity, and related titles. You can't copyright a title, but you aren't allowed to mooch off somebody else's title (*Return of the Wizard of OZ*) unless you get legal permission from the copyright holder. This doesn't stop companies from making "mockumentary" films (*Snakes on a Train,* by Asylum) which seems to come close – but as long as you do not confuse the audience, legally you are OK (in theory). It is possible to search the U. S. Copyright Office, Library of Congress records, and common law sources like IMDB, Amazon and Netflix to help prevent you from inadvertently choosing a title just like another movie or TV or video project. You will still need to pay a law firm or entertainment attorney to produce these for you if the project is going to be distributed. You might be able to get the distributor or sales agent to front these costs, but it's not a given.

If you plan on holding preview screenings to test audience response, include those costs as well, e.g., renting out a theater, hiring a projectionist, audience recruiting fee, your data gathering and questionnaire process.

## Hidden Expenses

Expenses can be hidden in plain sight. Ask vendors about things that may seem obvious:

- Catering: food for extra people (investors visiting sets, extras) and a place to eat it. Plates, napkins, silverware; what is required for access to water and electricity? How late can they take a head count?
- Return times, days for gear, OT charges
- After-hours contact information if equipment breaks or malfunctions
- Characteristics of the stock/format (there are lots of formats available now to shoot on and they have different quirks)
- If you are shooting on P2 cards, what's the workflow? Ask the Editor so the shoot isn't held up
- MUA and hair: quality prosthetics, wardrobe, make-up, and wigs. They don't have to cost a fortune but they're not cheap; discuss essential elements with make-up, hair and costume Department Heads. High definition formats are so great that they show everything. Everything — and it's not always pretty. An airbrush make-up system may be required
- Stunts — extra people, safety, insurance

*Union/guild*: residual deposits, pension, health and welfare, overtime, meal penalties, production fees, severance, turnaround times, travel requirements (1st class airfare?). Understand these way in advance so you don't get caught out later. If your production goes over the allocated guild/union approved budget, you will be billed after the fact for the bump up. Put a cap on cell phone reimbursement. Per diems are for distant shoots, and when the budget is snug, feed everyone as a group; keep the per diem for extra expenses (forgotten toothbrush, calling card).

*Garbage disposal*: Film production generates a lot of trash, and some of it is toxic. Depending where you are shooting, construction materials, and unused paints and fixatives aren't permitted to be left in any old trash can or poured down the drain: you can get fined, shut down, and it is bad for the environment. Plan your trash.

*Unused supplies*: Try to sell them if possible. For items that remain unsold, if it's expensive to dispose of items, call places like the Salvation Army, local high school and college art teachers, or Habitat for Humanity to find out if they can use them.

*Emotional vampires and power plays*: Everyone should know who's in charge and those in charge should be supported. Lose dead weight or negative energy as early as possible.

*Drugs and booze on set*: Put a clear policy in writing that everyone is aware of. Don't tolerate infractions — it's a safety issue.

*Safety and security*: Worth the price — medic, firemen, policemen, security guards, locks, accounting controls, as required by your insurer, or by the city or state where you are filming. Check with the film commission.

*Cast*: Do they require anything special or extra — entourage, perks, personal chef, trainer, hairdresser, children present, private house, trailer?

Just say **no** to "we'll fix it in post", a mentality that pushes responsibility and expense to post production. This usually moves the headache forward in time, and will disrupt the budget, eventually. Avoid this. This includes the affordable tendency with digital format to shoot so much footage, just because you can. Remember that someone has to go through all that footage.

*Bad weather* slows everything down; look at historical forecasts and the Farmer's Almanac for the regions and season you will be shooting in. Plan accordingly, taking into account recent weather pattern changes. Assign two people to check the Weather channel every day, and at night (in case one person forgets, or you get different forecasts).

*Legal formation*: You can save money in legal expenses by doing certain things yourself, if they are done correctly. Find a good entertainment attorney, recommended by fellow filmmakers, and start cultivating relationships with entertainment lawyers by attending legal seminars concerning film and entertainment law.

Your Producer may already have a production company, but it is common to form a company for each feature film, to offset taxes and protect members and investors. Don't rush to form a legal entity (you'll be on the radar to pay taxes), but *do budget* for it. Every state is a little different. Consult your CPA and attorney, as forming any business entity has tax consequences. *FYI: If you are using location-based incentives, they may have rules about this, so find out before spending a dime.*

*Minor actors*: There are strict rules about the amount of time a minor (18 and under) can work, and be present on set. Minors must have meal, rest, recreation and schooling breaks, as well. The Federal Department of Labor summarizes varying state laws regarding minor employment in a film, which can be found in their Table of Child Entertainment Provisions: www.dol.gov/whd/state/childentertain.htm

**Table 5.8**

| Age of Minor | Maximum Work Time on Set |
|---|---|
| 15 days–6 months | 20 minutes |
| 6 months–2 years | 2 hours |
| 2–5 years | 3 hours |
| 6–8 years | 4–6 hours |
| 9–15 years | 5–7 hours |
| 16–17 years | 6–8 hours |

There is hidden expense on top of the *extra time* it will take for a child's rehearsal and performance. The production must pay a guardian to accompany a minor. The shorter attention span of a young person means more short takes, more footage, more work in post. Babies are adorable, but unpredictable.

*Animal actors*: Require extra time to get from one place to another, and get acclimatized and comfortable in a new environment. They must be cast, trained (centered near major film industries), fed, watered, shaded, sheltered, and cared for, which can all add up. They may require fans, misters, appropriate crates, collars, and veterinarian examinations.

An American Humane Certified Animal Safety Representative™ must be on set (no charge for this within the U.S.) but you are expected to feed them.

Exporting or importing animals requires licenses from the U.S. Dept of the Interior, and a certificate of health is required when you are transporting an animal actor anywhere. Check with your local film commission regarding special permits needed for animals on your set in that region. Animals will incur additional insurance costs, including animal mortality insurance.

*Shipping*: Plan ahead, and make sure there is a human being responsible to account for your package on the other end. If at all possible, assign an office production person the duties so shipments have someone accountable for them at every point. Allocate a budget for shipping AFTER you have researched how much shipping you are likely to do, and to where.

Shipping is expensive even when you are not in a rush, particularly international shipping. Ask who needs it, why exactly, and when. Is this a document or file that can be made into a PDF, or scanned, or transferred online via FTP or the multiple FTP-type services like YouSendIt.com or Mobileme? (These FTP-type services are available for a one-time fee, you don't necessarily have to subscribe annually.)

## End of Chapter Five Review

The proportions of your budget should make sense, revealed on screen in production value, whatever the Producer and Director consider important to this particular film.

Strengthen your budget and schedule with these tips:

- Ask for help; get a second opinion;
- Look at the numbers;
- Make a picture.

The schedule will go through at least four major iterations:

- Preliminary;
- Fortified;
- Create a 6-day week versus a 5-day;
- Comparison;
- Can you take advantage of 3-day weekends?

The budget will go through at least four major iterations:

- Preliminary budget;
- Perfect world;
- Practical (with deals and favors called in) and "No matter what";
- Final approved budget.

Research in advance ways to save money and time on hidden expenses such as:

- Waste disposal;
- Insurance;
- Legal fees;
- Minor and animal actors;
- Shipping.

# Chapter Six
## *Managing Resources*

*"Of all the things I've done, the most vital is coordinating the talents of those who work for us and pointing them towards a certain goal."*

**Walt Disney**

Managing resources means keeping track of multiple priorities at the same time. On a day-to-day level, this means establishing organizational habits for yourself and your production office team to keep you on track. Routine, structure, and checklists are a means to staying on top of the schedule and budget. However you do it, set up a systematic way to keep payroll on time, and evaluate today, tomorrow, the next week of shooting, then yesterday.

*Today*:

- Schedule and budget
- Big deal
- Safety, food and comfort for cast and crew
- Payroll-related activity
- Place
- People
- Equipment

*Tomorrow*:

- Schedule and budget
- Big deal
- Safety, food and comfort for cast and crew
- Payroll-related activity
- Place
- People
- Equipment

Eve Honthaner's indispensible *The Complete Film Production Handbook* presents a brilliant checklist of weekly preproduction activities, as well as great systems to

**Week 1 Checklist and Duty Delegation**

____ Locate and set up production office

____ Team meeting: set preliminary schedule

____ Register business, open accounts: utility, bank

____ Stationery, business cards, web, contact info

____ Script reading and timing

____ Assign milestone tasks

**FIG. 6.1**

Detailed checklists help keep your team on track

order your paperwork (and pretty much everything else). Actionable checklists can help keep production meetings focused. They can be something very simple like the example in Figure 6.1.

Alternatively, create a detailed list to keep forward momentum. On smaller films, often the core team is a handful of people working multiple positions. Under the overall leadership of the Producer, producing staff spearheads business and administrative duties, while the directing unit leads artistic concerns, with everyone contributing to finding cast and crew. Table 6.1 illustrates a preproduction flow chart of tasks, which can be expanded or parsed down, allocated to a timeline, and assigned to team members.

**Table 6.1**

| Producer and LP | Director and AD |
|---|---|
| Where to shoot, contact film commissions | Review script, lock script |
| Breakdown and preliminary schedule | Schedule review and collaboration |
| Identify rates for Dept Heads, post ads for:<br>Location Scout/Manager<br>Casting Director<br>DP<br>Editor<br>Production Accountant<br>Art Director<br>Stunt Coordinator (if needed)<br>Special Effects Supervisor (if needed) | Recommend Dept Heads:<br>DP<br>AD<br>Editor<br>Art Director<br>Make-up/Hair/Wardrobe<br>Location Scout/Manager<br>Casting Director<br>Stunt Coordinator (if needed)<br>Special Effects Supervisor (if needed) |
| Review rates and reels, present best choices to Director and AD, choose 1st, 2nd, 3rd choices | Review rates and reels: choose 1st, 2nd, 3rd choices. Select DP, choose film format |
| Establish potential deals/offers to be extended | Approve offers/deals |
| Extend offers to Dept Heads and negotiate. Prepare deal memos | Create shooting schedule |
| Meeting w/ everyone on board to establish next milestones | Meeting w/ everyone on board to establish next milestones |
| Primary CASTING AUDITIONS | Scout locations, Art Director concepts, headshots |
| Research and identify key vendors. Obtain competitive bids | DP and Director plan setups and floor plans. Storyboard key scenes. Review location options |
| Prep all paperwork, permits, start union process if necessary | Dept Heads: preliminary art budget, location rates, equipment |
| Refine budget w/ Dept Heads' info | Refine budget items w/ feedback |
| Casting call backs | Casting call backs |
| Post ads for crew, identify catering | Dept Heads recommend crew |
| Review crew rates and reels, present best choices to Director and Dept Heads | Choices for crew, 1st, 2nd, 3rd |
| Extend offers and negotiate potential deals, and finalize crew and cast contracts. Open vendor accounts | Lighting plan: refine equipment requirements |
| Finalize paperwork with cast/crew/vendors. Obtain permits and releases | Rent and buy props, art supplies, construction materials |
| Finalize schedule, create transportation plan. If screenplay changed, print and distribute | Rehearsals and amendments to screenplay. Script re-timing |
| Finalize budget, with all deals | Storyboards, shot list, lighting designs, stunts |
| Lock in insurance, location paperwork | Begin construction if necessary and dressing sets as possible |
| Create online, social media campaign and website | Art department, and Make-up/Hair/Wardrobe |
| Safety meeting | Tech scout |

## Relationship between Script, Schedule and Budget

The *quickest* way to reduce your schedule and budget is by cutting: cut script pages, scenes, locations, and characters. In the best possible world, this happens as early as possible.

The *script, schedule* and *budget* are *interconnected*; whoever is responsible for making script changes must relay them to you on a regular basis. Once you learn of script changes, discuss with the AD and Director how this will influence the schedule and budget. This information needs to immediately flow to correct parties; print revised pages on different colored paper, and disseminate to Department Heads. Rental dates may need to be changed, call times shifted, and personnel schedules updated. Attend to this as quickly as possible, due to the ripple effect from script, to schedule, to budget. Hiring one less, or one more, actor will affect wardrobe, make-up and hair, lens choices, catering, space for dressing, and perhaps sets, props, transportation, and paperwork.

The UPM or Line Producer spends time in the production office, and on the set, and needs eyes and ears in both places at all times. Without up-to-date information, a link between the script, schedule and budget is lost. Make a point to schedule brief production meetings with the core team for whoever is available at the start, middle and end of the day; talk to the AD, Director, or script supervisor every day in order to stay abreast of the latest developments.

*Lock it up.* For a time, everything is in flux, then at some point during preproduction things get *locked* – the script, schedule and budget. Once locked, final decisions can be made, which can guide every decision. Initial efforts leading up to principal photography are to lock these items up, then create a shoot based on the final results.

People are the most powerful resource. Investigate personnel difficulties quickly. Most filmmakers want to do a good job, facilitated by a clear understanding of their duties and having a key crew member to answer to. If no resolution can be found, disruptors need to be let go.

## Production Accountant, AD and Line Producer

The Line Producer, AD and Production Accountant work together to maintain the integrity of the production by tending to different facets of the schedule and budget. The AD's focus is on the set and schedule on behalf of the Director's vision; the Accountant's focus is on the schedule and flow of money; and the Line Producer's focus is balancing the schedule and budget with input from both parties. Everyone works to stay on schedule and under the guiding hand of the Producer.

The Production Accountant (**AKA:** Key Production Accountant, or Production Auditor) pays the bills, directs payroll activities, signs checks, keeps the books, oversees petty cash, and prepares very specific budgeting and cost reports, like the cash flow report which shows how money is to be spent over time on a weekly basis, and reports showing where money was spent that week or day (hot costs). The Production Accountant is a critical team member, auditing spending, and keeping an eye on potential cost overruns. If you have a completion bond in place, the accountant reports to them as required.

In addition to providing reliable, timely information, and keeping them safe and fed, get your cast and crew paid properly and on time. This will generate goodwill, loyalty and hard work. Both the Line Producer and the Production Accountant must know who is working through a loan-out so the taxes are correct, as well as the union/non-union status of each employee.

Most films incur bills to be paid right away, so bring in an accountant early. While not required to be a CPA, that person should have experience *specifically* with film and TV production accounting, and understand location incentive requirements (if that is part of the financing plan). Production accounting is different from financial estate planning or tax return preparation. When interviewing potential accountants and accounting companies, ask which software they know, so that it works with your system.

Outsourcing payroll makes everyone's life easier, since your production revolves around the payroll cycle. If doing payroll yourself, discuss with your accountant how best to set it up. Payroll companies include: Indiepay, Entertainment Partners, Cast and Crew, Ease Entertainment, and Media Services, and the combination of payroll services and software is generally a package deal.

Meticulous attention to detail, accuracy and honesty are qualities to look for in your accounting team. When you interview accountants, find out if they provide the following services for all the phases of the project.

*Preproduction*:

Assist in production company set up/filing system

Obtaining Federal ID numbers

Set up bank accounts

Retain payroll company, etc.

Budget preparation

Cash flow analysis/reports

Purchase order/check requisition/invoice system

Bookkeeping: properly record and account transactions

*Production and Post*:

Budgeting

Accounts payable

Payroll

Petty cash

Cost reporting

Hot cost reporting

Bank reconciliations

Insurance claims

Bank reconciliations

Re-shoot accounting

Auditing: double-check that production financing was spent as planned

State tax rebate filing

Profit Participation Payout calculations and payment management

1099 filings

Taxation consultation

Union Deferment Payout calculations

Bookkeeping services

Record storage

Establishing a system of controls will help you keep an eye on money during production. *Purchase orders* are used to approve a cost in advance of actual payment. Knowing in advance what will be spent keeps money from flying out the window due to last minute requests not vetted through proper channels. Department heads have to sign off on purchase orders as pertains to their intentions and use, and their portion of the budget. When *invoices* come in, they get matched to the appropriate approved purchase order, approved by the Department Head (double-checked with time card if appropriate) and paid by check, then entered into the accounting system and filed. *Check requisitions* (or check requests) are requests for a check, or wire transfers, for an immediate purchase for a shoot, and are preferable to using petty cash, as you will have a paper trail. A *petty cash* system for requests and reimbursement, and department-approved and checked timecards for Payroll submission, help maintain order and ultimately save money.

The *First* Assistant Director (**AKA:** AD) runs the set. The AD helps establish the shooting schedule and maintain it, keeping things moving smoothly – working with the UPM to make the most efficient plan that will make the best use of the time and work of the Director, crew, equipment and cast. The AD shadows the Director – relaying information from Director to Crew, and vice versa. This is a key team member and together with the UPM they keep the production running. On shoots with inexperienced directors, a great AD helps keep the bus on the road.

Compact crews may just include one AD. Sometimes it's necessary to add another – a 2nd AD (**AKA:** Key 2nd AD) – to wrangle call sheets and other paperwork, oversee actors' preparation, and work with background actors.

Complex productions might utilize a 2nd 2nd AD and/or 3rd AD hired for a complicated day, or cumbersome situations like moving large groups, to supervise PAs (Production Assistants). Union ADs are members of the DGA.

The *Line Producer* runs the production office. A problem solver, the LP or UPM is responsible for all below-the-line costs. A UPM – Unit Production Manager – is a member of the DGA, a Line Producer is not, but their duties are similar. A UPM is usually hired by a Producer of a film or television show, and is responsible for watching all the costs of the project, with the intention of delivering the film or television show on budget at the end of principal photography. When the shooting begins, they may divide their time between the office and the set, or may work out of a trailer on the set.

A Line Producer or UPM's duties include: breaking down the script, preparing an initial schedule and budget, financial negotiations, preparing a preliminary shooting schedule which the AD takes over, hiring the crew, and overseeing Director-approved hires.

Management duties include approving production expenditures, negotiating salaries and equipment rates, approving time cards, call sheets and production reports, and settling conflicts.

## Optimize the Shoot

Every shoot is different, but it's common sense to plan ahead as much as possible. Communicate so everyone is on the same page, know the rules and parameters of your shoot, and conserve energy and money to any extent possible.

### No Unnecessary Movement

Every movement during the course of your shoot takes time – and production time is the most expensive of all. Every camera setup, relight, blocking and rehearsal, rigging, production meeting, eating, and traveling, all take time. The only time that actually makes it into your movie is the time when crew is working, actors are acting, and the Director's directing with camera and sound rolling. Create a map of your locations to guarantee the shortest route and most cost-efficient order.

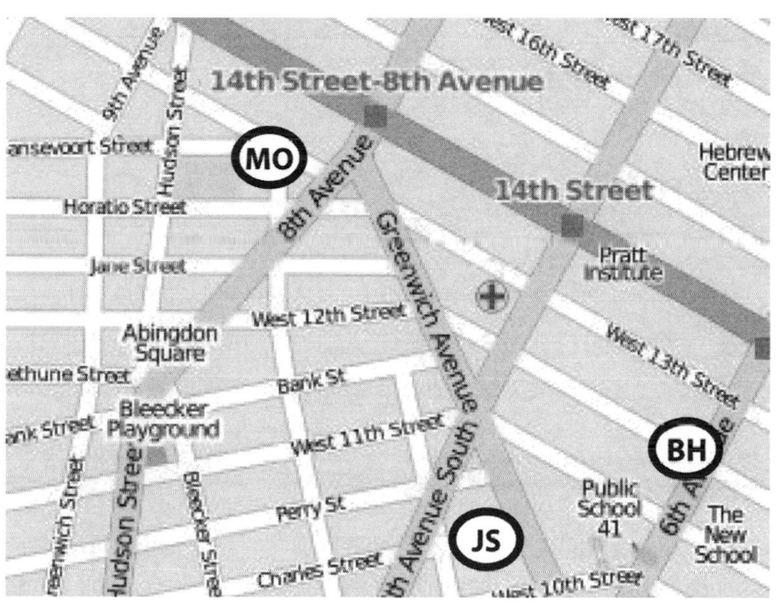


**FIG. 6.2**

Use a map to optimize shoot time, and reduce movement if possible


### Consider the Weather

Get a weather app on your phone, and put two people in charge of daily weather reports (from different sources). Check with the WeatherChannel.com periodically during shoot days to avert delays.

Check historical weather, Farmers' Almanac (www.FarmersAlmanac.com) one to two years back. For other historical weather information, the National Weather Service (www.weather.gov) will lend guidance for seasonality. You should plan weather backup plans in any case.

**Days Off, Turnaround, Meal Times**

If you are shooting union, learn the rules and plan to adhere to them strictly, otherwise penalties and fines will add up. When shooting non-union, use common sense, and use the union rules as a guide.

*Days off* give your cast and crew both a physical and emotional rest. Five-day weeks are standard on local shoots, and six-day weeks on distant shoots. Depending on the scope of the film, you may be able to double shift your production by hiring a second unit to get covers on the weekend.

Working with the union, pay strict attention to *turnaround* time (**AKA:** rest time) – the minimum time off between days of successive shooting.

- DGA – 8 hours
- SAG – 12 hours
- IATSE and Below the Line – 10 hours
- Teamsters – None

*Meal times* – must take place the standard six hours after starting work, lasting a minimum duration of half an hour for hot catered meal and an hour for anything else. In addition to the unions, state laws dictate meal intervals and length, so check the state Department of Labor website to make sure you are in compliance with the law. Really good hot breakfasts will get people to work on time, and it isn't unusual for crew to catalogue past work experiences according to quality and quantity of food. Catering = buffet and full meals; Kraft Services = snacks available all the time.

Overtime isn't just limited to time and a half; laws dictating double time over 12 hours are determined state by state (check the Department of Labor website for applicable state), and unions dictate overtime up to three times the established hourly rate for certain circumstances.

**Using a Second Unit**

A *second unit* is like a mini-crew, led by the second Unit Director and a Cinematographer. (The Director of the film is technically considered the First Unit Director.)

The second unit captures secondary footage, i.e., footage without key actors and dialogue (**AKA:** golden hour or magic hour). They may be sent out to capitalize on great weather, golden hour, or accommodate a tight schedule for a particular actor or location access, or film inserts, close-ups, handheld work, cutaways, exteriors, establishing shots, and sometimes stunts.

Second unit footage may not be considered the primary story-telling plot points, but it is critical in assisting the Editor, providing footage to build a story, as well as details, transitions, variety, character motivation, and perspective for the viewer.

Even though you are paying for additional crew (and support personnel if needed), and their gear, an efficient second unit saves time and money. Weighing the price of a second unit should be considered compared with how tight the schedule is (with shooting occurring in two places at once) and your Director's input.

A second unit is different from a multi-camera setup — when several cameras (A-Camera, B-Camera, etc.) shoot one scene at the same time. It is worth the expense when shooting a complex scene (particularly one that cannot be easily repeated), such as a crowd scene or one that involves choreography, stunts, action, explosions, special effects, and animals.

**Other Factors**

*Department budgets*: Department heads must sign off on their portion of the budget and keep to it, by reporting to the Line Producer or Production Manager. When new spending is mentioned, find out how it's going to be paid for — what other line items in the budget will be reduced to cover new costs? The Director, Producer and AD must support you in these efforts to safeguard the budget. When your team begins to make promises, remind them of the financial consequences.

*Lighting* incurs expense. Not only do you have to budget for the equipment but for electricity as well. Whenever possible, condense night shooting in your schedule. If there are many interior scenes, which take place at night in the screenplay, seek locations which may be dressed as night scenes (i.e., with fewer or no windows). Set up the schedule to shift to a night schedule, or, instead of starting late, discuss with the AD whether it makes sense to set call times in the late afternoon, just before dark.

During *sunrise* and *sunset*, natural lighting and shadow is the most beautiful, as opposed to outdoor lighting at high noon when shadows are harsh. Your DP and Director will most likely want to exploit sunrise and/or sunset during the schedule to achieve a specific effect. While there are hundreds of filters available, including a sunrise filter, you cannot pay for the quality of light during these times of day, and requests to schedule around these times should be accommodated. (Schedule these early on in case the weather doesn't cooperate). You can check sunrise and sunset times in advance to know how much daylight you will have available (www.sunrisesunset.com).

*Cloudy* and overcast days also create flattering light effects, and your DP and Director may want to adjust the schedule, if possible, on the fly to take advantage of these conditions.

Shooting *day for night*, or dusk for night, is an older technique that can be used as an effect, but audiences recognize it right away. Shooting outside at night is more expensive than day shooting, in terms of almost everything. The lighting equipment is more powerful and therefore more expensive, and neighbors can be touchy about noise and lights. Decisions to work outside at night should be weighed carefully.

*Effects* that are well planned can make you jump out of your seat, but poorly conceived effects just disrupt the story. They must be planned in advance – as early as possible – as to how each effect will be executed, and integrated with original photography. All of the following require sufficient planning time, and coordination with your Editor and post production facility; most have safety ramifications:

- Green screen/blue screen;
- Physical effects: models, miniatures, prosthetics, mechanically operated vehicles, puppets, robots, specialty props;
- Special make-up effects, used in preparation of prosthetics;
- Mechanical effects, like explosions, weather, crashes, bullets.

*Shooting outside the country* requires three times the planning of a domestic shoot: for research, finding partners and translators, understanding shipping regulations, pricing travel and lodging, and dealing with currency and tax issues. You will need to coordinate workflows and communication schedules with parties you are working with (bearing in mind the time difference), as well as build time pads for jet lag recovery (if possible).

Critical decisions include:

- Who goes and who stays;
- Currency and payment in native currency; language; translator;

- Laws, rules, regulations, working conditions;
- Threat of transportation strikes/safety;
- Insurance and bond demands re: travel;
- Import and export restrictions – money, equipment, medicine;
- Social customs – clothing, religious;
- Press censorship.

Do a thorough cost–benefit analysis of traveling abroad, and get in touch with filmmakers who have shot there. Begin discussions with native film commissions as soon as possible.

## End of Chapter Six Review

Establishing routines and detailed, actionable checklists assigned to specific people will improve the planning process, and the entire production as a whole.

*Establish your daily routine.* It should address tending to immediate tasks and tasks coming up that require a little attention, point by point. These will include: schedule and budget; the "big deal" of the day; safety, food and comfort for cast and crew; payroll-related activity; location; people and equipment. Recognize that this will continually be interrupted by the needs and requirements of various parties during production, so it's important to establish a rhythm.

*The script, schedule and budget are interconnected.* Staying abreast of changes to any of these should be discussed and communicated with the AD, Director, and Department Heads. The quickest way to reduce your schedule and budget is to cut pages, scenes, locations, and characters, as early as possible.

*The Line Producer, AD and Production Accountant work together.* The AD's focus is on the set and schedule; the Accountant's focus is on the money; and the Line Producer's focus is on the schedule and budget, with input from both the AD and Accountant.

*Optimizing the shoot* includes reducing unnecessary movement whenever possible, and being continually aware of weather forecasts and available outdoor light. Understand that infringing on required times off, such as days off, turnaround time, and meal times, can result in cost overages. Consider using a second unit to optimize the schedule and budget. Thoroughly consider and plan for other factors, like night shooting, effects and foreign travel, which have a significant impact on both the schedule and budget of the film.

# Chapter Seven
## *Special Considerations*

Each type of film presents challenges and will require special consideration. For example, some films take longer than others to make (features), require intermittent shoot schedules (documentaries), pose severely restrictive time and financial parameters (most films) or format (web and TV), or require use of non-actors (educational and corporate). The commonalities are to:

- Figure out what you know, and start from there;
- Ask questions;
- Apply logic and common sense;
- Consolidate resources (people, places, things) whenever possible.

Turn your schedule upside down and run different scenarios: "What if. . .longer days, shorter days, longer weeks, shorter weeks, non-union, union, 2nd unit, 3rd unit, etc."

Turn your budget upside down: "What if. . .different vendors, less overtime, rent kits instead of purchasing supplies, cast our own extras – when will we need funds?" Identify potential line items that are tight, or roomy, i.e., where there may be potential extra money. Budget line items are based on assumptions – using a certain location or number of background actors determines the lenses you must rent for that day; if you plan to rent equipment from several companies, cost savings may be achieved by consolidating an equipment order with one vendor.

Thorough knowledge of the budget will assist with *cash flow* (a schedule of when you will need funds and how much), the *cost report* (actual spending of costs to date), and the film's ultimate *audit*. Films are audited after the fact, so funders can see how their money was spent, e.g., on the film, not on vacation to Aruba. The Producer has to be able to account for every penny to their financiers. You don't want to go too much "under" budget (the financiers will want the balance of funds back), but you can't go over, because the Producer will be on the hook during production and it may damage the film. Working as the Line Producer, you will be counted upon as primary budget caretaker.

One way to do an up-close examination of the budget is to do comparisons, and make groups. While working on the budget, it is helpful to compare costs of specific *groups* of items. You can see what would happen if you omitted a certain group, or changed it in a fundamental way. Comparing local with distant shoot prices, and prep versus wrap, helps to discover potential savings.

When you set up your budget, create groups (Setup/Groups) for "Local" and "Distant", to compare their costs.

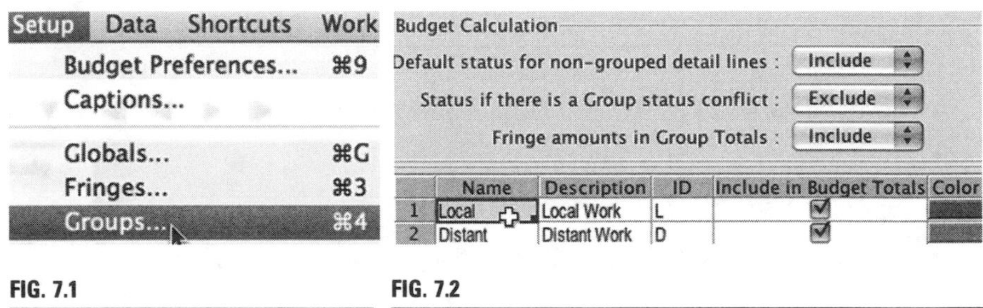


**FIG. 7.1**

Groups help you examine and compare expenses

**FIG. 7.2**

"Local" and "Distant" are commonly used groups

At the Detail level, apply groups to associated line items. Select "Local" lines (see Figures 7.3 and 7.4).

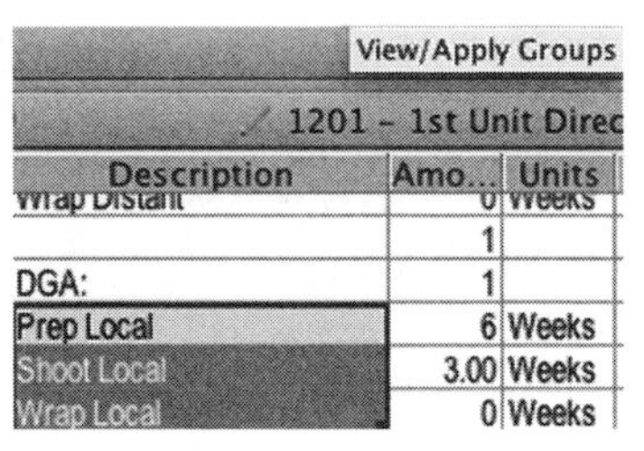


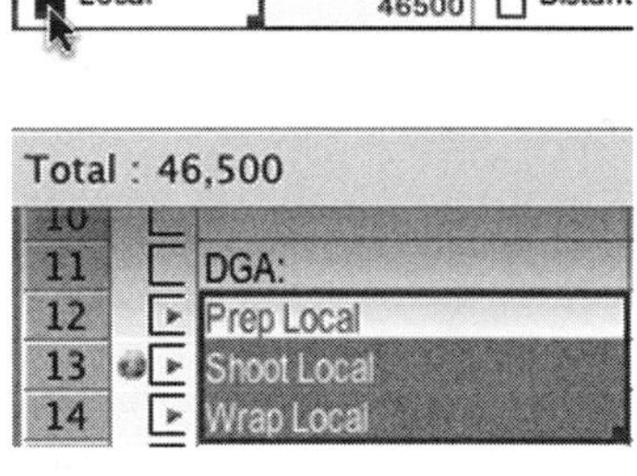


**FIG. 7.3**

Select "Local" line items in View/Apply Groups

**FIG. 7.4**

Tag "Local" and close

Repeat for "Distant". Highlight "Distant" lines, click View/Apply Groups, and tag "Distant".

Note totals (see Figure 7.8) — the complete budget total, in the lower left, and the total of Local and Distant Shoots on the lower right — to monitor changes.

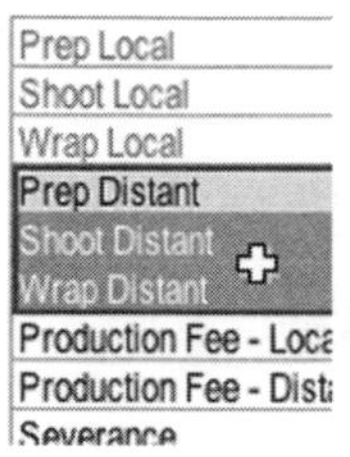


**FIG. 7.5**

Repeat for "Distant": select "Distant" lines

**FIG. 7.6**

View/Apply Groups

**FIG. 7.7**

Tag "Distant"

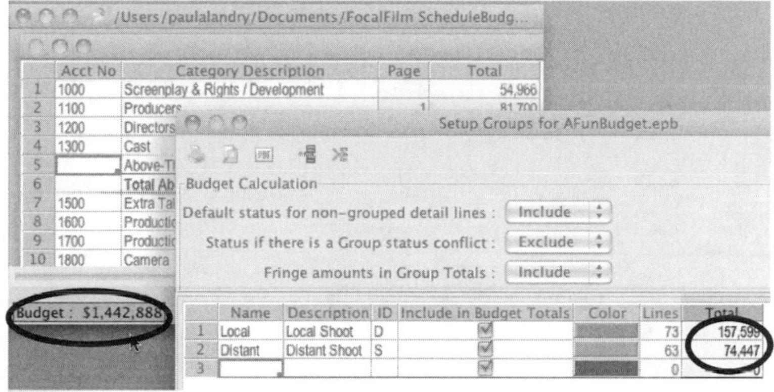


**FIG. 7.8**

Inside "Groups" there are totals, and at the bottom of your budgeting program, Budget totals and Session totals track recent changes. The Budget total is the entire budget amount at that moment, and Session totals consist of changes you have made since opening the file

All of the "Local Shoot" lines together adds up to 157,599; the Distant Shoot lines adds up to 74,447. (At this point, the Local Shoot is roughly twice as much as the Distant Shoot. Why don't 157,599 + 74,447 add up to the total budget number $1,442,888? Either because there are many non-location specific items within the budget, or you haven't assigned groups to everything yet.)

The meaning of these figures, in a broader sense, pertains to the screenplay. If scenes at the Distant Shoot are minor, would it be possible to send fewer crew or cast, or a second unit? Or hire locals and send a talented AD? That might reduce the "Distant" portion of the budget and related travel/lodging expenses. The reduction in cost must be weighed against reduced efficiencies of fewer people, or hiring unknown local crew. By hiding, or suppressing, the "Local Shoot" part of the budget, you can observe where the biggest changes occur, and in what categories (see Figure 7.9).

*Uncheck* "Local Shoot" to suppress it (see Figure 7.10).

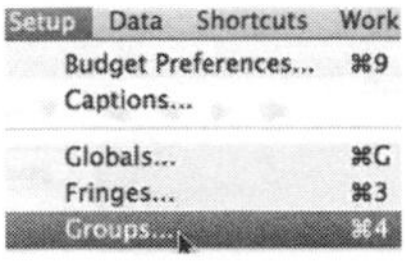

**FIG. 7.9**

Set up "Groups" to suppress different budget parts

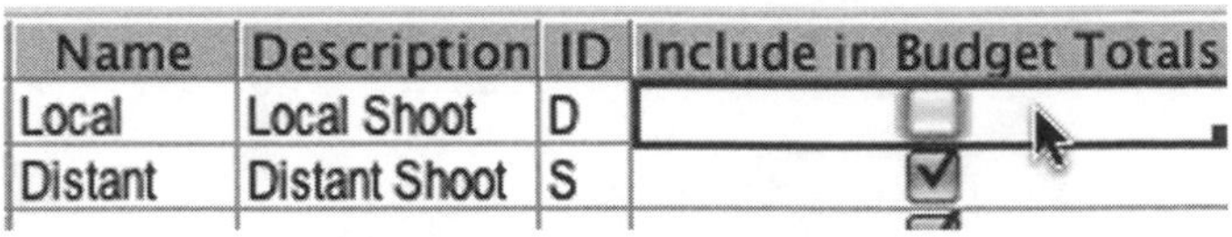

**FIG. 7.10**

Uncheck the part of the budget you want to suppress

And the overall budget total immediately updates *without* the Local Shoot cost.

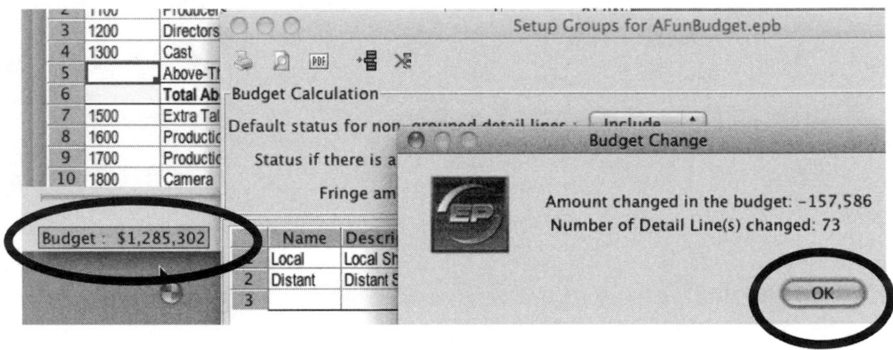


**FIG. 7.11**

Suppressing parts of the budget can help you and your team make important spending decisions

Most budgeting software shows updated totals, either at the top or the bottom of the page.

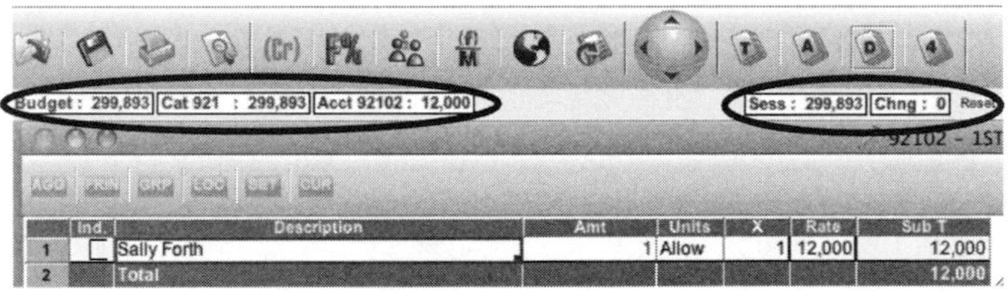


**FIG. 7.12**

Totals along the top show recent changes and the budget total

Create a *new* version of a budget and do a *comparison*. Open your budget, do a Save As, and name it something different, related to the experiment: for example, SpunOutLove_Budget_V2_ReducedTravel, SpunOutLove_Budget_V3_NonUnion, etc. Make changes to this new budget: recalculate, save and close. Now compare.

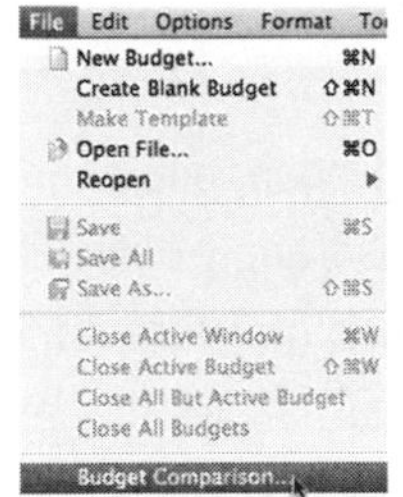


FIG. 7.13

Comparing budgets gives you an opportunity to find ways to save money

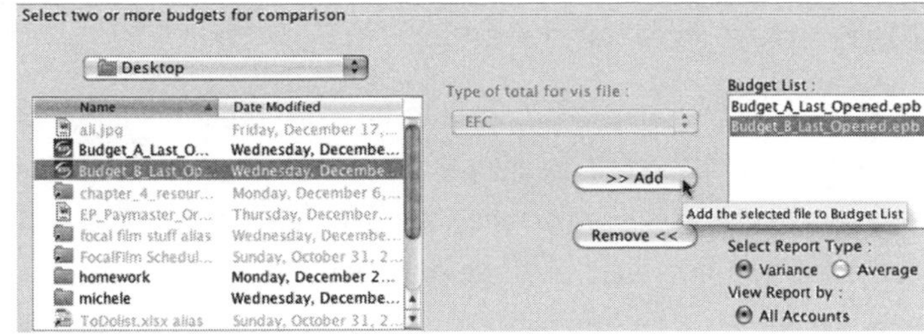


FIG. 7.14

Compare budgets with the same categories and numbering system

In Figure 7.15, it's easy to see that in Budget A the "Producers" and "Directors" figures are very different from Budget B. Now you can go investigate that – should figures be reduced, was something missing, why the discrepancy, and how to come up with a solution?

*FYI: If the comparison budgets (you can compare several) don't have the same account format, it is confusing and not useful: you're comparing apples with oranges.*

| Acct No | Category Description | Budget_A | Budget_B | Variance | Percent |
|---|---|---|---|---|---|
| 1000 | Screenplay & Rights / Development | $54,966 | $54,966 | 0 | 0% |
| 1100 | Producers | $913,638 | $81,700 | 831,938 | 91% |
| 1200 | Directors | $336,505 | $139,574 | 196,931 | 59% |
| 1300 | Cast | $109,346 | $109,346 | 0 | 0% |
| | Above-The-Line Travel/Other | $16,835 | $16,835 | 0 | 0% |
| | **Total Above-The-Line** | **$1,431,290** | **$402,421** | **1,028,869** | 72% |
| 1500 | Extra Talent | $30,000 | $30,000 | 0 | 0% |

FIG. 7.15

Producers and financiers often find it helpful to compare and contrast different budget scenarios

Scheduling and Budgeting Your Film

## Narrative Feature Film

In addition to the myriad of details to be worked out during preproduction, one priority is to *work the script*. Readings, rehearsals (once cast is identified and available) and rewrites will strengthen the material. The stronger the plot and structure, and the more vivid and believable the dialogue, the better the completed film will be, at any budget. All script preparation, such as videotaping rehearsals, previs and storyboarding important scenes, can save time and money during principal photography.

Tell everyone you know about the film, the story, cast, and crew; to draw support. Update them with email newsletters (*Constant Contact, YMLP, MailChimp, Mad Mimi*). In addition to appointing a Producer of Marketing and Distribution, you may also need a Producer of Social Media; the point is to make it a responsibility for a member of the team. Create a website, get on social media (e.g., *Facebook, YouTube, MySpace, Twitter, Bebo, Vimeo, 2nd Life, LinkedIn*) and start connecting to people. Solicit support from friends and family – they serve as valuable resources for locations, food, transportation, extras, even financing, and contribute to building momentum and awareness. If there is a facet of the production that would create a good story, consider crafting an article or series of articles for one of the independent websites/magazines/film communities.

*Marathon mentality*: Has everyone "trained" with a 5K or 10K run? Short races are training for marathons – short films are training for features.

*More money*: You can help the Producer, and the film, by exploiting every possible source of financing, whether location-, grant- or foundation-based or regional-, state-, or city-wide. Keep a Google alert set for contests and competitions, and join filmmaking communities online (distributors and agents of all sizes troll them), and keep your eyes out for new angel investors, partners and funding sources.

This activity will contribute to *both* the schedule and the *budget* in the form of an unlikely consequence, celebrity interest or involvement, a news story, winning publicity and free stock, lab time, access to equipment, locations, mentorship, or community involvement. Just like networking on a personal level leads to new opportunities, networking for a film leads to publicity and relationships that will improve the final product, and increase marketing and distribution opportunities.

*Don't wait to budget (time and cash) for marketing and distribution*: Often overlooked (until everyone is exhausted and the money is gone), this work should start as early as possible, hopefully during preproduction. Plan to take pictures – of cast, rehearsals, make-up, shoot, crew, construction, and the production office – to create the story of making the film; marketing and distribution require good stills. Videotape the production office; "vlogging," and creating "extra" DVD materials (the making of your great film), is fun and good experience for an intern/filmmaker.

Plan distribution deliverables for a feature along the way, so there's less scrambling at the end. Some of the items can only be completed before post, but others are available during preproduction – such as the synopsis, bios, crew and cast list, and certain contracts.

Here are just a few things you will be required to deliver to a distributor:

- Masters and prints, original negative, workprints, answer print, show prints, any interpositives or duplicates;
- Audio masters and sound elements;
- Videotape masters and screeners;
- Editing materials: EDLs (edit decision lists), code books, camera reports;
- Textless backgrounds, all footage, ends, trims, whether used or unused, dailies, source material;
- Quality report from the lab, lab access letter (if applicable);
- 20–30 color photos, 10–20 black and white photos; (all high resolution);
- Detailed written information regarding run time, aspect ratio and type of audio track;
- All marketing and publicity materials created, including a paper press kit and EPK (electronic press kit): synopsis, complete cast and crew list, bios of key filmmakers, final script, news hooks;
- Music – cue sheets, copies of music licenses, publishing rights and clearance agreements, song titles, the music publishers, run times, credits, names of the performing artists, songwriters and composers, lyrics;
- Trailers and bonus materials;
- Chain of title documents;
- M&E (music and effects) tracks;
- MPAA rating (if applicable);
- Key art, posters, logos, design elements related to the film;
- Access to online marketing materials created for the film;

- A list of contractual credits with corresponding agreements, releases, contracts and permissions related to the production;
- Guild and union paperwork, signed as required.

**Strengthening the Relationship with your Team**

One complaint I hear from cast and crew after a film's completion is that they want to know what's up with the production, i.e., its status, festival acceptances, access to clips for their own use — and this is even more important when everyone is paid little (or nothing). Automate and share this information whenever possible, for example by setting up and continuously updating a blog or feed about the film that interested cast and crew can subscribe to.

## Documentary Film

Docs don't usually have a traditional script. Wildlife, historical, technical, and political documentaries all have different styles, but are founded upon an outline, proposal, or treatment. Filmmakers have *some* idea of shots needed to structure the story, but not all; parts of the story emerge through a process of discovery built upon specific goals.

Documentaries have milestones — climactic and pivotal scenes — without which there would be no story, just like a feature. Schedule and budget for each important beat in the outline. Strive to capture important footage as early in the process as possible to maintain forward momentum. If there is no script, use different locations as "scenes" and number them. A narrator's voice-over, a host, interviews, research, archival, travel, and lodging are all concrete elements that can be scheduled and budgeted for. Often, a lot of shooting, then wading through footage happens before the storyline emerges — followed by more scripting and planning.

Documentary teams are generally smaller than features teams, and tend to be more mobile. Travel, interviews, or specific events are concrete items to schedule around, and budget for. It is natural for a doc. to be scheduled in fits and starts — similar to running a triathlon, i.e., a long race in disparate pieces. Use the same parameters you would for a feature, i.e., how much time will be allocated to each phase of production. Center your schedule around key events, interviews, good weather for outdoor scenes, and, to the best of the team's ability, schedule pivotal scenes first. Research is a significant (and sometimes expensive) aspect of the doc. process. Together with your team, identify a filmmaker to stylistically model the film after (e.g., Michael Moore, Michael Verhoeven Errol Morris, Morgan Spurlock), and pinpoint the expensive and time-consuming elements which get the story across.

A typical narrative film, whether long or short, generally progresses in a relatively linear fashion: development; prep; shoot; post/wrap (see Table 7.1).

**Table 7.1**

| Development | Financing | Prep Wk 1 | Prep Wk 2 | Prep Wk 3 | Prep Wk 4 | Prep Wk 5 | Shoot Wk 1 | Shoot Wk 2 | Post Wk 1 | Post Wk 2 | Post Wk 3 | Post Wk 4 |
|---|---|---|---|---|---|---|---|---|---|---|---|---|

Documentaries are iterative: development, financing, prep and shooting, *pause* — analyze footage — post production, and craft story, which leads to more prep and shoot (and possibly the search for more funding). It is not unusual for the overall schedule to look more like the one in Table 7.2, and there may be large gaps between shoots.

**Table 7.2**

| Development | Financing | Prep Wk 1 | Prep Wk 2 | Prep Wk 3 | Shoot Wk 1 | Post Wk 1 | Post Wk 2 | Financing | Prep Wk 4 | Prep Wk 5 | Shoot Wk 2 | Post Wk 3 |
|---|---|---|---|---|---|---|---|---|---|---|---|---|

Doc. budgets have line items that do not necessarily appear in feature film budgets:

- Research, stock footage and images;
- Historic experts, licensing audio and video clips;
- Permissions, clearances and releases of interview subjects;
- Motion graphics, animated sequences;
- Cast: narrator, voice-over, or host;
- E&O insurance (important);
- Fiscal sponsorship, grants, foundation funding;
- Cash donations, in-kind donations;
- Legal guidance on fair use elements incorporated into the story.

Look at other docs that match your team's concept; analyze how much footage should be interviews, establishing shots, stock footage, stills, personal stories. It's one thing to shoot Michael Moore style (with a mobile crew and lots of moxie), or like Lance Lipman directing *Dying to Live* (about organ donation), showing patience and finesse in a delicate situation, or *How's Your News* (Arthur Bradford) (close personal relationships, man on the street interviews in a new way) but quite another to shoot in the style of *March of the Penguins* (Luc Jacquet) or *Winged Migration* (Jacques Perrin, Jacques Cluzaud, Michel Debats). Will you need a lot of gear? A lot of people? Transport to the Arctic?

The same process applies as for the scheduling and budgeting of any other project — find out the intended end-plan for the project. ITVS, PBS, cable channels such as Discovery, or the BBC have technical delivery requirements. Do your homework to find out what that is: call and ask, and talk to other filmmakers.

Many docs do not pay interview subjects; make sure that is clearly understood by participants. When you are working with non-actors, plan extra time as the camera may make them nervous. Prepare your subjects as much as possible (unless your intention is the opposite), with a brief list of topics. Let them know what you are doing, the need for space or quiet, and approximately how much time you will need. Assure them that they do not need to memorize a script.

When scheduling to shoot rare, or one-time only, real-life events, prepare thoroughly — gear, stock, releases and people — and get as much footage as you can.

Figure 7.16 illustrates a Topsheet for a documentary.

| | | | | | |
|---|---|---|---|---|---|
| Program: | Bookem - A Library Restoration | | | | |
| Format: | DV 24P | | | | |
| Producer/Director: Joan Stindwcyk | | Research: | 10 | weeks | |
| Locations: NJ | | Prep: | 7 | weeks | |
| | | Shoot: | 22 | days (over 12 wks) | |
| Budget date: 14 Oct 2007 | | Wrap: | 2 | weeks | |
| | | Post: | 24 | weeks | |
| | | TOTAL: | 55 | weeks | |
| | ABOVE THE LINE | | | | TOTAL BUDGET |
| 1000 | Pre-Production and Development | | | | 2,500 |
| 2000 | Producing Staff | | | | 8,620 |
| 3000 | Rights, Music & Talent | | | | 3,927 |
| | TOTAL ABOVE THE LINE | | | | 15,047 |
| | BELOW THE LINE | | | | TOTAL BUDGET |
| 4000 | Crew & Personnel | | | | 15,387 |
| 5000 | Production Expenses | | | | 5,703 |
| 6000 | Travel and related expenses | | | | 7,304 |
| 7000 | Post-production | | | | 6,397 |
| 8000 | Insurance | | | | 1,640 |
| 9000 | Office & Administration costs | | | | 3,204 |
| 10000 | Other Required Items | | | | 420 |
| | TOTAL BELOW THE LINE | | | | 40,055 |
| | SUBTOTAL (ATL + BTL) | | | | 55,102 |
| | CONTINGENCY | | | | 5,510 |
| | FISCAL SPONSOR FEE | | | | 1,320 |
| | GRAND TOTAL | | | | 61,932 |

**FIG. 7.16**

Doc. budgets are often more streamlined

Note the line from the preceding budget, near the bottom, "FISCAL SPONSOR FEE". Many documentaries can apply for grant funding, but may need to incorporate as a non-profit company (501c3, IRS tax-exempt status). If you don't have non-profit status (which takes time, incurs expense and may not be practical when making one production), you can "borrow" (**AKA:** umbrella) 501c3 status from a fiscal sponsor. The production pays a percentage of funds raised through that entity to the sponsor.

While the majority of docs apply prior to preproduction, in some cases films in process can apply for fiscal sponsorship. The process typically consists of submitting a proposal, purpose or story description, schedule and budget, bios of your team, the documentary's target audience, marketing and distribution strategy, importance of the project, a funding strategy and supplemental materials (like a reel or news articles on the topic). The fiscal sponsor doesn't fund your film, it allows the film production to "borrow" their non-profit status during financing. Donations to the film will be tax deductible, which will be an incentive to potential funders.

Checks for your film are addressed to the fiscal sponsor; they deduct a fee (10–15%), and then send the remaining amount to the production company. You must include this item in the budget as the film must pay that amount out.

The Foundation Center (Foundationcenter.org) is a database and library of information about grants of all kinds – a valuable first stop when working on a doc.

Many associations offer fiscal sponsorship to documentary makers; search online and check out:

http://www.documentary.org/community/IDA-resources/fiscal_sponsorship

http://www.der.org/services/fiscal-sponsor/

http://www.wmm.com/filmmakers/applyforsponsorhip.shtml

www.fiscalsponsordirectory.org

http://www.ifp.org/fiscal-sponsorship/

www.fracturedatlas.org/site/fiscal

http://southerndocumentaryfund.org/fiscal-sponsorship/

Figure 7.17 shows a documentary budget for *Not a Feather But a Dot*, which includes a marketing budget. It was created in iterations, i.e., rounds of creation over time. The format is slightly different from the typical Topsheet and Detail level.

Budgeting tips for documentarians:

- Do include payment for your time and your team as is the norm for similar crew in your area.
- Do include the cost to create a study guide to accompany the film if intended for educational use.

| NOT A FEATHER BUT A DOT: BASE "A" Budget for 4/9/2009 | | | | | | |
|---|---|---|---|---|---|---|
| | # | | # | Unit | Price | Total Cost |
| **PRE-PRODUCTION TEAM** | | | | | | |
| Research | 1 | x | 17 | days | $175 | $2,975 |
| Production Coordinator | 1 | x | 10 | days | $200 | $2,000 |
| | | | | | | **$4,975** |
| | | | | | | |
| **PRODUCTION TEAM** | | | | | | |
| Director/Producer | 1 | x | 4 | weeks | $1,000 | $4,000 |
| Production Manager | 1 | x | 5 | days | $250 | $1,250 |
| Creative Consultants Fees | | | 1 | allow | $500 | $500 |
| Director of Photography with gear | 1 | x | 15 | days | $400 | $6,000 |
| Sound Recordist with gear | 1 | x | 11 | days | $300 | $3,300 |
| PA / Camera Assistant | 1 | x | 4 | days | $100 | $400 |
| | | | | | | **$15,450** |
| | | | | | | |
| **PRODUCTION TRAVEL** | | | | | | |
| Flights (Director) | 1 | x | 4 | Flights | $400 | $1,600 |
| Hotel (Director) | 1 | x | 4 | Nights | $100 | $400 |
| Per Diem (Director) | 1 | x | 8 | Days | $40 | $320 |
| | | | | | | **$2,320** |
| | | | | | | |
| **PRODUCTION EQUIPMENT & EXPENSES** | | | | | | |
| Studio Rental (for sketches) | | | 2 | days | $300 | $600 |
| Lighting rental (sketches & interviews) | 1 | x | 6 | days | $100 | $600 |
| Tape stock miniDV | | | 30 | tapes | $6 | $180 |
| Clone stock miniDV | | | 30 | tapes | $6 | $180 |
| Production Vehicle Rental & Gas | | | 8 | days | $150 | $1,200 |
| Meals | 4 | x | 5 | days | $25 | $500 |
| Parking, Taxis | | | 1 | allow | $100 | $100 |
| | | | | | | **$3,360** |
| **ARCHIVAL** | | | | | | |
| Researcher | 1 | x | 10 | days | $200 | $2,000 |
| Research Materials (books, videos, etc) | | | 1 | allow | $150 | $150 |
| Tape Transfers, Stock | 1 | x | 12 | allow | $50 | $600 |
| Licensing fees | | | 1 | allow | $2,500 | $2,500 |
| | | | | | | **$5,250** |
| | | | | | | |
| **POST PRODUCTION** | | | | | | |
| Editor with FCP suite & deck | 1 | x | 20 | days | $300 | $6,000 |
| Assistant Editor/Digitizer | 1 | x | 10 | days | $100 | $1,000 |
| Graphics, Titles | 1 | x | 3 | items | $150 | $450 |
| Animation | 1 | x | 2 | items | $600 | $1,200 |
| Stock and Masters | | | 1 | allow | $100 | $100 |
| Music/Composer | | | 1 | allow | $1,000 | $1,000 |
| | | | | | | **$9,750** |
| | | | | | | |
| **FINISHING** | | | | | | |
| Color Correct | 1 | x | 16 | hours | $300 | $4,800 |
| Sound Mix | 1 | x | 8 | hours | $250 | $2,000 |
| Video Cassette/DVD Masters | | | 1 | allow | $100 | $100 |
| | | | | | | **$6,900** |
| **MARKETING & DISTRIBUTION** | | | | | | |
| Press Packet | | | 1 | allow | $450 | $450 |
| Printing | | | 1 | allow | $250 | $250 |
| Festival Subissions | 1 | x | 20 | submiss | $30 | $600 |
| Stock and Dubs | | | 1 | allow | $150 | $150 |
| | | | | | | **$1,450** |
| **ADMINISTRATION** | | | | | | |
| Misc office/production supplies | | | 1 | allow | $100 | $100 |
| Shipping/Postage | | | 1 | allow | $100 | $100 |
| Production Insurance | | | 1 | allow | $1,400 | $1,400 |
| | | | | | | **$1,600** |
| | | | | | | |
| | | | | | **SUBTOTAL** | **$51,055** |
| | | | | | | |
| Incidentals | | | 1 | allow | $2,170 | $2,170 |
| | | | | | | |
| | | | | | **TOTAL** | **$53,225** |

**FIG. 7.17**

The format of this budget combines detail info on the Topsheet

- Don't include cost for *talent* in your budget or schedule, such as *personnel*, interview subjects, or actors.
- Don't include a contingency line item; rather, reinforce all line items of the budget by adding an additional 5–10%. Doc. funders are usually not financiers who read many film budgets and they may not trust it.
- Don't include equipment purchases, only rentals.
- Most filmmakers add their own money to the production; include this in individual donations rather than listing yourself as a donor.

*The Cost of Free*: Free isn't always free. If the film project is not going to be sold – and there are no plans for it to be placed into the marketplace for sale or rent – and if it is instructional, internal or educational, there is leeway. You may fly under the radar, but the minute a film is shown online it is broadcast to the world, and if the project utilizes another's copyrighted material, the owner may object and demand that it be removed. Copyrighted material includes logos, signs, art, magazine covers, music, images, video clips, and TV excerpts.

Most elements in a film will have to be paid for, one way or another (in time, money or both). The initial payment for footage, music and photos in the public domain (copyright has expired) is time. Financial costs may include research and a lawyer, possible transfer to a certain format, or picture and audio cleanup.

In the U.S., the owner of a copyright has "the right to reproduce or to authorize others to reproduce the work" (i.e., make copies). Fair use is outlined in Section 107 of the copyright law – "reproduction of a particular work may be considered fair, such as criticism, comment, news reporting, teaching, scholarship, and research" – and has been the subject of countless lawsuits worldwide. There is no "7-second rule" saying that it's OK to use just part of a song; the 10% rule (meaning you can use 10% of a work) of fair use applies to specific situations.

For commercial use, obtain permission from the copyright owner (or heirs, or estate), or consult an entertainment lawyer who specializes in clearances. Intellectual Property lawyers ($300–900 an hour) may save you money later if an issue comes up when you are in the process of securing distribution and you really need that E&O policy. Even if a clip seems like fair use, there may be SAG or AFTRA performers in it who require residual payments.

"The doctrine of fair use has developed through a substantial number of court decisions over the years and has been codified in section 107 of the copyright law.

Section 107 contains a list of the various purposes for which the reproduction of a particular work may be considered fair, such as criticism, comment, news reporting, teaching, scholarship, and research." Source: http://www.copyright.gov/fls/fl102.html as of July 22, 2011.

Criteria for fair use includes:

- Whether commercial nature or is for nonprofit educational purposes;
- The nature of the copyrighted work (obscure, well known);
- The amount and substantiality of the portion used in relation to the copyrighted work as a whole (e.g., a 10 minute film includes 9 minutes from someone else's film);
- The effect of the use upon the potential market for, or value of, the copyrighted work (i.e., your use of a clip from *Casablanca* reduces the studio's ability to sell *Casablanca*).

The distinction between fair use and infringement may be unclear and not easily defined. There is no specific number of words, lines, or notes that may safely be taken without permission. Acknowledging the source of the copyrighted material does not substitute for obtaining permission (http://www.copyright.gov/fls/fl102.html).

Copyright laws vary around the world, however the Berne Convention is a treaty to which the international community fosters copyright protection between nations. Everything pertaining to copyright is a very hot topic right now, and the issues are complex (www.WIPO.int for more info).

The Center for Social Media (www.centerforsocialmedia.org) is the first stop for questions regarding copyright, inclusion of other artistic works in a film, and public domain resources.

The Creative Commons (http://creativecommons.org) is building and developing a community of artists and content with a more flexible copyright definition to facilitate sharing of artistic works. When in doubt call an entertainment attorney.

*Transcription* is often required for documentaries and reality-style programming, and sometimes ad-lib, improvisatory-style shoots. Transcription creates a record of the film's dialogue after the fact. It can be used to analyze the material for storytelling purposes, or used by the Editor, and also to create a script. Professional transcription ranges from \$1+ per minute to \$20 an hour of recorded audio. Rush service costs more, as do noisy tapes, with low quality audio. You will want transcription *with* time code. The cost relates directly to the amount of footage to be transcribed, how quickly it needs to be turned around, and the quality of the audio. This is a good place to save money with interns who are interested in the subject matter, or in making documentaries. First-time Directors and Editors will benefit from doing it themselves, as they'll be very familiar with all of the footage.

## Shorts, Web Video and Webisodes

Short films (under 40 minutes, but more commonly under 10 minutes), web videos (films created specifically for Internet distribution), webisodes (series of short video films created to air initially as Internet television, for download or stream, rather than first airing on broadcast or cable) and mobisodes (short films to be viewed on a mobile phone or mobile wireless device) are great learning tools for filmmakers. As much creativity can be found on Vimeo, MyDamnChannel, Youtube, FunnyorDie.com as in movie theaters, but on a different scale.

Treat the short project as you would a feature with a delivery date, following the exact same breakdown, scheduling and budgeting steps. It's a good "first date" experience to see if you have a compatible working style with other filmmakers, producers, writers, actors, and DPs. It's a great way to hone scheduling and budgeting skills or learn new software. Shorts win Academy Awards, and there are many prestigious film festivals featuring shorts all over the world. Short film distribution online can be profitable, if not lucrative; Atomfilms is going strong, and YouTube, HowCast, and MyDamnChannel are funding and distributing select short films. Popular short films can earn money via advertising revenues, website traffic, or getting discovered as a result of their work online.

Many filmmakers working on shorts aren't paid; decide *what* you want to get out of the experience, and *how long* you will spend working.

What's the goal for the project? What's your goal with the project? For example:

- To deepen learning of current skills
- To grow new skills
- You love the story
- To have fun
- To meet new people
- To tell an important story
- Slow season, you have ample time to take new work
- Never before worked with. . .green screen, 3D technology, etc.
- To create a marketable representation of an idea for a feature film to use as a fundraising tool and you have a deal memo to get hired on that project should it come to fruition

- To do the scheduling and budgeting work in return for. . .a credit, seeing your screenplay made, producing, directing, etc.
- To build your reel
- To get in a festival
- To win awards
- To be seen by an audience
- To develop video for your Vimeo channel
- To showcase an idea for a mobile app
- To work in a new format or technology, such as an iPad or Vook project
- To put off working in positions outside of the film industry
- To collaborate with someone you like

Setting up a camera and pointing it at a "talking head" (like at a make-up artist demonstrating various styles of make-up application) is different from creating original scripted material, and the related scheduling and budgeting, and designing a shoot (which is not to say that make-up videos won't make you famous – Michelle Phan created an international career from her YouTube instructionals).

*Web budgets* are as varied as the videos themselves. The Internet sitcom *Break a Leg* by Yuri Baranovsky cost $500 an episode (with friends and favors). For 100 episodes of the web horror series *Buried Alive* (each episode 1–5 minutes long, 2½ hours total), creator John Norris spent approximately $500,000, averaging about $3,333 per minute, by Cynthia Littleton, Josef Adalian TV shows getting ambitious, Posted: Fri., Sep. 21, 2007, 4:05pm PT Variety Magazine. http://www.variety.com/article/VR1117972477?refCatid=14. Retrieved July 20, 2011.

At the high end of Internet films is the award-winning *Sanctuary*, an effects-laden sci-fi web series, costing $4.3 million to produce, for a total of 135 minutes (averaging $32,000 per minute). You can get good production value for $1,000 per finished minute, and with web pieces, shorter is usually better.

*Mobisodes:* If your team is producing a video for mobile devices make sure all the technical specs are clearly understood prior to shooting. Mobile video needs to be compressed appropriately for the available wireless network channel, so find out the proper CODEC the video must be delivered on, the length (average watching on web and mobile video is less than 5 minutes at a time), and appropriate frame rates and picture dimensions (3 inches on the diagonal is commonly used). The explosion of formats does not make this any easier. iPads have one screen size, cell phones another, and PS3 gaming devices have another. The popularity of smart phones, tablets, and faster connectivity are contributing to the mobisode resurgence.

The budget and schedule for a mobile film should not result in overproducing. Watch excellent mobile video and note stylistic differences: the editing pace is slower, and the props, setting, and camera moves are simpler than traditional films. Extremes do not translate to mobile video, due to the reduced size of the screen, so make sure to discuss equipment needs with your team (cranes, jibs, dollies, camera and lighting gear, any buzzers and whistles that may be unnecessary). Dialogue has to be ultra clear, and sound design sparing compared with a typical film. Check in with your entertainment lawyer regarding distribution agreements for any mobile or Telco carrier and ask about any unfamiliar terms — Digital Rights Management is a new area of the law and can be confusing.

Here is a brief list of companies funding and/or distributing shorts:

http://www.shortsinternational.com/
http://www.jaman.com/download/?f=submit
http://www.apollocinema.com/submit.htm
http://www.buzztaxi.com/
http://www.ifc.com/submissionpolicy/
http://www.sundancechannel.com/
www.mediakiller.com
www.elypsefilm.com
http://www.indiepixfilms.com/
http://indieflix.com/
http://www.cbc.ca/documentarychannel/
www.cfmdc.org
www.silenceoncourt.tv
www.customflix.com
www.themalls.com
http://www.cbc.ca/reflections/
http://www.movieola.ca/submit.php
http://www.ouatmedia.com/

www.mydamnchannel.com

www.bliptv.com

www.brightcove.com

www.cruxy.com

www.one.revver.com/revver

www.stage6.divx.com

www.iTunes.com

www.wamclips.com

www.amazon.com

www.youtube.com

www.bbc.co.uk/dna/filmnetwork

www.bango.com

www.atomicwedgietv.com

www.atomfilms.com

www.bigfilmshorts.com

www.labigfamily.com

www.bfi.org.uk

www.dazzlefilms.co.uk

www.futureshorts.com

www.microcinema.com

www.network-irl-tv.com

www.onedotzero.com

www.shortsinternational.com

www.sndfilms.com

## Television

The *type* of TV show your team is making will affect your scheduling and budgeting approach. The process of scheduling and budgeting a program that is a one-time, stand-alone show (not part of a series), such as a narrative movie for television, is similar to scheduling and budgeting any film.

Like film, TV scenes are scheduled in the most convenient and cost-effective order (as opposed to the order of the script). The budgeting process is the same as for a feature film or documentary, i.e., tailored to the material and resources available, and constrained by time. Typical budget construction and organization apply. Union versus non-union issues, (including AFTRA) must be considered.

When creating a program for a specific broadcaster, the submission of deliverables may include a back and forth period (you submit a rough cut of episode 1, they give notes and comments about how to improve it), and then additional editing (or shooting *and* editing) is done; then resubmission. Because of this review, allocate additional time and funding for re-shoots, editing, shipping and making dupes.

A documentary made for television is similar to budgeting a feature documentary, with exceptions made for length, delivery format, and any technical guidelines.

**Who's Driving the Bus?**

Producer credits in the television world have clearly defined duties compared with film. In filmmaking, the Executive Producer credit is given to the person who is instrumental in funding, and that person may, or may not, be involved in the hands-on making of the film. In TV, the Executive Producer (**AKA**: Show Runner) credit is often the person who created the concept, runs the production, and has the final say on everything – from hiring and creative issues to schedule and budgeting issues. The EP also supervises the show or series "bible" – a detailed universe of the show including characters, story, geography, back-story, art direction, stylistic notes, and information about the characters and settings that will inform the show. The EP may hire multiple writers or directors for different episodes. The production bible keeps everyone on the same artistic page.

Hopefully, any combination of the possible TV budgeting scenarios shown in Table 7.3, i.e., budgeting a sizzle reel, test tape, a pilot, or an entire series, will result in the network, media company, financiers or production company buying or

**Table 7.3** Possible TV Budgeting Scenarios

| The EP *plans* to pitch a show. | The EP wants to shoot a sizzle reel as a *sales* pitch of the show idea: | Your Executive Producer *pitched* a show, describing the idea. |
|---|---|---|
| The EP wants a budget created for the presentation. | to present to a network to get them interested. | The network is interested. |
| You create a *pattern* budget (a "typical episode") and an *amortization* budget: | You create a budget for the highlight reel, to shoot enough exciting material: | They give EP some money to shoot a pilot, or test tape, to see the idea in action. |
| to prove that the show can be made for a certain amount of money. | to prove the concept visually. | You create a budget for pilot episode, or to shoot some test tape for that amount:<br>to prove the concept visually. |

licensing the show from your team. TV executives receive so many ideas (and the public is fickle), that they must test them out before committing to the expense of making several episodes.

Series programming includes:

- Dramatic
- Situation comedy
- Reality program
- Documentary
- Game show
- News show
- Talk show
- Magazine format
- Educational
- Religious
- Sports
- How-to
- Variety
- Infomercial
- Music or arts programs

Budgeting for a series of episodes recurring periodically requires the same steps as budgeting for a narrative feature or documentry film, with a few additional line items.

Creating a budget for a series requires creating two budgets: a *pattern* budget (the hypothetical "average budget per episode") and an *amortization* budget (expensive line items you want to be divided over multiple episodes).

Pattern budget × Number of episodes = total budget for the series.

The *pattern* budget is similar to a feature budget and covers locations, crew, cast, catering, writers, equipment, film stock, typical production and post expenses – direct costs of that episode to be shot on that date at that time. It is organized into Above- and Below-the Line sections, just like any other film budget. Since it will be used as the *average* budget per episode, actual costs will vary.

The *amortization* budget contains only the costs that will be *spread over* (*amortized* or *reduced over*) all of the episodes in your series. If your multi-episode series show is set inside a castle, you will need to budget for construction of the castle as the set, or rent a castle-looking space for the time to shoot the entire series. You would budget to spread that cost *evenly* over all 13 episodes. It wouldn't be accurate to assign that large cost to one episode, or the pilot, as it is intended for use over the entire series of episodes. Any one-time, extraordinarily high cost that is utilized throughout the entire show (like sets, construction, puppets, devices, distinct props or even wardrobe, or rights to the underlying literary property upon which the material is based) could all be considered items to amortize over all of the episodes in the series.

Looking ahead, if you plan to shoot a second season of shows, based on this show, only spread the cost as far as your financing will carry it. Do not count on amortizing a cost over a second season if the team has not completed the first. Amortize costs only over the planned budget at a given time. If you are budgeting right now for six shows, amortize over that amount. Below is a list of accounts that could be used for amortization:

| | |
|---|---|
| 62031 | Amortization-Prep |
| 63032 | Amortization-Production |
| 62033 | Amortization-Post Production |
| 62034 | Amortization-Hiatus |
| 62035 | Amortization-Back 9 |
| 62036 | Amortization-Start up |
| 62037 | Amortization Wrap |

They might include preproduction costs, wrap costs, hiatus costs (break during shooting), audit, set and construction costs for items to be used throughout the entire series, auditing, scenery, storage, legal expenses, and other costs which apply to the whole show as opposed to one episode.

Take for example the creation of a large mechanical wheel for a game show based on a roulette game. The wheel lights up, spins, is designed and created solely for this show. The wheel will cost $30,000, and it can be amortized over several shows. If your initial series is six shows, spread the cost of the wheel over all six shows, and allocate $5,000 on the Amortization line for the wheel (see Table 7.4).

**Table 7.4** 6203-Series Amortization

| | Amount | Units | X | Rate | Subtotal |
|---|---|---|---|---|---|
| Roulette Game Wheel<br>Total $30,000<br>Amort. over 6 shows | 0.166667 | Allow | 1 | 30,000 | 5,000 |
| Total | | | | | 5,000 |

Budgeting for a series of episodes recurring periodically requires the same steps as budgeting for a narrative feature or documentary film, with a few additional line items. Like a film, every project is different; add or delete budgetary line items as necessary. If you are planning a show with a live studio audience, in your extras category include line items for casting, coordinating, feeding and warming up that audience.

| | |
|---|---|
| 5700-001 | EXTRAS/CROWD |
| 5700-002 | EXTRAS CASTING |
| 5700-003 | EXTRAS CASTING EXPENSES |
| 5700-004 | AUDIENCE COORDINATOR |
| 5700-005 | ASST. AUDIENCE COORDINATOR |
| 5700-006 | AUDIENCE WARM-UP |
| 5700-007 | AUDIENCE EXPENSES |
| 5700-008 | SEAT FILL COORDINATOR |
| 5700-009 | SEAT FILLERS |
| 5700-010 | CONTESTANT COORDINATOR |
| 5700-011 | ASST CONTESTANT COORDINATOR |
| 5700-012 | CONTESTANT EXPENSES |

Other unique budget line items include if you work with a talent agency to package a series (i.e., put together appropriate actors, a Director, or other significant attachments), insert an *"Agency Fee"* or *"Packaging Fee"* line in the Above the Line portion of the budget (occasionally it appears in the Below the Line: Other). This is typically a contractual payment, budgeted as 3–5% of the license fee a network will pay for the show. (*FYI, this might appear in a feature budget too if you are working with an agency.*)

**The Pilot**

One development scenario in television is that a Producer develops an idea into a script, attaches actors, a Director, and key crew, and creates a schedule and budget. (Just like development for a film.) If the Producer pitches this idea to a television network (premium or basic cable channel), and they like it, the network may commission a *pilot* — a first, sample episode that conveys the basic situation, concept and characters.

The budget of the pilot is usually one to three times higher than the cost of an average show. It must be completed as professionally as possible, including effects, music, great sound and visuals, but doesn't require vivid show opening graphics or complete end credits.

The pilot episode is a first impression, and must grab the audience with something — a great stunt, amazing set, or special effects. A pilot is your first (and only) shot at pulling in viewers and getting them hooked. A network will test the pilot with viewers over several months. If picked up by a network, a run of episodes may be ordered (anywhere from 5–13) to try out on audiences and get a reaction, then more ordered later — the "back nine" (golf term) — after a hiatus.

A TV show "season" was once considered to be 13 episodes. But to be on the safe side (cheaper and less risky), broadcasters may start by licensing only six episodes to see how audiences react. If everything goes well, they can always license more. If audiences don't respond, broadcasters look for something else. New television budgeters, unless asked otherwise, should start by budgeting 5–13 episodes.

Creating a pilot on spec (speculation) means that you don't have a client yet. You are creating the pilot to pitch to a client in the hopes that they will fund ongoing production of that show, or, in case of the web, the Producer is planning to distribute it, and build an audience — monetizing the venture by selling ads, or other sponsorship financing, or selling copies of the shows, or raising money some other way, such as by donations, in order to keep making the show. Pilot episodes created on speculation, if picked up, will likely get remade prior to airing. Nonetheless, the pilot (or test tape) has to be as high quality as possible.

More than 65 episodes equals syndication, i.e., you can predictably license the shows again, on a different network, and/or overseas, filling a substantial hole in any television schedule. With four seasons in a year of 52 weeks (each season being

**Table 7.5**

| Week | Monday – Friday nightly episode |
|---|---|
| 1 | 5 |
| 2 | 5 |
| 3 | 5 |
| 4 | 5 |
| 5 | 5 |
| 7 | 5 |
| 8 | 5 |
| 9 | 5 |
| 10 | 5 |
| 11 | 5 |
| 12 | 5 |
| 13 | 5 |
| 5 × 13 = | 65 episodes |

13 weeks long), 65 episodes means you can play a show every weeknight (see Table 7.5).

TV is big and growing, albeit in niche ways, so it's simultaneously getting bigger and smaller: there are a greater number of channels all the time, directed at increasingly focused, niche markets, for example the Food Network, Game Show channel, History channel, Home and Garden TV, Logo, VH1, and the Oprah Winfrey Network. IPTV (Internet integration with television) creates an opportunity for a limitless amount of channels; even if you don't have a broadcasting partner, your content can play online, and anyone with a television that accesses the Internet can watch. (Of course, you have to let viewers know about you – that's the hard part.)

An important component to budgeting television programming effectively is to know the audience demographic – and cater production values to their tastes. Prime time network television shows must cater to a varied and wide audience – and will be generally more expensive. This is one reason reality programming is so popular; it's cheap compared with scripted dramas and even successful sitcoms (*Everyone Loves Raymond, Friends, Two and a Half Men*) where actor salaries may run into the millions per episode.

Your show must insert appropriate commercial break points as are typical for programming on the network. Find out what the "clock" of the destination channel is, i.e., how many breaks and their length, as well as the length of each act in the show. For example, one cable channel stipulates that their 40-minute programs = 22:20 minutes of actual program, in four acts (with three breaks).

Act 1:5—7 minutes

Act 4: 4—5 minutes

Each commercial break: in black — 10 seconds long

## Educational and Corporate Films

An expense that can be significant in educational and corporate films relates to research and licensing stock footage, stills, historical images or video, and music.

Variations on a theme for corporate and educational use include some mix of:

- Demonstration or training;
- Talking heads or interviews;
- Incorporating graphics (e.g., motion graphics, animation, stills, composites, or something computer generated like PDFs or PowerPoint presentations);
- Scripted (generally with actors, or uncomplicated if using non-actors);
- Unscripted;
- You will need to find out when and how you will have access to: buildings, people, or insider situations.

When working with real people, not actors, you will need more time. You may have to shoot extra shots because they are nervous, or cannot memorize lines, and often appear stiff and unnatural. As these types of projects tend to be cheaper than a feature film (although not always), a single unit (i.e., Director, DP, Sound Person, Grip, Gaffer) and a few additional support staff are required.

When shooting in a corporate or school environment, plan on noise, disturbance, interruptions, and multiple light sources. Check in advance for freight elevators, where to enter, and limitations on size of gear. Depending on the end use of the project, these shoots span 1–5 days, and require back and forth with the client, so get to know what their expectations are in terms of what will be spent and how.

A typical budgeting approach is to establish the actual costs of the production, then build a profit margin above that – from 50% to 200%. This isn't usually added as a single line item, but rather is built into each line item of the project (**AKA:** cost plus). You could forgo that and just add a "profit line" to the bottom of the budget, but that is vulnerable to the client negotiating. If you are working with an educational partner, you may be expected to create study guides to accompany the film. Find out what is expected and budget accordingly.

Important questions to ask about corporate and educational projects include: who is going to watch the film, and what is the purpose of it? Is it internal or external? PR reels, sales meetings, and company training videos to relay company policies are often needed, and a good crew can bring some creativity and fun to these projects. Simple storyboards go a long way in communicating the creative aspect of these types of videos and can save time in the long run.

An *educational video* should match the instructor's intent, and relate to the materials it will accompany (whether lesson plans or online text and images), and include the appropriate learning points. Logistical challenges of shooting at schools include:

- Scheduling facilities around existing class schedules;
- Setting up equipment and light that doesn't disrupt the lesson;
- Finding students, teaching assistants, and faculty willing and available to participate on camera;
- Editing out any faculty or students who wouldn't sign releases.

Work with the educator to deliver any supplemental materials that can be used in their teaching. You may also want to make sure the Editor compresses the final video into different formats for a variety of uses.

## Working Without a Script

Conventional wisdom says there is no budgeting a project without a script, but it happens all the time. The more scripts you break down, schedule and budget, the more your mind will seek out costly items. Schedule and budget for what is on the page — and as you read a treatment, synopsis, or story outline, keep an eye out for expensive ingredients such as:

- Children and animal actors;
- Complex scenes with crowds, huge cast;
- Multitudes of locations;
- Long, elaborate story that will require a long script;
- Legal rights and permissions of famous songs, pre-existing movie footage, famous artwork or buildings;
- Night-time shooting outside;
- Epic stories, elaborate sets, period piece, sci-fi;
- Car chases, plane fights, marine scenes, helicopter footage;
- War scenes, race cars, pyrotechnics, explosions, destruction;
- New, untested machinery.

While the devil is in the details, the genre and scope of the story can give you a feel for the budget range. Compare the treatment or synopsis to: a dogme-type project — a drama about relationships using only natural light (*The Celebration*); or a coming-of-age comedy (*Napoleon Dynamite*) with a lot of hanging out; or a horror flick in one location, like *Paranormal Activity*. Drawing parallels between the basic story and existing films will establish guidelines.

Think of movies like *Clerks*. If you had access to one super-cheap, or nearly-free, location (a convenience store), with a strong script and talented, hungry actors, you could probably film it for $27,000, especially in a digital format and editing with a nonlinear program like Final Cut, i-Movie or Avid. (Note: there was a significant budget bump-up spent on the film in post, >$200,000, most likely by Miramax who distributed it, but at that point the film was made.)

If the schedule and budget depends in large part on your guess-timations of scene ingredients, and you have a Director to work with, talk it through with them so you are making educated conclusions. It depends on the scope of the project and your team's tenacity. Filming a play on a stage from several angles could be edited into a complete film and it would be relatively inexpensive.

For unscripted material, more cameras (that don't see each other in the frame) are good so you don't miss the unexpected.

Reality television or unscripted shows often work in a non-scripted environment — working toward a certain premise and related goals (conflict, drama, love, hate, backstabbing, frenemies, sorrow, apology). Ingredients may include a central location (and related expenses), crew, and a small cast, and the show is based on filming the relationships and conflict that takes place in that environment. The creators plot points, or an end-goal (who will win the race, be the last to survive — some climax to work toward), and the constantly running cameras look for, and encourage, those moments.

You can construct a film in the same way with actors who are comfortable improvising — using a basic template, or premise — and then really develop and sculpt the story through the editing process. With improvisatory-style projects, allot time for rehearsal and shooting multiple takes, to capture the magic when it appears.

As you might imagine, a loose shooting plan requires a lot of work on the post side, really diligent Assistant Editors to track and log footage, and Editors with patience and an eye for a story, so it is necessary to build extra time and money into the post process for the Editor to work their magic.

## End of Chapter Seven Review

To improve a budget:

- Use Groups to compare costs of specific groups of items for deep analysis;
- Create different versions;
- Compare different versions.

For narrative feature films:

- Work the script;
- Tell everyone you know;
- Adopt a marathon mentality;
- Network for your film;
- Don't wait to plan and budget for marketing and distribution.

Documentaries:

- The schedule may go in fits and starts;
- Unique budget line items include research, clip licensing, grant and foundation funding, fiscal sponsorship, donations;
- Similar to a triathlon – a long race in disparate pieces.

Shorts, web video, webisodes, mobisodes:

- Establish a goal for the project;
- Decide *what* you want to get out of it;
- Decide *how long* you will spend working on the project.

Television:

- The type of show affects the schedule and budget process. Treat stand-alone, one-off shows like a film;
- In television, the Executive Producer runs the show, much like the primary Producer in a film;
- As an LP, UPM or PM, you may be called upon to schedule and budget a sale or sizzle tape, and to highlight noteworthy moments or characters in the show;
- Schedule and budget a pilot (just like a feature);

- Create a budget for a series of episodes consisting of a *pattern* budget ("average budget per typical episode") and a separate *amortization* budget (for high costs to be *amortized*, or *spread over*, all of the episodes);
- Keep in mind at all times the target audience.

Educational and corporate films:

- Like documentary forms, you will need line items for licensing, and clearances;
- Direction for these types of films usually comes from a specific client, educational board, and subject matter;
- Keep the target audience in mind at all times, i.e., what they should take away from the film;
- Educational and corporate films are usually scheduled for short shoots, and often have to accommodate noisy environments with people who aren't used to being on camera (which takes a bit longer, and requires patience);
- These clients may be unfamiliar with the technology and require guidance regarding deliverables.

Working without a script:

- Schedule and budget what you read from the synopsis or treatment;
- Keep an eye out for expensive elements;
- Compare the material to pre-existing films and research their budgets;
- Work with the Director to form proper assumptions about locations, cast, and time factors;
- Reality TV and improvisatory style: you need some clear goals, multiple cameras, lots of time in post, and a great Editor.

# Chapter Eight

## *Additional Topics You Are Bound to Encounter*

---

*Costello*: I'm asking YOU who's on first.

*Abbott*: That's the man's name.

*Costello*: That's who's name?

*Abbott*: Yes.

---

We don't know what we don't know, and the funny thing about experience is that you only get it through repetition. In lieu of experience, *assume* circumstances will arise during prep and production that will incur additional expense, and take more time than initially planned for. The only insurance against the unknown is to build in additional time and budget reinforcements (and actually buy insurance).

In a collaborative art form such as filmmaking, many people work together toward a common goal, and need a system to do so efficiently. Your working practices need flexibility for you and your team. This chapter highlights some situations you may run into, and ways to design a working system that can handle whatever comes up.

## Scheduling

No two people will schedule one film the same: there is no right or wrong way. There's a first pass and then improvements – try this, that, and the other.

Like a Sudoku or a crossword puzzle, each new piece of knowledge provides clues to complete the entire puzzle. As you receive new information, ask how it could affect the schedule. Will cast and crew have sufficient time to do their work, rest, travel, eat? Are there any safety ramifications? Who else needs this information?

### Contrast and Compare

New information means having to select one thing over another; it is important to contrast and compare variables with your team. Solid decisions are made by first asking questions.

*Locations* are an important building block for the entire film. How does the look of the location suit the film, and is there enough physical space for cast and crew to eat, rest, prepare, and park?

Compare one location to another in terms of:

- Proximity to public transportation;
- Parking (space, availability, cost, access for large vehicles, security);
- Sufficient space for equipment;
- Power, electricity available, room for generator;
- Hard/easy to find and get to;
- Bathrooms (close by, far away, clean, quantity, size, public – Starbucks, McDonalds, library, hotels, or will you bring facilities like honeywagons?);
- Noise (planes, dogs, horns, train tracks nearby, sirens, traffic, dance clubs, zoos, school marching band practice, humming light fixtures, AC, fountains, church bells and clocks that sound the hour) and neighbors;
- Safety of neighborhood (check local police records);
- Food, access to food, places to eat;
- Cell phone reception;
- Physical space for cast and crew to eat, rest, prepare;
- Proximity to printer/copier/production office, Fedex Kinkos to run off call sheets, schedules, script change, or other required paperwork;

- Can the location serve for two or more sets? (Outdoor and indoor can be in different physical locations);
- What (bizarre, disruptive) calendar, or community events are going on during the shoot that may derail the schedule?

When planning to shoot someplace unfamiliar, do some sleuthing with a local connection through the film commission. Ask about rush hour times and direction, upcoming events, races and parades (closing bridges and rerouting traffic), and holiday celebrations (security and noise levels, tourists). Some of which you may be able to use. In NYC, events at the U.N. make shooting on the lower east side nearly impossible, and LA traffic at the 101/405 interchange makes people late. Even a local arts festival can wreak havoc on your schedule. Look into the future by using resources like last year's newspaper event listings, Chase's Calendar of Events, and Meetup.com. In international territories you need to be aware of local customs, like a periodic call to prayer over loudspeakers, transit strikes, or regional celebrations.

*Night versus Day*: Group exterior night scenes together, either at the end of the week, over a weekend, or for an entire week of night shooting. Avoid scheduling a night shoot followed immediately by a day shoot.

*Base camp*: In addition to a headquarters and information center online (whether a web site or through your scheduling/budgeting software) hold regular production meetings. Create communication and accountability loops so you can see the progress that others are making. The Line Producer, as the chief administrator of the film, one of the most important roles is to process and move information where it needs to go. Get everyone in your team used to the idea that you want to see what's going on, you trust them to do their jobs, and you want to see how they're doing it so you can improve yours.

Expect to be present at everything, but when that's impossible, gather your information from:

- Auditions, rehearsals, camera tests;
- Shot lists;
- Floor diagrams;
- Notes from Tech scouts of locations;
- Excel lists of equipment, props, prices, rates, due dates, terms;
- Passing someone in the hall is an opportunity to find out information – voila an instant production meeting.

Seeing into the future sometimes means asking the right questions, such as "What revisions do you plan to make to the script?" (This may save you scheduling and budgeting effort if the Producer and Director plan to cut out a significant, or expensive, section of the story.)

**Lock it UP**

*Locked script*: Once a script is locked, no more (major) changes will be made, and you can refine the schedule, select a start date for production, post and completion, then build a budget with concrete numbers.

*Locked budget*: Without a firm financial commitment, it's possible that you can lose the crew and vendors interested in working on your project, so keep good records of alternate choices. Stay abreast of the status of the project from the Producer, Director, and financiers, and what conditions are required for them to decide on a final figure, start date, and final script.

*Shooting Schedule*: Once the script, schedule and budget are locked, you have defined targets to aim at. Work with the AD to prepare paperwork outlining each day's activities during the shoot. A shooting schedule shows all the details of each shooting day, cast names and I.D. numbers, props, and page count. In duration a shooting schedule can be as long, or longer, than the script itself, due to the amount of detail. The shooting schedule is distributed only to key folks, such as Department Heads, at the production meeting to analyze the game plan for each scene. It's more detail than most crew and cast require, and a whole lot of paper, so it isn't distributed carelessly.

Figures 8.1 and 8.2 show how to view scheduling in Movie Magic.

Table 8.1 shows a sample shooting schedule for a 2-day marketing web video.

**Stay Practical**

As your team grows, relay and establish communication systems as appropriate. Sharing a production calendar on the Internet is one way to keep everyone up to date. Update it with important reminders, meetings and task milestones. Google (and others) offer shared calendars and documents, providing an online space for progress and shared production knowledge. Other Internet production tools for collaboration include Scenechronize, Gorilla, Celtx, Peepel, Scenios, Basecamp, OpenGoo, Zoho, OfficeLive, social media platforms or the film's website.

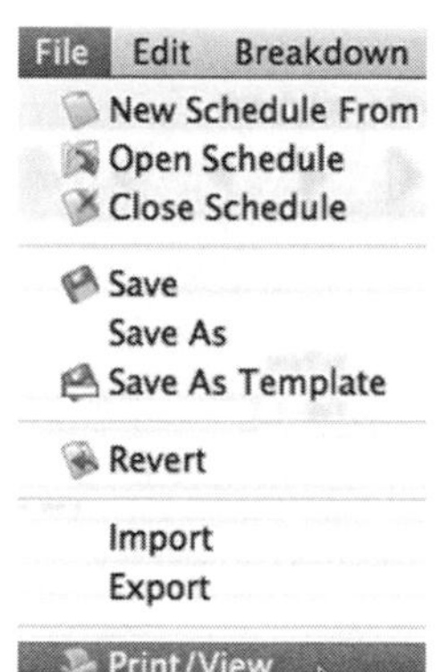


**FIG. 8.1**

File/Print

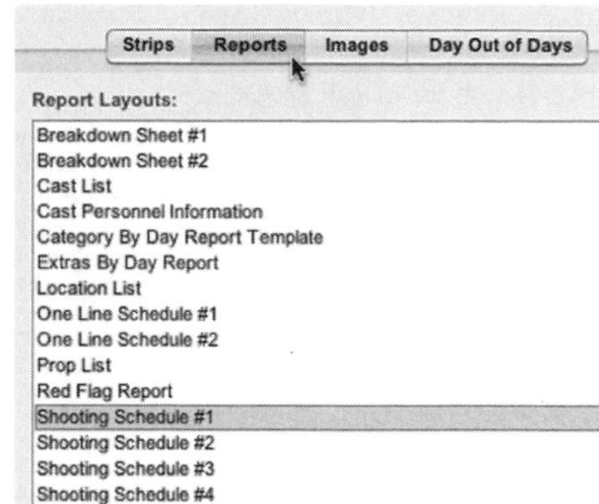


**FIG. 8.2**

Reports/Shooting Schedule

**Table 8.1**

Wed June 30

weather forecast – as of Monday, June 28: some clouds

9:30 AM ARRIVE via metro to Waterfront/Binghamton Shore Meetup point:
*74 W 1st. (corner of Jared Ave) :: (8 Train: 1st St. Stop)*

-SHOOT b-roll of financial district, fish market, sea front, Stark Street Seaport, park at the end of Stark St. *(map attached)*

11:45 AM BOAT travel on Binghamton Ferry. (Permission from owner, KayTrina McLightly, 212.555.1212, Ktrini_LightnUp38792@yahoo.com)

-SHOOT people drinking on deck, beauty shots of river, fishing club, kayaks, Statue of Freedom and Edgewater Island

2 PM BOAT back to shore (Binghamton Shore Meetup point), meal break

4 PM SHOOT 2929 Cubano Rest. (Stark St. Seaport) – interview Chef Kiki LaRue

6:30 PM magic light – SHOOT ON DECK, shots of boats in harbor, shots of seagulls, ferry traffic, INTERVIEW owner **KayTrina McLightly**

Fri July 2

weather forecast – as of Monday, June 28: lots of sunshine

10 AM CALL time for Historian interview at Friendship Temple

*will shoot using reflector and one light, and lav. Mic (2)*

(walk to Eternal Friendship Memorial construction site) tour and historic points of interest

INTERVIEW Historian: June Hendrickson 212.555.1212, 2798oldstuff@nychistory.org

11:45 AM SHOOT sequence of historian pondering memorial, shots of flag, memorial

– pans to the sea

1 PM WRAP

Mar 31, 2011 | Shooting Schedule | Page #: 1

EXT ROUTE 390 - U-HAUL TRUCK | Day | 1/8

Scene # 2

Jim drives U-Haul truck to get Betsy

**Cast Members**
2.JIM

**Vehicles**
V1.U-Haul truck
**Sound**
honks

---

EXT ROUTE 390 - U-HAUL TRUCK | Day | 3/8

Scene # 4

Jim hears clank in U-Haul truck

**Cast Members**
2.JIM

**Vehicles**
V1.U-Haul truck
**Sound**
clanking

---

INT SUBURBAN LIVING ROOM | Day | 3/8

Scene # 1

Betsy plays videos

**Cast Members**
1.BETSY
3.MRS. PICKLE

**Props**
drink
empty boxes
soup
straw
TV
video screen
videogame console
videogames

**Vehicles**
V1.U-Haul Truck
**Wardrobe**
slacker
**Sound**
Dr. Phil
honks
clanking
footsteps overhead

Mar 31, 2011 | Shooting Schedule | Page #: 2

**Set Dressing**
green sofa
**Greenery**
dying plant

---

INT U-HAUL TRUCK | Day | 1/8

Scene # 5

**Cast Members**
2.JIM

---

**FIG. 8.3**

Sample shooting schedule

**Table 8.2**

| Jan 1–7 | Jan 8–14 | Jan 15–21 | Jan 22–28 | Jan 29–Feb 4 | Feb 5–11 | Feb 12–18 | Feb 19–25 | Feb 26–Mar 3 | Mar 4–10 | Mar 11–17 |
|---|---|---|---|---|---|---|---|---|---|---|
| Prep Wk 1 | Prep Wk 2 | Prep Wk 3 | Prep Wk 4 | | | | | | | |
| | | | | Shoot Wk 1 Day1 | Shoot Wk 2 Day2 | | | | | |
| | | | | Shoot Wk 1 Day2 | Shoot Wk 2 Day2 | | | | | |
| | | | | Shoot Wk 1 Day3 | Shoot Wk 2 Day2 | | | | | |
| | | | | Shoot Wk 1 Day4 | Shoot Wk 2 Day2 | | | | | |
| | | | | Shoot Wk 1 Day5 | Shoot Wk 2 Day2 | | | | | |
| | | | | Shoot Wk 1 Day6 | Shoot Wk 2 Day2 | | | | | |
| | | | | | | Wrap Wk 1 | Wrap Wk 2 | Wrap Wk 3 | | |
| | | | | | | | Post Wk 1 | Post Wk 2 | Post Wk 3 | Post Wk 4 |
| | | | | | | | | | Rough Cut | Cast/Crew Screening |

Working *backward* is one of the best ways to arrive at a practical schedule. When you know the date for the film to be completed, count backward. Discuss with your team the ratio of preproduction to production, and production to post. A rudimentary schedule like this (see Table 8.2) can help keep everyone on point.

*Travel:* Be realistic. People need time to arrive, set up, break down and wrap, and possibly deal with jetlag. If you travel for 9 hours, it may be unrealistic to shoot 10 hours that same night. Plan ahead when shipping any production equipment. Unfamiliar equipment needs more time to operate and set up.

*Do it right the first time*: As much as possible, plan to make the day = shoot the scheduled amount of pages for that day. Plan to *shoot out*, or *wrap out*, a location, or a portion of a location (interior, side of the room, exterior, etc.), and move on. Plan your schedule and budget so that you don't double any efforts, i.e., no double moves, or double work (extra props and wardrobe OK). However careful the plan and its execution, re-shoots may be needed; make sure crew and actor contracts (and the schedule and budget) allow for that possibility.

### Questions about Eighths

Keep to the rule of only 8 eighths per one page as much as possible. When in doubt, simple scenes are fewer eighths, complex scenes are more. If something really funky comes up that is an exception, you can have more than 8 eighths. Think about it for a moment, then decide what makes sense to you. Apply logic and common sense, then make a decision and move on.

Insert shots, montage or cutaway shots may be extremely short; even if it takes up a quarter inch of a page, it is officially an eighth. In one script page comprised of 13 short scenes, each scene is considered an eighth. Once in a while a page will have more than 8 eighths, so go with it, and make sure to change it in your scheduling program.

For example, the page in Figure 8.4, as divided, has 11 eighths. It could be divided differently: scene 5, a series of yoga poses performed by one person, is a fairly simple scene, and the argument could be made that it only needs to be 1/8 long – with each pose as a scene part. Decide then check in with your Director and AD.

A scene that spans one page or longer is converted to one page + additional eighths. For example, a scene lasting 13 eighths (one full page plus 5/8 of the next page) = 1 and 5/8.

Scenes less than 1 inch long = 1/8. If you are using a ruler, do not include the slug line when measuring; start with the action description or dialogue right below.

### Script Inconsistency and New Versions

Script inconsistencies usually arise when the script didn't have scene or page numbers locked. Your original marked script and breakdown sheets (whether electronic or paper) serve as a touchstone to go back to when uncertainty arises, so keep them in a safe place with an obvious name (such as *ScriptTitle_OriginalBreakdown_14Jan2011.pdf*, or whatever you prefer). Inconsistencies can build into problems, so if you suspect something is out of whack, ferret it out and fix it. Inconsistencies in set and character names also create problems, so have another production office person take a look.

Create a production bible – whether it lives on a computer or in a three-ring binder with paperwork divided into tabs for the script, breakdown sheets, contracts, call sheets, production reports, day out of days reports, maps, contact information for all

| | | | |
|---|---|---|---|
| 1 | INT. PURPLE GARAGE - DAY<br>KIM HAMM, 70s, in revealing sweats, glides thru yoga. | 1 | 1/8 |
| 2 | EXT. SMALL TOWN LIBRARY - DAY<br>LAUGHING Middle school KIDS play kickball. | 2 | 1/8 |
| 3 | INT. PURPLE GARAGE - DAY<br>Kim moves into downward facing dog position. | 3 | 1/8 |
| 4 | EXT. SMALL TOWN LIBRARY - DAY<br>Tiny FIST winds up...<br>JIMMY, 10, SOCKED in the nose by the fist.<br>Kids cheer. | 4 | 2/8 |
| 5 | INT. PURPLE GARAGE - DAY<br>Yoga Pose: Warrior<br>Yoga Pose: Child's pose<br>Yoga Pose: Lotus<br>Yoga Pose: Handstand | 5 | 2/8 |
| 6 | EXT. SMALL TOWN LIBRARY - DAY<br>BIBI HAMM (10) sucks on a bleeding knuckle. | 6 | 1/8 |
| 7 | INT. SMALL TOWN LIBRARY - DAY<br>Jimmy cries in one corner, Bibi rolls her eyes. | 7 | 1/8 |
| 8 | EXT. SMALL TOWN LIBRARY - DAY<br>Kids peer in through the window. | 8 | 1/8 |
| 9 | INT. PURPLE GARAGE - DAY<br>Kim picks up numchucks, going through a vigorous routine. | 9 | 1/8 |

**FIG. 8.4**

Irregular eighths sometimes happen



cast and crew, account numbers, passwords, user names, phone numbers for primary team members, emergency contact information, press kit information, synopsis, bios, cell phone and walkie-talkie lists, logs for travel, releases, blank company letterhead, shipping labels, and mailing information.

### Honing Your Scheduling Skills

When just starting out, you may want to practice with a few short scripts. Offer to create schedules for free on a film-community website, or in the no-lo section of mandy.com (and similar sites) – the requests will come in by the dozen. Break scripts down then schedule them within a set (but reasonable) amount of time; without interruptions you should soon be able to break down a feature length script of 100 pages in a few hours. When you're learning, you can do it for free and many filmmakers will appreciate it. Start with short screenplays then build up to longer ones.

Many free scripts from completed feature films are available online (www.script-o-rama.com and www.simplyscripts.com); break them down and schedule them. Watch the film, and research the budget and grosses online on boxofficemojo.com and the-numbers.com. Test the assumptions you made about the screenplay (bearing in mind it probably changed during the process) against the resulting film. It is a tremendous amount of work and a great learning experience. You may want to start with *Sex, Lies and Videotape* as opposed to *Star Wars.* This is a less fulfilling process than working on a real production, but builds scheduling muscles. Practicing builds experience, and the more often you do it the faster and more automated the process will become.

To really gauge the effectiveness of the schedule you've created, ask Directors, UPMs, Line Producers, Producers' ADs, and production accountants to look at it. These personnel see many schedules and can give you practical tips and offer helpful suggestions. The next best way to test any schedule is to then work on making the film you scheduled with your team!

**Location, Location, Location**

Locations are important, and can be expensive and difficult to find. On low budget films, the PM may be charged with finding locations.

A *location scout* searches out the perfect locations for a film – a "reel" estate broker. Anyone can be a location scout, but someone who does it for a living will be familiar with types of location, saving you weeks, or months, of searching for the right place. If you can't afford a location scout, you can hire someone who's eager to drive around, take pictures of potential locations, make calls, and search the Internet – or you can do it yourself. Contact the film commission where you plan to shoot and ask if they have a location database.

A *location manager* manages the locations after you've found them. The location scout and location manager may be the same person, who acquires appropriate releases and permits, and makes sure proper insurance is in place. Location-based questions include:

- Is parking available for cast, crew, and equipment vehicles?
- Is it near bathroom facilities (a public park or a local restaurant)?
- Is it in a quiet location (away from traffic, train tracks, factories, and fountains)?
- Is there available electricity to plug in your lights? (If not, you'll need a generator.)
- If you're shooting out of town, are there overnight accommodations nearby?
- Is there air-traffic noise if the site is en route to the airport?
- Do you have space to set up a picnic area to feed your cast and crew?
- Can you get permission to shoot there? Do you need a permit? Can you afford to film there?
- Does using the site require the hiring of a police officer to stop foot or street traffic?
- Is there a photocopy store nearby?
- Is there cell phone reception?

Finding the perfect location that works as a few different sets is ideal. You can film the exterior of a house and then use a different house's interior. Once you have located primary locations for the most important scenes in the screenplay (i.e., the most frequently used ones), try to find secondary locations as close by as possible. 

## Budgeting

Budgeting is a combination of logic and common sense. Be sure to check your numbers with your eyes and a calculator. With numerous line items, and the gazillions of details involved in film budgeting, it is possible to overlook bizarre figures, doubled up costs, or general weirdness – which range from adding fringes to the wrong line items to adding in an extra zero or deleting equipment costs.

Almost *everything* affects the budget, whether it is related to the financing of a project, its distribution and related requirements, or aspects of production. *Department heads* are a great resource to vet and strengthen portions of a budget –they are the experts in that category. Below is a small list of terms which have budgetary ramifications in one way or another.

*Gross*: Income prior to any deductions;

*Adjusted Gross*: Income prior to defined deductions;

*Net*: Income after expenses are deducted, and those expenses should be defined and detailed down to the letter. "Net" can be a malleable term, subject to interpretations and 20 pages of legal definitions;

*Defined Proceeds*: Another term for a type of net profit, defining specific deductions may be taken from revenue (on its way into someone's pocket);

*Points*: Percentage point of a film's profits, usually promised / paid to someone Above the Line;

*Backend*: Participant in the profits of a film.

*Cashflowing*: Financing entity paying incremental amounts needed for upcoming expenses, instead of getting entire funding in one lump sum;

*Residuals*: Every distribution window *after* an initial theatrical release is considered secondary income, or residual income. SAG members earn residuals on all distribution after initial theatrical release. This varies by media, from 3–6% of the gross – higher on DVD, less from TV and Internet. In addition to SAG, other unions also receive residuals – DGA, WGA, IATSE, AFTRA and AFM – and it varies depending on the type of media the film will be exhibited upon.

*Random Rules of Thumb:*

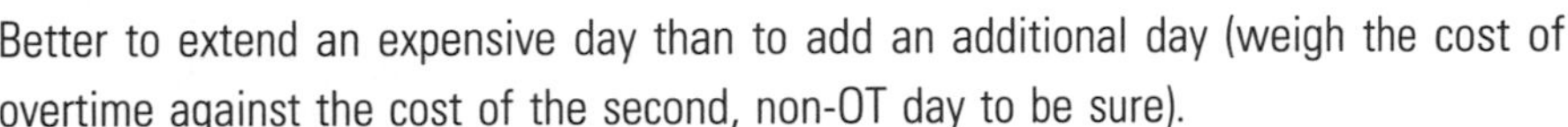

Better to extend an expensive day than to add an additional day (weigh the cost of overtime against the cost of the second, non-OT day to be sure).

Special cameras and equipment may be hard to find, and require specialized operators ($).

**Catering and Craft Service**

Supplying meals is referred to as catering, whereas supplying snack food is referred to as craft service.

- Hire a craft service person, and prepare food and expendables lists. Ask for everything and you may get something. Encourage craft service to approach local cafes and restaurants regarding donations.
- Identify the eating areas at each location.
- Secure a caterer (a catering company, restaurants, and so on); sort out the menu so that there is variety, and accommodation for special dietary needs.
- Compile a list of local restaurants near each location that might be able to provide second meals or extra food on larger set days.
- Have petty cash available daily for second meals or extra meal needs.
- Arrange for special meal needs if necessary.
- Make sure there are tables and chairs for the crew to sit at while eating lunch.

**Digital Format**

A quick note about the *digital* format — what is great about shooting digital is that it is relatively inexpensive to shoot. The tendency is to shoot and shoot and shoot, which sounds great — the Editor will have a lot of footage to choose from — but the flip side is that a lot of footage can be very time-consuming for the Assistant Editor and Editor (and Director) to work through. They now have a lot of footage to look at and take notes on, and more takes to choose from. Also, the more footage you have, the more space it will take up on the hard drive of the editing computer, and the longer the rendering time to upload it to the computer (unless you're shooting P2 cards).

Shooting on *P2 cards* is like videotaping direct-to-computer data files (eliminating the need to transfer from tape format into computer). In digital editing, you can *instantly transfer* footage into Final Cut or Avid, rather than having to go through the real time capture process — you can literally play the footage into your computer editing system.

Shooting solid-state memory cards (or sticks) has advantages over tape: it lacks the moving parts of a tape cassettes (less breakable), or the fragility of tape. However, as with every format, there is a downside. The number and size of cards is considerably more expensive than tape, and once you capture that footage in the computer, then record over it, the *original* recording is *gone* — which can be a scary thought.

Every format has its pros and cons. Together with the Producer, Director, Editor and DP, explore what those are, and the goals for the project. What makes life easy in production may make life difficult in post production (or vice versa), and it is vital that you plan for both.

**Transportation**

*Getting around:* Rent SUVs, vans or cars. For smaller shoots, you may not need a production truck. It is easier to drive and park smaller vehicles, and they require less gas. Make sure your driver knows the local road rules — in NYC you can't turn right on red (it's an expensive ticket) or drive trucks on the West Side Highway (another expensive ticket). Knowing the local road rules is another reason local film people can be great to have working with you.

Travel with the bare minimum of people. Only key crew needs to travel for a doc. Hiring local helpers means you don't have to pay for their lodging and travel, and they will know the area. If you need only B-Roll, hire a local to do it and have them send you the tapes or email the footage. Prior to interviewing subjects (friendly not hostile ones), ask if they can arrange to send you photos — do they have home video you could use? If they do allow you to use personal imagery, scan, copy and get it back to them safely and quickly (with a thank you note).

*Public Domain*: Free isn't always free. When incorporating clips, music, and art logos from others, make sure to clear them, or consult an entertainment attorney to verify whether material is in the public domain, or can be considered *fair use* (see Chapter 7).

*Music* can get expensive, and requires help from an attorney so that the production obtains the correct rights. There is a distinct difference between a Synchronization license and a Master license, requiring two separate negotiations. If you need the master rights, you must always secure the synch rights along with it. However, you may choose to rerecord the song to your specifications, in which case you will only be required to obtain the synch rights.

1. **Mechanical License Contract – you want to recreate a song to use it in a film**

   This contract provides permission from a copyright holder to a non-copyright holder of a musical work to reproduce a specific musical work for albums and soundtracks. It authorizes the manufacture and distribution of records, compact discs and cassette tapes for a specific copyrighted musical composition.
2. **Synchronization License Contract – you want to match pre-recorded music with visuals**

   This contract licenses musical works and the synching of the song with visuals – in a movie, video, or other multimedia production.
3. **Master Use License Agreement – you want to use a song someone else recorded in your film**

   Master Use Agreement is a general permission contract for a filmmaker to use a previously recorded piece of music in a film. This agreement must be used in conjunction with the Synch License Agreement. Specifically, the Master Use Agreement is used for a previously recorded piece of music, not an original work created specifically for the film.

## End of Chapter Eight Review

We cannot see into the future; however, to plan for the unforeseen we can:

- Build in additional time pads;
- Build in additional budget reinforcements;
- Get insurance.

*Scheduling* is like a puzzle that can be solved using many different approaches, and everyone will do it differently. With each piece of new information, contrast and compare different scenarios until you reach the optimal arrangement.

As you add new team members, cast, crew, investors, stakeholders, supporters, partners, and distributors, wrap them into the communication system appropriate for their role in the project.

Get involved in everything in order to spot potential bumps in the road. A three-sentence exchange in the hallway is an informal production meeting: get as much info as often as possible.

Plan backward, and build a calendar for everyone involved with the project. Take a little extra time now and do it right the first time (whatever it is) so you don't have to do it again, later.

Irregular script elements and inconsistencies will arise. Tackle them as fast as possible when you spot them, in a logical manner.

Capitalize on real life for the shoot if at all possible, and keep your eyes open to saving a buck at all times.

*Budgeting* is affected by almost everything, so be sure to understand (even if it means asking a million questions) the ramifications a decision will have on the film's financial plan. Better to plan for costs now than to be surprised by them later.

# Index

## D



## E

## T